International Criminal Evidence at the International Criminal Court

International Criminal Law Series

Founding Editor
M. Cherif Bassiouni †

Editor-in-Chief
William Schabas, Professor of International Law, Department of Law, Middlesex University; Professor of International Criminal Law and Human Rights, Leiden University; Honorary Chairman, Irish Centre for Human Rights, National University of Ireland, Galway; Canada/Ireland

Editorial Board

Kai Ambos, Judge at the Kosovo Specialist Chambers (KSC), The Hague; Professor of Law and Head, Department for Foreign and International Criminal Law, Georg August Universität; Gottingen, Germany

Mahnoush Arsanjani, Member, Institut de Droit International; former Director, Codification Division, United Nations Office of Legal Affairs, Iran

Mohamed Chande Othman, Chief Justice, Court of Appeal of Tanzania; Dodoma, Tanzania

Adama Dieng, Former Special Adviser on the Prevention of Genocide; former Registrar, International Criminal Tribunal for Rwanda; former Secretary General, International Commission of Jurists, Senegal

Mark Drumbl, Class of 1975 Alumni Professor of Law, Director, Transnational Law Institute, Washington and Lee University School of Law, USA

Chile Eboe-Osuji, former President, International Criminal Court and Distinguished International Jurist & Special Advisor to the President, Lincoln Alexander School of Law, Toronto Metropolitan University, Canada

Geoff Gilbert, Professor of Law and Head of the School of Law, University of Essex, Colchester UK

Philippe Kirsch, Ad hoc Judge, International Court of Justice; former President, International Criminal Court; Ambassador (Ret.) and former Legal Advisor, Ministry of Foreign Affairs of Canada; Sallèles d'Aude, Belgium/Canada

André Klip, Professor of Law, Department of Criminal Law and Criminology, Faculty of Law, Maastricht University; Maastricht, The Netherlands

Errki Kourula, Former Judge and President of the Appeals Division, International Criminal Court; The Hague, Finland

Motoo Noguchi, Former Chair of the Board of Directors, ICC Trust Fund for Victims and former UN International Judge at the Khmer Rouge Trials in Cambodia; Attorney at Law at Iwatagodo in Tokyo, Japan

Diane Orentlicher, Professor of International Law, Co-Director, Center for Human Rights and Humanitarian Law, Washington College of Law, American University; Washington, USA

Fausto Pocar, Judge and former President, International Criminal Tribunal for the Former Yugoslavia; President, International Institute of Humanitarian Law; Professor of International Law Emeritus, University of Milan; Italy

Leila Nadya Sadat, Henry H. Oberschelp Professor of Law, Director, Whitney R. Harris World Law Institute, Washington University School of Law; Alexis de Tocqueville Distinguished Fulbright Chair, University of Cergy-Pontoise; St. Louis, France/USA

Michael Scharf, Dean and John Deaver Drinko-Baker & Hostetler Professor of Law, Director, Frederick K. Cox International Law Center, Case Western Reserve University School of Law; Cleveland, USA

Ulrich Sieber, Director emeritus at the Max Planck Institute for the Study of Crime, Security and Law in Freiburg, Germany and honorary professor and faculty member at the law faculties of the University of Freiburg and the University of Munich, Germany

Goran Sluiter, Professor of Law, Department of Criminal Law and Criminal Procedure, Faculty of Law, University of Amsterdam; Amsterdam, The Netherlands

Françoise Tulkens, Former Vice-President, European Court of Human Rights; Strasbourg, France

Xuimei Wang, Professor of International Criminal Law, College for Criminal Law Science Beijing Normal University; Executive Director, ICC Project Office; Beijing, China

Christine van den Wyngaert, Judge Kosovo Specialist Chambers; former Judge, International Criminal Court; former Judge, International Criminal Tribunal for the Former Yugoslavia; former Ad hoc Judge, International Court of Justice, Belgium

Gert Vermeulen, Professor of Criminal Law, Director, Research Group Drug Policy, Criminal Policy and International Crime, Ghent University; Extraordinary Professor of Evidence Law, Maastricht University; Ghent, Belgium

Giuliana Ziccardi Capaldo, Professor International Law, Faculty of Law University of Salerno; Salerno, Italy

VOLUME 18

The titles published in this series are listed at *brill.com/icls*

International Criminal Evidence at the International Criminal Court

A Defense Perspective

By

Geert-Jan Alexander Knoops

BRILL | NIJHOFF

LEIDEN | BOSTON

Library of Congress Cataloging-in-Publication Data

Names: Knoops, Geert-Jan Alexander, 1960- author.
Title: International criminal evidence at the international criminal court : a defense perspective / Geert-Jan Alexander Knoops.
Description: Leiden ; Boston : Brill/Nijhoff, 2024. | Series: International criminal law series, 2213-2724 ; volume 18 | Includes bibliographical references and index.
Identifiers: LCCN 2024024534 (print) | LCCN 2024024535 (ebook) | ISBN 9789004364219 (hardback) | ISBN 9789004364226 (ebook)
Subjects: LCSH: Evidence, Criminal (International law) | Evidence, Expert. | Admissible evidence. | Defense (Criminal procedure) (International law) | International Criminal Court.
Classification: LCC KZ7422 .K59 2024 (print) | LCC KZ7422 (ebook) | DDC 345/.06--dc23/eng/20240602
LC record available at https://lccn.loc.gov/2024024534
LC ebook record available at https://lccn.loc.gov/2024024535

Typeface for the Latin, Greek, and Cyrillic scripts: "Brill". See and download: brill.com/brill-typeface.

ISSN 2213-2724
ISBN 978-90-04-36421-9 (hardback)
ISBN 978-90-04-36422-6 (e-book)
DOI 10.1163/9789004364226

Copyright 2024 by Koninklijke Brill BV, Leiden, The Netherlands.
Koninklijke Brill BV incorporates the imprints Brill, Brill Nijhoff, Brill Schöningh, Brill Fink, Brill mentis, Brill Wageningen Academic, Vandenhoeck & Ruprecht, Böhlau and V&R unipress.
All rights reserved. No part of this publication may be reproduced, translated, stored in a retrieval system, or transmitted in any form or by any means, electronic, mechanical, photocopying, recording or otherwise, without prior written permission from the publisher. Requests for re-use and/or translations must be addressed to Koninklijke Brill BV via brill.com or copyright.com.

This book is printed on acid-free paper and produced in a sustainable manner.

*To the best partner in my life, Carry,
and all my colleagues from my ICC defense team*

Contents

Preface XIII
Abbreviations XIV
Table of Cases XV

Introduction: Two Models of Criminal Law   1

PART 1
General

1   The Essence and Functioning of Criminal Evidence   5

2   The Admissibility and Weight of International Criminal Evidence at Trial   7
    2.1   Introduction   7
    2.2   Evidentiary Relevance and Probative Value within the ICC   7
    2.3   Procedural Aspects of 'Relevance' and 'Probative Value'   9

PART 2
Direct Evidence

3   (Eye)witnesses at ICC Trials   29
    3.1   Witness Dimensions   29
    3.2   The Evidentiary Value of (Eye)witnesses   29
    3.3   The Evidentiary Weight of (Eye)witnesses   33

4   Using (Anonymous) Hearsay Evidence   36
    4.1   Hearsay Evidence in Domestic Law   36
    4.2   Hearsay Evidence at the ICC   39
    4.3   Hearsay Evidence in ICTY Jurisprudence   45
    4.4   Analysis   46

5   Evidentiary Aspects of Insider Witnesses at the ICC   47
    5.1   The Evidentiary Risks and Pitfalls of Insider-Testimony at the ICC   48
    5.2   The Case Law on the Credibility and Reliability of Insider Witnesses   49

6   **Rule 68 and Prior Recorded Witness Testimony**   52
    6.1   Evolution and Context of ICTY Rules 92bis et seq.   52
    6.2   Other International ad hoc Tribunals   54
    6.3   Rules 92bis et seq. ICTY RPE   55
    6.4   ICC   74
    6.5   Analysis and Future Issues   120
    6.6   Conclusion   136

7   **Using Witness Preparation at the ICC**   141
    7.1   Introduction   141
    7.2   Statutory Law   142
    7.3   Witness Preparation in Other Common Law Jurisdictions   142
    7.4   Witness Preparation at the ad hoc Tribunals   144
    7.5   Witness Preparation at the ICC   146
    7.6   Conclusion   154

8   **(Crosss-)Examining Witnesses at the ICC**   156
    8.1   Types of Cross-examination   156
    8.2   ICTY Jurisprudence on Cross-examination of Witnesses   157
    8.3   Applying Cross-examination Techniques in Trials before the ICC   158

9   **The Defendant as Witness at His or Her Own Trial**   162

PART 3
Indirect Evidence

10   **Circumstantial Evidence at the ICC**   167
    10.1   Introduction   167
    10.2   Jurisprudential Denominations for Circumstantial Evidence   167
    10.3   Circumstantial Evidence within ad hoc Tribunals   170
    10.4   Challenging Circumstantial Evidence at Trial   171
    10.5   Evidentiary Value and Requirements for Circumstantial Evidence   172
    10.6   Increasing the Evidentiary Burden: the 'Shepherd Direction' Doctrine's Broad Application within the ICC   173
    10.7   Conclusion   174

11 Evidentiary Principles of Corroboration at the ICC 175
    11.1 Introduction 175
    11.2 The Purpose of Corroboration in Criminal Law 175
    11.3 An Example of the Corroboration Principle Applied in Criminal Law 177
    11.4 Corroboration under the ICC Framework 179
    11.5 Elements of Corroboration in International Criminal Law 184
    11.6 Conclusion 185

12 The Admissibility of 'Patterns of Conduct' as Evidence in (International) Criminal Cases 187
    12.1 The Pendergrass Jurisprudence 187
    12.2 'Pattern Evidence' at the ICC 189
    12.3 Conclusion 192

13 The Evidentiary Value and Admissibility of 'Bad Character Evidence' and 'Propensity Evidence' 193
    13.1 Introduction 193
    13.2 Common Law Parameters of 'Bad Character Evidence' 193
    13.3 Counterbalancing 'Bad Character Evidence' 195
    13.4 The Admissibility of 'Propensity Evidence' at Trial 197
    13.5 Conclusion 199

PART 4
The Admissibility of Expert Evidence

14 The Admissibility and Evidentiary Value of Expert Evidence 203
    14.1 Introduction 203
    14.2 Upcoming Role of Forensic Sciences at the ICC 203
    14.3 Towards a Uniform Admissibility Framework 208
    14.4 Substantive Requirements of Expert Evidence 212
    14.5 Testing Forensic Sciences in Court by Defense Counsel 214
    14.6 Challenging Expert Evidence: Strategic Guidelines 218
    14.7 Defense Strategies to Challenge Expert Witnesses before Trial 220
    14.8 Guidelines to (Cross-)examine and Test Forensic Experts at Trial 221

14.9   Defense Preparations to (Cross-)examine Experts at Trial   224
14.10 Joint Instructions to Forensic Experts   225
14.11 Disclosure Requirements   226
14.12 Cross-examination of Expert Witnesses   227
14.13 Examining Expert Evidence at Trial: the ECtHR Perspective   227
14.14 Conclusion   230

PART 5
Documentary Evidence

15 **Challenging Documentary Evidence at the ICC**   235
    15.1 Submission or Admission of Documentary Evidence at Trial   235
    15.2 Foundation Conditions for Documentary Evidence and Exhibits at Trial   240
    15.3 Conclusion   242

16 **The Evidentiary Value of NGO and IO Reports at the ICC**   243
    16.1 Introduction   243
    16.2 The Problematic Nature of NGO/IO Reports Used as Evidence   244
    16.3 The Use of NGO/IO Reports at Different Stages of ICC Proceedings   250
    16.4 The Admissibility of NGO Reports Based on Anonymous Sources   257
    16.5 Conclusion   259

17 **The Evidentiary Value of Social Media at the ICC**   260
    17.1 Introduction   260
    17.2 Definitions and Relevant Concepts   261
    17.3 General Evidentiary Pitfalls of Social Media Content   262
    17.4 Specificities of MIM Evidence   267
    17.5 Legal Framework in Construction   268
    17.6 Social Media Evidence and the Right to a Fair Trial: the ECtHR Perspective   273
    17.7 Conclusion   277

CONTENTS   XI

PART 6
The Extent of Disclosing Exculpatory Criminal Evidence

18 The Extent of Disclosing Exculpatory Criminal Evidence   281
    18.1 Introduction   281
    18.2 The Evidentiary Meaning of 'Exculpatory Evidence'   281
    18.3 Practical Implications Pertaining to the Defense
          Disclosure Burden   284
    18.4 Towards a Different Disclosure System   285
    18.5 Disclosure Mechanisms to Prevent Miscarriages of Justice   285
    18.6 Conclusion   288

PART 7
Weighing Evidence at ICC Trials

19 Evidence Presentation in ICC Trials   291
    19.1 Practices at the ICC   291
    19.2 Presentation of Evidence by Way of Leading Questions   294
    19.3 Presenting Evidence at Opening and Closing Statements   295
    19.4 Conclusion   296

20 No Case to Answer Proceedings at the ICC   297
    20.1 Introduction   297
    20.2 Historical Background on 'No Case to Answer' Motions   297
    20.3 Jurisprudence of International *ad hoc* Tribunals   300
    20.4 Overview of 'No Case to Answer' Proceedings at the ICC   308
    20.5 Conclusion   315

21 The Legal Position of the Acquitted Person at the ICC   317
    21.1 Introduction   317
    21.2 The (Non-)Right to Compensation for Any Acquitted Person
          at the ICC   318
    21.3 Establishing a 'Grave and Manifest Miscarriage of Justice'
          in Practice   326
    21.4 The Future of Acquitted Persons at the ICC: towards a Right
          to Compensation?   327
    21.5 Conclusion   329

Overall Concluding Remarks and Recommendations 330

Bibliography 333
Index 340

Preface

This book is meant to provide its readers with the 'state of the evidentiary art' within the system of the International Criminal Court (ICC). At the same time, it intends to provide both Prosecution and Defense counsel operating at the ICC with some guidance as regards several fundamental evidentiary subjects and how to perhaps best approach them. In particular, the role of Defense counsel at the ICC, bearing in mind that the ICC-system is still a developing mechanism, can be pivotal in the creation of case law in so far as it concerns the promulgation of evidentiary topics such as the admissibility of documentary and forensic evidence.

The contents of the book are a reflection of academic research but also of practical experience in the field from the perspective of the work as Defense counsel operating before the ICC. The ICC as an institution was set up to uphold the international rule of law and to serve international justice. Justice can be served by a conviction, but also by an acquittal. Sometimes the latter aspect of this 'justice coin' is underexposed or even ignored. Within the system of the ICC, and particularly in its search to justice, the subject-matter of "criminal evidence" – as this book will demonstrate – plays a decisive role in determining 'guilt' or 'innocence'. I hope therefore that the content of this work might assist both academics and practitioners in their respective roles operating in the field of international criminal law and especially within the ICC-system.

As author I am greatly indebted to my dear colleagues and friends of the ICC who so dedicatedly assisted me in the writing of this book and had a major part in the end result: Ms. Kelly Mae Smith, Ms. Myriam Hollant, Ms. Elsa Bohne, Ms. Alana Copier and Mr. Piet Seidenberg, all legal practitioners within this field. The book was born thanks to them.

Geert-Jan Alexander Knoops
August 2024

Abbreviations

Advisory Committee on Legal Texts (ACLT)
Appeal Chamber (A Ch)
Assembly of States Parties (ASP)
Call Data Records (CDRS)
Criminal Justice ACT of 2003 (CJA)
Elements of Crimes (EC)
European Convention on Human Rights (ECHR)
European Court of Human Rights (ECtHR)
European Court of Justice (ECJ)
Foreign Terrorist Fighters (FTF)
ICC Rules of Procedure and Evidence (ICC RPE)
ICTY Rules of Procedure and Evidence (ICTY RPE)
International Covenant on Civil and Political Rights (ICCPR)
International Criminal Court (ICC)
International Criminal Tribunal for Rwanda (ICTR)
International Criminal Tribunal for the Former Yugoslavia (ICTY)
Legal Representative for Victims (LRV)
Mobile Instant Messaging apps (MIM apps)
Office of the Prosecutor (OTP)
Pre-Trial Chamber (PT Ch)
Rome Statute of the International Criminal Court (RS)
Special Court for Sierra Leone (SCSL)
Special Tribunal for Lebanon (STL)
STL Rules of Procedure and Evidence (STL RPE)
Study Group on Governance (SGG)
Trial Chamber (T Ch)
Working Group on Lessons Learnt (WGLL)

Table of Cases

International Criminal Tribunal for the former Yugoslavia (ICTY)

Prosecutor v Aleksovski (Decision on Prosecutor's Appeal on Admissibility of Evidence) IT-95-14/1-A, A Ch (16 February 1999).

Prosecutor v Blagojević and Jokić (First Motion for Admission of Witness Statements and Prior Testimony Pursuant to Rule 92bis) IT-02-60-T, T Ch I(A) (12 June 2003).

Prosecutor v Blagojević and Jokić (Appeal judgment) I-02-60-A, A Ch (9 May 2007).

Blagojević and Jokić (Trial judgment) IT-02-60-T, T Ch I(A) (17 January 2005).

Prosecutor v Blaškić (Decision on the Production of Discovery Materials) IT-95-14, T Ch (27 January 1997).

Prosecutor v Blaškić (Trial judgment) IT-95-14-T, T Ch (3 March 2000).

Prosecutor v Brđanin (Decision on Motion for Acquittal pursuant to Rule 98 bis) IT-99-36-T, T Ch (28 November 2003).

Prosecutor v Brđanin (Decision on Motion for Acquittal pursuant to Rule 98 bis) IT-99-36-R77, T Ch (19 March 2004).

Prosecutor v Brđanin (Trial Judgment) IT-99-36-T, T Ch II (1 September 2004).

Prosecutor v Delalić et al. (Decision on Application of Defendant Zejnil Delalic for Leave to Appeal Against the Decision of the Trial Chamber of 19 January 1998 for the Admissibility of Evidence) IT-96-21-AR73.2, A Ch (4 March 1998).

Prosecutor v Delalić et al. (Decision on the Defence Motion to Compel the Discovery of Identity and Location of Witnesses) IT-96-21-T, T Ch (18 March 1997).

Prosecutor v Galić (Decision Concerning the Expert Witnesses Ewa Tableau and Richard Philipps) IT-98-29-T, T Ch I (3 July 2002).

Prosecutor v Galić (Decision on Interlocutory Appeal Concerning Rule 92bis(C)) IT-98-29-AR73.2, A Ch (7 June 2002).

Prosecutor v Galić (Decision on the Motion for the entry of Acquittal of the Accused Stanislav Galic) IT-98-29-T, T Ch (3 October 2002).

Prosecutor v Galić (Trial judgment) IT-98-29-T, T Ch I (5 December 2003).

Prosecutor v Hadžihasanović & Kubura (Trial judgment) IT-01-47-T, T Ch II (15 March 2006).

Prosecutor v Halilović (Decision on the Issuance of Subpoenas) IT-01-48-AR73, A Ch (21 June 2004).

Prosecutor v Haradinaj et al. (Appeal judgment) IT-04-84-A, A Ch (19 July 2010).

Prosecutor v Haradinaj et al. (Trial judgment with confidential annex) IT-04-84bis-T, T Ch II (29 November 2012).

Prosecutor v Haradinaj et al. (Trial judgment) IT-04-84-T, T Ch I (3 April 2008).

Prosecutor v Jelisić (Appeal judgment) IT-95-10-A, A Ch (5 July 2001).

Prosecutor v Kabashi (Sentencing judgment) IT-04-84-R77.1, T Ch I (16 September 2011).

Prosecutor v Karadžić (Appeal judgment) IT-95-5/18-AR98bis.1, A Ch (11 July 2013).

Prosecutor v Kordić and Čerkez (Decision on Appeal Regarding Statement of a Deceased Witness) IT-95-14/2-AR73.5, A Ch (21 July 2000).

Prosecutor v Kordić and Čerkez (Decision on Defence Motions for Judgment of Acquittal) IT-95-14/2-T, T Ch III (6 April 2000).

Prosecutor v Krajišnik (Decision on Appeal of Rule 98 bis Decision) IT-00-39-AR98bis.1, A Ch (4 October 2005).

Prosecutor v Krajišnik (Trial judgment) IT-00-39-T, T Ch I (27 September 2006).

TABLE OF CASES XVII

Prosecutor v Krnojelac (Trial Judgment) IT-97-25-T, T Ch II (15 March 2002).

Prosecutor v Krstić (Appeal judgment) IT-98-33-A, A Ch (19 April 2004).

Prosecutor v Kubura (Appeal judgment) IT-01-47-A, A Ch (22 April 2008).

Prosecutor v Kubura (Decision on Motions for Acquittal pursuant to Rule 98 bis of the Rules of Procedure and Evidence) IT-01-47-T, T Ch (27 September 2004).

Prosecutor v Kupreškić et al. (Decision on evidence of the good character of the accused and the defence of *Tu quoque*) IT-95-16-T, T Ch (17 February 1999).

Prosecutor v Kupreškić et al. (Appeal judgment) IT-95-16-A, A Ch (23 October 2001).

Prosecutor v Kvočka et al. (Appeal judgment) IT-98-30/1-A, A Ch (28 February 2005).

Prosecutor v Limaj et al. (Decision on Defence Motion on Prosecution Practice of 'Proofing' Witnesses) IT-03-66-T, T Ch II (10 December 2004).

Prosecutor v Ljubičić (Decision on Appeal Against Decision on Referral Under Rule 11 bis) IT-00-41-AR11bis.1, A Ch (4 July 2006).

Prosecutor v Martić (Decision on Appeal Against the Trial Chamber's Decision on the Evidence of Witness Milan Babić) IT-95-11-AR73.2, A Ch (14 September 2006).

Prosecutor v Mejakić et al. (Decision on Joint defence Appeal Against Decision on Referral under Rule 11bis) IT-02-65-AR11bis.1, A Ch (7 April 2006).

Prosecutor v Milošević (Decision on prosecution motion for the admission of transcripts in lieu of viva voce testimony pursuant to 92bis(d) – foca transcripts) IT-02-54-T, T Ch III (30 June 2003).

Prosecutor v Milošević (Appeal judgment) IT-98-29/1-A, A Ch (12 November 2009).

Prosecutor v Milošević (Decision on Admissibility of Prosecution Investigator's Evidence) IT-02-54-AR73.2, A Ch (30 September 2002).

Prosecutor v Milošević (Decision on Interlocutory Appeal of the Trial Chamber's Decision on the Assignment of Defence Counsel) IT-02-54-AR73.7, A Ch (1 November 2004).

Prosecutor v Milošević (Decision on Interlocutory Appeal on the Admissibility of Evidence-in-Chief in the Form of Written Statements) IT-02-54-AR73.4, A Ch (30 September 2003).

Prosecutor v Milošević (Decision on Prosecution Request to Have Written Witness Statements Admitted under Rule 92bis) IT-02-54-T, T Ch III (21 March 2002).

Prosecutor v Milošević (Dissenting Opinion of Judge David Hunt on Admissibility of Evidence-in-Chief in the Form of Written Statement (Majority Decision Given 30 September 2003)) IT-02-54-AR73.4, A Ch (21 October 2003).

Prosecutor v Milutinović et al. (Prosecution Motion for the Admission of Transcripts in Lieu of Viva Voce Testimony Pursuant to Rule 92bis (D)) IT-05-87-T, T Ch III (10 January 2003).

Prosecutor v Milutinović et al. (Decision on Ojdanic Motion to Prohibit Witness Proofing) IT-05-87-T, T Ch III (12 December 2006).

Prosecutor v Milutinović et al. (Decision on Evidence Tendered through Sandra Mitchell and Frederik Abrahams) IT-05-87-T, T Ch III (1 September 2006).

Prosecutor v Milutinović et al. (Decision on Lukic Defence Motions for Admission of Documents from Bar Table) IT-05-87-T, T Ch III (11 June 2008).

Prosecutor v Mladić (Public Redacted Version of Decision on Defence Interlocutory Appeal from the Trial Chamber Rule 98 bis Decision) IT-09-92-AR73.4, A Ch (24 July 2014).

Prosecutor v Mrkšić (Decision on Defence Interlocutory Appeal on Communication with Potential Witnesses of the Opposite Party) IT-95-13п-AR73, A Ch (30 July 2003).

Prosecutor v Mucić et al. (Appeal judgment) IT-96-21-A, A Ch (20 February 2001).

TABLE OF CASES XIX

Prosecutor v Naletilić and Martinović (Decision on the Admission of Witness Statements into Evidence) IT-98-34-T, T Ch I(A) (14 November 2001).

Prosecutor v Naletilić and Martinović (Decision on the Prosecutor's Request for Public Version of Trial Chamber's "Decision on the Motion to Admit Statement of Deceased Witnesses [...]" of 22 January 2002) IT-98-34-T, T Ch I(A) (27 February 2002).

Prosecutor v Popović et al. (Decision on Prosecution Motion for Admission of Evidence Pursuant to Rule 92 quarter) IT-05-88-T, T Ch II (21 April 2008).

Prosecutor v Popović et al. (Decision on the Admissibility of the Borovcanin Interview and the Amendment of the Rule 65 ter Exhibit List) IT-05-88-T, T Ch II (25 October 2007).

Prosecutor v Popović et al. (Trial judgment) IT-05-88-T, T Ch II (10 June 2010).

Prosecutor v Prlić et al. (Appeal judgment) IT-04-74-A, A Ch (29 November 2017).

Prosecutor v Prlić et al. (Decision on the Application of Rule 92ter of the Rules) IT-04-74-T, T Ch III (25 June 2007).

Prosecutor v Prlić et al. (Separate Opinion of Presiding Judge Jean-Claude Antonetti Regarding the Decision on the Application of Article 92ter of the Rules) IT-04-74-T, T Ch III (25 June 2007).

Prosecutor v Šešelj (Redacted version of the "Decision on the prosecution's consolidated motion pursuant to Rules 89 (F), 92 bis, 92 ter and 92 quater of the Rules of Procedure and Evidence" filed confidentially on 7 January 2008) IT-03-67-T, T Ch III (21 February 2008).

Prosecutor v Sikirica et al. (Decision on Prosecution's Application to Admit Transcripts Under Rule 92bis) IT-95-8-T, T Ch III (23 May 2001).

Prosecutor v Stakić (Appeal judgment) IT-97-24-A, A Ch (22 March 2006).

Prosecutor v Strugar (Decision on Defence Motion requesting Judgment of Acquittal pursuant to Rule 98 bis) IT-01-42-T, T Ch II (21 June 2004).

Prosecutor v Tadić (Decision on the Defence Motion on Hearsay) IT-94-1-T, T Ch I (5 August 1996).

Prosecutor v Tolimir (Partial Decision on Prosecution's Rule 92bis and Rule 92ter Motion for Five Witnesses) IT-05-88/2-T, T Ch II (27 August 2010).

Prosecutor v Vasiljević (Appeal judgment) IT-98-32-A, A Ch (25 February 2004).

International Criminal Tribunal for Rwanda (ICTR)

Prosecutor v Akayesu (Appeal judgment) ICTR-96-4-A, A Ch (1 June 2001).

Prosecutor v Bagosora et al. (Decision on Admissibility of Proposed Testimony of Witness DBY) ICTR-98-41-T, T Ch I (18 September 2003).

Prosecutor v Bagosora et al. (Decision on Motions for Judgment of Acquittal) ICTR-98-41-T, T Ch I (2 February 2005).

Prosecutor v Barayagwiza (Decision on Prosecution Request for Review of Reconsideration) ICTR-97-19-AR72, A Ch (3 March 2000).

Prosecutor v Bikindi (Appeal judgment) ICTR-01-72-A, A Ch (18 March 2010).

Prosecutor v Gatete (Appeal judgment) ICTR-00-61-A, A Ch (9 October 2012).

Prosecutor v Kamuhanda (Decision on Kamuhanda's Motion for Partial Acquittal Pursuant to Rule 98 bis of the Rules of Procedure and Evidence) ICTR-99-54A-T, T Ch II (20 August 2002).

Prosecutor v Kanyarukiga (Appeal judgment) ICTR-02-78-A, A Ch (8 May 2012).

Prosecutor v Karemera et al. (Decision on Interlocutory Appeal Regarding Witness Proofing) ICTR-98-44-AR73.8, A Ch (11 May 2007).

Prosecutor v Karemera et al. (Decision on Defence Motions to Prohibit Witness Proofing, Rule 73 of the Rules of Procedure and Evidence) ICTR-98-44-T, T Ch III (15 December 2006).

Prosecutor v Karemera et al. (Decision on Prosecutor's Interlocutory Appeal of Decision on Judicial Notice) ICTR-98-44-AR73(C), A Ch (16 June 2006).

TABLE OF CASES XXI

Prosecutor v Karera (Appeal Judgment) ICTR-01-74-A, A Ch (2 February 2009).

Prosecutor v Mpambara (Decision on the Defence's Motion for Judgement of Acquittal) ICTR-2001-65-T, T Ch I (21 October 2005).

Prosecutor v Munyakazi (Appeal Judgment) ICTR-97-36A-A, A Ch (28 September 2011).

Prosecutor v Munyakazi (Decision on the Prosecutor's Request for Referral of Case to the Republic of Rwanda) ICTR-97-36-R11bis, T Ch III (28 May 2008).

Prosecutor v Muvunyi (Decision on Tharcisse Muvunyi's Motion for Judgement of Acquittal Pursuant to Rule 98 bis) ICTR-2000-55A-T, T Ch II (13 October 2005).

Prosecutor v Nahimana et al. (Appeal Judgment) ICTR-99-52-A, A Ch (28 November 2007).

Prosecutor v Nchamihigo (Decision on Defence Motion for Judgement of Acquittal) ICTR-2001-63-T, T Ch III (8 March 2007).

Prosecutor v Ndahimana (Appeal judgment) ICTR-01-68-A, A Ch (16 December 2013)

Prosecutor v Ndindiliyimana et al. (Decision on Defence Motions for Judgement of Acquittal) ICTR-2000-56-T, T Ch II (20 March 2007).

Prosecutor v Ntagerura et al. (Appeal judgment) ICTR-99-46-A, A Ch (7 July 2006).

Prosecutor v Nyiramasuhuko et al. (Decision on Defence Motions for Acquittal Under Rule 98 bis) ICTR-98-42-T, T Ch II (16 December 2004).

Prosecutor v Rukundo (Appeal Judgment) ICTR-2001-70-A, A Ch (20 October 2010).

Prosecutor v Rwamakuba (Decision on Defence Motion for Judgement of Acquittal) ICTR-98-44C-T, T Ch III (28 October 2005).

Prosecutor v Setako (Appeal judgment) ICTR-04-81-A, A Ch (28 September 2011).

Prosecutor v Zigiranyirazo (Decision on the Defence Motion Pursuant to Rule 98 bis) ICTR-2001-73-T, T Ch III (21 February 2007).

International Criminal Court (ICC)

Prosecutor v Abd-Al-Rahman (Public redacted version of the Decision on the Prosecution's request to introduce prior recorded testimonies under Rule 68(2)(c)) ICC-02/05-01/20-603-Red, T Ch I (21 February 2022).

Prosecutor v Abu Garda (Decision on the Confirmation of Charges) ICC-02/05-02/09-243-Red, PT Ch I (8 February 2010).

Prosecutor v Al Bashir (Decision on the Prosecution's Application for a Warrant of Arrest against Omar Hassan Ahmad Al Bashir) ICC-02/05-01/09-3, PT Ch I (4 March 2009).

Prosecutor v Al Hassan (Annex A to the Decision on the conduct of proceedings) ICC-01/12-01/18-789-AnxA, T Ch X (6 May 2020).

Prosecutor v Al Hassan (Annex to the Decision on witness preparation and familiarisation) ICC-01/12-01/18-666, T Ch X (17 March 2020).

Prosecutor v Al Hassan (Decision on Defence's proposed expert witnesses and related applications seeking to introduce their prior recorded testimony under Rule 68(3) of the Rules) ICC-01/12-01/18-2206, T Ch X (1 June 2022).

Prosecutor v Al Hassan (Decision on the Defence's request for variation of the time limit related to the accompanying declarations of Rule 68(2)(b) witnesses and the introduction into evidence of the prior recorded testimony of D-0002 and D-0146 pursuant to Rule 68(2)(c) of the Rules) ICC-01/12-01/18-2445-Red, T Ch X (16 December 2022).

Prosecutor v Al Hassan (Decision on Prosecution's proposed expert witness) ICC-01/12-01/18-989-Red, T Ch X (21 October 2020).

Prosecutor v Al Hassan (Decision on the introduction into evidence of P-0125's prior recorded testimony pursuant to Rule 68(2)(c) of the Rules) ICC-01/12-01/18-1413-Conf, T Ch X (14 April 2014).

Prosecutor v Al Hassan (Decision on the introduction of evidence of witness P-0643) ICC-01/12-01/18-1409-Red, T Ch X (12 April 2021).

Prosecutor v Al Hassan (Decision on witness preparation and familiarisation) ICC-01/12-01/18-666, T Ch X (17 March 2020).

Prosecutor v Al Hassan (Public redacted version of 'Decision on requests related to the submission into evidence of Mr Al Hassan's statements') ICC-01/12-01/18-1475-Red, T Ch X (20 May 2021).

Prosecutor v Al Hassan (Public Redacted Version of 'Decision on Defence application to exclude the evidence of or recall P-0547') ICC-01/12-01/18-2344-Red, T Ch X (21 September 2022).

Prosecutor v Al Hassan (Public redacted version of "Decision on the introduction into evidence of P-0570's prior recorded testimony pursuant to Rule 68(2)(c) of the Rules") ICC-01/12-01/18-1588-Red, T Ch X (11 August 2021).

Prosecutor v Al Hassan (Rapport du Greffe en application de la Décision du 20 mars 2019) ICC-01/12-01/18-359, Registrar (29 May 2019).

Prosecutor v Al Mahdi (Trial judgement and Sentence) ICC-01/12-01/15-171, T Ch VIII (27 September 2016).

Prosecutor v Al-Werfalli (Warrant of Arrest) ICC-01/11-01/17-2, PT Ch I (17 August 2017).

Prosecutor v Banda (Public redacted version Judgment on the appeal of Mr Abdallah Banda Abakaer Nourain against Trial Chamber IV's issuance of a warrant of arrest) ICC-02/05-03/09-632-Red, A Ch (3 March 2015).

Prosecutor v Banda and Jerbo (Corrigendum of the "Decision on the Confirmation of Charges") ICC-02/05-03/09-121-Corr-Red, PT Ch I (7 March 2011).

Prosecutor v Banda and Jerbo (Judgement on the appeal of Mr Abdollah Banda Abakaer Nourain and Mr Salah Mohammed Jerbo Jamus against the decision of Trial Chamber IV of 23 January 2013 entitled "Decision on the Defence's Request for Disclosure of Documents in the Possession of The Office of the Prosecutor") ICC-02/05 03/09-501, A Ch (28 August 2013).

Prosecutor v Bemba et al. (Appeal judgment) ICC-01/05-01/13-2275-Red, A Ch (8 March 2018).

Prosecutor v Bemba et al. (Decision on Narcisse Arido's Request to Preclude the Prosecution from Using Private Communications) ICC-01/05-01/13-1711, T Ch VII (10 March 2016).

Prosecutor v Bemba et al. (Decision on Prosecution Request to Exclude Defence Witness D22-0004) ICC-01/05-01/13-1653, T Ch VII (24 February 2016).

Prosecutor v Bemba et al. (Decision on Relevance and Propriety of Certain Kilolo Defence Witnesses) ICC-01/05-01/13-1600, T Ch VII (4 February 2016).

Prosecutor v Bemba et al. (Decision on Request in Response to Two Austrian Decisions) ICC-01/05-01/13-1948, T Ch VII (14 July 2016).

Prosecutor v Bemba et al. (Decision on Requests to Exclude Western Union Documents and other Evidence Pursuant to Article 69(7)) ICC-01/05-01/13-1854, T Ch VII (29 April 2016).

Prosecutor v Bemba et al. (Decision on the Unified Protocol on the practices used to prepare and familiarise witnesses for giving testimony at trial) ICC-01/05-01/08-1016, T Ch III (18 November 2010).

Prosecutor v Bemba et al. (Decision on Witness Preparation and Familiarisation) ICC-01/05-01/13-1252, T Ch VII (15 September 2015).

Prosecutor v Bemba et al. (Directions on the conduct of the proceedings) ICC-01/05-01/13-1209, T Ch VII (2 September 2015).

Prosecutor v Bemba et al. (Judgment on the appeal of Mr Jean-Jacques Mangenda Kabongo against the decision of Pre-Trial Chamber IT of 17 March 2014 entitled "Decision on the 'Requete de mise en liberte' submitted by the Defence for Jean-Jacques Mangenda") ICC-01/05-01/13-560, A Ch (11 July 2014).

Prosecutor v Bemba et al. (Separate opinion of Judge Geoffrey Henderson) ICC-01/05-01/13-2275-Anx, A Ch (8 March 2018).

Prosecutor v Bemba Gombo (Appeal judgment) ICC-01/05-01/08-3636-Red, A Ch (8 June 2018).

Prosecutor v Bemba Gombo (Decision on "Prosecution's Motion to Exclude Defence Political-Military Strategy Expert") ICC-01/05-01/08-2273, T Ch III (21 August 2012).

Prosecutor v Bemba Gombo (Decision on Mr. Bemba's claim for compensation and damages) ICC-01/05-01/08-3694, PT Ch II (18 May 2020).

TABLE OF CASES   XXV

Prosecutor v Bemba Gombo (Decision on the "Defence Motion on Prosecution contact with its witnesses") ICC-01/05-01/08-3070, T Ch III (22 May 2014).

Prosecutor v Bemba Gombo (Decision on the "Prosecution Application for Leave to Submit in Writing Prior-Recorded Testimonies by CAR-OTP-WWWW-0032, CAR-OTP-WWWW-0080, and CAR-OTP-WWWW-0108") ICC-01/05-01/08-886, T Ch III (16 September 2010).

Prosecutor v Bemba Gombo (Decision on the Admissibility and Abuse of Process Challenges) ICC-01/05-01/08-802, T Ch III (24 June 2010).

Prosecutor v Bemba Gombo (Decision on the Admission into Evidence of Items Deferred in the Chamber's « Decision of the Prosecution's Application for Admission of Materials into Evidence Pursuant to Article 64(9) of the Rome Statute ») ICC-01/05-01/08-2721, T Ch III (27 June 2013).

Prosecutor v Bemba Gombo (Decision on the admission into evidence of materials contained in the prosecution's list of evidence) ICC-01/05-01/08-1022, T Ch III (19 November 2010).

Prosecutor v Bemba Gombo (Decision on the admission into evidence of items deferred in the Chamber's "First decision on the prosecution and defence requests for the admission of evidence" (ICC-01/05-01/08-2012)) ICC-01/05-01/08-2793, T Ch III (03 September 2013).

Prosecutor v Bemba Gombo (Decision on the Confirmation of Charges) ICC-01/05-01/08-424, PT Ch II (15 June 2009).

Prosecutor v Bemba Gombo (Decision on the procedures to be adopted for instructing expert witnesses) ICC-01/05-01/08-695, T Ch III (12 February 2010).

Prosecutor v Bemba Gombo (Defence submissions on the proposed admission of Witness CHM-01's statement) ICC-01/05-01/08-2936, Defense (13 January 2014).

Prosecutor v Bemba Gombo (Dissenting Opinion of Judge Kuniko Ozaki on the Decision on the admission into evidence of materials contained in the prosecution's list of evidence) ICC-01/05-01/08-1028, T Ch III (23 November 2010).

Prosecutor v Bemba Gombo (Judgment on the appeals of Mr Jean-Pierre Bemba Gombo and the Prosecutor against the decision of Trial Chamber III entitled "Decision on the admission into evidence of materials contained in the prosecution's list of evidence") ICC-01/05-01/08-1386, A Ch (3 May 2011).

Prosecutor v Bemba Gombo (Order on the procedure relating to the submission of evidence) ICC-01/05-01/08-1470, T Ch III (31 May 2011).

Prosecutor v Bemba Gombo (Order seeking observations on the admission into evidence of written statement of Witness CHM-01) ICC-01/05-01/08-2923, T Ch III (13 December 2013).

Prosecutor v Bemba Gombo (Partly Dissenting Opinion of Judge Kuniko Ozaki on the Decision on the Unified Protocol on the practices used to prepare and familiarise witnesses for giving testimony at trial) ICC-01/05-01/08-1039, T Ch III (24 November 2010).

Prosecutor v Bemba Gombo (Prosecution's Observations on the admission into evidence of the written statement of witness CHM-01) ICC-01/05-01/08-2930, T Ch III (10 January 2014).

Prosecutor v Bemba Gombo (Public Redacted Version of "Decision on the Prosecution's Application for Admission of Materials into Evidence Pursuant to Article 64(9) of the Rome Statute" of 6 September 2012) ICC-01/05-01/08-2299-Red, T Ch III (8 October 2012).

Prosecutor v Bemba Gombo (Public Redacted Version of "Decision on the admission into evidence of items deferred in the Chamber's previous decisions, items related to the testimony of Witness CHM-01 and written statements of witnesses who provided testimony before the Chamber") ICC-01/05-01/08-3019-Red, T Ch III (26 August 2014).

Prosecutor v Bemba Gombo (Public redacted version of Decision on the presentation of additional testimony pursuant to Articles 64(6)(b) and (d) and 69(3) of the Rome Statute) ICC-01/05-01/08-2863, T Ch III (6 November 2011).

Prosecutor v Bemba Gombo (Public redacted version of the First decision on the prosecution and defence requests for the admission of evidence, dated 15 December 2011) ICC-01/05-01/08-2012-Red, T Ch III (9 February 2012).

TABLE OF CASES   XXVII

Prosecutor v Bemba Gombo (Separate Opinion of Judge Van den Wyngaert and Judge Morrison) ICC-01/05-01/08-3636-Anx2, A Ch (8 June 2018).

Prosecutor v Bemba Gombo (Trial judgment) ICC-01/05-01/08-3343, T Ch III (21 March 2016).

Prosecutor v Bemba Gombo (Victims and Witnesses Unit's Unified Protocol on the practices used to prepare and familiarise witnesses for giving testimony at trial) ICC-01/05-01/08-972, Registrar (22 October 2010).

Prosecutor v Blé Goudé (Decision on Mr. Blé Goudé's request for compensation) ICC-02/11-01/15-1427, Article 85 Ch (10 February 2022).

Prosecutor v Gbagbo (Decision adjourning the hearing on the confirmation of charges pursuant to article 61(7)(c)(i) of the Rome Statute) ICC-02/11-01/11-432, PT Ch I (3 June 2013).

Prosecutor v Gbagbo (Decision on the Confirmation of Charges) ICC-02/11-01/11-656-Red, PT Ch I (12 June 2014).

Prosecutor v Gbagbo (Judgment on the appeal of Côte d'Ivoire against the decision of Pre-Trial Chamber I of 11 December 2014 entitled 'Decision on Côte d'Ivoire's challenge to the admissibility of the case against Simone Gbagbo'") ICC-02/11-01/12-75-Red, A Ch (27 May 2015).

Prosecutor v Gbagbo and Blé Goudé (Corrigendum of Party Dissenting Opinion Of Judge Henderson) ICC-02/11-01/15-950-Anx-Red-Corr, T Ch I (23 June 2017).

Prosecutor v Gbagbo and Blé Goudé (Decision on 'Defence's Motion to Preclude and Exclude the prospected Evidence of Witness P-369, or, in the alternative, to restrict the Scope of Witness P-0369's intended Evidence') ICC-02/11-01/15-539, T Ch I (13 May 2016).

Prosecutor v Gbagbo and Blé Goudé (Decision on the submission and admission of evidence) ICC-02/11-01/15-405, T Ch I (29 January 2016).

Prosecutor v Gbagbo and Blé Goudé (Decision on witness preparation and familiarisation) ICC-02/11-01/15-355, T Ch I (2 December 2015).

Prosecutor v Gbagbo and Blé Goudé (Defence's Motion to Preclude and Exclude the prospected Evidence of Witnesses P-369, or, in the alternative, to restrict the Scope of Witness P-0369's intended Evidence) ICC-02/11-01/15-509, T Ch I (10 May 2016).

Prosecutor v Gbagbo and Blé Goudé (Directions on the conduct of the proceedings) ICC-02/11-01/15-205, T Ch I (3 September 2015).

Prosecutor v Gbagbo and Blé Goudé (Dissenting Opinion of Judge Henderson) ICC-02/11-01/15-355-Anx1, T Ch I (3 December 2015).

Prosecutor v Gbagbo and Blé Goudé (Judgment in the appeal of the Prosecutor against Trial Chamber I's decision on the no case to answer motions) ICC-02/11-01/15-1400, A Ch (31 March 2021).

Prosecutor v Gbagbo and Blé Goudé (Judgment on the appeals of Mr Laurent Gbagbo and Mr Charles Blé Goudé against the decision of Trial Chamber I of 9 June 2016 entitled "Decision on the Prosecutor's application to introduce prior recorded testimony under Rules 68(2)(b) and 68(3)", 1 November 2016) ICC-02/11-01/15-744, A Ch (1 November 2016).

Prosecutor v Gbagbo and Blé Goudé (Judgment on the appeals of Mr Laurent Gbagbo and Mr Charles Blé Goudé against Trial Chamber I's decision on the submission of documentary evidence) ICC-02/11-01/15-995, A Ch (24 July 2017).

Prosecutor v Gbagbo and Blé Goudé (Second public redacted version of "Annex 1 – Prosecution's Consolidated Response to the Defence No Case to Answer", 10 September 2018, ICC-02/11-01/15-1207-Conf-Anx1) ICC-02/11-01/15-1207-Conf-Anx1, T Ch I (8 November 2018).

Prosecutor v Gbagbo and Blé Goudé (Public Redacted Version of Reasons of Judge Geoffrey Henderson) ICC-02/11-01/15-1263-AnxB-Red, T Ch I (16 July 2019).

Prosecutor v Gbagbo and Blé Goudé (Separate Opinion of Judge Henderson annexed to 'Decision on the Prosecutor's Application to protect the confidentiality of the sources of P-0369') ICC-02/11-01/15-466-Conf-Anx, T Ch I (21 March 2016).

Prosecutor v Gicheru (Public Redacted Version of Decision On The Request To Exclude Audio Recordings Pursuant To Article 69(7) of The Statute) ICC-01/09-01/20-284-Red2, T Ch III (18 February 2022).

TABLE OF CASES   XXIX

Prosecutor v Katanga (Decision on the Defence Requests Set Forth in Observations 3379 and 3386 of 3 and 17 June 2013) ICC-01/04-01/07-3388-tENG, T CH II (26 June 2013).

Prosecutor v Katanga (Trial judgment) ICC-01/04-01/07-3436-tENG, T Ch II (7 March 2014).

Prosecutor v Katanga (Version publique expurgée de « Décision relative à trois requêtes tendant à la production d'éléments de preuve supplémentaires et à un accord en matière de preuve » (ICC-01/04-01/07-3217-Conf)) ICC-01/04-01/07-3217-Red, T Ch II (4 January 2012).

Prosecutor v Katanga and Ngudjolo Chui (Annex I – Minority Opinion of Judge Christine Van den Wyngaert) ICC-01/04-01/07-3436-AnxI, T Ch II (7 March 2014).

Prosecutor v Katanga and Ngudjolo Chui (Corrigendum – Directions for the conduct of the proceedings and testimony in accordance with rule 140) ICC-01/04-01/07-1665-Corr, T Ch II (1 December 2009).

Prosecutor v Katanga and Ngudjolo Chui (Corrigendum to Defence Request to Admit into Evidence Entirety of Document DRC-OTP-1017-0572) ICC-01/04-01/07-2839-Corr, T Ch II (18 April 2011).

Prosecutor v Katanga and Ngudjolo Chui (Corrigendum to the Decision on the Prosecution Motion for admission of prior recorded testimony of Witness P-02 and accompanying video excerpts) ICC-01/04-01/07-2289-Corr-Red, T Ch II (27 August 2010).

Prosecutor v Katanga and Ngudjolo Chui (Decision on Defence Request to Admit into Evidence Entirety of Document DRC-OTP-1017-0572) ICC-01/04-01/07-2954, T Ch II (25 May 2011).

Prosecutor v Katanga and Ngudjolo Chui (Decision on Prosecutor's request to allow the introduction into evidence of the prior recorded testimony of P-166 and P-219) ICC-01/04-01/07-2362, T Ch II (3 September 2010).

Prosecutor v Katanga and Ngudjolo Chui (Decision on Request to admit prior recorded testimony of P-30 as well as related video excerpts) ICC-01/04-01/07-2233, T Ch II (30 June 2010).

Prosecutor v Katanga and Ngudjolo Chui (Decision on the Confirmation of Charges) ICC-01/04-01/07-717, PT Ch I (30 September 2008).

Prosecutor v Katanga and Ngudjolo Chui (Decision on the Prosecutor's Bar Table Motions) ICC-01/04-01/07-2635, T Ch II (17 December 2010).

Prosecutor v Katanga and Ngudjolo Chui (Jugement rendu en application de l'article 74 du Statut) ICC-01/04-01/07-3436, T Ch II (7 March 2014).

Prosecutor v Katanga and Ngudjolo Chui (Public Judgment In the Appeal by Mathieu Ngudjolo Chui of 27 March 2008 against the Decision of PreTrial Chamber I on the Application of the Appellant for Interim Release) ICC-01/0401/07-572, A Ch (9 June 2008).

Prosecutor v Kenyatta (Decision on Prosecution's applications for a finding of non-compliance pursuant to Article 87(7) and for an adjournment of the provisional trial date) ICC-01/09-02/11-908, T Ch V(B) (31 March 2014).

Prosecutor v Kenyatta (Decision on witness preparation) ICC-01/09-02/11-588, T Ch V (2 January 2013).

Prosecutor v Kenyatta (Judgment on the Prosecutor's appeal against Trial Chamber V(B)'s 'Decision on Prosecution's application for a finding of non-compliance under Article 87(7) of the Statute') ICC-01/09-02/11-1032, A Ch (19 August 2015).

Prosecutor v Kenyatta and Ali (Annex: Victims' response to Prosecution's application for an adjournment of the provisional trial date) ICC-01/09-02/11-879-Anx-Red, Victim (13 January 2014).

Prosecutor v Kenyatta and Ali (Decision on the Confirmation of Charges) ICC-01/09-02/11-382-Red, PT Ch II (23 January 2012).

Prosecutor v Kenyatta and Ali (Victims' response to Prosecution's application for an adjournment of the provisional trial date) ICC-01/09-02/11-879-Red, Victim (13 January 2014).

Prosecutor v Kony, Otti, Odhiambo, and Ongwen (Public Judgment on the appeal of the Defence against the "Decision on the admissibility of the case under article 19 (1) of the Statute" of 10 March 2009) ICC-02/04-01/05-408, A Ch (16 September 2009).

TABLE OF CASES   XXXI

Prosecutor v Lubanga Dyilo (Appeal judgment) ICC-01/04-01/06-3121-Red, A Ch (1 December 2014).

Prosecutor v Lubanga Dyilo (Corrigendum to Decision on the admissibility of four documents) ICC-01/04-01/06-1399, T Ch I (20 January 2011).

Prosecutor v Lubanga Dyilo (Corrigendum to redacted Decision on the defence request for the admission of 422 documents) ICC-01/04-01/06-2595, T Ch I (8 March 2011).

Prosecutor v Lubanga Dyilo (Decision on the admissibility of four documents) ICC-01/04-01/06-1399, T Ch I (13 June 2008).

Prosecutor v Lubanga Dyilo (Decision on the admission of material from the "bar table") ICC-01/04-01/06-1981, T Ch I (24 June 2009).

Prosecutor v Lubanga Dyilo (Decision on the Confirmation of Charges) ICC-01/04-01/06-803-tEN, PT Ch I (29 January 2007).

Prosecutor v Lubanga Dyilo (Decision on the Practices of Witness Familiarisation and Witness Proofing) ICC-01/04-01/06-679, PT Ch I (9 November 2006).

Prosecutor v Lubanga Dyilo (Decision on the procedures to be adopted for instructing expert witnesses) ICC-01/04-01/06-1069, T Ch I (10 December 2007).

Prosecutor v Lubanga Dyilo (Decision on the prosecution's application for the admission of the prior recorded statements of two witnesses) ICC-01/04-01/06-1603, T Ch I (15 January 2009).

Prosecutor v Lubanga Dyilo (Decision on the prosecution's request for an order on the disclosure of tu quoque material pursuant to Rule 77) ICC-01/04-01/06-2147, T Ch I (2 October 2009).

Prosecutor v Lubanga Dyilo (Decision on the request by the legal representative of victims a/0001/06, a/0002/06, a/0003/06, a/0049/06, a/0007/08, a/0149/08, a/0155/07, a/0156/07, a/0404/08, a/0405/08, a/0406/08, a/0407/08, a/0409/08, a0149/07 and a/0162/07 for admission of the final report of the Panel of Experts on the illegal exploitation of natural resources and other forms of wealth of the Democratic Republic of the Congo as evidence) ICC-01/04-01/06-2135, T Ch I (22 September 2009).

Prosecutor v Lubanga Dyilo (Decision Regarding the Practices Used to Prepare and Familiarise Witnesses for Giving Testimony at Trial) ICC-01/04-01/06-1049, T Ch I (30 November 2007).

Prosecutor v Lubanga Dyilo (Instructions to the Court's expert on child soldiers and trauma) ICC-01/04-01/06-1671, T Ch I (6 February 2009).

Prosecutor v Lubanga Dyilo (Judgment on the appeals of the Prosecutor and Mr Thomas Lubanga Dyilo against the "Decision on Sentence pursuant to Article 76 of the Statute") ICC-01/04-01/06-3122, A Ch (1 December 2014).

Prosecutor v Lubanga Dyilo (Prosecution's Application for a Preliminary Ruling on the Admission of Prior Recorded Statements) ICC-01/04-01/06-1262, Prosecution (5 April 2008).

Prosecutor v Lubanga Dyilo (Prosecution's Response to « Requête de la Défense aux fins d'admission en preuve des éléments relatifs à D-0041 ») ICC-01/04-01/06-3091, Prosecution (14 May 2014).

Prosecutor v Lubanga Dyilo (Redacted Decision on the "Cinquième requête de la Défense aux fins de dépôt de documents") ICC-01/04-01/06-2702-Red, T Ch I (6 April 2011).

Prosecutor v Lubanga Dyilo (Redacted Decision on the "Troisième requête de la Défense aux fins de dépôt de documents") ICC-01/04-01/06-2664-Red, T Ch I (16 March 2011).

Prosecutor v Lubanga Dyilo (Redacted Decision on the Prosecution's Application to Admit Rebuttal Evidence from Wihiess DRC-OTP-WWWW-0005) ICC-01/04-01/06-2727-Red, T Ch I (28 April 2011).

Prosecutor v Lubanga Dyilo (Requête de la Défense aux fins d'admission en preuve des éléments relatifs à D-0041) ICC-01/04-01/06-3088, Defense (12 May 2014).

Prosecutor v Lubanga Dyilo (Trial judgment) ICC-01/04-01/06-2842, T Ch I (14 March 2012)

TABLE OF CASES   XXXIII

Prosecutor v Mbarushimana (Decision on the Confirmation of Charges) ICC-01/04-01/10-465-Red, PT Ch I (16 December 2011).

Prosecutor v Mbarushimana (Public Judgment on the appeal of Mr Callixte Mbarushimana against the decision of Pre-Trial Chamber I of 19 May 2011 entitled 'Decision on the 'Defence Request for Interim Release'") ICC-01/04-01/10-283, A Ch (14 July 2011).

Prosecutor v Ngudjolo Chui (Annex A_Joint Dissenting Opinion of Judge Ekaterina Trendafilova and Judge Cuno Tarfusser) ICC-01/04-02/12-271-AnxA, T Ch II (27 February 2015).

Prosecutor v Ngudjolo Chui (Judgment on the Prosecutor's appeal against the decision of Trial Chamber II entitled "Judgment pursuant to article 74 of the Statute") ICC-01/04-02/12-271-Corr, A Ch (7 April 2015).

Prosecutor v Ngudjolo Chui (Decision on the "Requête en indemnisation en application des dispositions de l'article 85(1) et (3) du Statut) ICC-01/04-02/12-30/ENG, T Ch II (16 December 2015).

Prosecutor v Ngudjolo Chui (Décision relative aux requêtes du Procureur aux fins d'admission de pièces qu'il entend verser directement aux débats), ICC-01/04-01/07-2635-tFRA, T Ch II (17 December 2010).

Prosecutor v Ngudjolo Chui (Trial judgment) ICC-01/04-02/12-3-tENG, T Ch II (18 December 2012).

Prosecutor v Ntaganda (Annex A Protocol on the practices to be used to familiarise witnesses for giving testimony at trial) ICC-01/04-02/06-656-AnxA, T Ch VI (17 June 2015).

Prosecutor v Ntaganda (Annex B Protocol on the practices to be used to familiarise witnesses for giving testimony at trial) ICC-01/04-02/06-656-AnxB, T Ch VI (17 June 2015).

Prosecutor v Ntaganda (Annex to Decision on witness preparation) ICC-01/04-02/06-652-Anx, T Ch VI (16 June 2015).

Prosecutor v Ntaganda (Decision on Admissibility of Evidence and Other Procedural Matters) ICC-01/04-02/06-308, PT Ch II (8 June 2014).

Prosecutor v Ntaganda (Decision on Defence Preliminary Challenges to Prosecution's Expert Witnesses) ICC-01/04-02/06-1159, T Ch VI (9 February 2016).

Prosecutor v Ntaganda (Decision on the protocol on witness familiarisation) ICC-01/04-02/06-656, T Ch VI (17 June 2015).

Prosecutor v Ntaganda (Decision on witness preparation) ICC-01/04-02/06-652, T Ch VI (16 June 2015).

Prosecutor v Ntaganda (Dissenting Opinion of Judge Christine Van den Wyngaert) ICC-01/04-02/06-271-Anx2, A Ch (5 March 2014).

Prosecutor v Ntaganda (Judgment – Annex 5: Partly Concurring Opinion of Judge Eboe-Osuji) ICC-01/04-02/06-2666-Anx5-Corr, A Ch (31 March 2021).

Prosecutor v Ntaganda (Judgment on the appeal of Mr Bosco Ntaganda against the "Decision on Defence request for leave to file a 'no case to answer' motion") ICC-01/04-02/06-2026, A Ch (5 September 2017).

Prosecutor v Ntaganda (Judgment on the appeal of Mr Bosco Ntaganda against the "Decision on Defence requests seeking disclosure orders and a declaration of Prosecution obligation to record contacts with witnesses") ICC-01/04-02/06-1330, A Ch (20 May 2016).

Prosecutor v Ntaganda (Prosecution's Response to the « Requête de la Défense relative à l'admissibilité de certains éléments de preuve que le Procureur entend présenter à l'audience de confirmation des charges et en radiation de certaines parties du Document contenant les charges") ICC-01/04-02/06-269, Prosecution (3 March 2014).

Prosecutor v Ntaganda (Public redacted version of 'Decision on admission of prior recorded testimony of Witness P-0773 under Rule 68', 2 December 2016, ICC-01/04-02/06-1667-Conf) ICC-01/04-02/06-1667-Red, T Ch VI (27 February 2017).

Prosecutor v Ntaganda (Public redacted version of Judgment on the appeals of Mr Bosco Ntaganda and the Prosecutor against the decision of Trial Chamber VI of 8 July 2019 entitled 'Judgment') ICC-01/04-02/06-2666-Red, A Ch (30 March 2021).

Prosecutor v Ntaganda (Trial judgment) ICC-01/04-02/06, T Ch VI (8 July 2019).

Prosecutor v Ongwen (Decision on Defence Request for Remedies in Light of Disclosure Violations) ICC-02/04-01/15-1734, T Ch IX (22 April 2020).

Prosecutor v Ongwen (Decision on Prosecution Request to Submit Interception Related Evidence) ICC-02/04-01/15-615, T Ch IX (1 December 2016).

Prosecutor v Ongwen (Decision on the Defence Request to Order a Medical Examination of Dominic Ongwen) ICC-02/04-01/15-637-Red, T Ch IX (16 February 2016).

Prosecutor v Ongwen (Decision on the Prosecution's Applications for Introduction of Prior Recorded Testimony under Rule 68(2)(b) of the Rules) ICC-02/04-01/15-596-Red, T Ch IX (18 November 2016).

Prosecutor v Ongwen (Initial Directions on the Conduct of the Proceedings) ICC-02/04-01/15-497, T Ch IX (13 July 2016).

Prosecutor v Ongwen (Public Judgment on the appeal of the Prosecutor against the decision of Pre-Trial Chamber II entitled 'Decision Setting the Regime for Evidence Disclosure and Other Related Matters') ICC-02/04-01/15-251, A Ch (17 June 2015).

Prosecutor v Ongwen (Public Redacted Version of "Defence Appeal Brief Against the Convictions in the Judgment of 4 February 2021) ICC-02/04-01/15-1866-Red, Defense (19 October 2021).

Prosecutor v Ruto and Sang (Annex I Dissenting Opinion of Judge Herrera Carbuccia) ICC-01/09-01/11-2027-AnxI, T Ch V(A) (5 April 2016).

Prosecutor v Ruto and Sang (Annex: Decision on witness preparation) ICC-01/09-01/11-524-Anx, T Ch V (7 February 2013).

Prosecutor v Ruto and Sang (Decision No. 5 on the Conduct of Trial Proceedings (Principles and Procedure on 'No Case to Answer' Motions)) ICC-01/09-01/11-1334, T Ch V(A) (3 June 2014).

Prosecutor v Ruto and Sang (Decision on Prosecutor's Application for Witness Summonses and resulting Request for State Party Cooperation) ICC-01/09-01/11-1274-Corr2, T Ch v(A) (17 April 2014).

Prosecutor v Ruto and Sang (Decision on Sang Defence Application to Exclude Expert Report of Mr Herve´ Maupeu,) ICC-01/09-01/11-844, T Ch v(A) (7 August 2013).

Prosecutor v Ruto and Sang (Decision on the appeals of Mr William Samoei Ruto and Mr Joshua Arap Sang against the decision of Pre-Trial Chamber II of 23 January 2012 entitled "Decision on the Confirmation of Charges Pursuant to Article 61(7)(a) and (b) of the Rome Statute"), ICC-01/09-01/11-414, A Ch (24 May 2012).

Prosecutor v Ruto and Sang (Decision on the Conduct of Trial Proceedings (General Directions)) ICC-01/09-01/11-847, T Ch v(A) (9 August 2013).

Prosecutor v Ruto and Sang (Decision on the Confirmation of Charges) ICC-01/09-01/11-373, PT Ch I (23 January 2012)

Prosecutor v Ruto and Sang (Decision on the Prosecution's Application for Admission of Documentary Evidence Related to the Testimony of Witness 13) ICC-01/09-01/11-1804, T Ch v(A) (4 February 2015).

Prosecutor v Ruto and Sang (Decision on the Prosecution's Request for Admission of Documentary Evidence) ICC-01/09-01/11-1353, T Ch v(A) (10 June 2014).

Prosecutor v Ruto and Sang (Decision on Witness Preparation) ICC-01/09-01/11-524, T Ch v (2 January 2013).

Prosecutor v Ruto and Sang (Decision on witness preparation: Partly Dissenting Opinion of Judge Oboe-Osuji) ICC-01/09-01/11-524, T Ch v (2 January 2013).

Prosecutor v Ruto and Sang (Defence Submissions on the Conduct of the Proceedings) ICC-01/09-01/11-795, Defense (3 July 2013).

Prosecutor v Ruto and Sang (ICC-01/09-01/11-T-87-ENG ET WT 17-02-2014 1-36 SZ T) ICC-01/09-01/11-T-87, T Ch v(A) (17 February 2014).

TABLE OF CASES XXXVII

Prosecutor v Ruto and Sang (Judgment on the appeals of Mr William Samoei Ruto and Mr Joshua Arap Sang against the decision of Trial Chamber v(A) of 19 August 2015 entitled "Decision on Prosecution Request for Admission of Prior Recorded Testimony") ICC-01/09-01/11-2024, A Ch (12 February 2016).

Prosecutor v Ruto and Sang (Judgment on the appeals of William Samoei Ruto and Mr Joshua Arap Sang against the decision of Trial Chamber v (A) of 17 April 2014 entitled "Decision on Prosecutor's Application for Witness Summonses and resulting Request for State Party Cooperation") ICC-01/09-01/11-1598, A Ch (9 October 2014).

Prosecutor v Ruto and Sang (Prosecution submissions on the conduct of the proceedings) ICC-01/09-01/11-794, T Ch v(A) (3 July 2013).

Prosecutor v Ruto and Sang (Prosecution's Application for Admission of Documents from the Bar Table Pursuant to Article 64(9)) ICC-01/09-01/11-819, Prosecution (19 July 2013).

Prosecutor v Ruto and Sang (Prosecution's Application for Admission of Documents from the Bar Table Pursuant to Article 64(9)) ICC-01/09-01/11-1121, Prosecution (2 December 2013).

Prosecutor v Ruto and Sang (Prosecution's further submissions pursuant to the Prosecution's request under article 64(6)(b) and article 93 to summon witnesses) ICC-01/09-01/11-1202, Prosecution (4 March 2014).

Prosecutor v Ruto and Sang (Public redacted version of "Corrected Version of Prosecution's Application for Admission of Documentary Evidence Related to the Testimony of Witness P-0013",28 October 2014, ICC-01/09-01/11-1619-Conf-Corr) ICC-01/09-01/11-1619, Prosecution (12 November 2014).

Prosecutor v Ruto and Sang (Public redacted version of "Prosecution's request for the admission of prior recorded testimony of [REDACTED] witnesses", 29 April 2015, ICC-01/09-01/11-1866-Conf + Annexes) ICC-01/09-01/11-1866-Red, Prosecution (21 May 2015).

Prosecutor v Ruto and Sang (Public redacted version of "Corrigendum of Ruto Defence Request for Judgment of Acquittal", ICC-01/09-01/11-1990-Conf-Corr, 26 October 2015) ICC-01/09-01/11-1990-Corr-Red, T Ch v(A) (26 October 2015).

Prosecutor v Ruto and Sang (Public redacted version of "Corrigendum of Ruto Defence response to the 'Prosecution's request for the admission of prior recorded testimony of [REDACTED] witnesses'", 12 June 2015, ICC-01/0901/11-1908-Conf) ICC-01/09-01/11-1908-Corr-Red, Defense (23 June 2015).

Prosecutor v Ruto and Sang (Public Redacted Version of Corrigendum to Sang Defence Response to Prosecution's Request for the Admission of Prior Recorded Testimony of [Redacted] Witnesses, filed on 12 June 2015) ICC-01/09-01/11-1911-Corr-Red, Defense (30 June 2015).

Prosecutor v Ruto and Sang (Public redacted version of Decision on Prosecution Request for Admission of Prior Recorded Testimony) ICC-01/09-01/11-1938-Corr-Red, T Ch v(A) (19 August 2015).

Prosecutor v Ruto and Sang (Public Redacted Version of Sang Defence 'No Case to Answer' Motion, filed on 23 October 2015) ICC-01/09-01/11-1991-Red, T Ch v(A) (6 November 2015).

Prosecutor v Ruto and Sang (Public redacted version of: Decision on Defence Applications for Judgments of Acquittal) ICC-01/09-01/11-2027-Red-Corr, T Ch v(A) (5 April 2016).

Prosecutor v Ruto and Sang (Sang Defence Response to the Prosecution's Application for Admission of Documents from the Bar Table Pursuant to Article 64(9)) ICC-01/09-01/11-1130, T Ch v(A) (24 December 2013).

Prosecutor v Ruto and Sang (Sang Defence response to the request pursuant to article 63(1) of the Rome Statute and rule 134quarter of the Rules of Procedure and Evidence to excuse Mr. William Samoei Ruto from attendance at trial, and the Office of the Prosecutor's Application [...]) ICC-01/09-01/11-1127, Defense (19 December 2013).

Prosecutor v Ruto and Sang (Sang Defence Submissions on the Conduct of the Proceedings) ICC-01/09-01/11-796, Defense (3 July 2013).

Prosecutor v Ruto and Sang (Separate, Partly Concurring Opinion of Judge Eboe-Osuji on the "Decision on Prosecution Request for Admission of Prior Recorded Testimony") ICC-01/09-01/11-1938-Anx-Red, T Ch v(A) (19 August 2015).

Prosecutor v Ruto, Kosgey, and Sang (Decision on the Confirmation of Charges) ICC-01/09-01/11-373, PT Ch II (23 January 2012).

TABLE OF CASES   XXXIX

Prosecutor v Said (Decision on the Prosecution's First, Second and Fourth Requests Pursuant to Rule 68(2)(b) of the Rules, filed on 20 October 2022 (ICC-01/14-01/21-507-Conf)) ICC-01/14-01/21-507-Red , T Ch VI (21 October 2022).

Prosecutor v Said (Public Redacted Version of Decision on the Prosecution's Request under Rule 68(2)(c) to Introduce the Prior Recorded Testimony of Six Witnesses) ICC-01-14-01-21-506-RED, T Ch VI (26 October 2022).

Prosecutor v Yekatom and Ngaïssona (Decision on Motions on the Scope of the Charges and the Scope of the Evidence at Trial) ICC-01/14-01/18-703-Red, T Ch V (30 October 2020).

Prosecutor v Yekatom and Ngaïssona (Decision on the Prosecution Requests for Formal Submission of Prior Recorded Testimonies under Rule 68(3) of the Rules concerning Witnesses P-1962, P-0925, P-2193, P-2926, P-2927, P-1577 and P 0287, and the Ngaïssona Defence Motion to Limit the Scope) ICC-01/14-01/18-907-Red, T Ch V (1 April 2021).

Prosecutor v Yekatom and Ngaïssona (Decision on the Yekatom Defence Request to Exclude Expert Witness P-2926) ICC-01/14-01/18-881, T Ch V (11 February 2021).

Prosecutor v Yekatom and Ngaïssona (First Decision on the Prosecution Requests for Formal Submission of Prior Recorded Testimonies pursuant to Rule 68(2)(b) of the Rules) ICC-01/14-01/18-1833-Corr-Red, T Ch V (17 April 2023).

Prosecutor v Yekatom and Ngaïssona (First Decision on the Prosecution Requests for Formal Submission of Prior Recorded Testimonies pursuant to Rule 68(2)(c) of the Rules) ICC-01/14-01/18-1975-Red, T Ch V (12 July 2023).

Prosecutor v Yekatom and Ngaïssona (Further Directions on the Conduct of the Proceedings (Presentation of Evidence by the CLRV and the Defence)) ICC-01/14-01/18-1892, T Ch V (29 May 2023).

Prosecutor v Yekatom and Ngaïssona (Initial Directions on the Conduct of the Proceedings) ICC-01/14-01/18-631, T Ch V (26 August 2020).

Prosecutor v Yekatom and Ngaïssona (Prosecution's Response to the Yekatom Defence Urgent request for access to evidentiary materials in possession of the Office of the Prosecutor (ICC-01/14-01/18-1604-Conf) ICC-01/14-01/18-1609, T Ch V (13 October 2022).

Prosecutor v Yekatom and Ngaïssona (Public Redacted Version of the "Request for the Exclusion of Fabricated Evidence", 5 December 2023, ICC-01/14-01/18-2240-Conf) ICC-01/14-01/18-2240-Red, T Ch V (9 February 2024).

Prosecutor v Yekatom and Ngaïssona (Public redacted version of "Prosecution Response to the Yekatom Defence 'Request for the Exclusion of Fabricated Evidence' (ICC-01/14-01/18-2240-Conf)", ICC-01/14-01/18-2313-Conf, 18 January 2024) ICC-01/14-01/18-2313-Red, OTP (12 February 2024).

Prosecutor v Yekatom and Ngaïssona (Public redacted Judgment on the appeal of Mr Patrice Edouard Ngaïssona against the decision of Trial Chamber V of 6 October 2023 entitled "Decision on the Prosecution Request for Formal Submission of Prior Recorded Testimony pursuant to Rule 68(2)(d) of the Rules") ICC-01/14-01/18-2501-Red, A Ch (20 May 2024).

Prosecutor v Yekatom and Ngaïssona (Public redacted Judgment on the appeal of Mr Patrice Edouard Ngaïssona against the decision of Trial Chamber V of 6 October 2023 entitled "Third Decision on the Prosecution Requests for Formal Submission of Prior Recorded Testimonies pursuant to Rule 68(2)(c) of the Rules") ICC-01/14-01/18-2502-Red, A Ch (20 May 2024).

Situation in the Democratic Republic of Congo, (Under Seal Ex parte, Prosecutor only Judgment on the Prosecutor's appeal against the decision of Pre-Trial Chamber I entitled "Decision on the Prosecutor's Application for Warrants of Arrest, Article 58") ICC-01/04-169-US-Exp, A Ch (13 July 2006).

Other International Courts and Tribunals

Special Court for Sierra Leone (SCSL)

Prosecutor v Taylor (Appeal judgment) SCSL-03-01-A, A Ch (26 September 2013).

Prosecutor v Taylor (Decision on Prosecution Motion for Admission of Part of the Prior Evidence of TF1-362 and TF1-371 Pursuant to Rule 92ter) SCSL-03-01-T-399, T Ch II (25 January 2008).

Prosecutor v Sesay et al. (Decision on Defence Motion Seeking the Disqualification of Judge Robertson from the Appeals Chamber) SCSL-2004-AR15-15, T Ch I (13 March 2003).

Prosecutor v Sesay et al. (Trial judgment) SCSL-04-15-T, T Ch I (25 February 2009).

Special Tribunal for Lebanon (STL)
Prosecutor v Ayyash et al. (Decision on the admissibility of documents published on WikiLeaks website) STL-11-01/T/TC, T Ch (21 May 2015).

Prosecutor v Ayyash et al. (Trial judgment) STL-11-01/T/TC, T Ch (18 August 2020).

Kosovo Specialist Chambers (KSC)
Prosecutor v Gucati and Haradinaj (Decision on the Defence Request for Admission of Items through the Bar Table and Related Matters) KSC-BC-2020-07/F00502, TP II (17 December 2021).

European Union

Persia International Bank PLC v Council of the European Union, Case T-493/10, Judgment of the General Court (Fourth Chamber), 6 September 2013.

European Court of Human Rights (ECtHR)

Adamčo v Slovakia App no 19990/20 (ECtHR, 1 June 2023).

Al-Khawaja and Tahery v the United Kingdom App nos. 26766/05 and 22228/06 (ECtHR, 15 December 2011).

Danilov v Russia App no 88/05 (ECtHR, 1 March 2021).

Del Río Prada v Spain App no 42750/09 (ECtHR, 21 October 2013).

Doorson v the Netherlands App no 20524/92 (ECtHR, 26 March 1996).

Ellis and Simms and Martin v. United Kingdom App nos 46099/06 and 46699/06 (ECtHR 10 April 2012).

Keskin v the Netherlands App no 2205/16 (ECtHR, 19 January 2021).

Kostovski v the Netherlands App no 11454/85 (ECtHR, 20 November 1989).

Lucà v Italy App no 33354/96 (ECtHR, 27 February 2001).

Saïdi v France App no 14647/89 (ECtHR, 20 September 1993).

Schatschaschwili v Germany App no 9154/10 (ECtHR, 15 December 2015).

Sekanina v Austria App no 13126/87 (ECtHR, 25 August 1993).

Unterpertinger v Austria App no 9120/80 (ECtHR, 24 November 1986).

Van Mechelen and Others v the Netherlands App nos. 21363/93, 21364/93, 21427/93 and 22056/93 (ECtHR, 23 April 1997).

Yüksel Yalçınkaya v Türkiye App no 15669/20 (ECtHR, 26 September 2023).

National Jurisdictions

Canada
R v Aksidan, 2006 BCCA 258.

R v J.-L.J., 2000 SCC 51.

R v Trochym, 2007 SCC 6

United States
Daubert v Merrell Dow Pharmaceuticals, Inc., 509 U.S. 579 (1993).

Frye v United States, 293 F. 1013 (D.C. Cir. 1923).

Hamdi & Ibrahim Mango Co v Fire Association of Philadelphia, 20 FRD 181 (SONY, 1957)

Mapp v Ohio, 367 U.S. 643 (1961).

Murray v United States, 487 U.S. 533 (1988).

Neil v Biggers, 409 U.S. 188 (1972).

State v McCormick, 259 S.E. 2d 880 (1979)

The State v Smith, 192 So.3d 836 (4h Cir. 2016).

Tienda v State, 479 S.W.3d 863 (Tex. App. 2015).

Renee vs State of Texas 49SO.3D.248. (2010)

United States v Huskisson, 926 F.3d 369 (7th Cir. 2019).

United States v Pendergrass, 991 F.3d 1327 (11th Cir. 2021).

United States v Vayner, 2014 WL 4942227 (2d Cir. 2014)

England and Wales
R v Allan [2017] MBCA 88.

R v Davis [2008] UKHL 36

R v Ditta [2016] EWCA Crim 8.

R v Farooqi [2013] EWCA Crim 1649.

R v Gilmour [2005] EWCA Crim 824.

R v Hanson [2005] EWCA Crim 824.

R v M [2012] EWCA Crim 1588.

R v McNeill [2007] EWCA Crim 2927.

R v Mouncher and others [2011] EWCA 1367.

R v Sule [2012] EWCA Crim 1130.

Australia
Barca v The Queen (1975) 133 CLR 82.

Davidson v R (2009), 75 NSWLR 150.

Gwilliam v R [2019] NSWCCA 5.

Peacock v The King (1911) 13 CLR 619.

Questions of Law Reserved on Acquittal (No 2 of 1993) 61 SASR 1 [Supreme Court of South Australia, Full Court].

The Queen v Baden-Clay (2016) 258 CLR 308.

Wiggins v R [2020] NSWCCA 256.

Italy
Corte di Cassazione, 36080/15, Judgment 27/03/2015.

Finland
District court of Kanta-Häme (22 March 2016) Judgment no. 16/112863.

District Court of Pirkanmaa (18 March 2016) Judgment no. 16/112431.

Germany
German Federal Court of Justice (27 July 2017) Judgment no. StR 57/17.

Higher Regional Court of Berlin 2a Criminal Division (1 March 2017) Case no. (2A) 172 OJs 26/16 (3/16).

The Netherlands
Judgment Supreme Court of the Netherlands, ECLI:HR:1998:ZD0917, 27/01/1998.

Sweden
Scania and Blekinge Court of Appeal (11 April 2017) Case no. B 3187-16.

Svea Court of Appeal (31 May 2017) Case no. B 3787-16.

Transcripts

Prosecutor v Blé Goudé, Transcript ICC-02/11-01/15-T-242-Red-ENG CT WT, Article 85 Ch (13 December 2021).

Prosecutor v Boskoski, Transcript IT-04-82-T, T Ch III (14 November 2007).

TABLE OF CASES   XLV

Prosecutor v Gbagbo and Blé Goudé, Transcript ICC-02/11-01/15-T-42-ENG ET WT, T Ch I (19 May 2016).

Prosecutor v Haradinaj et al., Transcript IT-04-84bis-T, T Ch II (24 August 2011) <http://icty.org/x/cases/haradinaj/trans/en/110824ED.htm> accessed 13 July 2023.

Prosecutor v Haradinaj et al., Transcript IT-04-S4-T, T Ch I (5 June 2007) <http://icty.org/x/cases/haradinaj/trans/en/070605ED.htm> accessed 13 July 2023.

Prosecutor v Haradinaj et al., Transcript IT-04-S4-T, T Ch I (20 November 2007) <http://www.icty.org/x/cases/haradinaj/trans/en/071120ED.htm> accessed 13 July 2023.

Prosecutor v Lubanga, Transcript ICC-01/04-01/06-T-170-ENG, T Ch I (7 May 2009).

Prosecutor v Yekatom and Ngaïssona, Transcript ICC-01/14-01/18-T-023-Red2-ENG, T Ch V (29 March 2021).

Prosecutor v Yekatom and Ngaïssona, Transcript ICC-01/14-01/18-T-016-ENG, T Ch V (18 February 2021).

Prosecutor v Al Mahdi, Transcript ICC-01/12-01/15-T-4-Red-ENG (22 August 2016).

Prosecutor v Mladić, Transcript IT-09-92-T, T Ch II (30 August 2012).

Prosecutor v Lubanga Dyilo, Transcript ICC-01/04-01/06-T-333-Red2-ENG, T Ch I (12 November 2010).

Prosecutor v Lubanga Dyilo, Transcript ICC-01/04-01/06-T-350-Red2-ENG, T Ch I (14 April 2011).

Prosecutor v Lubanga Dyilo, Transcript ICC-01/04-01/06-T-125-Red3-ENG, T Ch I (12 February 2009).

Prosecutor v Lubanga Dyilo, Transcript ICC-01/04-01/06-T-170-ENG, T Ch I (7 May 2009).

Prosecutor v Katanga and Ngudjolo Chui, Transcript ICC-01/04-01/07-T-211-RED2-ENG, T Ch II (2 November 2010).

Prosecutor v Kenyatta, Muthaura and Ali, Transcript ICC-01/09-02/11-T-27-ENG, T Ch V(B) (5 February 2014).

Prosecutor v Katanga and Ngudjolo Chui, Transcript ICC-01/04-01/07-T-97-Red-ENG, T Ch II (8 February 2010).

Prosecutor v Kordić & Čerkez, Transcript IT-95-14/2-T, T Ch II (28 January 2000).

Introduction: Two Models of Criminal Law

The choice for a certain model of legal thinking in a country, for example a restriction model or a protection model, is a philosophical choice: how do we view the role of the government in a free society?

Underlying the restriction model, which underlies American legal thought, and which assumes that the power of the government vis-à-vis the citizen must be curtailed, is a more fundamental legal philosophical idea, namely the "social compact" theory. This assumes a pre-political state of nature in which man is "governed" only by natural laws. It assumes that man is born free and therefore carries with him natural rights. These natural rights (the right to life, to liberty, to equality, to livelihood and the right to the pursuit of happiness) cannot be limited by laws invented by humanity itself. We are born with these natural rights; they are ours simply by virtue of being born as human and cannot be taken away from us by other human forces.

This principle is consistent with the ideas of eighteenth-century philosopher and social contract-theorist John Locke, who argued that citizens willingly surrender some of their freedom (by authorizing a government to use coercive means) in exchange for protection. Government as such is thus based on a (hypothetical) social contract between man and government – and its authority is thus also based on this very same contract. By extension, its authority to bend the natural rights of man through these coercive means should not be used for political ends, but only towards realizing those ends for which such authority was extended – namely protecting life, liberty and property.[1]

In European legal thinking, for politico-pragmatic reasons, there is a preference not for the restriction model, but for the protection model. In this model, the priority is to protect the citizen from the criminal, with the government having a monopoly on 'the truth'. The accused is more an object of investigation, and less a person with unalienable human rights.

Why should one prefer the restriction rationale over the protection rationale? The restriction model has the potential to reduce the risk of miscarriages of justice. It forces the judiciary and police to assume a fundamentally different mentality and approach to the criminal law system. In a criminal case, the focus is then not on the search for evidence to convict the citizen (who is then a suspect), but on the idea that the citizen, even if suspected of a serious crime,

---

[1] John Locke, *The Second Treatise of Civil Government and A Letter Concerning Toleration* (Blackwell 1948).

could well be innocent and that his natural rights must be protected – during the investigation process, but especially also during the criminal trial itself.

Advocates of the protection model point out that even in the U.S. restriction model, miscarriages of justice occur due to false confessions, shaky eyewitness testimony, errors in forensics and so on. Sure, that happens. But it is only a half to one percent of the total number of criminal cases in the U.S. Deeper analysis of the U.S. stray cases show that things went wrong there precisely because the restriction model was not adequately applied, and investigators worked from a tunnel vision. Alternative scenarios, which might have demonstrated the innocence of the accused citizen, were therefore not properly considered. The pitfall of this tunnel vision presents itself much earlier in the protection model.

In the protection model – stemming from the inquisitorial model – the government has a monopoly on "truth-telling". In the restrictive model, truth-telling is something for the parties to the criminal proceedings themselves and not just for the government. Both the Defense and the Prosecution have the right to conduct their own investigations and bring witnesses to the hearing. Truth-telling takes place entirely at the public hearing and has a dual nature. Within the protection model, for the time being, the citizen must lose out to the power of the government.

Let us return to the key question: what should a legal system stand for? For preventing miscarriages of justice. Why? Because wrongful convictions are a far more fundamental assault on the natural rights of human beings than not hearing a victim during a criminal trial, or not having to cooperate in decrypting a computer in a child sex offender case.

PART 1

General

CHAPTER 1

The Essence and Functioning of Criminal Evidence

International criminal trials are all about evidence. What is criminal evidence and how to assess the strength or weakness thereof? The answers to these questions depend on the type of evidence which is submitted to the Court. Two main types of evidence can be detected: testimonial and documentary evidence. The latter embraces also forensic evidence and evidence based upon digital and social media sources.

This book intends to present the most important implications of these types of criminal evidence as featuring before the International Criminal Court (ICC). One should bear in mind that criminal evidence does not have the pretention to prove a certain fact with mathematical certainty. Therefore, a judgment in a criminal case cannot identify nor not-identify a certain crime scenario with such certainty. It only indicates the most likely scenario based upon the assessment of the available evidence. In other words, criminal evidence is nothing more or less than "(...) an item which a litigant produces to make the existence of a fact more or less probable."[1]

The introduction of what is supposed to be criminal evidence by one of the litigants should be governed by fixed legal principles in order to create legal certainty and to strike a balance between the interests of the Prosecution and the rights of the accused person. The common interest within any criminal trial should be that in order to be perceived as 'criminal evidence' one has to assure the reliability and accuracy of the specific item which is submitted to the Court to prove a certain fact.

At the ICC, as at virtually any modern criminal court, the truth-seeking nature of the proceedings is pivotal. While never explicitly stating as such, the truth-seeking nature of the proceedings is evidenced by Art. 54(1)(a) of the Rome Statute (RS), which states that the Prosecutor shall 'In order to establish the truth, extend the investigation to cover all facts and evidence relevant to an assessment of whether there is criminal responsibility under this Statute, and, in doing so, investigate incriminating and exonerating circumstances equally'. The truth-seeking nature of proceedings is also evidenced by the requirement of each witness to 'give an undertaking as to the truthfulness' of evidence given by them (Art. 70(1)) and that false testimony given under such

---

[1] 'Evidence', *Legal Information Institut* (Cornell University insignia) <https://www.law.cornell.edu/wex/evidence#content> accessed 20 July 2023.

oath is considered an 'offence against the administration of justice' pursuant to Art. 70(1)(a). Additionally, under Art. 70(1)(b) knowingly presenting false or forged evidence by a party is also considered as such an offence.

This observation touches upon a fundamental question; what is the real essence of the Rules of Procedure and Evidence which govern a criminal trial? From a legal-philosophical perspective, there are two approaches. First, there is the approach of the so-called protection model which implies that criminal law, and its underlying evidentiary rules, should serve society in that it should protect it against any criminality which affects the world. Second, there is the approach of the restriction model. This model perceives criminal law as a set of rules to protect the individual against the power of the State. It is premised upon the thought of the philosopher John Locke (1632–1704): a population delegates powers to a government so that this government can create order in society. Yet, the population should be protected against abuse of power by this very government. Therefore, the law is simply there to assure that the government remains within the boundaries of the powers given to it/delegated to it.[2]

---

[2] Geert-Jan Knoops, 'De Rechtsstaat in Het Geding; Essay Gerechtelijke Dwalingen' (*De Groene Amsterdammer*, 24 April 2013) <https://www.groene.nl/artikel/de-rechtsstaat-in-het-geding> accessed 20 July 2023.

CHAPTER 2

The Admissibility and Weight of International Criminal Evidence at Trial

2.1 Introduction

The contours of criminal evidence rely on two different concepts: admissibility and weight. Admissibility pertains predominantly to the authenticity of materials and second to 'probative value' thereof.[1] Probative value on its turn embraces two factors:
- Relevance of evidence
- Reliability of evidence[2]

Yet, the reliability element, as being part of the admissibility test, has been subject of diverging views by several Trial Chambers.[3] The ultimate position at the time of the International Criminal Tribunal for the former Yugoslavia (ICTY) and International Criminal Tribunal for Rwanda (ICTR) seems to be ventilated by the ICTY Appeals Chamber (A Ch) in the case of the *Prosecutor v Kordić and Čerkez* of 21 July 2000, where it was held that the reliability of a statement is of relevance to admissibility, not just to weight.[4]

2.2 Evidentiary Relevance and Probative Value within the ICC

When it concerns the approach of the ICC, Art. 64(9)(a) RS attributes to the ICC Trial Chambers the power to rule on the admissibility or relevance of evidence. This power is seemingly unfettered since the Rules ICC of Procedure

---

1 Richard May and Marieke Wierda, *International Criminal Evidence*, vol 9 (Brill 2021) 107 <https://brill.com/display/title/13900#navigation> accessed 14 June 2023.
2 Ibid.
3 Ibid.
 The authors mention various ICTY and ICTR cases expressing different views on whether reliability constitutes a separate condition of admissibility. Cf. Richard May and Marieke Wierda, *International Criminal Evidence*, vol 9 (Brill 2021) 108 <https://brill.com/display/title/13900#navigation> accessed 14 June 2023.
4 *Prosecutor v Kordić and Čerkez* (Decision on Appeal Regarding Statement of a Deceased Witness) IT-95-14/2-AR73.5, A Ch (21 July 2000) para. 24; *Ibid* 109.

and Evidence (ICC RPE) authorize the ICC judges '(...) to assess freely all evidence submitted'.[5]

The ICC system is meant to function such that the Trial Chamber, upon submission of evidence by the parties, will assess the probative value of such evidence.[6] The ICC system seems to follow a two-prong test before admitting evidence. First, there is a relevance-test, after which the probative value thereof is to be determined.[7] According to the case law of the ICC, evidence to be considered is relevant if it makes the existence of a fact at issue more or less probable:

> Although under articles 64(9)(a) and 69(4) relevance is a legal precondition to admissibility, it is primarily a logical standard. If the evidence tendered makes the existence of a fact at issue more or less probable, it is relevant. Whether or not this is the case depends on the purpose for which the evidence is adduced. Unless immediately apparent from the exhibit itself, it is the responsibility of the party tendering it to explain: (1) the relevance of a specific factual proposition to a material fact of the case; (2) how the item of evidence tendered makes this factual proposition more probable or less probable. If submissions on these points are not sufficiently clear or precise, or if the Chamber cannot ascertain the relevance of an item of evidence with reasonable precision, it may decide to reject it on those grounds.[8]

Therefore, the relevance of a certain piece of evidence is context-related, i.e. it should be determined in light of the Prosecution of the case of the Defense. In other words, a certain piece of evidence might not be relevant to the Prosecution case, yet it could well be relevant from the perspective of the Defense.

After having established that a certain evidentiary item is deemed to be relevant, the ICC Trial Chambers look into the probative value thereof. In the cases of the *Prosecutor v Bemba Gombo* and of the *Prosecutor v Katanga and Ngudjolo Chui*, the term 'probative value' was described as:

---

5 Rule 63(2) ICC RPE.
6 Art. 69(3) and Art. 69(4) RS.
7 Lindsay Freeman and Raquel Llorente, 'Finding the Signal in the Noise: International Criminal Evidence and Procedure in the Digital Age' (2021) 19 Journal of International Criminal Justice 163, 180.
8 *Prosecutor v Katanga and Ngudjolo Chui* (Decision on the Prosecutor's Bar Table Motions) ICC-01/04-01/07-2635, T Ch II (17 December 2010) para. 16.

Under the second part of the admissibility test, the Chamber must consider, on a preliminary basis, whether the item in question has probative value. This will always be a fact-specific inquiry and may take into account innumerable factors, including the indicia of reliability, trustworthiness, accuracy or voluntariness that inhere in the item of potential evidence, as well as the circumstances in which the evidence arose. It may also take into account the extent to which the item has been authenticated. While it is not necessary that each item of evidence be authenticated via witness testimony, the Chamber needs to be satisfied that the item is what it purports to be, either because this is evident on its face or because other admissible evidence demonstrates the item's provenance.[9]

The contours of what one should understand to be "the ability to establish a given fact" is hardly to be made more specific. One can only say in the negative what 'amount' of probative value is insufficient. The indication thereof can be found in Art. 69(7) RS which says that evidence has to be excluded when it was obtained in violation of the statute or of internationally recognized human rights, presupposed that the violation casts substantial doubt on the reliability of the evidence or the admission of the evidence would be antithetical to and would seriously damage the integrity of the proceedings.

2.3 Procedural Aspects of 'Relevance' and 'Probative Value'

2.3.1 *Introduction*

Within an international criminal trial, one of the questions of perennial concern pertains to the procedural moment at which 'probative value' is to be determined. In this regard, ICC Trial Chambers are endowed with wide discretionary powers as to this temporal aspect of probative value.[10] The consequence of this power is that Trial Chambers have applied it differently, both as regards to the timing of ruling on admissibility of the evidence and as to whether the Trial Chamber (T Ch) has to look into each item of evidence individually or in conjunction.

---

9   *Prosecutor v Bemba Gombo* (Public Redacted Version of "Decision on the Prosecution's Application for Admission of Materials into Evidence Pursuant to Article 64(9) of the Rome Statute" of 6 September 2012) ICC-01/05-01/08-2299-Red, T Ch III (8 October 2012); *Prosecutor v Ngudjolo Chui* (Décision relative aux requêtes du Procureur aux fins d'admission de pièces qu'il entend verser directement aux débats), ICC-01/04-01/07-2635-tFRA, T Ch II (17 December 2010) paras 21 and 34.
10 Referring to Art. 64(3)(a) RS.

2.3.2 *The Concepts of Admission or Submission*

With regard to the first aspect, two law finding models are perceivable. In the case of the *Prosecutor v Bemba et al.*, the A Ch affirmed:

> The above provisions accord the Trial Chamber discretion when admitting evidence at trial. As home out by the use of the word "may" in article 69 (4), the Trial Chamber has the power to rule or not on relevance or admissibility when evidence is submitted to the Chamber. Consequently, the Trial Chamber may rule on the relevance and/or admissibility of each item of evidence when it is submitted, and then determine the weight to be attached to the evidence at the end of the trial. In that case, an item will be admitted into evidence only if the Chamber rules that it is relevant and/or admissible in terms of article 69 (4), taking into account "the probative value of the evidence and any prejudice that such evidence may cause to a fair trial or to a fair evaluation of the testimony of a witness". Alternatively, the Chamber may defer its consideration of these criteria until the end of the proceedings, making it part of its assessment of the evidence when it is evaluating the guilt or innocence of the accused person.[11]

The first model relates to the so-called 'admission' model. This model has the aim that each item of evidence is determined in the context of admissibility by the Court at the moment it is produced by the Prosecution or the Defense at trial.[12] Some ICC Trial Chambers opted for this approach; for instance, in the first ICC case against Mr Lubanga Dyilo.[13] A similar decision was adopted by another ICC Trial Chamber in the case of the *Prosecutor v Katanga and Ngudjolo Chui*.[14] Yet, this approach was not adopted by the ICC Appeals Chamber.

---

11 *Prosecutor v Bemba Gombo* (Judgment on the appeals of Mr Jean-Pierre Bemba Gombo and the Prosecutor against the decision of Trial Chamber III entitled "Decision on the admission into evidence of materials contained in the prosecution's list of evidence") ICC-01/05-01/08-1386, A Ch (3 May 2011) para. 37.
12 Freeman and Llorente (n 7) 163, 181.
13 *Prosecutor v Lubanga Dyilo* (Decision on the admissibility of four documents) ICC-01/04-01/06-1399, T Ch I (13 June 2008) para. 27.
14 *Prosecutor v Katanga and Ngudjolo Chui* (Decision on the Prosecutor's Bar Table Motions) ICC-01/04-01/07-2635, T Ch II (17 December 2010).

Indeed, in the case of the *Prosecutor v Bemba et al.*, the A Ch endorsed the 'submission' model.[15] Within this second model, all evidence brought into the trial by the parties is supposed to be submitted to the Court, and the decision on the admissibility of evidence is prolonged to the final judgment in the particular case.[16] In the case of the *Prosecutor v Gbagbo and Blé Goudé*, the judges held as follows:

> Contrary to the arguments raised by the parties, the Chamber is not persuaded that this approach will be beneficial to the fairness and expeditiousness of the trial, or, even more fundamentally, effectively instrumental to its ultimate duty to determine the truth. Several factors militate instead in favour of a solution whereby, as a matter of principle, the assessment of both the admissibility and the relevance or probative value of the evidence is deferred until the moment when the Chamber will be deliberating its judgment, pursuant to Article 74(2) of the Statute.[17]

These factors were well outlined in the initial Direction on the Conduct of the Proceedings in the case of the *Prosecutor v Ongwen*, where the Trial Chamber explained that "such an approach ... is done, inter alia, because: (i) the Chamber is able to assess more accurately the relevance and probative value of a given item of evidence after having received all of the evidence being presented at trial; (ii) a significant amount of time is saved by not having to assess an item's relevance and probative value at the point of submission and again at the end of the proceedings; (iii) there is no reason for the Chamber to make admissibility assessments in order to screen itself from considering materials inappropriately and (iv) there is no reason to assume that professional judges would consider irrelevant or unduly prejudicial material, noting in particular that the requirement of a reasoned judgment enables the participants to verify precisely how the Chamber evaluated the evidence".[18] Therefore, it is to be concluded that the submission regime is the prevailing one at the ICC.

---

15 *Prosecutor v Bemba et al.* (Appeal judgment) ICC-01/05-01/13-2275-Red, A Ch (8 March 2018) paras 599–601; Freeman and Llorente (n 7) 163, 181.
16 Freeman and Llorente (n 7) 163, 181.
17 *Prosecutor v Gbagbo and Blé Goudé* (Decision on the submission and admission of evidence) ICC-02/11-01/15-405, T Ch I (29 January 2016) para. 12.
18 *Prosecutor v Ongwen* (Initial Directions on the Conduct of the Proceedings) ICC-02/04-01/15-497, T Ch IX (13 July 2016) para. 25.

2.3.3 The Concept of the Holistic and Atomistic Approach

As to the second topic, this pertains to how the submitted evidence is to be weighed. Like before, two different approaches are perceivable, namely the 'holistic' or 'intuitive holistic' and the 'atomistic' or 'deconstruction' methods.[19] While the latter approach entails that each piece of evidence be evaluated at the moment of judgment by the judges as an isolated document,[20] the former approach entails that the judges consider the evidence as a whole, that is to say in its entirety.[21]

ICC judges are far from unanimous on which method is most suitable, as exemplified by the Court's jurisprudence. While the majority of the Appeals Chamber in the case of the *Prosecutor v Ngudjolo Chui* adopted the atomistic approach,[22] the majority of the Appeals Chamber in *Bemba et al.* followed the holistic view.[23] Moreover, several Trial Chambers deemed this holistic view more suitable as opposed to the atomistic view.[24]

The reason why Trial Chambers – although the holistic method seems dominant among ICC judges – may prefer one approach over the other lies in the purpose of the Drafters of the Rome Statute to attribute to the judges quite some leeway on how to accommodate trial proceedings.[25] This might even imply that ICC judges interchange between the two methods in that for certain specific documents the admission is to be followed, while at the end of the trial the evidence will be adjudicated according to the holistic method.[26]

---

[19] Freeman and Llorente (n 7) 163, 181–182.
[20] *Ibid* 182.
[21] *Ibid* 182.
[22] *Prosecutor v Ngudjolo Chui* (Annex A Joint Dissenting Opinion of Judge Ekaterina Trendafilova and Judge Cuno Tarfusser) ICC-01/04-02/12-271-AnxA, T Ch II (27 February 2015) paras 44–51.
[23] *Prosecutor v Bemba et al.* (Appeal judgment) ICC-01/05-01/13-2275-Red, A Ch (8 March 2018) paras 600–601; Freeman and Llorente (n 7) 163, 182.
[24] *Prosecutor v Ntaganda* (Trial judgment) ICC-01/04-02/06, T Ch VI (8 July 2019) para. 45; *Prosecutor v Gbagbo and Blé Goudé* (Public Redacted Version of Reasons of Judge Geoffrey Henderson) ICC-02/11-01/15-1263-AnxB-Red, T Ch I (16 July 2019) paras 31, 255, 1056, 1121, 1667, and 1864; Freeman and Llorente (n 7) 163, 182.
[25] Art. 64(3)(a) and Art. 64(3)(b) RS.
[26] *Prosecutor v Bemba et al.* (Separate opinion of Judge Geoffrey Henderson) ICC-01/05-01/13-2275-Anx, A Ch (8 March 2018) paras 38 and 39, where the Judge supports the existence of a hybrid approach, which would better reflect the compromise reached by the ICC States Parties between the Common Law and the Romano-Germanic legal traditions. Cf. also Freeman and Llorente (n 7) 163, 182–183.

2.3.4 Towards a Differentiation?

Situations may arise, whereby an immediate resolution on admissibility may accelerate Court's proceedings. This may be the case with digital evidence, which requires an early understanding of this type of evidence.[27] Such a situation arose in the ICC case of the *Prosecutor v Yekatom and Ngaïssona* with regard to the introduction by the Prosecution of numerous pages of Facebook messages. In the opening statement of the Defense at trial, the Defense argued in this regard:

> The Chamber, as we submit, will learn during this trial that Facebook evidence is, as we will prove, not reliable at its face, it's not self-authenticating, partly due to the anonymity resulting in the use of pseudonyms as usernames. Other risks we will submit during this trial will appear and were already identified by also the Court of Appeals of Texas in the Tienda v State case, 2012, an important case when it concerns the veracity of Facebook messages and the value of those messages as criminal evidence. And also that court ruled that that type of evidence, without more, is not sufficient to support a finding of authenticity. Mr President, your Honours, it is our submission that this Chamber should keep these reasonings in mind, these rulings in mind when the Prosecution will ask you to look at Facebook evidence, whether Messenger or posts, such as evidence the Prosecution has already quoted and displayed in its opening statement on Tuesday. With regard to Facebook messages and posts emanating from unknown individuals, such as from the account, quote, "coordination des Anti-Balaka", (Speaks English) the Chamber should also keep in mind what the Pre-Trial Chamber in this case already held in paragraph 202, where the judges ruled that Facebook entries must be assigned limited weight in the absence of evidence led as to the identity of the person using the account entitled "coordination des Anti-Balaka.[28]

During the trial, the Defense – at the time when the Prosecution during the presentation of its case, first introduced Facebook messages through a Prosecution witness – raised an objection in court as to the admissibility of those messages. The court transcripts of this discussion read as follows:

---

27 Freeman and Llorente (n 7) 163, 183.
28 *Prosecutor v Yekatom and Ngaïssona*, Transcript ICC-01/14-01/18-T-016-ENG, T Ch V (18 February 2021) pages 23–24.

> Secondly, the Facebook messages we are confronted with are forensically not independently authenticated, as such. There is an abundance of jurisprudence to say that the communication which takes place allegedly between Facebook accounts cannot, as such, demonstrate that these accounts were actually used by their legitimate owners. It's also mentioned in our opening statement, as your Honours know.[29]

In the opening statement of the Defense, the argument as to the inadmissibility of the Facebook messages was already introduced, as follows:

> Now, Mr President, your Honours, we asked the Chamber that the issue of admissibility of social media evidence, which we will argue at trial, of course, has already led to relevant jurisprudence in the United States of America, indicating that Facebook messages become a main concern and has impacted upon the judicial findings of several courts.[30]

The presiding judge responded to the aforementioned objection, preferring a holistic approach when evaluating the evidence, also in regard to Facebook-evidence:

> First of all – and this is something that we would have to – the Chamber would have to ascertain later, and I think there will be further evidence and further discussions about the probative value or if it is – has a probative value at all.[31]

One should bear in mind that to build its cases, the Prosecution is increasingly relying on social media evidence such as Facebook and Twitter messages, which in turn involves an assessment of the authenticity of this material. In light of this, early admissibility deliberations would seem more appropriate.[32] Lindsay Freeman and Raquel Vazquez Llorente provide an additional argument for potential early admissibility decisions:

---

29 *Prosecutor v Yekatom and Ngaïssona*, Transcript ICC-01/14-01/18-T-023-Red2-ENG, T Ch V (29 March 2021) p. 69.
30 *Prosecutor v Yekatom and Ngaïssona*, Transcript ICC-01/14-01/18-T-016-ENG, T Ch V (18 February 2021), p. 23.
31 *Prosecutor v Yekatom and Ngaïssona*, Transcript ICC-01/14-01/18-T-023-Red2-ENG, T Ch V (29 March 2021) p. 70.
32 ICC-01/14-01/18-T-016-ENG 163, 183.

If evidence is manifestly irrelevant or unreliable, judges may have to exercise their discretion under Article 69(4) and exclude it in order to avoid cluttering the evidentiary record.[33]

Additionally, the authors alert to the risk of the "[...] cumulative effect (that) may generate inefficiencies in the proceedings [...]" if one does not engage in early admissibility decisions on digital evidence which equally applies to social media.[34]

2.3.5 *The Admissibility of 'Antithetically Obtained' Evidence*

The afore going illustrates that the system of the ICC lacks a clear and consistent regime on the admissibility of criminal evidence.[35] Yet, the nature and impact on individual rights is far more invasive with regard to the enforcement of (international) criminal law than with reference to the application of Public International Law, the area of law that mainly governs inter-state relations. Indeed, the latter discipline is less concerned with individual rights of citizens, since it aims at protecting State rights.[36] This section will analyse how the ICC approaches the issue of evidence which is (potentially) obtained in violation of human rights norms.

2.3.5.1   General Principles of 'Antithetical' Evidence

The starting point lies in Art. 69(7) RS, which introduces an exclusionary rule on the admissibility of evidence. Its primary goal is to not admit evidence which was obtained through a violation of the principles of the Rome Statute or 'internationally recognized human rights'. Within this context, Art. 69(7) RS stipulates two parameters for the non-admission of evidence:

i.   The violation at stake must cast 'substantial' doubt on the reliability of the evidence, or
ii.   Such admission would be 'antithetical' to and would 'seriously damage the integrity of the proceedings'.

---

33   *Ibid* 185–186.
34   *Ibid* 186.
35   Sara Mansour Fallah, 'The Admissibility of Unlawfully Obtained Evidence before International Courts and Tribunals', *The Law & Practice of International Courts and Tribunals* (Brill 2020) 147–176, 151, where the author observes that 'The lack of rules on admissibility is, however, not a problem in all fields of international law. Clearer guidelines exist in the context of international human rights law and international criminal law'.
36   *Ibid.*

The interpretation of this provision raises a controversial question which was already outlined in chapter 1: does the criminal law system aim to protect one's individual rights, which entails that evidence obtained in violation of these rights and even the 'fruits' of such violations, should be excluded? Or, should the criminal law system aim to provide that the accused is guilty and thus in the interest of societal protection against crime, admit any evidence irrespective of its origin?

This apparent controversiality was evidenced during the establishment of the Rome Statute, where some delegations suggested that evidence obtained through human rights violations be excluded. In contrast, other delegations deemed this notion to be too broad, and that the ICC framework should differentiate minor violations of human rights from more serious violations.[37]

2.3.5.2 Minor versus 'Serious' Human Rights Violations

The question, though, is how one should differentiate minor human rights violations from more severe ones. One criterion could be whether the particular violation related to an infringement of the accused's fair trial rights or, alternatively, constituted an invasion of one's privacy rights.

In this regard, a parallel can be drawn from the approach of the European Court of Human Rights (ECtHR). The Court of Strasbourg, in its assessment of whether a domestic court in a national criminal proceeding has violated one or more fair trial rights, looks into the 'overall fairness' of a criminal trial. This approach could be derived from the ECtHR's view on the examination of incriminating witnesses.

In its landmark judgment, *Al-Khawaja & Tahery v United Kingdom*,[38] the Court developed a three-pronged test to assess whether the not being able to (cross-)examine incriminating witnesses constitutes an infringement of fair trial rights. The test was later also more broadly applied, in regards to the question whether the use of evidence obtained in violation of one's human rights amounts to an infringement of fair trial rights. The Court further elucidated upon and clarified this test in *Schatschaschwili v Germany*:

> According to the principles developed in the Al-Khawaja and Tahery judgment, it is necessary to examine in three steps the compatibility with Article 6 §§ 1 and 3 (d) of the Convention of proceedings in which

---

[37] Mark Klamberg (ed), *Commentary on the Law of the International Criminal Court* (Torkel Opsahl Academic EPublisher (TOAEP) 2017) 537.

[38] *Al-Khawaja and Tahery v the United Kingdom* App nos. 26766/05 and 22228/06 (ECtHR, 15 December 2011).

statements made by a witness who had not been present and questioned at the trial were used as evidence (ibid., § 152). The Court must examine

i. whether there was a good reason for the non-attendance of the witness and, consequently, for the admission of the absent witness's untested statements as evidence (ibid., §§ 119–25);
ii. whether the evidence of the absent witness was the sole or decisive basis for the defendant's conviction (ibid., §§ 119 and 126–47); and
iii. whether there were sufficient counterbalancing factors, including strong procedural safeguards, to compensate for the handicaps caused to the defence as a result of the admission of the untested evidence and to ensure that the trial, judged as a whole, was fair (ibid., § 147).[39]

Further, In the ECtHR's case of *Keskin v the Netherlands*, one can find the following paragraphs further clarifying the test developed in *Al-Khawaja and Tahery*:

The Court further explained that "good reason for the absence of a witness" must exist from the trial court's perspective, that is, the court must have had good factual or legal grounds not to secure the witness's attendance at the trial. If there was a good reason for the witness's non-attendance in that sense, it followed that there was a good reason, or justification, for the trial court to admit the untested statements of the absent witness as evidence (see Schatschaschwili, cited above, § 119). While the absence of a good reason for the non-attendance of the witness could not of itself be conclusive of the unfairness of the applicant's trial, it was a very important factor to be weighed in the balance when assessing the overall fairness of a trial, and one which might tip the balance in favour of finding a breach of Article 6 §§ 1 and 3 (d) of the Convention (ibid., § 113).

As regards the question whether the evidence of the absent witness whose statements were admitted in evidence was the sole or decisive basis for the defendant's conviction (second step of the Al-Khawaja and Tahery test), the Court reiterated that "sole" evidence is to be understood as the only evidence against the accused and that "decisive" should be narrowly interpreted as indicating evidence of such significance or importance as is likely to be determinative of the outcome of the case. Where the untested evidence of a witness is supported by other corroborative evidence, the assessment of whether it is decisive will depend on the strength of the supporting evidence; the stronger the corroborative

---

[39] *Schatschaschwili v Germany* App no 9154/10 (ECtHR, 15 December 2015) para. 107.

evidence, the less likely that the evidence of the absent witness will be treated as decisive (ibid., § 123).

It further held that it is not for the Court to act as a court of fourth instance, its starting-point for deciding whether an applicant's conviction was based solely or to a decisive extent on the depositions of an absent witness being the judgments of the domestic courts. The Court must review the domestic courts' evaluation in the light of the meaning it has given to "sole" and "decisive" evidence and ascertain for itself whether the domestic courts' evaluation of the weight of the evidence was unacceptable or arbitrary. It must further make its own assessment of the weight of the evidence given by an absent witness if the domestic courts did not indicate their position on that issue or if their position is not clear (ibid., § 124).

Furthermore, given that its concern is to ascertain whether the proceedings as a whole were fair, the Court should not only review the existence of sufficient counterbalancing factors in cases where the evidence of the absent witness was the sole or the decisive basis for the applicant's conviction, but also in cases where it found it unclear whether the evidence in question was sole or decisive but nevertheless was satisfied that it carried significant weight and its admission might have handicapped the defence. The extent of the counterbalancing factors necessary in order for a trial to be considered fair would depend on the weight of the evidence of the absent witness. The more important that evidence, the more weight the counterbalancing factors would have to carry in order for the proceedings as a whole to be considered fair (ibid., § 116).[40]

As a result, a mere infringement of Art. 8 ECHR (right to privacy) does not automatically constitute a violation of Art. 6 ECHR (right to a fair trial); the particular improper act of part of the Prosecution Service has to affect the overall fairness of the criminal proceedings. This view could be of guidance for the ICC proceedings. This does not mean that one specific violation of, for example, privacy rights through an illegal search of someone's premises should never lead to the conclusion that the 'overall' fairness of the proceedings is infringed. This could largely depend on whether an illegal search resulted in discovering 'potential' incriminating evidence and if so, on whether the Prosecution would benefit from such a search in building a case against a civilian. The latter criterium derives from U.S. criminal law, while other courts such as

---

40 *Keskin v the Netherlands* App no 2205/16 (ECtHR, 19 January 2021) paras 48–51.

the Dutch Supreme Court, do not believe there is any right for the defendant to be protected against 'a discovery of a crime'.

2.3.5.3   'Clean Hands' as an Admissibility Factor?

The issue of benefitting from unlawful behaviour by the Prosecution, also features in international case law through the doctrine of 'clean hands'. This doctrine transpired with respect to the Wikileaks documents. In November 2010, the online platform Wikileaks disseminated approximately 250.000 confidential diplomatic cables from 274 embassies and other diplomatic services of the United States. A member of the U.S. Army was responsible for this leak. Such disclosure of confidential cables was illegal under U.S. law, particularly under the Espionage Act of 1917.[41]

Notably, according to Art. 69(8) RS, a State's national law is not binding when it concerns the determination of relevance or admissibility of evidence.[42] On this point, international courts follow different views. The European Court of Justice (ECJ) decided to admit these cables as evidence in the case of *Persia International Bank PLC v Council*. In particular, the Court held that the possible unlawful nature of these documents could not be held against the applicant, since the latter was not involved in leaking these documents.[43] Therefore, if the party using the evidence in court was the one who unlawfully obtained or acquired it, under this doctrine, this may lead to its inadmissibility.[44]

Within the context of ICC proceedings, this would imply that it has to be established that the Prosecution Service itself were (in)directly involved in the unlawful acquirement of the evidence. For the Defense, this is quite a heavy burden to meet, especially in the absence of access to the communication between the members of the Prosecution and their investigators. As a result, within the ICC framework the 'clean hands' doctrine does not appear to be the most suitable to preserve the rationale of Art. 69(7) RS.

2.3.5.4   Probative Value as Touchstone for Art. 69(7) RS

Rather than assessing the gravity of the potential breach of human rights or looking into the role of the party introducing the evidence, one could also opt for a focus on solely the probative value of the evidence. This approach was

---

41   Mansour Fallah (n 35) 147–166, 160.
42   Cf. also Klamberg (n 37) 537.
43   *Persia International Bank PLC v Council of the European Union*, Case T-493/10, Judgment of the General Court (Fourth Chamber), 6 September 2013, para. 95; Mansour Fallah (n 35) 147–176, 163.
44   Mansour Fallah (n 35) 147–176, 164.

followed by the Special Tribunal for Lebanon (STL) in the case of the *Prosecutor v Ayyash et al.* in its Decision on the Admissibility of Documents published on the Wikileaks website.[45]

Within the system of the STL, Rule 149(d) of the Rules of Procedure and Evidence (STL RPE) governed the exclusion of evidence on the basis of the criterion that the probative value be substantially outweighed by the need to ensure a fair trial. The judges of the STL did not accentuate the unlawfulness as to how the Wikileaks cables were obtained or disclosed; instead, the Court's decisive criterion for the admissibility of these documents was their reliability.

In its decision, the STL judges considered that the particular Wikileaks documents could not proclaim to have the *prima facie* requirements for reliability, which the Court defined as having to bear authenticity and accuracy. For this reason, the Court denied the Defense motion to admit the documents into evidence.[46] Yet, if one would accept this admissibility approach based upon the probative value criterion, it could also result in admitting evidence which meets the standard of admissibility but still might be tainted in the way it was obtained, and this could affect the integrity of the proceedings.

2.3.5.5 Differentiation Based on the Due Process Notion

Another potential solution to the dilemma of how to differentiate between violations which cast 'substantial doubt on the reliability of evidence' pursuant to Article 69(7) RS and which violations do not, or between what is 'antithetical' and what is not, perhaps lies in the view of the U.S. Supreme Court.

In its landmark judgment of *Mapp v Ohio*, rendered on June 19, 1961, the Court held that the exclusionary rule, which forbids the use of unconstitutionally obtained evidence in federal courts, should also extend to evidence presented before State Courts as being a fundamental due process right. Accordingly, the U.S. Supreme Court ruled that such unconstitutionally obtained evidence should be suppressed (also) in State criminal trials.[47] The U.S. Supreme Court reasoned that 'the exclusionary rule is an essential part of both the Fourth and Fourteenth Amendments'.[48]

---

45   *Prosecutor v Ayyash et al.* (Decision on the admissibility of documents published on WikiLeaks website) STL-11-01/T/TC, T Ch (21 May 2015); Mansour Fallah (n 35) 147–176, 161–162.

46   *Prosecutor v Ayyash et al.* (Decision on the admissibility of documents published on WikiLeaks website) STL-11-01/T/TC, T Ch (21 May 2015) paras 35 and 43.

47   *Mapp v Ohio*, 367 U.S. 643 (1961).

48   Ibid.

Yet, this exclusionary rule has been nuanced through exceptions such as the independent source doctrine. In *Murray v United States*, the Supreme Court held that evidence initially detected during an unlawful search could nonetheless be admitted under this doctrine, provided that it would later be rediscovered through some legal channel – for instance a search based upon a valid search warrant – which legal course of notion was 'genuinely independent' from the original illegal search.[49]

In *Murray v United States*, a two-part test was developed in order to decide if a warrant is to be seen as an independent legal basis to retrieve evidence. This test, also confirmed by the Seventh Circuit in *United States v Huskisson* in its ruling of June 5 2019,[50] implies that a search warrant is considered to be an independent source if:

i. The illegally obtained evidence did not undermine the determination by the Court that probable cause existed to justify the search, and
ii. The illegal search did not affect the decision of the government to pursue the search warrant.[51]

As to the first question, for the search to be legal under this doctrine, it must be established that the application for a search warrant entail sufficient non-tainted evidence to substantiate probable cause.[52] For ICC proceedings, such

---

49   *Murray v United States*, 487 U.S. 533 (1988).
50   *United States v Huskisson*, 926 F.3d 369 (7th Cir. 2019).
     In this case, the scope of the independent source doctrine was expanded, underlining the tension between such doctrine and the protection from warrantless searches of the home as guaranteed by the Fourth Amendment. The Huskisson court's broad reading of the Murray test has the practical effect that government officials may engage in an initial search to confirm their suspicion and may then rationalize these searches ex post If they have probable cause to justify a later-issued application, as they are now allowed to include the information discovered during the initial search in the affidavit for the subsequent warrant; this means that even if Tainted Evidence Is Described in the Warrant Application, the unlawfully obtained evidence may still be admitted at trial. In doing so, the exclusionary rule and the exception of the 'genuinely independent' source from the original, unconstitutional search as conceptualized in *Murray v United States* are watered down, thus further eroding the due process rights and constitutional protections. For a comment on this case, cf. Akua Abu et al. (eds), 'United States v. Huskisson: Seventh Circuit Holds That Evidence Gathered Through an Unlawful Search of a Home May Be Admissible Under the Independent Source Doctrine Even If Tainted Evidence Is Described in the Warrant Application. COMMENT ON:926 F.3d 369 (7th Cir. 2019)' (2020) 133 Harvard Law Review <https://harvardlawreview.org/print/vol-133/united-states-v-huskisson/> accessed 2 August 2023.
51   *Murray v United States*, 487 U.S. 533 (1988).
52   *Ibid*.

an approach would mean that the Prosecution, in order to remedy a piece of evidence which was obtained in violation of Art. 69(7) RS, would need to present other evidence of the same nature or to the same extent as the tainted evidence.

Yet, this theory leaves unsanctioned the violation of human rights as such, in so far as it damages the integrity of the proceedings. Therefore, the U.S. Supreme Court approach on the exclusionary rule doesn't seem the most suitable one within the ICC system, as it would defeat the purpose of Art. 69(7) RS at the very least.

Suppose the Prosecution would be able to retrieve a witness statement through a payment to this witness or in exchange for assisting the witness in obtaining a stay permit, which statement it would not have obtained in the absence of the aforementioned actions: this could 'cast substantial doubt on the reliability' of this type of evidence. Yet, the Prosecution presents another witness who testifies, along the same lines as the first witness. Can one say that this non-tainted evidence could remedy the potential breach of the integrity of the proceedings regarding the first witness, such that the Court could ignore this breach by saying that the Prosecution did present further evidence? Such an approach would undermine the *raison d'être* of Art. 69(7) RS.

2.3.6 Presenting the Defense of 'Exclusion of Evidence' at the International Criminal Court

An important question to consider relates to the presentation of the defense of 'exclusion of evidence'. As recently recalled, the power to exclude evidence is a cornerstone of the Court's ability to both 'protect the accuracy and reliability of the Court's fact-finding by requiring that evidence of questionable credibility be excluded', and safeguard 'the moral integrity and the legitimacy of the proceedings by requiring that the process of collecting and presenting evidence is fair towards the accused and respects the procedural and human rights of all those who are involved in the trial'.[53] In this regard, in the Court's jurisprudence it has been consistently reiterated that 'the party bringing the motion under Art. 69(7) of the Statute bears the burden of showing that the criteria for the exclusion of evidence has been met'',[54] which further entails,

---

53 *Prosecutor v Yekatom and Ngaïssona* (Public Redacted Version of the "Request for the Exclusion of Fabricated Evidence", 5 December 2023, ICC-01/14-01/18-2240-Conf) ICC-01/14-01/18-2240-Red, T Ch v (9 February 2024) para. 32.

54 *Prosecutor v Yekatom and Ngaïssona* (Public redacted version of "Prosecution Response to the Yekatom Defence 'Request for the Exclusion of Fabricated Evidence'(ICC-01/14-01/18-2240-Conf)", ICC-01/14-01/18-2313-Conf, 18 January 2024) ICC-01/14-01/18-2313-Red, OTP (12 February 2024) para. 7; *Prosecutor v Al Hassan* (Public redacted version of 'Decision

in accordance with the plain wording and intent of Art. 69(7) RS, demonstrating at the outset that the challenged evidence was obtained through unlawful means.[55] In the concrete case, this burden will most probably rest upon the Defense.

The Appeal Chamber in *Bemba et al.* held that 'Article 69(7) of the Statute envisages two consecutive inquiries. First, in accordance with the chapeau of this provision, it must be determined whether the evidence at issue was "obtained by means of a violation of th[e] Statute or internationally recognized human rights". An affirmative answer to this question is, however, not sufficient for the concerned evidence to be inadmissible. When the conditions of the chapeau of article 69(7) of the Statute are met, the second step is to consider whether "[t]he violation casts substantial doubt on the reliability of the evidence" (article 69 (7) (a) of the Statute) or "[t]he admission of the evidence would be antithetical to and would seriously damage the integrity of the proceedings" (article 69 (7) (b) of the Statute). The evidence concerned is inadmissible in case of an affirmative answer to either of these two questions'.[56] Therefore, as recalled by the Appeal Chamber, 'the fact that evidence was obtained by means of a violation of the Statute or internationally recognised human rights is a necessary pre-condition for the exclusion of such evidence under this legal basis'.[57]

A further important consideration concerns the fact that the party seeking the exclusion of the contaminated evidence also bears the burden to show a causal link between the alleged violation and the specific portion of the evidence. Indeed, as observed by Trial Chamber X in *Al Hassan*, 'The chapeau of Article 69(7) of the Statue provides that the provision applies where evidence

---

on requests related to the submission into evidence of Mr Al Hassan's statements') ICC-01/12-01/18-1475-Red, T Ch X (20 May 2021) para. 37; *Prosecutor v Bemba Gombo* (Public redacted version of the First decision on the prosecution and defence requests for the admission of evidence, dated 15 December 2011) ICC-01/05-01/08-2012-Red, T Ch (9 February 2012) para. 17.

55 *Prosecutor v Yekatom and Ngaïssona* (Public redacted version of "Prosecution Response to the Yekatom Defence 'Request for the Exclusion of Fabricated Evidence'(ICC-01/14-01/18-2240-Conf)", ICC-01/14-01/18-2313-Conf, 18 January 2024) ICC-01/14-01/18-2313-Red, OTP (12 February 2024) para. 7; *Prosecutor v Al Hassan* (Public redacted version of 'Decision on requests related to the submission into evidence of Mr Al Hassan's statements') ICC-01/12-01/18-1475-Red, T Ch X (20 May 2021) para. 37.

56 *Prosecutor v Bemba et al.* (Appeal Judgment) ICC-01/05-01/13-2275-Red, A Ch (8 March 2018) para. 280; *Prosecutor v Yekatom and Ngaïssona* (Public Redacted Version of the "Request for the Exclusion of Fabricated Evidence", 5 December 2023, ICC-01/14-01/18-2240-Conf) ICC-01/14-01/18-2240-Red, T Ch V (9 February 2024) para. 33.

57 *Prosecutor v Bemba et al.* (Appeal Judgment) ICC-01/05-01/13-2275-Red, A Ch (8 March 2018) para. 351.

was 'obtained by means of a violation' (emphasis added). The Chamber observes that this, by its plain wording, requires a breach of the Statute or internationally recognised human rights as well as, a causal link between the violation and the gathering of the evidence'.[58] In particular, the Chamber noted that, consistent with the aforementioned Appeal Chamber's findings in *Bemba et al.*, '(T)he first determination for the Chamber is whether it has been shown that the evidence in question was gathered, or its gathering was facilitated by, such a breach or violation'.[59] Moreover, The Chamber explained that '(T)he exclusionary rule under the Statute warrants an assessment focused on the investigative activities of the ICC Prosecution which generated this particular evidence. Such an analysis may include consideration of the general context in which the evidence was gathered and interaction with, or influence of other authorities, but only insofar as those factors are relevant to the gathering of the specific evidence in this case by the ICC Prosecution. This construction of Article 69(7) is consistent with its plain language and with the practical realities which surround evidence gathering with respect to alleged atrocity crime in the different situations within the jurisdiction of the Court. ICC investigators are dependent on the cooperation of States to conduct investigative activities and their control with respect to the overall conditions and circumstances in which those activities are carried out will be limited. Article 69(7) in its plain wording recognises that distinction by focusing not on the general conditions applicable in the situation where the investigations and evidence gathering are occurring but rather those specific to the way in which evidence is actually obtained'.[60]

Such an approach would seem to be confirmed by the general interpretation of Art. 69(7) endorsed by ICC Chambers, whereby '(A) factor in the separate assessment under Article 69(7)(b) of the Statute is the Prosecution's degree of control over the evidence gathering process or power to prevent any improper

---

58 *Prosecutor v Al Hassan* (Public redacted version of 'Decision on requests related to the submission into evidence of Mr Al Hassan's statements') ICC-01/12-01/18-1475-Red, T Ch X (20 May 2021) para. 33; *Prosecutor v Yekatom and Ngaïssona* (Public redacted version of "Prosecution Response to the Yekatom Defence 'Request for the Exclusion of Fabricated Evidence' (ICC-01/14-01/18-2240-Conf)", ICC-01/14-01/18-2313-Conf, 18 January 2024) ICC-01/14-01/18-2313-Red, OTP (12 February 2024) para. 21; *Prosecutor v Gicheru* (Public Redacted Version of Decision On The Request To Exclude Audio Recordings Pursuant To Article 69(7) of The Statute) ICC-01/09-01/20-284-Red2, T Ch III (18 February 2022) para. 45.

59 *Prosecutor v Al Hassan* (Public redacted version of 'Decision on requests related to the submission into evidence of Mr Al Hassan's statements') ICC-01/12-01/18-1475-Red, T Ch X (20 May 2021) para. 41.

60 *Ibid* para. 42.

or illegal activity. While that is not necessarily a consideration in assessing whether a breach or violation has occurred, it supports that the exclusionary rule, especially to the extent that it is intended to discipline or deter irregular or unlawful conduct by authorities, must be construed narrowly with focus on the circumstances pertaining to gathering of the specific evidence'.[61]

In light of the foregoing, Defense Counsel at the ICC, bearing the burden to argue that the criteria of Art. 69(7) are met, should therefore secure arguments to make such a causal link probable in order for the exclusionary rule to operate.

2.3.7 Towards a New Exclusionary Rule

Within international courts jurisprudence, it is difficult to detect an overarching criterion for the admissibility of evidence, especially for the exclusion thereof. The exclusionary rule has been subjected to erosion, in that national and international courts have at times tried to nuance this rule by introducing factors such as the gravity of the law which was infringed, the (non) male fides intention by the party breaching it, the existence of non-tainted evidence, and whether the party invoking the evidence had clean hands.[62]

Yet, every attenuation of the exclusionary rule would disseminate a non-deterrent signal to the parties in a criminal trial, especially to the Prosecution.[63] Hence, the only way to protect the integrity of the criminal justice system is to unconditionally exclude evidence which is obtained by unlawful or antithetical methods, without any exceptions or factors which could be balanced against the effects of the exclusion of evidence to mitigate such exclusion.

---

61 Ibid para. 43; *Prosecutor v Lubanga Dyilo* (Decision on the admission of material from the "bar table") ICC-01/04-01/06-1981, T Ch I (24 June 2009) paras 45–47; *Prosecutor v Bemba et al.* (Decision on Requests to Exclude Western Union Documents and other Evidence Pursuant to Article 69(7)) ICC-01/05-01/13-1854, T Ch VII (29 April 2016) paras 65, 68–69; *Prosecutor v Bemba et al.* (Decision on Request in Response to Two Austrian Decisions) ICC-01/05-01/13-1948, T Ch VII (14 July 2016) paras 33, 36–37, 39; *Prosecutor v Bemba et al.* (Separate Opinion of Judge Geoffrey Henderson) ICC-01/05-01/13-2275-Anx, A Ch (8 March 2018) para. 34.

62 Mansour Fallah (n 35) 147–176, 174.

63 Ibid 147–176, 176.

PART 2

Direct Evidence

CHAPTER 3

(Eye)witnesses at ICC Trials

3.1 Witness Dimensions

Up to now, in every case which was brought before the ICC, the Prosecution did rely on lay-witnesses, some of which qualify as 'eye'-witnesses. The ICC RPE do not contain a clear definition about the exact competency of a witness who can be called before the Court.

One of the most important questions is whether a lay witness can be examined on their opinion or perceptions concerning certain events, apart from eliciting from this witness factual observations. However, like before, no clear guidance can be found in the ICC RPE. In some law systems such as the federal law system of the United States, a lay witness may testify in the form of opinions or inferences, if the testimony can rationally be based on the perception of such witness.[1]

Nonetheless, the line between 'rationally perceived' and 'mere speculation' is quite thin. Therefore, in principle, a witness is someone who did observe certain events relevant to the charges and, thus, can assist the Court with factual observations.

3.2 The Evidentiary Value of (Eye)witnesses

In the book *You might go to prison, even though you're innocent*, Justin Brooks writes:

> When multiple victims make an identification, the evidence to convict is compelling, but that still doesn't mean it's accurate. In the Luis Vargas case, not one, not two, but three separate women identified our client Luis as the man who raped them. On December 7, 1999, just before being sentenced to fifty-five years-to-life for three crimes he didn't commit, Luis addressed the Los Angeles Superior Court, stating, "I will pray for God's

---

[1] Thomas Mauet, *Trials: Strategy, Skills, And the New Powers of Persuasion* (1st edn, Aspen Publishers 2005) 123, where the author discusses Rule 701 of the U.S. Federal Rules of Evidence.

mercy on all of you ... but as far as I'm concerned, the individual who really did these crimes might really be raping someone out there."

Luis was right. The victims who testified that they had been raped by Luis had in fact been attacked by a man who came to be known as the "Teardrop Rapist." That man continued to rape women long after Luis went to prison.[2]

Eyewitness error is the leading cause of wrongful convictions, with empirical studies suggesting that one in three eyewitnesses makes an erroneous eyewitness identification. This conclusion was put forward in 2016 by Safer et al. based upon several scientific experiments,[3] and is relevant also for ICC proceedings. The authors ascribe the following reasons to eyewitness errors:

(i) Firstly, legal professionals, like jurors, have limited knowledge of factors that affect the accuracy of what eyewitness purport to have seen. This specifically relates to lack of knowledge of proper identification procedures.[4]

(ii) Secondly, the scientific research reveals the inability of legal professionals to apply their knowledge of the eyewitness factors – if existing – to the facts of a criminal case.[5]

(iii) Thirdly, research indicates that, within the criminal law system, no effective legal safeguard is available to sensitize jurors and legal professionals to the potential risks of eyewitness testimony, which in turn contributes to misunderstanding potential errors.[6]

To prevent such errors from being overlooked by jurors (or legal professionals), the U.S. Supreme Court in the case of *Neil v Biggers* in 1972 set forth five eyewitness factors that jurors should consider when assessing eyewitness testimony. These factors are the following:

(i) The opportunity of the witness to view the criminal at the time of the crime;
(ii) The witness' degree of attention;
(iii) The accuracy of the witness' prior description of the criminal;

---

2 Justin Brooks, *You Might Go to Prison, Even Though You're Innocent* (1st edn, University of California Press 2023) 64.
3 Martin Safer et al., 'Educating Jurors about Eyewitness Testimony in Criminal Cases with Circumstantial and Forensic Evidence' (2016) 47 International journal of law and psychiatry 86. Cf. Also Richard Wise et al., 'An Examination of the Causes and Solutions to Eyewitness Error' 5 Frontiers in Psychlatry 102.
4 *Ibid* 86.
5 *Ibid.*
6 *Ibid.*

(iv) The level of certainty demonstrated by the witness at the confrontation, and
(v) The length of time between the crime and the confrontation.[7]

Particularly relevant is the Court's statement according to which "it is the likelihood of misidentification which violates a defendant's right to due process, and it is this which was the basis of the exclusion of evidence in Foster. Suggestive confrontations are disapproved because they increase the likelihood of misidentification, and unnecessarily suggestive ones are condemned for the further reason that the increased chance of misidentification is gratuitous. But as *Stovall* makes clear, the admission of evidence of a showup without more does not violate due process".[8]

In *Neil v Biggers*, the accused was convicted of rape on evidence that consisted in part of testimony concerning the victim's visual and voice identification of the accused during a show up at a station-house seven months after the rape. The victim had been in the presence of her assailant a considerable amount of time and had directly observed him indoors and under a full moon outdoors and testified that she had 'no doubt' that the accused was her assailant. Additionally, she had previously given the police a description of the assailant and had not identified others presented at previous showups, lineups or by way of photographs. Police stated they had used the showup technique in lieu of a lineup due to difficulties in finding individuals matching the victim's description.

The U.S. Supreme Court delved into the procedural details of the identification and discussed the impact of those details upon the evidentiary weight. The following three paragraphs from the ruling are instructive of how eyewitness identification could be approached in the context of international criminal proceedings:

> In part, as discussed above, we think the District Court focused unduly on the relative reliability of a lineup as opposed to a showup, the issue on which expert testimony was taken at the evidentiary hearing. It must be kept in mind also that the trial was conducted before Stovall, and that therefore the incentive was lacking for the parties to make a record at trial of facts corroborating or undermining the identification. The testimony was addressed to the jury, and the jury apparently found the identification reliable. Some of the State's testimony at the federal evidentiary hearing may well have been self-serving in that it too neatly fit the case

---

7   *Neil v Biggers*, 409 U.S. 188 (1972) paras 199–200.
8   *Ibid* para. 199.

law, but it surely does nothing to undermine the state record, which itself fully corroborated the identification.

We find that the District Court's conclusions on the critical facts are unsupported by the record, and clearly erroneous. The victim spent a considerable period of time with her assailant, up to half an hour. She was with him under adequate artificial light in her house and under a full moon outdoors, and at least twice, once in the house and later in the woods, faced him directly and intimately. She was no casual observer, but rather the victim of one of the most personally humiliating of all crimes. Her description to the police, which included the assailant's approximate age, height, weight, complexion, skin texture, build, and voice, might not have satisfied Proust, but was more than ordinarily thorough. She had "no doubt" that respondent was the person who raped her. In the nature of the crime, there are rarely witnesses to a rape other than the victim, who often has a limited opportunity of observation. The victim here, a practical nurse by profession, had an unusual opportunity to observe and identify her assailant. She testified at the habeas corpus hearing that there was something about his face 'I don't think I could ever forget".

There was, to be sure, a lapse of seven months between the rape and the confrontation. This would be a seriously negative factor in most cases. Here, however, the testimony is undisputed that the victim made no previous identification at any of the showups, lineups, or photographic showings. Her record for reliability was thus a good one, as she had previously resisted whatever suggestiveness inheres in a showup. Weighing all the factors, we find no substantial likelihood of misidentification. The evidence was properly allowed to go to the jury.[9]

The five factors enunciated by the U.S. Supreme Court can also be helpful to ICC judges and especially to Defense counsel, to question an eyewitness of an incident with which the accused is charged, like in the case of war crimes of rape or pillaging. Eyewitness testimony can pay an important role in proving such type of charges.

Additionally, scientific psychological research in this area has brought forward a three-prong test in evaluating eyewitness evidence by the jurors, which is equally applicable in the context of international criminal trials.

(i) First, one should determine how Prosecution investigators conducted the eyewitness interviews. In particular, this first step entails determining:

---

9   *Ibid* paras 200–201.

a. If the investigators obtained the information as mentioned by the U.S. Supreme Court in *Neil v Biggers*;
b. If the eyewitness' memory was contaminated by post-event information, for instance by press articles;
c. If the investigators encouraged the eyewitness in his or her identification.[10]

(ii) Second, one should determine how the Prosecution investigators performed the identification procedure;
(iii) Third, one should assess how potential situational factors at the time of the crime scene might have affected the accuracy of the testimony[11]

All of these factors in combination, should be further explored at trial when the Prosecution presents an eyewitness who claims to have identified a certain individual perpetrator.

3.3 The Evidentiary Weight of (Eye)witnesses

Apart from the determining factors for the evaluation of (eye)witnesses, as described in the previous paragraph, the evidentiary weight of this type of evidence depends also on other elements. These factors can be derived from the available impeachment methods as accepted in Common Law.

Within the U.S. Federal Rules of Evidence and Common Law Jurisprudence, there are seven categories of impeachment features. Five of them are relevant to lay witnesses since they shed light on the credibility of the witness evidence, thus contributing to the evaluation of its evidentiary weight. These categories are the following:

a. The existence of bias or improper motive;
b. The potential contradiction with prior statements given by the witness;
c. Contradictions given at trial;
d. Prior convictions;
e. Prior bad acts by the witness (without convictions).[12]

For Defense counsel, the following guidelines are instructive of how to introduce these factors:

Sub a.) Bias, which concerns a pre-dispositional frame of (negative) mind towards the accused, can be established by showing a previous relationship

---

10 Safer et al. (n 3) 86, 86.
11 *Ibid* 86, 87.
12 For these categories, cf. Mauet (n 1) 214–215.

with the accused which can make probable that the witness has a certain interest in the outcome of the case.[13] Motive pertains to a specific reason of the witness, such as revenge, to settle a score with the accused which fuels his or her testimony. It is important that in order to show such incentive on the part of a witness, Defense counsel preferably introduced 'extrinsic evidence' such as documentary or witness evidence.

In the context of ICC proceedings, the elements of bias and motive deserve special attention, considering that certain witnesses appearing at trial may have taken sides for one of the (fighting) parties in an international or internal armed conflict. The political background of the witness is equally relevant in these proceedings, and should be a focus for Defense investigations.

Sub b.) At the ICC, the Prosecution conducts its investigations, which may result in prior statements given by witnesses. These statements are not made under oath before a judge. Nonetheless, the Defense may use them, according to case law, during the examination of a witness, particularly in two instances:
- To refresh the memory of a witness, if the witness no longer has a clear recollection of a particular fact at trial;
- To confront the witness with a clear contradiction with such a prior statement of the witness.[14]

In this regard, ICC proceedings are familiar with the concept of 'investigatory notes', which are not official statements by the witness, but a summary of a contact between ICC investigators and the witness. The status of those investigatory notes is such that Trial Chambers at the ICC do allow the Defense to confront a witness with either such notes taken from this very witness or from another witness.[15] To conclude, these prior statements and investigatory notes can be useful pieces of evidence to challenge the credibility of an (eye)witness

Sub d. and e.) Prior convictions or 'bad acts' on the part of a witness can affect the credibility of the witness.[16] Obviously, not every prior conviction automatically reflects on such credibility. Convictions which say something about potential dishonesty or falsehood of the witness merit attention, for instance convictions for fraud or false information given to the authorities.[17] Such convictions can shed a light on the integrity of the witness and their mentality to tell the truth. For Defense counsel, it is important to seek disclosure

---

13   *Ibid* 214.
14   See, inter alia, *Prosecutor v Yekatom and Ngaïssona*, trial transcript.
15   See, inter alia, *Prosecutor v Yekatom and Ngaïssona*, trial transcript.
16   Cf. Rule 609 and Rule 608(6) of the U.S. Federal Rules of Evidence; Mauet (n 1) 215.
17   *Ibid*.

from the Prosecution of the criminal record, if existing, of the witness, or try to find in open sources, all material available on the witness on this area.

To sum up, this chapter has delved into several factors which can impact upon the evidentiary weight of (eye)witness testimony either as to identification evidence or as to the substance of a witness testimony. In particular, these factors may assist the Defense at the ICC when preparing an examination of Prosecution witnesses.

CHAPTER 4

Using (Anonymous) Hearsay Evidence

4.1 Hearsay Evidence in Domestic Law

4.1.1 *Hearsay Evidence in Common Law Jurisdictions*

Similar to documentary evidence, which is discussed in Part v, evidentiary challenges arise with respect to evidence which rests upon hearsay. Hearsay evidence is a form of indirect evidence that is typically admissible before international criminal jurisdictions such as the ICC and the *ad hoc* tribunals.

In common law jurisdictions, hearsay evidence is in principle not admissible. This is known as the 'hearsay rule', which is an exclusionary rule "prohibiting hearsay (out of court statements offered as proof of that statement) from being admitted as evidence because of the inability of the other party to cross-examine the maker of the statement".[1] However, common law jurisdictions have developed clearly delineated exceptions to the rule.

In the UK, hearsay evidence may be admissible if it falls under one of the exceptions listed in the *Criminal Justice Act of 2003* (CJA 2003).[2] An example is when all parties agree to the admission of the evidence;[3] another example is the so-called business documents exception.[4]

4.1.2 *The Business Documents Exception in (International) Criminal Law*

In the UK, the business documents exception was introduced in response to the realities of information generation and storage in modern commercial enterprises.[5] Indeed, it appears difficult to trace the flow of information after many years since the moment it was entered into the computer database. Therefore, according to this exception, a statement in a business record can be

---

1 'Hearsay Rule', *Legal Information Institut* (Cornell University insignia) <https://www.law.cornell.edu/wex/hearsay_rule#content> accessed 4 August 2023; John Spencer, *Hearsay Evidence in Criminal Proceedings*, vol 5 (1st edn, Hart Publishing 2008) 173, where the author explains: "the basic problem with hearsay is that it cannot usually be subjected to the three tests which the law applies to test the sincerity and accuracy of disputed evidence : the oath, cross-examination and the ability of the court to observe the demeanour of the witness".
2 Criminal Justice Act 2003, chapter 2, Part 11; Paul Roberts and Adrian Zuckerman, *Criminal Evidence* (3rd edn, Oxford University Press 2022) 408–412.
3 Section 114(1)(c) CJA 2003 provides that a statement is not excluded by the hearsay rule where 'all the parties are in agreement to it being admissible.'
4 Section 117 CJA 2003.
5 Roberts and Zuckerman (n 2) 446–447.

produced at trial "without requiring its proponent to produce percipient witnesses to every detail of the statement's provenance".[6] However, as pointed out by Roberts and Zuckerman, it is difficult to understand why the mere receipt of a document in the course of business should guarantee the reliability of its contents, as the CJA 2003 would seem to presuppose.[7]

In federal[8] and most state courts in the United States, the business records exception is a statutory exception which "allows parties to enter regularly compiled records within an organization that meet a certain level of trustworthiness".[9] According to the federal system, 4 requirements must be fulfilled for the exception to be applicable. First, the information in the record, in a written form, must come from someone who had first-hand knowledge of the event as part of their job;[10] second, the records must be ordinarily produced in the normal course of business of an organization or workplace (according to the STL, official governmental records can also be viewed as a form of business record as they are the product of the 'business' of government);[11] thirdly, the person must be able to testify to the standards of record keeping for the organization;[12] Lastly, the records must not give rise to untrustworthiness. In this regard, Courts often consider whether records appear to be self-serving, holding to be more skeptical when records are, for instance, made in anticipation of litigation.[13]

The last requirement is the most interesting to Defense council; indeed, parallels can be drawn with ICC proceedings and a recent practice by the Prosecution to submit self-authenticating documents like Call Data Records (CDRs), that are recorded data from a specific phone number produced by a telephone exchange.[14] In this regard, Defense council should pay particular attention to

---

6   *Ibid* 447.
7   *Ibid*.
8   Rule 803(6) of the U.S. Federal Rules of Evidence.
9   'Business Records Exception', *Legal Information Institut* (Cornell University insignia) <https://www.law.cornell.edu/wex/business_records_exception#content> accessed 15 August 2023.
10 *Ibid*.
11 *Ibid*; *Prosecutor v Ayyash et al.* (Trial judgment) STL-11-01/T/TC, T Ch (18 August 2020) paras 358 and 364.
12 'Business Records Exception', *Legal Information Institut* (Cornell University insignia) <https://www.law.cornell.edu/wex/business_records_exception#content> accessed 15 August 2023.
13 *Ibid*.
14 'The Application of Call Data Records in Corporate Forensic Investigations' (*CYFOR*) <https://cyfor.co.uk/the-application-of-call-data-records-in-corporate-investigations/> accessed 18 August 2023.

whether these records were made or adapted in view of litigation, in other words, to whether CDRs were shaped in light of the Prosecution case.

In 2020, the STL was confronted with the admissibility of Call Data Records. In its judgment of 18 August 2020, the STL defined these CDRs as follows: "Call data records provide information about communications, such as the source and destination telephone numbers, the type of communication (voice call or text message), the date and time of the communication, the duration of the voice call, the IMEI number of the handset relevant to the communications, and the cell towers to which the mobiles connected. Call data records are the business records of telecommunication companies generated and retained automatically and legally in the normal course of their business".[15]

The STL distinguished between records produced by a corporation or other entity for an investigation or for the purposes of litigation, such as for use in court, and archive business records produced for everyday operational reasons.[16] While the fact of being produced in the normal course of business provides the latter records with a *prima facie* degree of reliability, "documents created for specific court use, or in response to an investigation, could potentially have been shaped or even manipulated with the intention to produce a desired result favourable to someone such as the tendering party. This could lessen or even deprive them of probative value".[17]

Therefore, it is very important for Defense council to verify format and producer of the CDR, as this may make a difference in terms of probative value. Additionally, Defense council should be aware that this type of business records might contain double hearsay, which is not allowed through the business exception.

4.1.3 *Hearsay Evidence in Civil Law Jurisdictions*

In European civil law systems, by contrast, a widely adopted concept is the 'directness principle' or 'immediacy principle'.[18] This principle is an inclusionary rule that does not prevent from hearing hearsay evidence. However, if the person is still available, the Court is obliged to hear evidence from the original source of the information.[19] This is because the immediacy principle, in its substantive view, requires evidence to be based on the most primary source so

---

15 *Prosecutor v Ayyash et al.* (Trial judgment) STL-11-01/T/TC, T Ch (18 August 2020) paras 373–374.
16 *Ibid* paras 362 and 363.
17 *Ibid* para. 363.
18 Simon De Smet, 'A Structural Analysis of the Role of the Pre-Trial Chamber in the Fact-Finding Process of the ICC' in Carsten Stahn and Göran Sluiter (eds), *The Emerging Practice of the International Criminal Court* (Brill 2009) 401–440, 412.
19 Spencer (n 1) 23.

as to ensure the verifiability of the information contained therein.[20] Therefore, hearsay evidence is in principle not inadmissible, but it should be handled with caution.[21] For instance, in Germany a conviction shall be corroborated by more reliable evidence and not be based on hearsay evidence only.[22]

As anticipated, there is a consensus that hearsay evidence must be approached with circumspection, since it cannot be challenged at trial. Indeed, tensions with an accused's right to confront the evidence presented against him or her are clearly perceivable, which stands at odds with this essential requirement of a fair trial.[23] The right to confrontation is codified in international instruments like Art. 6(3)(d) ECHR and Art. 14(3) of the International Covenant on Civil and Political Rights (ICCPR).

4.2 Hearsay Evidence at the ICC

At the ICC, it is settled practice that hearsay evidence is not *ab initio* inadmissible; nonetheless, it is typically approached with caution and its probative value – which is usually lower – is determined "on the basis of the context and conditions in which it was obtained, and with due consideration of the impossibility of cross-examining the information source".[24]

In contrast to the ICTY Rules of Procedure and Evidence (ICTY RPE),[25] the ICC system does not provide specific rules governing the admission of hearsay evidence,[26] which must be assessed on a case-by-case basis; it is left to the judges' discretionary powers and interpretation. Rule 63(2) ICC RPE provides

---

20 Marc Groenhuijsen and Hatice Selçuk, 'The Principle of Immediacy in Dutch Criminal Procedure in the Perspective of European Human Rights Law' (2014) 126 Zeitschrift für die Gesamte Strafrechtswissenschaft 248, 250–251, where the authors recall that Prof. Gare explained: "the principle of immediacy is based on the idea that the use of original evidence is preferable to any reproduction of evidence which bears the risk of distortion".
21 Spencer (n 1) 23.
22 *Ibid.*
23 *Ibid* 12.
24 *Prosecutor v Katanga and Ngudjolo Chui* (Decision on the confirmation of charges) ICC-01/04-01/07-717, PT Ch I (30 September 2008) para. 137; *Prosecutor v Ngudjolo Chui* (Trial judgment) ICC-01/04-02/12-3-tENG, T Ch II (18 December 2012) para. 55; *Prosecutor v Katanga* (Trial judgment) ICC-01/04-01/07-3436-tENG, T Ch II (7 March 2014) para. 90; *Prosecutor v Lubanga Dyilo* (Trial judgment) ICC-01/04-01/06-2842, T Ch I (14 March 2012) para. 108.
25 Rule 89(D) ICTY RPE "A Chamber may exclude evidence if its probative value is substantially outweighed by the need to ensure a fair trial".
26 The only formal exclusionary rule is found in Articles 69(7) (a) and (b) RS, which apply to cases where evidence is obtained by means of a violation of the Statute or internationally recognized human rights.

for the judges' discretionary power "to assess freely all evidence submitted in order to determine its relevance or admissibility in accordance with article 69." Judges at the ICC have typically approached hearsay evidence as a matter of probative value rather than of admissibility,[27] reflecting a rather inclusionary (albeit *sui generis*) approach to evidence.

The case law of the ICC provides for several conditions in order for hearsay to have sufficient probative value:
– The first requirement relates to the fact that adequate information is provided as to the reliability and credibility of the original source.[28]
– The second requirement is that identity of the original source must be known. This enables the Defense and the Chamber to find out how the source came to know the information, and also to verify potential motives on the part of the source to incriminate the accused.[29]

This means that if the hearsay evidence is based on anonymous hearsay or hearsay without adequate information on the reliability and credibility of the source, a trial chamber must find that the information provided by the hearsay witness is unsupported.[30] To conclude otherwise, it would be impossible to assess the trustworthiness of the witness. These two elements create for Defense counsel a solid argument to challenge hearsay evidence.

4.2.1   *Anonymous Hearsay Evidence at the Pre-trial Stage*

At the pre-trial stage, ICC chambers have indicated that "there is nothing in the Statute or the Rules which expressly provides that the evidence which can be considered hearsay from anonymous sources is inadmissible *per se*"[31] but have warned that "it may cause difficulties for the Defence because it is deprived of the opportunity to challenge its probative value".[32]

---

[27]   E.g. *Prosecutor v Lubanga Dyilo* (Decision on the confirmation of charges) ICC-01/04-01/06-803-tEN, PT Ch I (29 January 2007) paras 101–103.

[28]   *Prosecutor v Gbagbo and Blé Goudé* (Public Redacted Version of Reasons of Judge Geoffrey Henderson) ICC-02/11-01/15-1263-AnxB-Red, T Ch I (16 July 2019) para. 42.

[29]   Ibid para. 44.

[30]   Ibid para. 45.

[31]   *Prosecutor v Lubanga Dyilo* (Decision on the confirmation of charges) ICC-01/04-01/06-803-tEN, PT Ch I (29 January 2007) paras 101–103; *Prosecutor v Bemba Gombo* (Decision on the confirmation of charges) ICC-01/05-01/08-424, PT Ch II (15 June 2009) para. 50.

[32]   *Prosecutor v Bemba Gombo* (Decision on the confirmation of charges) ICC-01/05-01/08-424, PT Ch II (15 June 2009) para. 50 (citing *Prosecutor v Lubanga Dyilo* (Decision on the confirmation of charges) ICC-01/04-01/06-803-tEN, PT Ch I (29 January 2007) para. 106); *Prosecutor v Katanga and Ngudjolo Chui* (Decision on the confirmation of charges) ICC-01/04-01/07-717, PT Ch I (30 September 2008) para. 119.

In *Lubanga Dyilo*, the Pre-Trial Chamber (PT Ch) held that as a general rule, it will only rely on anonymous hearsay evidence (citing the examples of NGO reports and press articles), to *corroborate* other evidence, "mindful of the difficulties that such evidence may present to the Defence in relation to the possibility of ascertaining its truthfulness and authenticity".[33]

In *Bemba Gombo*, the PT Ch found that the use of anonymous witness statements was permitted at the pre-trial stage due to the lower evidentiary threshold (than at trial) but that this evidence must be given low probative value because of the disadvantage caused to the Defense:

> With regard to direct evidence emanating from an anonymous source, the Chamber shares the view, adopted in other pre-trial decisions, that it may cause difficulties to the Defence because it is deprived of the opportunity to challenge its probative value. This also holds true for summaries of witness statements. The Chamber is fully aware that the use of anonymous witness statements and summaries is permitted at the pre-trial stage, particularly because the evidentiary threshold is lower than the threshold applicable at the trial stage. However, to counterbalance the disadvantage that it might cause to the Defence, such evidence is considered as having a rather low probative value. More specifically, the probative value of anonymous witness statements and summaries is lower than the probative value attached to the statements of witnesses whose identity is known to the Defence.[34]

---

33 *Prosecutor v Lubanga Dyilo* (Decision on the confirmation of charges) ICC-01/04-01/06-803-tEN, PT Ch I (29 January 2007) para. 106; *Prosecutor v Katanga and Ngudjolo Chui* (Decision on the confirmation of charges) ICC-01/04-01/07-717, PT Ch I (30 September 2008) paras 159–160 (cited by the Pre-Trial Chamber in *Prosecutor v Banda and Jerbo* (Corrigendum of the "Decision on the Confirmation of Charges") ICC-02/05-03/09-121-Corr-Red, PT Ch I (7 March 2011) para. 41); *Prosecutor v Mbarushimana* (Decision on the confirmation of charges) ICC-01/04-01/10-465-Red, PT Ch I (16 December 2011) para. 49; *Prosecutor v Ruto, Kosgey, and Sang* (Decision on the confirmation of charges) ICC-01/09-01/11-373, PT Ch II (23 January 2012) para. 78; *Prosecutor v Kenyatta and Ali* (Decision on the confirmation of charges) ICC-01/09-02/11-382-Red, PT Ch II (23 January 2012) para. 90. Similarly, the Trial Chamber in *Mladić* at the ICTY held that "the Chamber considers that it is most appropriate to allow the parties to clarify any unclear, vague, or hearsay portions of a statement during the testimony of the witnesses. In the absence of any clarification, the Chamber may attach less weight, if any, to such portions", see *Prosecutor v Mladić*, Trial Chamber II, Transcript of 30 August 2012.

34 *Prosecutor v Bemba Gombo* (Decision on the confirmation of charges) ICC-01/05-01/08-424, PT Ch II (15 June 2009) (citing the *Lubanga Dyilo* and *Katanga* confirmation decisions); *Prosecutor v Katanga and Ngudjolo Chui* (Decision on the confirmation of charges) ICC-01/04-01/07-717, PT Ch I (30 September 2008) paras 159–161, where the PT Ch held

Similarly, in *Lubanga Dyilo,* the PT Ch held, relying on ECtHR jurisprudence, that the use of anonymous statements *as sufficient evidence to found a conviction* can be irreconcilable with Art. 6 ECHR:

> Furthermore, ECHR jurisprudence evinces that the European Convention does not preclude reliance at the investigation stage of criminal proceedings on sources such as anonymous informants. Nevertheless, the ECHR specifies that the subsequent use of anonymous statements as sufficient evidence to found a conviction is a different matter in that it can be irreconcilable with article 6 of the European Convention, particularly if the conviction is based to a decisive extent on anonymous statements.
>
> Accordingly, the Chamber considers that objections pertaining to the use of anonymous hearsay evidence do not go to the admissibility of the evidence, but only to its probative value.[35]

4.2.2 Anonymous Hearsay Evidence at Trial

In assessing the admissibility of a NGO report,[36] the T Ch in *Lubanga Dyilo* rejected the admission of a document both on the basis of its low probative value and of it causing material prejudice to the parties:

> the authors of the report are not to be called, and counsel will be unable, through questioning, to investigate the significant criticisms that have been made of its contents [...] it follows that, if admitted, this document is likely to cause material prejudice to the parties.[37]

---

that "while the Chamber does take note of the Prosecution's reference to rule 63(4) of the Rules which states that the Chamber "shall not impose a legal requirement that corroboration is required in order to prove any crime within the jurisdiction of the court", it is of the view that, this provision notwithstanding, the Chamber may, pursuant to article 69(4) of the Statute, determine that the evidence will have a lower probative value if the Defence does not know the witness's identity and only a summary of the statement, and not the entire statement, may be challenged or assessed".

[35] [emphasis added] *Prosecutor v Lubanga Dyilo* (Decision on the confirmation of charges) ICC-01/04-01/06-803-tEN, PT Ch I (29 January 2007) paras 101–103, citing *Kostovski v the Netherlands* App no 11454/85 (ECtHR, 20 November 1989) para. 44. Cf. also *Prosecutor v Mbarushimana* (Decision on the confirmation of charges) ICC-01/04-01/10-465-Red, PT Ch I (16 December 2011) para. 49.

[36] "Report of the Panel of Experts on the illegal exploitation of natural resources and other forms of wealth of the Democratic Republic of the Congo", S/2001/357, 12 April 2001.

[37] *Prosecutor v Lubanga Dyilo* (Decision on the request by the legal representative of victims a/0001/06, a/0002/06, a/0003/06, a/0049/06, a/0007/08, a/0149/08, a/0155/07, a/0156/07, a/0404/08, a/0405/08, a/0406/08, a/0407/08, a/0409/08, a0149/07 and a/0162/07 for admission of the final report of the Panel of Experts on the illegal exploitation of natural

In *Bemba Gombo*, in the context of an abuse of process motion, the T Ch held that NGO reports had little, if any, evidential weight, given that their provenance and reliability were entirely not investigated and untested.[38] Interestingly, the motion was determined on the standard of balance of probabilities, rather than beyond reasonable doubt; as a logical extension, if NGO reports are found to be unreliable on this lower standard, they would then surely not meet the more rigorous one of beyond reasonable doubt as applied in the course of trial.[39]

In the *Bemba Gombo* Appeal Judgment, Judges Van den Wyngaert and Morrison specifically addressed the issue of anonymous hearsay evidence in their separate opinion. Regarding the Trial Chamber's finding in relation to the existence of a widespread or systematic attack against a civilian population, the Judges indicated that the Trial Chamber cross-referenced a large number of hearsay or anonymous hearsay evidence and that it "failed to properly analyse this evidence and address its potentially extremely low probative value".[40] They found that the Trial Chamber also failed to give even an indication of the approximate number of crimes that were committed at these locations.[41] The judges noted that:

> when the evidence is analysed properly, it is only possible to identify seven witnesses who speak directly about the number of criminal acts. The vast majority of this testimony is based on (anonymous) hearsay. The same applies to the documentary evidence the Trial Chamber relied upon. It is true that the evidence shows that a large number of crimes were reported, but this cannot, in our view, prove beyond reasonable doubt that they actually took place, let alone that the MLC was solely responsible for them.[42]

Further, the Judges also noted the inherent unreliability of hearsay evidence, underlying the distinction between hearsay and *anonymou*s hearsay

---

      resources and other forms of wealth of the Democratic Republic of the Congo as evidence) ICC-01/04-01/06-2135, T Ch I (22 September 2009) paras 33–34.

38   *Prosecutor v Bemba Gombo* (Decision on the Admissibility and Abuse of Process Challenges) ICC-01/05-01/08-802, T Ch III (24 June 2010) paras 235, 254–255.

39   This was argued by the Sang Defence in its Response to the Prosecution's Application for Admission of Documents from the Bar Table Pursuant to Article 64(9), para. 34.

40   *Prosecutor v Bemba Gombo* (Separate Opinion of Judge Van den Wyngaert and Judge Morrison) ICC-01/05-01/08-3636-Anx2, A Ch (8 June 2018) para. 8.

41   *Ibid* para. 68.

42   *Ibid* footnote 5.

evidence, and concluding that in the latter case, reliability could simply not be established:

> One of the central findings of the Conviction Decision is contained in paragraph 563, where the Trial Chamber found that there was "consistent and corroborated evidence that MLC soldiers committed many acts of rape and murder against civilians throughout the 2002–2003 CAR operation. However, closer inspection of the relevant footnote reveals that the evidence in question consists mainly of documentary and testimonial hearsay evidence. As set out above, we have grave concerns about excessive reliance on hearsay evidence, especially if the reliability of the source of the information cannot be established. We also reject the Trial Chamber's apparent conclusion that weak testimonial evidence can somehow be corroborated by weak documentary evidence, especially if one or both are based on (anonymous) hearsay.[43]

Significantly, the Judges found that the Prosecution's argument of the application of a 'holistic' or 'cumulative' approach to the evidence "cannot counteract the absence of clear and convincing evidence" and that it "creates the risk that the Chamber may consider evidence that is not relevant or has no evidentiary weight to speak of and make findings under the "illusion of corroboration":[44]

> There is indeed a difference between claiming that one has 'twenty' coins and that one has 'many' such coins. However, in the end one can only legally prove that one has 'many' coins by defining how much 'many' is and then presenting evidence to prove the existence of each individual coin. It is thus certainly not true that a 'piecemeal' approach would lead the Chamber to exclude potentially relevant evidence. On the contrary, the Prosecutor's proposed 'cumulative' approach creates the risk that the Chamber may consider evidence that is not relevant or has no evidentiary weight to speak of and make findings under the illusion of corroboration. As indicated above, the dangers of the Prosecution's suggested approach are illustrated by the impugned Conviction Decision. We refer to our concerns expressed above about the opacity of the reasoning, the reliance on (anonymous) hearsay evidence and the findings beyond a reasonable doubt based on dubious circumstantial evidence.[45]

---

43   *Ibid* para. 64.
44   *Ibid* para. 67.
45   [emphasis added] *Ibid* para. 67.

4.3 Hearsay Evidence in ICTY Jurisprudence

At the ICTY, with respect to documentary evidence, i.e. reports containing anonymous statements such as HRW or UNOCI reports, the ICTY has indicated that the opportunity to examine the author of a report "does not overcome the absence of the opportunity to cross-examine the person who made them". The T Ch also considers the importance of verifying whether the hearsay is "first hand" – a fact that simply cannot be known when the hearsay is anonymous:

> Where the material summarised consists of statements made by others (other than written statements by prospective factual witnesses for the purposes of legal proceedings), so that the material summarised would be admissible pursuant to Rule 89(C), the summary still consists of hearsay evidence of those statements made by others, and the reliability of the statements made by those other persons (which are themselves hearsay) is relevant to the admissibility of the summary. As stated in the Aleksovski Decision (in a passage upon which the prosecution did not rely), the Trial Chamber must consider whether the summary is "first-hand" hearsay (that is, whether the persons who made the statements summarised personally saw or heard the events recorded in their statements), and whether the absence of the opportunity to cross-examine those persons affects the reliability of their statements. Contrary to the submission of the prosecution, the opportunity to cross-examine the person who summarised those statements does not overcome the absence of the opportunity to cross-examine the persons who made them.[46]

Similarly, the Trial Chamber in *Milutinovic*, with respect to HRW reports, denied the admission of the report on the basis that it was not "in a position to assess the reliability of the factual contentions contained therein".[47] The T Ch added that "neither the report's acknowledgement of these problems, nor the opportunity to cross-examine one of the authors and editors of the report, can adequately replace the opportunity to test the reliability of any of the person's making the statements. The Trial Chamber does not have sufficient material to satisfy it of the general reliability of the information on which this report is

---

46 [emphasis added] *Prosecutor v Milošević* (Decision on Admissibility of Prosecution Investigator's Evidence) IT-02-54-AR73.2, A Ch (30 September 2002) para. 22.
47 *Prosecutor v Milutinović et al.* (Decision on Evidence Tendered through Sandra Mitchell and Frederik Abrahams) IT-05-87-T, T Ch I (1 September 2006) para. 21.

based".[48] In *Krajisnik*, the T Ch indicated that although hearsay evidence is not inadmissible *per se*, "in those cases where a witness did not specify the source of the hearsay, the Chamber has generally not relied on the hearsay".[49]

4.4 Analysis

From the aforementioned jurisprudence, it follows that anonymous hearsay evidence is inherently unreliable (given that it is impossible to establish the trustworthiness of the source(s), or whether it is first-hand). Hearsay *where the source is known* and anonymous hearsay evidence must be distinguished from one another: the latter is inherently unreliable and must be excluded, as both the parties and the Judges have absolutely no way of testing it.

The potential use of anonymous hearsay evidence at the pre-trial and trial stages must equally be distinguished: if at the pre-trial stage anonymous hearsay evidence could be used – *at best* (cf. Judge Henderson's opinion, below) – to corroborate other evidence (e.g. PT Ch *Lubanga Dyilo* approach), the same cannot be affirmed for the trial stage, where the evidentiary threshold is much higher. Within no case to answer (NCTA) proceedings, anonymous hearsay evidence should also be excluded given the evidentiary threshold, or should be given extremely little weight in the Chamber's assessment of the NCTA.

Basing a conviction (or a NCTA) on anonymous hearsay evidence may amount to a breach of Art. 6 ECHR, as highlighted in *Lubanga Dyilo*. Moreover, in NCTA proceedings, it could be argued that relying on this type of evidence may amount to a breach of both Art. 6 ECHR and Art. 67 RS (this aspect will be further developed below).

---

48 [emphasis added] *Ibid* para. 22.
49 *Prosecutor v Krajišnik* (Trial judgment) IT-00-39-T, T Ch I (27 September 2006) para. 1190.

CHAPTER 5

Evidentiary Aspects of Insider Witnesses at the ICC

In almost every proceeding before the ICC, the OTP resorts to the use of so-called 'insider' or 'linkage' witnesses to prove its case. The cases prosecuted by international criminal tribunals are often large systemic crimes that are unlikely to be perpetrated by a single individual, but instead are much more frequently perpetrated by organized groups. Mapping organizational links and identifying the most responsible individuals within such criminal structures is a difficult task for any judicial body; for international criminal courts this can be even more difficult, as they often lack the investigative tools available to domestic law enforcement agencies. This results in often limited availability of documentary or forensic evidence. In order to be able to identify key figures within such organizations, the Office of the Prosecutor (OTP) often resorts to the use of insider witnesses, namely individuals with inside knowledge of the said organizations.[1]

In 2015, the ICTY acknowledged that the evidence obtained from this type of witnesses is often crucial for establishing the degree of responsibility of the accused.[2] Apart from the ICTY, both the ICTR and Special Court for Sierra Leone (SCSL) have relied upon insider witnesses to support their case, especially to prove the existence of command structures within armed groups and the planning of military operations.[3]

Within the Rome Statute, the term 'insider' or 'linkage' witness does not appear. Indeed, this is terminology that has been created in the practice of the various international criminal tribunals. The qualification 'insider' witness pertains to individuals who are willing to testify for the Prosecution (or sometimes for the Defense) and meet the following two requirements:

(i) The witness belonged to the 'inner circle' of the accused or was otherwise in a close relationship with the accused, while being potentially also implicated in the acts with which the accused is charged, and

(ii) The witness is allegedly in the possession of 'valuable information' concerning the acts and conduct of the accused.[4]

---

1 Gabriele Chlevickaite and Barbora Hola, 'Empirical Study of Insider Witnesses' Assessments at the International Criminal Court' (2016) 16 International Criminal Law Review 673, 674.
2 'Witnesses' (United Nations, International Criminal Tribunal for the former Yugoslavia) <https://www.icty.org/sid/158#main-content> accessed 2 August 2023; Ibid 673, 679.
3 Chlevickaite and Hola (n 1) 673, 679–680.
4 Ibid 673, 676.

The use of this type of witnesses by the Prosecution at the ICC or at any other international criminal tribunal can be of assistance to the Prosecution, particularly when it has to prove a political structure or plan within the context of committing crimes against humanity or war crimes. After all, no crime-base witness can fulfil this role while normally only the individuals who were close to advent of such a structure or plan can provide inside information.[5] It was not without reason that the former Chief Prosecutor of the SCSL David Crane, qualified this engagement as "dancing with the devil".[6] One should also bear in mind, as highlighted by the practice of the international criminal tribunals, that insider witnesses may well be criminally responsible themselves for the very acts with which the accused is charged and, thus, may play "the 'Devil' towards the accused to distract the international judiciary from their own acts".

5.1 The Evidentiary Risks and Pitfalls of Insider-Testimony at the ICC

As mentioned above, at the ICC there is no case in which the Prosecution has not resorted to insider testimony.[7] Determining the credibility of insider witnesses and at the same time their trustworthiness – which are two different concepts – remains one of the most vulnerable tasks for judges, given the likelihood of false testimony due to improper motives on the part of the insider witness; this may potentially lead to miscarriages of justice. Incentives to give false testimony may stem from membership in certain ethnic groups, political motivations or personal animosity toward the accused, or even self-promotion, revenge or obtaining asylum or protection.[8]

In addition to the aspects of credibility and trustworthiness, there is the question of the moral justification for the admission of insider witnesses in an international criminal trial, in which the defendant could face a serious sentence. Moreover, one cannot rule out a scenario in which insiders testifying against a defendant before the ICC seek to evade their responsibilities, therefore being willing to give false testimony (e.g., because of political bias or because they have been bribed).[9]

How can an ICC judge, or any other judge, verify that an insider is speaking the truth, without being aware of political manipulations that cannot be found

---

5   *Ibid.*
6   *Ibid* 673, 678 (footnote 22).
7   *Ibid* 673, 698.
8   For further details, cf. *Ibid* 673, 685, 687, 698
9   *Ibid.*

in the case file or in any documents assembled by the Prosecution? This means that assessing an insider's credibility is perhaps more important than simply verifying his trustworthiness.[10] As a result, the determination of the evidentiary value of insiders should first be based on an assessment of their credibility, and only if this test is met, the reliability test should then apply.

Credibility pertains to the capability of belief which has to do with the trustworthiness of an individual as witness. Part of this determination is the personal or political background of the witness and his or her incentive to testify against the accused. The question here is whether the Court can (dis)believe the witness.[11] In contrast to credibility, which relates to subjective elements of the witness, reliability is related to the objectification of the content of the witness statement.

5.2 The Case Law on the Credibility and Reliability of Insider Witnesses

Regarding the determination of reliability, the case law of the International Criminal Tribunals revolves around the 'internal consistency' of the insider's testimony, that is to say, around 'its consistency with other evidence in the case'.[12]

From the empirical study conducted by Chlevickaite and Hola in 2016, two important factors were identified within ICC case law that may constitute the reliability of an insider's testimony:

(i) Consistency and corroboration, meaning not only the internal consistency of the testimony but also whether the testimony is corroborated by other witnesses and/or documents.[13] One recent example is the ICC case against Charles Blé Goudé who stood trial before the ICC for alleged participation in crimes against humanity during the civil war in Cote d'Ivoire in 2011. In the acquittal judgment, the majority of ICC Trial Chamber I, held that:

> It is noted that the Prosecutor alleged that the information from the call centre reports about this incident is 'consistent' with the evidence of the jeunes patriotes being identified as the perpetrators of the 'killings and

---

10   Ibid 673, 699.
11   Ibid 681.
12   Ibid 673, 683.
13   Ibid 673, 689.

burnings at roadblocks'. However, from the documents cited in support, there is no mention of this incident having taken place at a roadblock following an identity check, as alleged by the Prosecutor. There is no other information pointed out by the Prosecutor that could lead one to draw this inference.[14]

Therefore, absence of consistency and contradictions within the testimony or contradictions with other witnesses, undermine the link between the alleged crimes.[15]

(ii) The second reliability factor is the element of the level of 'knowledge and detail', whereby proximity to the events charged seems to increase the reliability of insider testimony.[16] Yet, the fact that an insider witness seems to proclaim to have high level of knowledge or detail, should not exempt the court from making sure that the witness did not obtain these details from other witnesses with whom he or she had contact with before testifying.

Credibility of an insider witness as being another evidentiary element, could and should be subjected to a separate test, in combination with reliability. The aforementioned empirical study[17] indicates that the elements of 'bias and motivation' were of relevance in some of the ICC rulings.[18]

This study concluded that ICC trial chambers predominantly make their assessments on the basis of reliability, whereas the aspect of credibility has been attributed with a less prominent role.[19] Since this analysis of 2016, some ICC decisions have appeared, whereby the credibility of insider witnesses was deemed relevant.[20]

For Defense council at the ICC, during the preparation of the examination of insider witnesses it is important to focus not only on reliability factors, but also on credibility aspects. Although it could be argued that "high reliability can outweigh concerns about credibility",[21] and even if an insider's statement appears to be consistent and corroborated by other evidence, reliability cannot

---

14 *Prosecutor v Gbagbo and Blé Goudé* (Public Redacted Version of Reasons of Judge Geoffrey Henderson) ICC-02/11-01/15-1263-AnxB-Red, T C I (16 July 2019) para. 1620.
15 Chlevickaite and Hola (n 1) 690.
16 Ibid.
17 Ibid.
18 Ibid 692–693.
19 Ibid 695.
20 See for example *Prosecutor v Gbagbo and Blé Goudé* (Public Redacted Version of Reasons of Judge Geoffrey Henderson) ICC-02/11-01/15-1263-AnxB-Red, T Ch I (16 July 2019) paras. 39–45.
21 Chlevickaite and Hola (n 1) 673.

completely replace the issue of credibility. Therefore, insider testimony should be approached with caution, and credibility should be at the fore of witness evaluation. The danger of potential wrongful convictions based on the insider's (malicious) evidence should in any case outweigh the presence of reliability, once the insider is likely to testify on the basis of dubious ulterior motives.

In its June 1, 2023 decision in *Adamčo v Slovakia*, the European Court of Human Rights was faced with a conviction of the appellant for murder based on statements of insider witnesses including the appellant's accomplices. The ECtHR made the following observations, which foreshadow their relevance to ICC proceedings as well:

> As that evidence came from accomplices who had been said to have obtained advantages in return for incriminating the applicant, the Court must enquire into how the applicant's objections in relation to that evidence were addressed at domestic level and whether the domestic authorities subjected the matter to an adequate degree of scrutiny (see *Adamčo v Slovakia*, no. 45084/14, § 59, 12 November 2019), bearing in mind that the required intensity of such scrutiny correlates with the importance of the advantage that the accomplice obtains in return for the evidence he or she gives (see *Erdem v Germany* (dec.), no. 38321/97, 9 December 1999).[22]

The ECtHR held that the national courts did not pay any discernible individual attention to the scope and nature of the advantages obtained by any of these witnesses in return for incriminating the applicant, despite his specific arguments on that point and despite his ability to cross-examine these witnesses, while the advantages were significant.[23] It is critically important that Defense counsel employ this reasoning should such a situation arise.

---

22 *Adamčo v Slovakia* App no 19990/20 (ECtHR, 1 June 2023), para. 62.
23 *Ibid* para. 73.

CHAPTER 6

Rule 68 and Prior Recorded Witness Testimony

6.1 Evolution and Context of ICTY Rules 92bis et seq.

Initially, the most significant rule of evidence at the ICTY was Rule 89(C) which provided that a Chamber may admit any material it deemed to have probative value. This permissive rule was born of an early fear of difficulties in obtaining evidence. Although the ICTY procedural framework was early recognised as *sui generis*, neither purely inquisitorial nor purely adversarial, in the beginning it leaned more towards the common law preference for orality in the form of *viva voce* witness testimony.[1]

As ICTY RPE were adopted by judges and not – as is the case at the ICC – by states, the evolution of Rule 92*bis et seq* followed the development of ICTY case law. A number of early cases established the admissibility of hearsay evidence; thus, a number of more specific rules emerged in the years, with the most important innovations being Rule 92*bis* in 2000 (later amended), Rule 92*ter* and Rule 92*quater* in 2006, and Rule 92*quinquies* in 2009.

In brief, Rule 92*bis allowed* for the admission of limited hearsay evidence in lieu of oral testimony provided that the statement went to proof of a matter other than the acts and conduct of the accused. Later, rule 92*ter* provided that even hearsay evidence in the form of written statements going to the acts and conduct of the accused could be admissible, without cross examination, provided that the witness would be present to confirm the accuracy of the statement under oath and available for cross-examination. Rule 92*quater allowed* for written statements from unavailable witnesses, including the deceased ones, provided that the chamber considered the evidence reliable. The provision did not provide for an opportunity of cross-examination; moreover, whether or not the statement went directly to the guilt of the accused was not a condition for admissibility, but a factor in deciding whether or not to allow such evidence. Adopted following cases where witnesses were intimidated and allegedly killed, and subsequent witnesses were therefore unwilling to testify, Rule 92*quinquies* allowed for the use of statements from witnesses who have been subject to interference. Like before, there was no cross-examination, and the statement may go to the proof of the acts and conduct of the accused.

---

[1] See Rule 90(A) of original ICTY RPE, later repealed.

There has been much practice on Rules 92bis and 92ter, although the latter has been less controversial in practice since the witness would be present and available for cross-examination. Rule 92*quater* has been less frequently used, and Rule 92*quinquies has never been used* (at least publicly).

In addition to the desire to expedite proceedings and to the needs related to the 'Completion Strategy', the ICTY was also faced with overlapping trials which mitigated in favour of introducing evidence from earlier proceedings rather than having the same witnesses appear multiple times over many years in different but related trials.[2]

The sum of these changes is that ICTY trials tended to involve large amounts of documentary evidence. These have, in some cases, expedited trials and avoided witness reappearances; moreover, they have been "important in understanding the sequence and precise nature of the events which took place during that conflict, as well as in promoting the efficient use of the tribunal's time and resources".[3]

The changes, cumulatively, are also a major departure from the earlier rules. The development of Rules 92*bis et seq*, together with other important rules (especially Rule 89(F) which allowed Trial Chambers to *receive the evidence of a witness orally or, where the interests of justice allowed, in written form*) have shifted the focus away from the initial preference for orality – the express reference to it in the RPE was even repealed – and gradually moved to contain more features of inquisitorial systems. In the scientific literature, some commentators generally welcomed these changes. For example, Gaynor noted that the preference for orality developed in jury trials in common law jurisdictions at a time when many jurors were illiterate but all spoke the same language. In such circumstances, which are very far removed from modern international criminal trials, it made sense for evidence to be presented in oral form.[4]

Others have been more concerned. Writing after the introduction of Rule 92*bis*, ICTY Judge Wald called the amendments a *"180 degree turn from earlier emphasis on the 'principle' of live testimony*' and categorised the '*emerging dominance of written testimony*".[5] Judge Wald took this position in 2001, well

---

2   Fergal Gaynor, "Law of Evidence: Admissibility of Documentary Evidence" in Göran Sluiter and others (eds), *International Criminal Procedure: Principles and Rules* (Oxford University Press 2013) 1049.
3   Karim Khan, Caroline Buisman, and Christopher Gosnell (eds), *Principles of Evidence in International Criminal Justice* (Oxford University Press 2010) 449.
4   Gaynor (n 2) 1076.
5   Patricia Wald, 'To "Establish Incredible Events by Credible Evidence": The Use of Affidavit Testimony in Yugoslavia War Crimes Tribunal Proceedings' (2001) 42 Harvard International Law Journal 535, 545 and 548.

before the introduction of 92*ter*, *quater* and *quinquies*, which further enlarged the scope of admissible documentary evidence.

It is interesting to note that commentators who assessed the adoption of 92*bis more favourably*, did so on the basis that it covered only evidence going to the proof of a matter *other* than the acts and conduct of the accused, meaning that "*live testimony remains indispensable to prove the individual guilt of the accused*".[6] Similarly, in 2002 May and Wierda noted that documentary evidence was supplementary to and not a substitute for live evidence, considering it unlikely that an accused would ever be convicted solely on the basis of documentary evidence.[7] In this regard, it is undeniable that in order to accelerate proceedings, there has been a gradual evolution towards much greater reliance on documentary evidence,[8] with inevitable impact on the right of the accused to examine witnesses.

6.2   Other International ad hoc Tribunals

Although not always in exactly the same terms, the evolution on documentary evidence at the ICTY was broadly adopted by other tribunals: the ICTR, the SCSL, and the STL. Reflecting, among other things, the different literacy rates among the concerned populations, the ICTY had a greater focus on documentary evidence than was the case at the ICTR, where a stronger preference for orality was retained: Rules 92*ter* and *quater* were not adopted at the ICTR, therefore it was not possible to have non-cross examined statements.[9]

---

6   Kai Ambos, 'International Criminal Procedure: "Adversarial", "Inquisitorial" or Mixed?' (2003) 3 International Criminal Law Review 1, 28.
7   Richard May and Marieke Wierda, *International Criminal Evidence*, vol 9 (Brill 2021) 210 <https://brill.com/display/title/13900#navigation> accessed 14 June 2023.
8   Alexander Heinze and Goran Sluiter, *International Criminal Law: A Critical Introduction* (Oxford University Press 2008) 388–389, referring to 92bis as 'a significant departure from the initial flexible nature of the ICTY's law of evidence'.
9   When the ad hoc tribunals were established, the literacy rate was over 90% in the countries making up the Former Yugoslavia compared with only around 60% in Rwanda. Thus, in terms of the reliability of a written statement at the ICTR, it was possible that the witness would have to rely on someone else telling them what they were signing. The ICTR Rules retained a provision expressing a preference for orality, although this was deleted from the ICTY Rules (ICTR Rule 90(A)).
    Nevertheless, as noted in Gaynor (n 2) 1046, some cases at the ICTR, as in the case of *Bagosora et al.*, involved large amounts of documentary evidence.

Although both were created after the adoption of the Rome Statute, the SCSL and the STL had versions of the ICTY's Rules 92*bis, ter* and *quater*.[10] Prior to the amendment of ICC Rule 68, no other international criminal tribunal had a rule comparable to ICTY's Rule 92*quinquies*.[11] Having set out the context of the ICTY rules 92*bis et seq*, the next sections will look at each of the rules in turn, focussing on the main features and key jurisprudence.

6.3 Rules 92bis et seq. ICTY RPE

6.3.1 *Rule 92bis*

The first and most frequently used Rule was 92bis, which regulated the case of written statements in lieu of oral testimony, provided that the statement would go to proof of a matter other than the acts and conduct of the accused. It outlined a list of factors to guide the admissibility of such evidence, and set out safeguards.

Rule 92*bis* was titled 'Admission of Written Statements and Transcripts in Lieu of Oral Testimony',[12] and read as follows:

> (A) A Trial Chamber may dispense with the attendance of a witness in person, and instead admit, in whole or in part, the evidence of a witness in the form of a written statement or a transcript of evidence, which was given by a witness in proceedings before the Tribunal, in lieu of oral testimony which goes to proof of a matter other than the acts and conduct of the accused as charged in the indictment.
> (i) Factors in favour of admitting evidence in the form of a written statement or transcript include but are not limited to circumstances in which the evidence in question:
> (a) is of a cumulative nature, in that other witnesses will give or have given oral testimony of similar facts;

---

[10] In relation to the admission of written evidence, the STL RPE for example, are modeled to a large extent on the ICTY RPE; cf. Matthew Gillett and Matthias Schuster, 'The Special Tribunal for Lebanon Swiftly Adopts Its Rules of Procedure and Evidence' (2009) 7 Journal of International Criminal Justice 884, 885–909.

[11] If the lower literacy rates in Rwanda were among the reasons why the Tribunal maintained a greater preference for orality, this raises the question as to why the ICC adopted the ICTY Rules, when a number of ICC situation countries had literacy rates much lower than those in Rwanda.

[12] Adopted 1 December 2000, amended 13 December 2000, amended 13 September 2006.

        (b) relates to relevant historical, political or military background;
        (c) consists of a general or statistical analysis of the ethnic composition of the population in the places to which the indictment relates;
        (d) concerns the impact of crimes upon victims;
        (e) relates to issues of the character of the accused; or
        (f) relates to factors to be taken into account in determining sentence.
    (ii) Factors against admitting evidence in the form of a written statement or transcript include but are not limited to whether:
        (a) there is an overriding public interest in the evidence in question being presented orally;
        (b) a party objecting can demonstrate that its nature and source renders it unreliable, or that its prejudicial effect outweighs its probative value; or
        (c) there are any other factors which make it appropriate for the witness to attend for cross-examination.
(B) If the Trial Chamber decides to dispense with the attendance of a witness, a written statement under this Rule shall be admissible if it attaches a declaration by the person making the written statement that the contents of the statement are true and correct to the best of that person's knowledge and belief and
    (i) the declaration is witnessed by:
        (a) a person authorised to witness such a declaration in accordance with the law and procedure of a State; or
        (b) a Presiding Officer appointed by the Registrar of the Tribunal for that purpose; and
    (ii) the person witnessing the declaration verifies in writing:
        (a) that the person making the statement is the person identified in the said statement;
        (b) that the person making the statement stated that the contents of the written statement are, to the best of that person's knowledge and belief, true and correct;
        (c) that the person making the statement was informed that if the content of the written statement is not true then he or she may be subject to proceedings for giving false testimony; and
        (d) the date and place of the declaration.
The declaration shall be attached to the written statement presented to the Trial Chamber.

(C) The Trial Chamber shall decide, after hearing the parties, whether to require the witness to appear for cross-examination; if it does so decide, the provisions of Rule 92 ter shall apply.

The genesis of 92*bis* is to be found in a number of cases where documentary evidence was admitted, subject to limitations, under the existing Rule 89 framework.

In the case of *Blaskić* in 1998, the Trial Chamber admitted the statement of a deceased witness, without deciding at that point on its probative value. Later in *Kordić, the same statement was admitted by the Trial Chamber, but only for this to be overturned* in 2000 by the Appeals Chamber. Indeed, the latter considered that the statement was so lacking indicia of reliability as to be devoid of probative value, thereby being inadmissible.[13]

This case law was subsequently codified into Rule 92*bis*, setting out the admissibility regime for recorded testimonial evidence, including the limits and safeguards.[14] As noted above, the adoption of Rule 92*bis* was a decisive moment in the shift towards greater reliance on documentary evidence. Rule 92*bis* was *lex specialis* to the general admissibility framework in Rule 89.[15] While it was initially adopted to establish rules for the admissibility of statements taken by a party to the proceedings, "its standards have gradually come to be applied to any post facto eyewitness description of events".[16]

Some limited case law on the application of Rule 92*bis* developed throughout 2001 and early 2002.[17] In two key decisions in 2002, *Galić* and *Milošević*, the ICTY Appeals Chamber looked in detail at the rationale for and conditions of use of the rule.

---

13   *Prosecutor v Kordić & Čerkez* (Decision on Appeal Regarding Statement of a Deceased Witness) IT-95-14/2-AR73.5, A Ch (21 July 2000) paras 19–28 (cf. in particular paras 19, 27, and 28).

14   Cf. generally Karim Khan, Caroline Buisman, and Christopher Gosnell, *Principles of Evidence in International Criminal Justice* (Oxford University Press 2010) 460; Deirdre Montgomery and Eugene O'Sullivan, 'The Erosion of the Right to Confrontation Under the Cloak of Fairness at the ICTY' (2010) 8 Journal of International Criminal Justice 511, 511–538.

15   *Prosecutor v Galić* (Decision on Interlocutory Appeal Concerning Rule 92bis(C)) IT-98-29-AR73.2, A Ch (7 June 2002) para. 31.

16   Khan, Buisman, and Gosnell (n 4) 375.

17   *Prosecutor v Sikirica et al.* (Decision on Prosecution's Application to Admit Transcripts Under Rule 92bis) IT-95-8-T, T Ch III (23 May 2001); *Prosecutor v Naletilić and Martinović* (Decision on the Prosecutor's Request for Public Version of Trial Chamber's "Decision on the Motion to Admit Statement of Deceased Witnesses [...]" of 22 January 2002) IT-98-34-T, T Ch I(A) (27 February 2002).

6.3.1.1   Galić – 'Acts and Conduct of the Accused', Particularly in the Context of Command Responsibility

In this case, at issue was the admissibility into evidence of written statements by two witnesses who had later died. Following an interlocutory appeal, the A Ch allowed the admission into evidence of one of the statements, while rejected the admission of the other. Notably, Rule 92*bis*(C), which related to written statements by persons who by reason of death or otherwise could not give oral evidence, was later amended (as discussed below in relation to Rule 92*quater*). The *Galić* decision is remarkable for its interpretation of what constitute 'acts and conduct of the accused', particularly in the context of a case involving command responsibility.[18]

A statement under Rule 92*bis* may only contain 'proof of a matter other than the acts and conduct of the accused as charged in the indictment'. In *Galić*, the appellant had challenged the admissibility of written statements under 92*bis* on, *inter alia*, the ground that they did go toward proof of his acts and conduct. In relation to the charge of command responsibility, Galić had further argued that insofar as the statements went to proof of the acts and conducts of others, where those others were his subordinates, it would be unfair to him if those statements were admitted in written form, because his own acts and conduct encompassed the acts and conduct of his co-perpetrators and/or subordinates.[19]

However, the A Ch interpreted the requirement of the Rule 92*bis* statement not pertain to the acts and conduct of the accused as not excluding that statements dealing with the 'acts and conduct of others who commit the crimes for which the indictment alleges that the accused is individually responsible'; in this regard, only statements dealing with the 'acts and conduct of the accused as charged in the indictment which establish his responsibility for the acts and conduct of those others' would fall outside the scope of the Rule.[20] The A Ch further specified that 'conduct' may also include the omission of the accused person to act as well as necessarily including the accused's state of mind.[21] This latter statement was relevant in that 'there is often but a short step from a finding that the acts constituting the crimes charged were committed by such subordinates to a finding that the accused knew or had reason to know that those crimes were about to be or had been committed by them'.[22]

---

18   *Prosecutor v Galić* (Decision on Interlocutory Appeal Concerning Rule 92bis(C)) IT-98-29-AR73.2, A Ch (7 June 2002).
19   *Ibid* para. 8.
20   *Ibid* para. 9.
21   *Ibid*.
22   *Ibid* para. 14.

The A Ch found that the fact that the written statement goes to proof of the acts and conduct of a subordinate of the accused, or of some other person for whose acts and conduct the accused is charged with responsibility, is nevertheless relevant to the Trial Chamber's decision under Rule 92bis. The A Ch held that the proximity to the accused of the acts and conduct described in the written statement was relevant to the determination as to whether the maker of the statement should appear for cross-examination and to whether the evidence should be admitted in written form at all: "where the evidence is so pivotal to the prosecution case, and where the person whose acts and conduct the written statement describes is so proximate to the accused, the Trial Chamber may decide that it would not be fair to the accused to permit the evidence to be given in written form".[23]

Referring to the 'special and sensitive situation posed by a charge of command responsibility', the A Ch affirmed that the exercise of the discretion as to whether the evidence should be at all admitted in written form becomes more difficult as it may be that the subordinates of the accused (or alleged subordinates) are so close to the accused that *either* (i) the evidence of their acts and conduct which the Prosecution seeks to prove by a Rule 92bis statement becomes sufficiently pivotal to the Prosecution case that it would not be fair to the accused to permit the evidence to be given in written form, *or* (ii) the absence of the opportunity to cross-examine the maker of the statement would in fairness preclude the use of the statement in any event.[24]

Given the manner in which prior recorded statements are transcribed in the multilingual environment of an international tribunal, the *Galić* Appeals Chamber – as other chambers would later echo – highlighted that such statements were often of dubious reliability: "(...) the decision to encourage the admission of written statements prepared for the purposes of such legal proceedings in lieu of oral evidence from the makers of the statements was nevertheless taken by the Tribunal as an appropriate mixture of the two legal systems, but with realisation that any evidentiary provision specifically relating to that material required considerable emphasis upon the need to ensure its reliability. This is particularly so in relation to written statements given by prospective witnesses to OTP investigators, as questions concerning the reliability of such statements have unfortunately arisen, from knowledge gained in many trials before the Tribunal as to the manner in which those written statements are compiled".[25]

---

23   *Ibid* para. 13.
24   *Ibid* paras 14–15.
25   *Ibid* para. 30.

6.3.1.2   Milošević – Statement Going to 'Acts and Conduct of the Accused' Where Witness Is Present

Rule 92*bis* was relevant also throughout the *Milošević* trial. In a 2002 decision, the T Ch interpreted the phrase 'acts and conduct of the accused' by holding that it was a plain expression which should be given its ordinary meaning, and that if the phrase had been intended to 'cover the acts and conduct of alleged co-perpetrators or subordinates, it would have said so'.[26]

Later, in January 2003, the Prosecution sought the admission of Transcripts of evidence given by 11 witnesses who had previously testified in the *Krnojelac* and *Kunarac* cases. The T Ch admitted the statements – the majority without cross-examination – holding that: "cross-examination should not be permitted mechanically and as a matter of course. Where the rights of the accused are protected, as in this case, by earlier cross-examinations, the balance, as here, should be struck on the side of the victims and witnesses".[27]

However, the most notable decision regarding Rule 92*bis* in the *Milošević* case, which then came to be codified as Rule 92*ter, is from 2003*. Earlier rulings of the Appeals Chamber, in both *Galić* and *Milošević*, had determined that a written witness statement or the summary of a statement signed and later produced by the maker of the statement when testifying, were inadmissible under 92*bis* if containing material going to proof of the acts and conduct of the accused as charged in the indictment. However in 2003, the A Ch found, by majority, that such material was admissible under Rule 89(F). The fact that the evidence may relate to the acts and conduct of the accused did not bar its admission, but became a factor to consider when deciding whether to admit the statement – or the weight to be attached to it.[28] The A Ch argued that when a witness is present and can orally attest to the accuracy of the written statement, this is beyond the scope of Rule 92*bis*, and the evidence entered into the record cannot be considered to be exclusively written within the meaning of Rule 92*bis*.[29]

The *Milošević* trial came at a time when the ICTY was facing pressure to conduct trials more expeditiously, especially in light of the mandated Completion Strategy. Commenting on the usefulness of Rule 92*bis*, the A Ch noted: "the

---

[26] *Prosecutor v Milošević* (Decision on Prosecution Request to Have Written Witness Statements Admitted under Rule 92bis) IT-02-54-T, T Ch III (21 March 2002) para. 22.

[27] *Prosecutor v Milošević* (Decision on prosecution motion for the admission of transcripts in lieu of viva voce testimony pursuant to 92bis(d) – foca transcripts) IT-02-54-T, T Ch III (30 June 2003) para. 48.

[28] *Prosecutor v Milošević* (Decision on Interlocutory Appeal on the Admissibility of Evidence-in-Chief in the Form of Written Statements) IT-02-54-AR73.4, A Ch (30 September 2003).

[29] *Ibid* para. 16.

length of the trials, the amount of evidence, and the complexity of the proceedings in this jurisdiction, ha[ve] made it necessary for Trial Chambers to consider expeditious methods for the presentation of evidence, whilst at all times ensuring that the trial is fair – both to the accused and Prosecution. The proper application of Rule 92*bis* is one such method by which this may be achieved".[30]

In his Dissenting opinion, Judge Hunt considered that utilitarian concerns such as the Completion Strategy were not a sufficient reason for the Appeals Chamber to depart from its earlier practice. His view was that the earlier practice had developed in order to ensure the reliability of evidence and respect the rights of the accused by not admitting written statements that would go to the proof of the acts and conduct of the accused.[31] Despite Judge Hunt's criticism, the Decision[32] was codified in Rule 92*ter*, introduced in 2006, along with an amended version of Rule 92*bis* and the inclusion of Rule 92*quater*.[33]

6.3.1.3 Blagojevic and Jokic – Unnecessarily Cumulative Evidence

In another case from 2003 also involving 92*bis*, a further clarification to the rule was added, regarding the notion of cumulative evidence. Rule 92*bis* stated that the fact that evidence that 'is of a cumulative nature, in that other witnesses will give or have given oral testimony of similar facts' was a factor in favour of its admission. In *Blagojević and Jokić*, the T Ch noted that: "(…) while Rule 92bis permits for the admission of cumulative evidence on matters other than the acts and conduct of the accused through written statements, this Rule should not be interpreted by any of the parties to these proceedings as an invitation to tender *unnecessarily* cumulative or repetitive evidence. The admission of *unnecessarily* cumulative or repetitive evidence may affect the expeditious nature of the proceedings, and therefore will not be admitted".[34]

---

30   *Prosecutor v Milošević* (Decision on prosecution motion for the admission of transcripts in lieu of viva voce testimony pursuant to 92bis(d) – foca transcripts) IT-02-54-T, T Ch III (30 June 2003) para. 25.

31   *Prosecutor v Milošević* (Dissenting Opinion of Judge David Hunt on Admissibility of Evidence-in-Chief in the Form of Written Statement (Majority Decision Given 30 September 2003)) IT-02-54-AR73.4, A Ch (21 October 2003).

32   *Prosecutor v Milošević* (Decision on Interlocutory Appeal on the Admissibility of Evidence-in-Chief in the Form of Written Statements) IT-02-54-AR73.4, A Ch (30 September 2003).

33   For a view in agreement with Judge Hunt's position, cf. O'Sullivan and Montgomery (n 14) 511.

34   *Prosecutor v Blagojević and Jokić* (First Decision on Prosecution's Motion for Admission of Witness Statements and Prior Testimony Pursuant to Rule 92bis) IT-02-60-T, T Ch I(A) (12 June 2003) para. 20 (emphasis in original).

6.3.1.4   Karemera – a Balance between Accused's Rights and Expediency

As noted, the ICTR Rule 92*bis* is very similar to that of the ICTY.[35] In a 2006 decision in *Karemera*, the ICTR A Ch used 92*bis* as an analogy in the context of judicial notice.[36] The Appeals Chamber explained that Rule 94(B) (governing judicial notice) and Rule 92*bis* were procedural mechanisms adopted essentially for the same purpose and that both struck 'a balance between the procedural rights of the Accused and the interest of expediency'.[37] Regarding reliability, the A Ch stated that: "there is reason to be particularly skeptical about facts adjudicated in other cases when they bear specifically on the actions, omissions, or mental state of an individual not on trial in those cases. As a general matter, the defendants in those other cases would have had significantly less incentive to contest those facts than they would facts related to their own actions; indeed, in some cases such defendants might affirmatively choose to allow blame to fall on another".[38]

The Appeals Chamber also recalled the *Galić* finding that 92*bis* excluded written statements going to proof of the acts and conduct of the accused which establish his responsibility for the acts and conduct of others, but not those statements going to proof of the acts and conduct of those others who commit the crimes for which the indictment alleges that the accused is individually responsible. It found by analogy that the same distinction applied to Rule 94(B).[39] In *Popovic*, the ICTY T Ch found that this fashioning of a 'fair limitation in light of the principles balanced in Rule 92*bis*' was instructive.[40]

6.3.2   *Rule 92ter*

On 13 September 2006, Rule 92*ter* was adopted. It was titled 'Other Admission of Written Statements and Transcripts', and held:

---

35   Note that the ICTR Rule 92*bis*(C) is based on the ICTY version of this rule that allows statements from deceased witnesses. As discussed below, at the ICTY, Rule 92*bis*(C) was later replaced by 92*quater*. In Karemera, this rule was used to admit three statements from deceased witnesses.
36   *Prosecutor v Karemera et al.* (Decision on Prosecutor's Interlocutory Appeal of Decision on Judicial Notice) ICTR-98-44-AR73(C), A Ch (16 June 2006).
37   *Ibid* para. 51.
38   *Ibid*.
39   *Ibid* para. 52.
40   *Prosecutor v Popović et al.* (Decision on the Admissibility of the Borovcanin Interview and the Amendment of the Rule 65 ter Exhibit List) IT-05-88-T, T CH II (25 October 2007) para. 71.

(A) A Trial Chamber may admit, in whole or in part, the evidence of a witness in the form of a written statement or transcript of evidence given by a witness in proceedings before the Tribunal, under the following conditions:
(i) the witness is present in court;
(ii) the witness is available for cross-examination and any questioning by the Judges; and
(iii) the witness attests that the written statement or transcript accurately reflects that witness' declaration and what the witness would say if examined.
(B) Evidence admitted under paragraph (A) may include evidence that goes to proof of the acts and conduct of the accused as charged in the indictment.

Rule 92ter specifically allowed for the introduction of statements into evidence – even when the evidence went to proof of the acts and conduct of the accused – as long as the witness would be present to confirm the accuracy of the statement and the latter reflected what the witness would say if examined, and would be available for cross-examination (though this need not necessarily take place). From a Defense perspective, the requirement that the witness be available for examination made Rule 92*ter* less problematic compared with the two rules which followed. While 92*ter* was used extensively at the ICTY, the only request to use it before the SCSL was rejected.[41]

While Rule 92*bis* required the witness to affirm the truth and content of his statement before a judicial body or the Registrar,[42] this was no longer the case with regard to Rule 92*ter*, as the ICC Prosecution later noted in an application in *Lubanga Dyilo*: "it is noted that Rule 92*ter* of the ICTY Rules of Procedure and Evidence specifically allows for the introduction of statements into evidence without examination-in-chief as long as the witness is present to confirm the accuracy of the statement under oath. This Rule was amended in

---

41 *Prosecutor v Taylor* (Decision on Prosecution Motion for Admission of Part of the Prior Evidence of TF1-362 and TF1-371 Pursuant to Rule 92*ter*) SCSL-03-01-T399, T Ch II (25 January 2008).

42 According to Rule 92bis, "(B) If the Trial Chamber decides to dispense with the attendance of a witness, a written statement under this Rule shall be admissible if it attaches a declaration by the person making the written statement that the contents of the statement are true and correct to the best of that person's knowledge and belief and (i) the declaration is witnessed by: (a) a person authorised to witness such a declaration in accordance with the law and procedure of a State; or (b) a Presiding Officer appointed by the Registrar of the Tribunal for that purpose".

light of the Appeals Decision in Milosevic, where such practice was rendered permissible".[43]

Critically, this Rule negated the necessity of the witness to affirm the truth and content of his statement before a judicial body or the Registrar, as prescribed by Rule 92*bis*, precisely because the statement or prior testimony was not being presented in lieu of oral testimony; because the witness would be available for cross-examination and questions from the Bench, such a requirement was redundant as the veracity of the statement would be confirmed under oath by the witness. This procedure has been used with all categories of witnesses, to wit: vulnerable witnesses, crime base, insiders, and UN personnel.[44]

6.3.2.1   Prlić – 92ter Not a New Avenue for the Admission of Documents through Written Statements Rather Than through a Witness

In the Prlić case, the T Ch stated that the 'main objective of Rule 92ter was to ensure an effective and expeditious trial while respecting the rights of the accused,'[45] and affirmed that the rationale of the Rule RELATED TO the need to limit the Prosecution's examination of a witness about issues mentioned in summaries compiled in accordance with Rule 65ter.

The Chamber acknowledged that after encouraging the Prosecution to apply Article 92ter in the presentation of its evidence, the Prosecution was now doing so; in particular, in accordance with a common practice that once a witness has confirmed that a written statement accurately reflects his or her statement and what he or she would say if examined, the Prosecution may ask the witness questions in order to clarify the points referred to in the written statement. In addition, the Chamber stated that the Prosecution may question a witness on points not mentioned in the written statement, but which were raised during the proofing, provided that certain requirements would be met.

The Chamber stated that it had, however, noticed a "new practice by the Prosecution to introduce documents by means of a witness written statement without these documents being discussed in court". Hence, the Chamber recalled that "a party wishing to tender a document into evidence should do it, as a rule, through a witness which can testify to its authenticity, relevance and

---

43   *Prosecutor v Milošević* (Decision on Interlocutory Appeal on the Admissibility of Evidence-in-Chief in the Form of Written Statements) IT-02-54-AR73.4, A Ch (30 September 2003).

44   *Prosecutor v Lubanga Dyilo* (Prosecution's Application for a Preliminary Ruling on the Admission of Prior Recorded Statements) ICC-01/04-01/06-1262, Prosecution (5 April 2008) footnote 7.

45   *Prosecutor v Prlić et al.* (Decision on the application of Rule 92ter of the Rules) IT-04-74-T, T Ch III (25 June 2007).

probative value, and that this document should be presented to the witness in court";[46] moreover, it recalled that there could be no question of opening a new avenue for the admission of documents through written statements submitted pursuant to Rule 92ter.[47]

Judge Antonetti submitted a separate opinion, agreeing with – but going further – the Decision. Judge Antonetti advocated for 92ter to be used only in specific cases and under the supervision of the Chamber. He recalled that 92ter had been adopted, on his initiative, by the Judges in order to speed up proceedings, but that its subsequent use had not been in this spirit. He contended that it had been used by the Prosecution in a manner that not only could lengthen proceedings, but also impinge on the rights of the Defense: "the Chamber authorised the Prosecution to put to a witness any relevant question concerning written statements. Nevertheless, this practice has shown its limitations. Instead of a few clarifying questions or some new questions being put to a 92ter witness, these became very lengthy testimonies. Thus, the objective of Article 92ter, which is to save time, may be reversed if a party is allowed to present the maximum number of written exhibits while still asking a number of oral questions. As a result, the opposing party, in this case the Defence, must prepare not only for the written statements, but also – and very quickly – for new oral questions, in addition to cross-examining the witness on numerous documents presented at the hearing".[48]

A part from this cautious approach on the part of the Chamber, the ICTY's report to the UN General Assembly the same year took a positive view on the efficiency gains realised through 92ter: "the addition of rule 92ter, which authorizes a Trial Chamber to consider written statements and transcripts of witnesses in lieu of oral testimony that go to proof of the acts and conduct of the accused, resulted in substantial savings of court time in both the Milutinovic et al. and Popovic et al. multi-accused trials. Additionally, in the multi-accused Prlic et al. trial, the Trial Chamber revised and reduced the time allocated to the parties for their cases".[49]

---

46 Unless the Prosecution decides to present the document through a written request in conformity to guideline 6 as cited in the Chamber's Decision of 29 November 2006.

47 *Prosecutor v Prlić et al.* (Decision on the application of Rule 92ter of the Rules) IT-04-74-T, T Ch III (25 June 2007).

48 *Prosecutor v Prlić et al.* (Separate Opinion of Presiding Judge Jean-Claude Antonetti Regarding the Decision on the Application of Article 92ter of the Rules) IT-04-74-T, T Ch III (25 June 2007).

49 'Report of the International Tribunal for the Prosecution of Persons Responsible for Serious Violations of International Humanitarian Law Committed in the Territory of the Former Yugoslavia since 1991', A/62/172-S/2007/469 (1 August 2007).

6.3.3 Rule 92quater

Rule 92quater, which was adopted on 13 September 2006 as well, allowed statements from unavailable persons, including those who are deceased, as reflected in the text of the Rule:

> (A) The evidence of a person in the form of a written statement or transcript who has subsequently died, or who can no longer with reasonable diligence be traced, or who is by reason of bodily or mental condition unable to testify orally may be admitted, whether or not the written statement is in the form prescribed by Rule 92bis, if the Trial Chamber:
> (i) is satisfied of the person's unavailability as set out above; and
> (ii) finds from the circumstances in which the statement was made and recorded that it is reliable.
> (B) If the evidence goes to proof of acts and conduct of an accused as charged in the indictment, this may be a factor against the admission of such evidence, or that part of it.

Under this Rule, whether a written statement or transcript went directly to proof of the guilt of an accused was no longer a condition, but a factor in deciding whether or not to allow such evidence – even though there would be no possibility of cross-examination. The key conditions were that the maker of the statement be truly unavailable and that the evidence be considered to be reliable.

6.3.3.1 Naletilić and Martinović

Rule 92*quater* was adopted following a decision in *Naletilić and Martinović*.[50] In this case, the Prosecutor sought to have admitted two statements from deceased witnesses. The T Ch found that a combined reading of Rule 92*bis*(C) and Rule 92*bis*(A) meant that statements from deceased witnesses could only be admissible when they did not go to the acts and conduct of the accused. Therefore, the Chamber rejected the motion, affirming that it would "not admit the written evidence of these witnesses in lieu of oral testimony since it would be prejudicial to the rights of the Accused to cross-examine his accuser and, consequently, his right of a fair trial".

---

50   Codifying Prosecutor v Naletilić and Martinović, IT-98-34-A.
    Cf. Mark Klamberg, *Evidence in International Criminal Trials: Confronting Legal Gaps and the Reconstruction of Disputed Events*, vol 2 (Brill 2013) 391, noting that the SCSL has the same rule as 92quater and relied on it in the case of Charles Taylor in 2002.

The Chamber further noted that it shared concerns with regard to the general reliability of witness statements taken by investigators of the Prosecution, "namely the fact that such statements are not given under oath, that they never have been subject to cross-examination, that they are given by a witness not contemporaneously with the events in question but only some years afterwards; finally, and in a particular way, that the taking of these statements regularly involves the process of multiple translations whose reliability as such appears to be questionable".[51]

Following this case, Rule 92*bis*(C) was abolished and Rule 92*quater* adopted to codify *Naletilić and Martinović*; however, evidence going directly to the guilt of an accused would not be inadmissible as such, but would be considered as a factor against its admission. Three notable cases where the conditions of Rule 92*quater* were expounded are *Vojislav Šešelj*,[52] *Popović et al.*[53] and *Tolimir*.[54]

6.3.3.2 Vojislav Šešelj – Retroactive Application

In *Šešelj*, in addition to the evidence of 61 witnesses under 92*ter*, the Prosecution sought to have admitted the evidence of three deceased witnesses under 92*quater*. The accused had been charged by indictment issued in February 2003; that is, some three and half years prior to the adoption of Rules 92*ter* and *quater*. He objected to the "(…) retroactive application of Rules 92ter and 92quater of the Rules which would be prejudicial and would contravene Rule 6 (D) of the Rules and Article 51(4) of the Statute of the International Criminal Court codifying customary international law on this matter, this principle of security in judicial matters and the existing principle of presenting evidence orally that exists in adversarial proceedings".[55]

The Prosecution argued that the new Rules were simply the codification of the practice of the ICTY relating to Rule 92*bis* and Rule 89; thus, there was no prejudice in this case to the accused.[56] The Trial Chamber recalled how Rule 6(D) of the ICTY Rules provided that any amendments shall enter into

---

51   *Prosecutor v Naletilić and Martinović* (Decision on the Prosecutor's Request for Public Version of Trial Chamber's "Decision on the Motion to Admit Statement of Deceased Witnesses […]" of 22 January 2002) IT-98-34-T, T Ch I(A) (27 February 2002).
52   *Prosecutor v Šešelj*, IT-03-67.
53   *Prosecutor v Popović et al.*, IT-05-88.
54   *Prosecutor v Tolimir*, IT-05-88/2.
55   *Prosecutor v Šešelj* (Redacted version of the "Decision on the prosecution's consolidated motion pursuant to Rules 89 (F), 92 bis, 92 ter and 92 quater of the Rules of Procedure and Evidence" filed confidentially on 7 January 2008) IT-03-67-T, T Ch III (21 February 2008) para. 19 (internal citations omitted).
56   *Ibid* para. 21 (internal citations omitted).

force seven days after being officially issued, *"but shall not operate to prejudice the rights of the accused [...] in any pending case"*. The Chamber explained that unless it is proven that the right of the accused are prejudiced, there is no bar to retroactive application of the rules. In the case at hand, although the indictment was issued in 2003, the trial did not begin until December 2007 – namely, more than a year after the adoption of the new rules. Thus, the accused was on notice for at least a year before the commencement of his trial that the new rules may be applied.

While the Prosecution had initially filed to have evidence admitted under Rules 92*bis*, 92*quater* and 89, it later sought to retain its applications with regard to 92*quater* and to replace its applications made under 92*bis* and 89 with requests to admit the same evidence under Rule 92*ter* instead. Thus at least with regard to the 92*ter* applications, the accused in fact only had notice of these two weeks before the Pre-Trial Conference.[57] Nonetheless, the Chamber held that retroactive application was permissible. According to the Chamber, the accused was also allowed to request the application of rules 92*ter* and *quater* at any time; hence, the application of those rules in the present instance did not prejudice the rights of the Accused, 'since he may invoke the same rights as the Prosecutor and has not shown the existence of any prejudice'.[58] The issue of retroactivity will be further explored in relation to Rule 68 at the ICC.

6.3.3.3   Popović et al. – Meaning of 'Unavailable'

Another notable instance involving Rule 92*quater* was the case of *Popović et al*.[59] In a 2007 decision, the Trial Chamber discussed at length the relationship between Rules 92 *bis et seq*, and the meaning of 'unable to testify' in 92*quater*. The Chamber made it clear that this meant unavailability for *'reasons beyond control', 'uncontrollable circumstances'*.[60]

At a later point, the Prosecution sought to have admitted the prior testimony of a deceased witness.[61] Its testimony, which had been given during the case of *Blagojević and Jokić*, related to, among other things, an alleged conversation with the defendant in the course of which the latter would have suggested to

---

57 *Ibid* para. 35.
58 *Ibid* para. 37.
59 *Prosecutor v Popović et al.*, IT-05-88.
60 *Prosecutor v Popović et al.* (Decision on the Admissibility of the Borovcanin Interview and the Amendment of the Rule 65 ter Exhibit List) IT-05-88-T, T CH II (25 October 2007) para. 74.
61 *Prosecutor v Popović et al.* (Decision on Prosecution Motion for Admission of Evidence Pursuant to Rule 92 quarter) IT-05-88-T, T Ch II (21 April 2008).

put the bodies of killed Bosnian Muslims into a bauxite mine.[62] The Accused claimed that the testimony was unreliable.

The Trial Chamber accepted that it 'contained inconsistencies, admissions of prior false statements, and uncorroborated claims'.[63] Furthermore, it acknowledged that the evidence of the meeting and conversation were uncorroborated.[64] Nonetheless, the T Ch said that it had proceeded with caution in considering these factors and the multiple cross-examinations in *Blagojevic and Jokic*, thereby finding that the evidence bore 'sufficient indicia of reliability for admission pursuant to Rule 92quater'.[65]

However, it should be noted that in the case of *Krstić*, the Appeals Chamber held that 'the discrepancies in the evidence given ... and the ambiguities surrounding some of the statements, [...] caution the Appeals Chamber against relying on his evidence alone'.[66]

Eventually, after being admitted under rule 92*quater*, this written evidence – going to proof of the acts and conduct of the accused, uncorroborated and from a deceased witness, so without cross-examination – was relied on in the judgment in the *Popović and others*.[67] This clearly shows that although less frequently used than Rules 92*bis* and *ter*, rule 92*quater has equally played an important role*.

As Nerenberg and Timmermann noted: "if there may have been some merit to Judge Hunt's concerns [...] about the erosion of the accused's rights with the expanded use of Rule 89(F) to admit statements going to the acts and conduct of the accused, contrary to the express provisions of Rule 92*bis*, then perhaps there is further cause for concern with Rules 92*quater* and 92*quinquies*'s authorisation of the admission of such statements with not even a remote possibility of cross"-examination.[68]

6.3.3.4 Tolimir – Meaning of 'Unavailable'

Another case where the use of Rule 92*quater* arose is *Tolimir*.[69] In this instance, the Prosecution sought to have admitted the testimony that had been provided

---

62 *Ibid* para. 58; *Prosecutor v Popović et al.* (Trial judgment) IT-05-88-T, T Ch II (10 June 2010) para. 1268 and footnote 4157.
63 *Prosecutor v Popović et al.* (Decision on Prosecution Motion for Admission of Evidence Pursuant to Rule 92 quarter) IT-05-88-T, T Ch II (21 April 2008) para. 61.
64 *Ibid* para. 62.
65 *Ibid* paras 63–64.
66 *Prosecutor v Krstić* (Appeal judgment) IT-98-33-A, A Ch (19 April 2004) para. 94, cited in *Prosecutor v Popović et al.* (Trial judgment) IT-05-88-T, T Ch II (10 June 2010) para. 1214.
67 *Ibid* para. 1268 and footnote 4157.
68 Khan, Buisman, and Gosnell (n 4) 474.
69 *Prosecutor v Tolimir*, IT-05-88/2.

in *Popović* and/or *Krstic* by three witnesses initially subject to Rule 92*ter*. Then, the Prosecution sought to convert the same three witnesses to Rule 92*bis* and have the testimony admitted in lieu of *viva voce* testimony. This motion was on the basis that two of the three witnesses were 'unavailable' for reasons of psychological health, whereas the remaining witness was 'unwilling' due to fears that his family would be harmed as a consequence of his testimony; therefore, these circumstances had prevented the Prosecution from prevailing upon the witnesses to testify.[70]

Agreeing with the Defense that the situation better fitted Rule 92*quater*, the T Ch proceeded to assess the merits of the admission on that basis, affirming that 'otherwise, the stringent requirements in Rule 92quater would be circumvented'.[71]

The Chamber recalled that 92*quater* had two cumulative requirements, namely that the witness must be unavailable for 'reasons beyond control'[72] and the evidence must be reliable. The evidence was considered to be reliable in that it had already been provisionally admitted under Rule 92*ter* before the witnesses were considered by the Prosecution to be unavailable. However, the Chamber was not satisfied that the Prosecution had shown the witnesses were truly unavailable and thus the motion for admission of their evidence, submitted under 92*bis* but decided under 92*quater*, was rejected.

6.3.4 Rule 92quinquies

Rule 92quinquies was adopted in 2009, after alleged and actual difficulties in securing witness testimonies in cases like *Popović, Haradinaj, Limaj* and *Šešelj*. The Rule was titled 'Admission of Statements and Transcripts of Persons Subjected to Interference',[73] and contained the following:

> (A) A Trial Chamber may admit the evidence of a person in the form of a written statement or a transcript of evidence given by the person in proceedings before the Tribunal, where the Trial Chamber is satisfied that:
> (i) the person has failed to attend as a witness or, having attended, has not given evidence at all or in a material respect;

---

70 *Prosecutor v Tolimir* (Partial Decision on Prosecution's Rule 92bis and Rule 92ter Motion for Five Witnesses) IT-05-88/2-T, T Ch II (27 August 2010).
71 *Ibid* para. 32.
72 *Prosecutor v Popović et al.* (Decision on the Admissibility of the Borovcanin Interview and the Amendment of the Rule 65 ter Exhibit List) IT-05-88-T, T CH II (25 October 2007) para. 74.
73 Adopted 10 December 2009.

(ii) the failure of the person to attend or to give evidence has been materially influenced by improper interference, including threats, intimidation, injury, bribery, or coercion;
(iii) where appropriate, reasonable efforts have been made pursuant to Rules 54 and 75 to secure the attendance of the person as a witness or, if in attendance, to secure from the witness all material facts known to the witness; and
(iv) the interests of justice are best served by doing so.
(B) For the purposes of paragraph (A):
(i) An improper interference may relate inter alia to the physical, economic, property, or other interests of the person or of another person;
(ii) the interests of justice include:
(a) the reliability of the statement or transcript, having regard to the circumstances in which it was made and recorded;
(b) the apparent role of a party or someone acting on behalf of a party to the proceedings in the improper interference; and
(c) whether the statement or transcript goes to proof of the acts and conduct of the accused as charged in the indictment.
(iii) Evidence admitted under paragraph (A) may include evidence that goes to proof of the acts and conduct of the accused as charged in the indictment.
(C) The Trial Chamber may have regard to any relevant evidence, including written evidence, for the purpose of applying this Rule.

It allowed the admission of the prior recorded testimony of a witness who, due to interference, either did not testify as a witness, or if present, did not give evidence 'at all or in a material respect'. Under this sub-rule, the chamber need not necessarily find the evidence reliable, but may admit it in the 'interests of justice'. Reasonable efforts must have been made to secure the attendance of the witness or, if they are present in Court but have failed to testify, to secure their testimony.

The scope of Rule 92*quinquies* was even broader than that of Rule 92*quater*: in applying 92*quinquies*, the chamber may take into account any relevant evidence, including written evidence.[74] Rule 92*quinquies* mirrored changes in the

---

74 Rule 92 quinquies (C) ICTY RPE.

law of evidence in several common law jurisdictions, particularly regarding the admission of prior witness statements in situations where witnesses subject to interference later recant the testimony.[75] However, Rule 92*quinquies* has never publicly been used at the ICTY.[76] Nevertheless, it has been referred in submissions at the ICC since the adoption of ICC Rule 68(2)(d) so as to duplicate 92*quinquies* – as will be discussed below.

6.3.4.1 (i) Haradinaj

One case where Rule 92*quinquies* might have been expected to be used was the *Haradinaj* re-trial. The trial judgment had noted the problems of witnesses unwilling to testify due to fear:

> throughout the trial, the Trial Chamber encountered significant difficulties in securing the testimony of a large number of witnesses. Many witnesses cited fear as a prominent reason for not wishing to appear before the Trial Chamber to give evidence. The Trial Chamber gained a strong impression that the trial was being held in an atmosphere where witnesses felt unsafe.[77]

In the case at hand, two key witnesses for the Prosecution refused to testify; therefore, the accused were acquitted on almost all the counts that the testimonies could have helped to establish.[78] Mr. Kabashi, for example, refused to testify on multiple occasions, stating that although some witness had been killed, he did not want 'protective measures because such measures do not exist in reality; they only exist within the boundaries of this courtroom, not

---

75   Australia, Ireland, Canada and the United States. Jurisdictions have endorsed different solutions; for example, the 6th Amendment to the US Constitution provides for a right to confront witnesses which does not exist in most common law jurisdictions (where it is generally referred to as right to examine witnesses).
    Cf. Gaynor (n 2) 1072–1073. Cf. also the discussion on domestic jurisdictions in the ECtHR case of *Al-Khawaja and Tahery*.
76   The public record shows, for example, that at least one Prosecution 92*quinquies* motion was filed in the *Karadžić* case. However, neither the motion, nor its response, nor the reply, nor the decision, appear to be public. In this regard, cf. <http://www.icty.org/x/cases/karadzic/trans/en/120502IT.htm> accessed 13 July 2023, 28322–23.
77   *Prosecutor v Haradinaj et al.* (Trial judgment) IT-04-84-T, T Ch I (3 April 2008) para. 6 (internal citations omitted).
78   *Ibid* paras 502–504; *Prosecutor v Haradinaj et al.* (Appeal judgment) IT-04-84-A, A Ch (19 July 2010) para. 38.

outside it'.[79] In 2011, Mr. Kabashi was convicted of interfering with the Tribunal's administration of justice.[80]

While the trial took place prior to the adoption of 92*quinquies*, the (partial) re-trial was ordered in July 2010 – some seven months after the adoption of 92*quinquies*. The Prosecution claimed a breach of its own fair trial rights and, by majority, the Appeals Chamber found that *'particularly in the context of the serious witness intimidation that formed the context of the Trial, it is clear that the Trial Chamber seriously erred in failing to take adequate measures to secure the testimony of Kabashi and the other witness'*. The Appeals Chamber emphasised that Mr. Kabashi, as well as the other protected witness who had refused to testify in the original trial, should be called to testify in the retrial.[81]

The re-trial took place over 2011–12. Mr. Kabashi was recalled, and again refused to answer questions. From the transcripts, there are indications that 'something' else – possibly Rule 92*quinquies*, was under consideration. This partial RE-trial was ordered on the grounds, *inter alia*, that not enough had been done to secure the testimony of intimidated witnesses. Given that it took place after the adoption of Rule 92*quinquies*, it may be expected that the new rule would have been applied in relation to the testimony of Mr. Kabashi.

However, although the Prosecution successfully sought to admit under *92bis* the transcript of the evidence given by Mr. Kabashi in the *Limaj* case,[82] there appears to be nothing on the public record to suggest that 92quinquies was also used. This opens up three different scenarios: (i) that such use is simply not on the public record; (ii) that the Prosecution did not seek to use it, perhaps because the introduction of the *Limaj* transcript under *92bis* was deemed to be sufficient; or (iii) because the Chamber considered it inappropriate to use the new rule, considering that it was adopted only after the initial trial. In light of the timing, the first two options would seem the most likely; the fact remains that the absence of a public record is an unfortunate circumstance for future jurisprudence in relation to the similar Rule 68(2)(c) ICC RPE.

---

79 *Prosecutor v Haradinaj et al.*, Transcript IT-04-S4-T, T Ch I (5 June 2007) <http://icty.org/x/cases/haradinaj/trans/en/070605ED.htm> accessed 13 July 2023; *Prosecutor v Haradinaj et al.*, Transcript IT-04-S4-T, T Ch I (20 November 2007) <http://www.icty.org/x/cases/haradinaj/trans/en/071120ED.htm> accessed 13 July 2023.
80 *Prosecutor v Kabashi* (Sentencing judgment) IT-04-84-R77.1, T Ch I (16 September 2011).
81 *Prosecutor v Haradinaj et al.* (Appeal judgment) IT-04-84-A, A Ch (19 July 2010) para. 49.
82 *Prosecutor v Haradinaj et al.*, Transcript IT-04-84bis-T, T Ch II (24 August 2011) <http://icty.org/x/cases/haradinaj/trans/en/110824ED.htm> accessed 13 July 2023; *Prosecutor v Haradinaj et al.* (Trial judgment with confidential annex) IT-04-84bis-T, T Ch II (29 November 2012).

Having addressed the development and practice of Rules 92 *bis et seq.* at the ICTY, the next section will turn to Rule 68 of the ICC Rules of Procedure and Evidence.

6.4 ICC

6.4.1 *Rule 68*
6.4.1.1   Relationship with Other Relevant Articles of the Rome Statute
As with ICTY Rules *92bis et seq.*, Rule 68 ICC RPE on prior recorded testimony does not exist in a vacuum. Article 67 RS sets out the rights of the accused person,[83] while Article 68 RS outlines witness and victim protection, and Article 69(2) RS enshrines the principle of orality prescribing that witness testimony at the ICC shall be given in person '*except to the extent provided by the measures set forth in Article 68 or in the Rules of Procedure and Evidence*'.[84]

Depending on the circumstances, Rule 68 may overlap with other provisions of the ICC normative framework; in cases where Rule 68 is inapplicable, other provisions may allow for the admission of, for example, written statements.[85]

---

[83] The right to examine witnesses is set out in Article 67(e)RS as the right "To examine, or have examined, the witnesses against him or her and to obtain the attendance and examination of witnesses on his or her behalf under the same conditions as witnesses against him or her. The accused shall also be entitled to raise defences and to present other evidence admissible under this Statute".

[84] Article 69(2) RS.

[85] Article 68(2) RS provides for an exception to public hearings in order to protect victims and witnesses or an accused, in that the Court may conduct any part of the proceedings in camera or allow the presentation of evidence by electronic or other special means. In *Prosecutor v Lubanga Dyilo* (Decision on the prosecution's application for the admission of the prior recorded statements of two witnesses) ICC-01/04-01/06-1603, T Ch I (15 January 2009) para. 20, the T Ch stated that "... *in the right circumstances, Article 68(2) of the Statute and Rule 68(b) of the Rules create separate routes whereby prior recorded testimony can replace, in full or in part, live testimony. However, these provisions, although potentially overlapping, are clearly different in scope, since the focus of Article 68(2) is specifically directed at protecting victims and witnesses whilst Rule 68 is a general provision for the introduction of prior recorded testimony, subject to specific safeguards*". In a Status conference in *Prosecutor v Bemba Gombo* on 17 March 2014, Judge Steiner noted: "... *as is also stressed by the jurisprudence of Trial Chamber I, Rule 68 of the Rules is not the only provision of the Court's legal framework under which the admissibility of written statements may be assessed. When Rule 68 of the Rules is not applicable, the Chamber is not precluded from considering that written statements may be admissible under other provisions. In particular, Articles 69(4) and 64(9) of the Statute and Rule 63(2) of the Rules give the Chamber the authority and discretion to freely assess all evidence submitted – including written statements – and rule on their relevance and admissibility, taking into account, inter alia,*

6.4.1.2 Original Rule 68: Evolution and Assessment

It is somewhat of a banality to say that The ICC has looked at the practice before ad hoc international tribunals and sometimes drawn inspiration from them. However in this instance, the ICC RPE were promulgated through a preparatory committee in mid-2000, that is, before the adoption of Rule 92*bis* ICTY RPE in December of that year.[86] ICC RPE eventually entered into force on 9 September 2002 – prior to the adoption of ICTY Rules 92*ter, quarter* and *quinquies*.

In its original formulation, Rule 68 was concise, and its requirements were considerably stricter than the provisions of the ICTY's Rule 92*bis et seq.* as evidenced by the text:

> When the Pre-Trial Chamber has not taken measures under article 56, the Trial Chamber may, in accordance with article 69, paragraph 2, allow the introduction of previously recorded audio or video testimony of a witness, or the transcript or other documented evidence of such testimony, provided that:
> (a) If the witness who gave the previously recorded testimony is not present before the Trial Chamber, both the Prosecutor and the defence had the opportunity to examine the witness during the recording; or
> (b) If the witness who gave the previously recorded testimony is present before the Trial Chamber, he or she does not object to the submission of the previously recorded testimony and the Prosecutor, the defence and the Chamber have the opportunity to examine the witness during the proceedings.

Notably, prior recorded testimony was allowed provided that there would be an opportunity to confront the witness: original Rule 68(A) required that in the event that a witness were not present in Court, the parties would have the opportunity to examine the witness during the recording of the testimony; Alternatively in case the witness were present, sub-rule B provided that such witness would be available for examination by the parties, having consented to the introduction of the evidence.[87]

---

any prejudice that the admission of such evidence may cause to a fair trial or to a fair evaluation of the testimony of a witness".

86   Khan, Buisman, and Gosnell (n 4) 380.
87   *Prosecutor v Lubanga Dyilo* (Decision on the prosecution's application for the admission of the prior recorded statements of two witnesses) ICC-01/04-01/06-1603, T Ch I (15 January 2009) para. 19.

One commentator, writing prior to the amendment of Rule 68, referred to the original ICC evidence regime as to a 'a welcome return to the principle that witnesses should testify in person, in court'.[88] In contrast, another scholar assessed that the practice of the ICC had moved in favour of witness evidence-in-chief being provided in writing and that the ICC, even before amending rule 68, 'has shown a tendency to follow the same path' and that 'elements of the experience gained at the ICTY, ICTR and SCSL are beginning to appear in the ICC's practice'.[89]

However, this tendency should not be overstated. Regarding less controversial admissions of prior recorded testimonies, ICTY Rule 92*ter* was in essence similar to original ICC Rule 68(b) in that both allowed for the introduction of prior testimonies from witnesses present before the Court and available for examination. As for the more controversial elements, namely where prior recorded testimonies are admitted without any possibility of cross-examination (92*quater* and *quinquies*), these were not possible at the ICC under original rule 68.

6.4.1.3 Amended Rule 68: Development and Process of Adoption

The ICC RPE were amended in November 2013, during the twelfth Assembly of States Parties.[90] Among the amendments was the revised and considerably lengthened Rule 68 on prior recorded testimony:

1. When the Pre-Trial Chamber has not taken measures under article 56, the Trial Chamber may, in accordance with article 69, paragraphs 2 and 4, and after hearing the parties, allow the introduction of previously recorded audio or video testimony of a witness, or the transcript or other documented evidence *of* such testimony, provided that this would not be prejudicial to or inconsistent with the rights of the accused and that the requirements of one or more of the following sub-rules are met.
2. If the witness who gave the previously recorded testimony is not present before the Trial Chamber, the Chamber may allow the introduction of that previously recorded testimony in any one of the following instances:

---

88 Colleen Rohan, 'Protecting the Rights of the Accused in International Criminal Proceedings: Lip Service or Affirmative Action?' in William Schabas and Yvonne McDermott (eds), *Critical perspectives* (Routledge 2013) 303.
89 Gaynor (n 2) 1062 and 1071.
90 'Amendments to the Rules of Procedure and Evidence' (International Criminal Court 2013) ICC-ASP/12/Res.7.

(a) Both the Prosecutor and the defence had the opportunity to examine the witness during the recording.
(b) The prior recorded testimony goes to proof of a matter other than the acts and conduct of the accused. In such a case:
  (i) In determining whether introduction of prior recorded testimony falling under sub-rule (b) may be allowed, the Chamber shall consider, inter alia, whether the prior recorded testimony in question:
    – relates to issues that are not materially in dispute;
    – is of a cumulative or corroborative nature, in that other witnesses will give or have given oral testimony of similar facts;
    – relates to background information;
    – is such that the interests of justice are best served by its introduction; and
    – has sufficient indicia of reliability.
  (ii) Prior recorded testimony falling under sub-rule (b) may only be introduced if it is accompanied by a declaration by the testifying person that the contents of the prior recorded testimony are true and correct to the best of that person's knowledge and belief. Accompanying declarations may not contain any new information and must be made reasonably close in time to when the prior recorded testimony is being submitted.
  (iii) Accompanying declarations must be witnessed by a person authorised to witness such a declaration by the relevant Chamber or in accordance with the law and procedure of a State. The person witnessing the declaration must verify in writing the date and place of the declaration, and that the person making the declaration:
    – is the person identified in the prior recorded testimony;
    – assures that he or she is making the declaration voluntarily and without undue influence;
    – states that the contents of the prior recorded testimony are, to the best of that person's knowledge and belief, true and correct; and
    – was informed that if the contents of the prior recorded testimony are not true then he or she may be subject to proceedings for having given false testimony.

(c) The prior recorded testimony comes from a person who has subsequently died, must be presumed dead, or is, due to obstacles that cannot be overcome with reasonable diligence, unavailable to testify orally. In such a case:
  (i) Prior recorded testimony falling under sub-rule (c) may only be introduced if the Chamber is satisfied that the person is unavailable as set out above, that the necessity of measures under article 56 could not be anticipated, and that the prior recorded testimony has sufficient indicia of reliability.
  (ii) The fact that the prior recorded testimony goes to proof of acts and conduct of an accused may be a factor against its introduction, or part of it.
(d) The prior recorded testimony comes from a person who has been subjected to interference. In such a case:
  (i) Prior recorded testimony falling under sub-rule (d) may only be introduced if the Chamber is satisfied that:
    – the person has failed to attend as a witness or, having attended, has failed to give evidence with respect to a material aspect included in his or her prior recorded testimony;
    – the failure of the person to attend or to give evidence has been materially influenced by improper interference, including threats, intimidation, or coercion;
    – reasonable efforts have been made to secure the attendance of the person as a witness or, if in attendance, to secure from the witness all material facts known to the witness;
    – the interests of justice are best served by the prior recorded testimony being introduced; and
    – the prior recorded testimony has sufficient indicia of reliability.
  (ii) For the purposes of sub-rule (d)(i), an improper interference may relate, inter alia, to the physical, psychological, economic or other interests of the person.
  (iii) When prior recorded testimony submitted under sub-rule (d)(i) relates to completed proceedings for offences defined in article 70, the Chamber may consider adjudicated facts from these proceedings in its assessment.

(iv) The fact that the prior recorded testimony goes to proof of acts and conduct of an accused may be a factor against its introduction, or part of it.

3. If the witness who gave the previously recorded testimony is present before the Trial Chamber, the Chamber may allow the introduction of that previously recorded testimony if he or she does not object to the submission of the previously recorded testimony and the Prosecutor, the defence and the Chamber have the opportunity to examine the witness during the proceedings.

Notwithstanding some differences as will be discussed below, this new ICC rule adopted the relevant rules of the ICTY. Stated differently, new ICC Rule 68(2)(b) parallels ICTY Rule 92*bis*; new ICC Rule 68(2)(c) parallels ICTY Rule 92*quater*, and ICC Rule 68(2)(d) is ICTY Rule 92*quinquies*. While these three sub-rules are new additions, new ICC Rule 68(3) replicates the old ICC Rule 68(b) and serves the same rationale as ICTY Rule 92*ter*.[91] Consequently, the amendments add three situations in which prior recorded testimony of an absent witness may be used at the ICC: where the testimony goes to proof of a matter other than the acts and conduct of the accused; where the witness is unavailable (for example deceased); or was subject to interference.[92]

According to the Chair of the Working Group on Amendments, the proposal emanated from the Court itself, and aimed: "(…) at allowing the judges of the Court to reduce the length of Court proceedings and streamline the presentation of evidence by increasing the instances in which prior recorded testimony could be introduced instead of hearing the witness in person, while paying due regard to the principles of fairness and the rights of the accused".[93]

---

91   Since the language of Rule 92ter ICTY RPE is clearer than that contained in Rule 68(3) ICC RPE, it is surprising that when the ICTY adopted Rules 92bis, quater and quinquies, 92ter was not also adopted. Instead, the new ICC RPE Rule 68(3) reproduces the old language of ICC RPE Rule 68(b). The difference between 92ter and 68(b)/68(3) lies in the fact that while 92ter(a)(iii) requires the witness to attest that the past statement accurately reflects the witness's statement and what the witness would say if examined, Rule 68(b) requires the witness not to object to the admission of previously recorded testimony.

92   'Working Group on Lessons Learnt: Second Report of the Court to the Assembly of States Parties' (International Criminal Court 2013) ICC-ASP/12/37/Add.1, executive summary and para. 3 of the proposed amendments to Rule 68.

93   *Ibid* para. 11.
     Note that the report used the expression '*due regard*' to the principles of fairness and the rights of the accused, whereas Article 64(2) RS provides that "The Trial Chamber shall ensure that a trial is fair and expeditious and is conducted with full respect for the rights of the accused and due regard for the protection of victims and witnesses".

Given that Rule 68 has now been amended and is in force, this section will focus on how the rules on which it is based have been used in the past, so as to predict its possible use in the future practice of the ICC. Although the section will not dwell on the process that led to the adoption of the amendments, a few words are needed in order to better understand that context and the limited debate around the impact of the amendments on the rights of the Defense. As will be discussed, the amendments appear to have been enacted relatively rapidly, without substantial consultation of those outside the decision-making process such as civil society or Defense counsel, and at a time when other significant issues on the agenda were likely of higher priority. The fact that the changes were presented as the established practice of the ICTY likely facilitated the process.

The amendments were formally submitted to Assembly of States Parties (ASP) 12 through the proposal of the Working Group on Lessons Learnt (WGLL Report), which had recommended their adoption to the Study Group on Governance (SGG). This SGG was created for dialogue between states parties to the Rome Statute and the ICC.[94] The Report – issued less than 30 days before the amendments were adopted – notes that the preliminary discussions began in May 2013, while the discussions on the amendments took place in September 2013 between the Study Group, the Court and the Advisory Committee on Legal Texts (ACLT).[95] The ACLT does have one member representing those on the list of external counsel before the ICC, although this person must represent both Defense counsel and counsel for victims on the list – two groups whose interests may not always coincide. The Report states that the amendment to rule 68 *'was prepared in consultation with major stakeholders and received broad support'* and that *'in particular, its text was adopted by the Advisory Committee on Legal Texts, and thereafter discussed with the*

---

94 The Study Group on Governance was established by resolution of the Assembly of the States Parties "to conduct a structured dialogue between States Parties and the Court with a view to strengthening the institutional framework of the Rome Statute system and enhancing the efficiency and effectiveness of the Court while fully preserving its judicial independence". 'Establishment of a Study Group on Governance' (International Criminal Court 2010) ICC-ASP/9/Res.2.

95 'Working Group on Lessons Learnt: Second Report of the Court to the Assembly of States Parties' (International Criminal Court 2013) ICC-ASP/12/37/Add.1, para. 12 and executive summary of the amendments to Rule 68; Regulation 4 (1) of the Regulations of the Court: "1. There shall be an Advisory Committee on Legal Texts comprised of: (a) Three judges, one from each Division, elected from amongst the members of the Division, who shall be members of the Advisory Committee for a period of three years; (b) One representative from the Office of the Prosecutor; (c) One representative from the Registry; and (d) One representative of counsel included in the list of counsel."

Study Group on Governance'.[96] Thus, the 'relevant stakeholders' envisaged by the report appear to be the states parties to the Rome Statute and the Court (or at least certain elements thereof), with very limited engagement with externals. The few documents available from civil society are all dated very close to the date of actual adoption, suggesting unawareness of the proposals until a few weeks before the ASP.[97]

In general, the impact of the amended Rule 68 on the rights of the accused is addressed in a cursory manner in the WGLL Report. This notes that these rights must be upheld, without providing details on how this goal might be achieved in light of the new rules, other than recalling that it would be up to the Chambers to ensure the respect of fair trial rights. For example, the Report notes that in amending Rule 68, 'an explicit reference to the rights of the accused was added, to draw attention expressly to this fundamental protection in the context of exceptions to the principle of orality',[98] but it does not address how the reference might be implemented. Regarding Rule 68(2)(b),[99] the Report states that 'provided that certain procedural steps are met', allowing such testimony would 'expedite proceedings and have additional budgetary benefits'.[100]

The balance to be struck in these amendments was clearly between the need to enhance the efficiency of the Court, while FULLY ensuring the rights of the accused. Those consulted who might be expected to have advocated for the latter appear to have been very much a minority, compared with those whose interests might be expected to have been more attuned to the former objectives of expediency.[101]

The Report recommending the amendments to the ASP does say, in a footnote, that 'although meaningful insight can be gained from the ICTY in constructing this amendment proposal, the tensions created by adding exceptions to the right of the accused to examine witnesses against him or her should be

---

96   *Ibid* para. 8.
97   E.g. Amnesty International, Human Rights Watch, and the International Bar Association all have documents dated November 2013.
98   'Working Group on Lessons Learnt: Second Report of the Court to the Assembly of States Parties' (International Criminal Court 2013) ICC-ASP/12/37/Add.1, para. 12 of the amendments to Rule 68.
99   Evidence of an absent witness going to proof of a matter other than the acts and conduct of the accused.
100 'Working Group on Lessons Learnt: Second Report of the Court to the Assembly of States Parties' (International Criminal Court 2013) ICC-ASP/12/37/Add.1, para. 18 of the amendments to Rule 68.
101 Namely, the States Parties to the ICC, especially in a year when budget increases were sought for the operation of the ICC.

borne in mind', but it also presents the amendments as based on ICTY rules and reflecting the practice in international criminal tribunals.[102] Presenting the Rule 68 amendments as the established practice of the ICTY undoubtedly facilitated their adoption – regardless of the fact that there is no published practice on one of the sub-rules and that some elements of the others have been controversial. For example at the ICTY, on multiple occasions judges reprimanded the tendency to use Rule 92bis et seq. to submit excessive amounts of prior recorded material, thereby frustrating the aim of shorter, streamlined trials.[103] Similarly, the linguistic differences between many of the Court's Situations and the ICTY's region of jurisdiction were not addressed. As previously discussed, the ICTR retained a stronger preference for orality than was the case at the ICTY due to the lower literacy rates in Rwanda. Indeed, these low rates meant that illiterate witnesses would not be able to personally verify the accuracy of a transcribed oral statement. Yet, the literacy rates in some of the ICC situation countries have been lowr than in Rwanda. As a result, low literacy rates, coupled with possible translation problems associated with countries where multiple languages are spoken, reduce the reliability of prior recorded evidence. However, this difference with the ICTY (where literacy was well over 90%) was never mentioned in the WGLL Report.

Two further differences not referred to in the Report were the specific drivers behind the developments of the ICTY Rules. As noted, overlapping trials were an impetus behind the development of the ICTY rules on prior recorded testimony, in that admitting transcripts of evidence given in a previous trial would avoid the need for the same witness to testify multiple times on the same issues.[104] However, the same situation is not, generally, the case at the ICC, although this difference in context seems to have been overlooked in the process of adoption of the ICC rules. Furthermore, the ICTY rules were adopted in the context of the UNSC-mandated Completion Strategy – an impetus not present in the case of the permanent mandate of the ICC.[105]

---

102 'Working Group on Lessons Learnt: Second Report of the Court to the Assembly of States Parties' (International Criminal Court 2013) ICC-ASP/12/37/Add.1, para. 20 of the amendments to Rule 68 (footnote 4).

103 E.g. *Prosecutor v Blagojević and Jokić* (First Decision on Prosecution's Motion for Admission of Witness Statements and Prior Testimony Pursuant to Rule 92bis) IT-02-60-T, T Ch I(A) (12 June 2003); *Prosecutor v Prlić et al.* (Separate Opinion of Presiding Judge Jean-Claude Antonetti Regarding the Decision on the Application of Article 92ter of the Rules) IT-04-74-T, T Ch III (25 June 2007).

104 Gaynor (n 2) 1049.

105 Nonetheless, notwithstanding its permanency, the ICC is under intense pressure to improve and expedite its work and, given that excessively long proceedings are neither in the interests of the Court nor in the interest of the accused, this is an imperative for both

The Report argued that Rule 68 needed to be amended to be '*more flexible and efficient*' in allowing the admission of witness testimony without that witness subsequently appearing before the Court because, unlike the ICTY, the ICC had no power to compel a witness to appear before the Court.[106] Indeed, the mainstream view prior to 17 April 2014 was that the ICC did not have any subpoena power to compel witness attendance. However, Trial Chamber V(a) in *Ruto and Sang* found that the ICC does have power to compel the testimony of witnesses who did not voluntarily wish to attend.[107] This finding was later upheld by the Appeals Chamber, which found that Article 64 (6) (b) RS gives Trial Chambers the power to compel a witness to appear before it, thereby creating a legal obligation for the individual concerned.[108] Therefore, the arguments made in support of Rules 68(2)(c) and 68(2)(d) would no longer seem to hold true.

Finally, it should be noted that other significant items were also on the agenda of the ASP, not least those relating to the case against Kenyan President Kenyatta, and thus many participants at the meeting appear to have accorded higher priority to other issues such as the Court's relationship with Africa, the relevance of official capacity to Prosecution, and the presence of the accused at trial.

The resolution by which the amendments were adopted was decided by consensus.[109] In a preambular paragraph, it recognised 'that enhancing the

---

parties. "Criticisms of drawn-out courtroom proceedings have long dogged international criminal tribunals, and the International Criminal Court (ICC) is no exception. We call on, and work with, the ICC and states to enhance the efficiency and effectiveness of its courtroom proceedings. While a measure of feet-finding was to be expected for the Court's first proceedings, it is vital that their duration is significantly reduced to bolster confidence in the Rome Statute system of international justice" ('Delivering Justice, Faster' (*Coalition for the International Criminal Court*) <https://www.coalitionfortheicc.org/fight/strong-icc/delivering-justice-faster#main-content> accessed 29 August 2023).

106 'Working Group on Lessons Learnt: Second Report of the Court to the Assembly of States Parties' (International Criminal Court 2013) ICC-ASP/12/37/Add.1, para. 6 of the amendments to Rule 68.

107 *Prosecutor v Ruto and Sang* (Decision on Prosecutor's Application for Witness Summonses and resulting Request for State Party Cooperation) ICC-01/09-01/11-1274-Corr2, T Ch V(a) (17 April 2014) paras 88ff. In particular, cf. para. 100.

108 *Prosecutor v Ruto and Sang* (Judgment on the appeals of William Samoei Ruto and Mr Joshua Arap Sang against the decision of Trial Chamber V (A) of 17 April 2014 entitled "Decision on Prosecutor's Application for Witness Summonses and resulting Request for State Party Cooperation") ICC-01/09-01/11-1598, A Ch (9 October 2014) para. 113. Cf. also paras 101ff, and in particular paras 107–108.

109 'Amendments to the Rules of Procedure and Evidence' (International Criminal Court 2013) ICC-ASP/12/Res.7.

efficiency and effectiveness of the Court is of common interest both for the Assembly of States Parties and the Court' – although it made no reference to the Defense as party to proceedings before the Court. As outlined, the Defense had very little voice in the process of the adoption of the resolution. Those states parties that made reference to Rule 68 in their General Debate statements did so in positive terms, calling on the Court to increase efficiency.[110] Other participants at the ASP and commentators, including civil society, academics and journalists, were also supportive of the change to Rule 68 on efficiency grounds, although some warned that elements of the amendment could undermine the accused's right to a fair trial.[111] While it is not possible to gauge whether the process might have been different had it taken place over a longer period of time and with a broader range of voices involved, the amended Rule 68 largely seems to have been well accepted, but with limited caution for the impact on the rights of the Defense.

6.4.2   ICC Practice: Original Rule 68

The WGLL Report, in recommending the amendments to Rule 68 to the ASP, argued that the original Rule 68 was not particularly effective at expediting trials and that the Rule 68(a) requirement that the non-tendering party would

---

110   E.g. statements of Australia, Norway, and the United Kingdom.
111   Cf. International Bar Association (IBA), which, although supportive of the amendment to Rule 68, recommended a cautious approach to its implementation; cf. Amnesty International, which expressed concerns about respect for the rights of the accused (such as the right to cross-examination); cf. also 'Human Rights Watch Memorandum for the Twelfth Session of the International Criminal Court Assembly of States Parties' (*Human Rights Watch*, 12 November 2013) <https://www.hrw.org/news/2013/11/12/human-rights-watch-memorandum-twelfth-session-international-criminal-court-assembly#main-content> accessed 14 July 2023, which recommended to "consider carefully proposals to amend the Rules of Procedure and Evidence with regard to the presence at trial of defendants, bearing in mind the need to ensure sufficient consultation on proposals and their consistency with the Rome Statute, and whether adopting amendments at this time would be premature given evolving practice at the court". Along the same lines, Beth Van Schaack, 'ICC Assembly of States Parties Rundown' (*A Forum on Law, Rights, and U.S. National Security*, 27 November 2013) <https://www.justsecurity.org/3862/icc-assembly-states-parties-rundown/#primary> accessed 14 July 2023, who said: "*Rule 68 has been amended to allow pre-recorded testimony rather than viva voce testimony in certain circumstances, an amendment that will no doubt address witness protection concerns, but will also implicate defendants' confrontation rights. During ASP12, Kenya and the defendants' defence counsel raised strong objections to the Rule 68 proposal. Language indicating that "Rule 68 will not be applied retroactively to the detriment of the person who is being investigated or prosecuted" was necessary to enable Kenya to ultimately join consensus. The new rules now mirror Rules 92bis, 92ter, and 92quater from the International Criminal Tribunal for the former Yugoslavia's RPEs, which were employed to good effect*".

be given the opportunity to examine the absent witnesses during the recording of the testimony was *'demanding'* and *'difficult to satisfy'*.[112] As will be discussed in relation to each case, Rule 68(a) was used twice in *Lubanga Dyilo*, and was considered – but eventually rejected – in *Bemba Gombo* and *Katanga*. Original Rule 68(a) remains in the new Rule 68, in essentially the same form, as Rule 68(2)(a).

In contrast to the limited use of original Rule 68(a) at the ICC, original Rule 68(b) was more frequently used – unsurprisingly, given that as with ICTY Rule 92*ter*, it was predicated on the witness who provided the prior recorded evidence being present for later examination, if necessary. Original Rule 68(b) was also replicated in essentially the same terms in the new Rule 68(3).

While Rule 68(a) was too infrequently used for any consistent procedure to develop, the procedure adopted in cases where the original Rule 68(b) was used was, in essence, that 21 days prior to the date of the witness' appearance in Court, the party seeking to introduce the evidence pursuant to Rule 68(b) should file an application, accompanied by a copy of the prior recorded testimony that identified the exact passages that the party sought to have admitted into evidence. The opposing party would then have 10 days following the notification of the application to respond.[113]

---

112 "*Rule 68, in its current form, has not been particularly effective in increasing the expeditiousness of the Court's first trials. Rule 68(a) is currently the only avenue for introducing prior recorded testimony in the absence of a witness, and has demanding requirements. In particular, it is difficult to satisfy the requirement that the non-tendering party had the opportunity to examine the absent witnesses during the recording of the testimony. The difficulty in fulfilling the conditions of rule 68(a) is evidenced by the limited jurisprudence applying the provision. Rule 68(a) has only been successfully invoked twice in the history of the Court, and even then the provision was applied under arguably unusual circumstances*" ('Working Group on Lessons Learnt: Second Report of the Court to the Assembly of States Parties' (International Criminal Court 2013) ICC-ASP/12/37/Add.1, para. 6 of the amendments to Rule 68).

113 In *Ruto and Sang*, for example, the Prosecutor argued for recourse to Rule 68 claiming that '*in certain circumstances, recourse to Rule 68 could be beneficial to the interests of justice, as it aids the judicial economy of the proceedings by allowing for the introduction of evidence in an efficient yet fair manner*'. Regarding Rule 68(b), the Prosecutor submitted that the procedure for the conduct of proceedings set down in *Prosecutor v Katanga and Ngudjolo Chui* (Corrigendum – Directions for the conduct of the proceedings and testimony in accordance with rule 140) ICC-01/04-01/07-1665-Corr, T CH II (1 December 2009) paras 92–94, should be adopted in Ruto and Sang, with any necessary modifications (*Prosecutor v Ruto and Sang* (Prosecution submissions on the conduct of the proceedings) ICC-01/09-01/11-794, T Ch v(A) (3 July 2013)).

In its decision – which came only three months before Rule 68 was amended – the Chamber essentially adopted the procedure set out in the Prosecution's submissions

6.4.2.1 Lubanga Dyilo

Issues regarding Rule 68 arose at various stages throughout the trial in *Lubanga Dyilo*. The Chamber took a pragmatic approach to the admission of prior recorded testimony with attention to the non-tendering party, who would be given the opportunity to examine the source of such evidence.

As for the scope of the physical material covered by original Rule 68, in *Lubanga Dyilo* this was first interpreted broadly, with subsequent trials more or less endorsing this approach.

In *Lubanga Dyilo*, the Trial Chamber affirmed that Rule 68 specifically included audio or video records, transcripts or other documented evidence of the testimony of a witness. The Chamber was persuaded by the fact that Rule 68 permitted the introduction of written statements of a witness' testimony, in addition to video or audio-taped records or transcripts, *'because these are all clear examples of the "documented evidence" of a witness' testimony'*.[114]

6.4.2.1.1 *Rule 68(a) – Supervised Deposition*

The WGLL Report stated that the original Rule 68(a) was only used twice at the ICC, both times in the *Lubanga Dyilo* case, under *'arguably unusual circumstances'*.[115] These two instances related to an abuse of process application.[116] Two witnesses testified at the Court at a time when the chamber was unable to be present and the depositions were supervised by the Legal Advisor.[117] The parties were in agreement; the Chamber permitted the recording of the depositions in this manner on the basis of, *inter alia*, Rule 68(a) and later admitted the depositions into evidence under this Rule, without the need to call either witness to testify before the Chamber.[118]

---

on 68(b). Cf. *Prosecutor v Ruto and Sang* (Decision on the Conduct of Trial Proceedings (General Directions)) ICC-01/09-01/11-847, T Ch V(A) (9 August 2013) para. 28.

The Prosecutor also submitted that where a party seeks to introduce evidence pursuant to Rule 68(a), it should be required to file a written application. The Chamber did not comment specifically on Rule 68(a) in its decision on the conduct of proceedings.

114 *Prosecutor v Lubanga Dyilo* (Decision on the prosecution's application for the admission of the prior recorded statements of two witnesses) ICC-01/04-01/06-1603, T Ch I (15 January 2009) para. 18.
115 'Working Group on Lessons Learnt: Second Report of the Court to the Assembly of States Parties' (International Criminal Court 2013) ICC-ASP/12/37/Add.1, para. 6 of the amendments to Rule 68.
116 *Ibid* para. 20 of the amendments to Rule 68.
117 *Prosecutor v Lubanga Dyilo*, Transcript ICC-01/04-01/06-T-333-Red2-ENG, T Ch I (12 November 2010), 18–21.
118 'Working Group on Lessons Learnt: Second Report of the Court to the Assembly of States Parties' (International Criminal Court 2013) ICC-ASP/12/37/Add.1, para. 20 of the amendments to Rule 68.

6.4.2.1.2 Rule 68(b)

The original Rule 68(b) was used in *Lubanga Dyilo* following an application by the Prosecution to admit two written statements in lieu of oral testimony. In considering the motion, the Chamber stated that fact-specific decisions would need to be made to resolve applications under this Rule.[119]

The Chamber discussed at length the advantages and disadvantages of *viva voce* and written evidence, noting that '*there can be material advantages in testimony being given in its entirety viva voce before the Court*'. The Chamber also noted that '*there can be equal material advantages in having evidence read, in whole or in part*' and '*[o]n occasion there will be little, if any advantage, to evidence being given* in toto *orally*', but that '*the right of the accused to a fair trial must not be undermined by decisions of this kind*'.[120]

In that instance, the Trial Chamber did admit the statements under Rule 68(b), for reasons of efficiency and expediency of the proceedings, and provided that the Defense and the Chamber could later examine the witnesses in court. In the decision, the factors the Chamber considered to be in favour of allowing the introduction of prior recorded testimony included, (i) that the testimony relates to issues which are not materially in dispute; (ii) that it is

---

119 *Prosecutor v Lubanga Dyilo* (Decision on the prosecution's application for the admission of the prior recorded statements of two witnesses) ICC-01/04-01/06-1603, T Ch I (15 January 2009) para. 21.

120 *Ibid* paras 21–24: "Depending on the circumstances, there can be material advantages in testimony being given in its entirety viva voce before the Court, particularly when evidence of significance is challenged or requires comprehensive investigation. The live questioning of a witness in open court on all aspects of his or her evidence can have a material impact on the Chamber's overall assessment of the evidence, since oral testimony is, for obvious reasons, of a different nature to a written statement: most importantly the evidence can be fully investigated and tested by questioning, and the Court is able to assess its accuracy, reliability and honesty, in part by observing the conduct and demeanour of the witness. However, there can be equal material advantages in having evidence read, in whole or in part. In the context of this application, relevant examples are that it avoids witnesses unnecessarily repeating their evidence once it has been recorded. Furthermore, there is a real potential for war crimes trials to last an excessive period of time and the court is entitled to bear this issue in mind when weighing the possibility of receiving non-oral evidence. On occasion there will be little, if any advantage, to evidence being given in toto orally, for instance when there is likely to be limited challenge or where the testimony is not of central significance. However, the right of the accused to a fair trial must not be undermined by decisions of this kind, and the Chamber must ensure that the accused's rights are appropriately protected. For instance, if, as here, Article 69 is relied on, any measures which the Chamber implements "shall not be prejudicial to or inconsistent with the rights of the accused" (Article 69(2) of the Statute)."

not central to core issues in the case, but rather provides relevant background information; and (iii) that it is corroborative of other evidence.[121]

6.4.2.1.3 Importance of Witness Being Present

Deciding on a later Defense request for the admission of 422 documents, the Chamber admitted some interview transcripts of Prosecution witnesses who had testified before the Chamber, but rejected the transcripts of individuals not called as witnesses.[122] The Chamber noted that under Article 69(2)RS, it could admit, *inter alia*, documents and written transcripts, applying the three-prong test of relevance, probative value and fairness. Since the interviews had been conducted as part of an information-gathering exercise and the witnesses had not been called to give oral testimony, the Chamber held that 'there are insufficient indications as to whether the prosecution's questions were sufficiently comprehensive or penetrating to provide a balanced and reliable picture'. For the documents to be admitted, the Chamber said that the individuals should be called as witnesses so that a proper assessment could be made of their reliability and credibility.[123] Later applications were similarly rejected on the grounds that the source of the evidence would not be called to testify.[124]

In another instance in *Lubanga Dyilo*, a statement was admitted into evidence, although the witness had not been called to testify. Admittedly, this happened under special circumstances; moreover, the admission was under Article 69(4) RS instead of Rule 68, because the requirements of the latter had not been met.[125] In that case (which related to the abuse of process issues involving intermediaries), the Chamber noted that the statement had been taken under the supervision of the Prosecution and signed by the witness, and that its admission would not be prejudicial to the Prosecution who had been

---

121 *Ibid* paras 7, 22 and 24.
122 *Prosecutor v Lubanga Dyilo* (Corrigendum to redacted Decision on the defence request for the admission of 422 documents) ICC-01/04-01/06-2595, T CH I (8 March 2011); *Prosecutor v Lubanga Dyilo* (Redacted Decision on the "Cinquième requête de la Défense aux fins de dépôt de documents") ICC-01/04-01/06-2702-Red, T CH I (6 April 2011) footnote 16.
123 *Prosecutor v Lubanga Dyilo* (Corrigendum to redacted Decision on the defence request for the admission of 422 documents) ICC-01/04-01/06-2595, T CH I (8 March 2011) para. 58.
124 *Prosecutor v Lubanga Dyilo* (Redacted Decision on the "Troisième requête de la Défense aux fins de dépôt de documents") ICC-01/04-01/06-2664-Red, T Ch I (16 March 2011) para. 50.
125 *Prosecutor v Lubanga Dyilo* (Redacted Decision on the "Cinquième requête de la Défense aux fins de dépôt de documents") ICC-01/04-01/06-2702-Red, T CH I (6 April 2011), as cited, for example, in *Prosecutor v Lubanga Dyilo* (Redacted Decision on the Prosecution's Application to Admit Rebuttal Evidence from Wihiess DRC-OTP-WWWW-0005) ICC-01/04-01/06-2727-Red, T Ch I (28 April 2011) footnote 96.

given the opportunity to examine the witness while recording the statement. The Defense requested the admission of the statement and indicated that it did not consider that the accused would be prejudiced by virtue of the lack of opportunity to examine the witness. Hence, the Chamber found that the statement, while not meeting the requirements of Rule 68, could however be admitted under Article 69(4) RS.

6.4.2.1.4 A 'Real as Opposed to a Symbolic or Theoretical Opportunity' to Examine the Source of the Statement

At a late stage of the *Lubanga Dyilo* trial, the Prosecution sought to have admitted under Rule 68 the transcript of an interview with a witness who had been brought to The Hague to be questioned by the Prosecution, in the presence of the Defense, but who was later not called to testify in Court.

While the Prosecution submission acknowledged the fact that the preferred course of action would have been to call the witness to testify, this had not happened for various reasons.[126] The Prosecution claimed that the requirements of Rule 68 were met because the Defense was present at the meeting, thus having the opportunity to question the witness.

The Defense denied, submitting that the Prosecution had never implied that it would use the contents of the meeting as evidence. The Defense claimed that had it been informed that the meeting would take place within the context of Rule 68, it would have considered asking questions as had been the case with other witnesses.[127]

In responding to the application, the Chamber reviewed the approaches taken with reference to the admissibility of prior recorded statements into evidence.[128] It recalled a number of the aforementioned instances where decisions to allow or refuse the admissibility of documentary evidence had been taken throughout the case, to then concluded that: "for Rule 68 to be applied, it is necessary that both the prosecution and the defence have had – or will have – an opportunity to examine the witness, whether at the Court or elsewhere. However, this opportunity must be real, and not symbolic or theoretical. Additionally, the questioning must have occurred under circumstances in

---

126 *Prosecutor v Lubanga Dyilo*, Transcript ICC-01/04-01/06-T-350-Red2-ENG, T Ch I (14 April 2011), 24 (lines 7–13) and 26 (lines 6–10).
127 *Ibid* 27–28.
128 *Prosecutor v Lubanga Dyilo* (Redacted Decision on the Prosecution's Application to Admit Rebuttal Evidence from Wihiess DRC-OTP-WWWW-0005) ICC-01/04-01/06-2727-Red, T Ch I (28 April 2011) para. 45.

which the parties were aware that they were to exercise their right or, alternatively, that allowed for its sufficient exercise".[129]

The Chamber held that the Prosecution's application under Rule 68 was ill-founded and, thus, that the question of admissibility had to be decided under the Article 64(9) test of *prima facie* relevance, probative value, and fairness.[130] The Chamber found in this instance that the probative value was far outweighed by its prejudicial effect: "the party not calling the witness was not at any stage warned of the need to ask questions (to avoid adverse evidential consequences), nor did counsel avail themselves of this opportunity. In such circumstances, it would be unfair to admit evidence that is potentially of real significance when the Defense had been denied the opportunity to test the material by questioning".[131]

6.4.2.2 Katanga and Ngudjolo Chui

6.4.2.2.1 *Rule 68(a)*

Although the procedure was eventually not applied in *Katanga and Ngudjolo Chui*, the possibility of using original Rule 68(a) was evoked at several times throughout the case, including in the final judgment against Mr Katanga, with the Chamber noting that if other measures to ensure the timely presence of a witness were unsuccessful, the use of Rule 68(a) to admit prior testimony could be considered.[132] Presumably, the 'other measures' the Chamber had in

---

129   *Ibid* para. 53.
130   *Ibid* para. 54.
131   *Ibid* para. 55.
132   *Prosecutor v Katanga* (Decision on the Defense Requests Set Forth in Observations 3379 and 3386 of 3 and 17 June 2013) ICC-01/04-01/07-3388-tENG, T CH II (26 June 2013) para. 65: "The Chamber does also not rule out, pursuant to the provisions of rule 67 of the Rules, hearing these witnesses' testimonies by audio or video link, by virtue of the modalities used on 2 November 2010 when Witness P-323 was recalled. Such modalities for hearing testimony shall be employed where it would prove particularly difficult for a witness to travel to The Hague, or where, for reasons including the witness's availability, he or she is unable to appear when required by the Chamber. Lastly, where manifest that a witness is unable to appear within such time as to comply with the duty of celerity cast on the Chamber, the Bench will assess whether recourse must be had to the provisions of rule 68(a) of the Rules. It will then be for the Defense for Germain Katanga and the Prosecution to liaise forthwith so as to take such testimonies within the time frame determined by the Chamber."

The final Katanga Trial Chamber judgment recalled this possibility (*Prosecutor v Katanga and Ngudjolo Chui* (Jugement rendu en application de l'article 74 du Statut) ICC-01/04-01/07-3436, T Ch II (7 March 2014) para. 1571): "The Chamber also wishes to recall that it had mentioned, even before the additional Defense investigations started, that it was possible to use means of evidence other than physical appearance in the room. On that occasion, it also said that 'if the appearance of a witness could not occur within

mind included video-links, given that this tool was used to hear witness testimony of a witness who had to be recalled for further questioning.[133]

6.4.2.2.2 *Rule 68(b)*

In the Directions for the conduct of the proceedings in *Katanga and Ngudjolo Chui*, the Chamber had instructed that a party requesting the admission of parts of prior recorded testimony attached any other material to which references are made in those parts.[134] This led to a series of motions under Rule 68, with focus on the extent to which this rule could be used to admit documentary evidence, particularly video excerpts, prior to the testimony of the witness to which they related. In general, the Chamber endorsed a case-by-case approach, finding that Rule 68 cannot be used as a catch-all to admit documentary evidence without first going through a witness. In line with the *Lubanga Dyilo* Trial Chamber, it did not accept that the scope of Rule 68 was limited to written statements.

In a confidential filing in 2010, the Prosecution sought to use Rule 68(b) to introduce several passages of a witness statement and excerpts from videos allegedly made by the witness itself, before it had testified at the trial.[135] The Defense for Katanga submitted in response that rule 68(b) could not be used to tender documentary evidence; similarly, the Defense for Ngudjolo Chui submitted that Rule 68(b) is not aimed at the admission of exhibits. Both

---

a period compatible with the requirement of promptness held by the Chamber, it will consider whether it is appropriate to use the provisions of Rule 68(a) of the Rules", unofficial translation, original text: "La Chambre tient aussi à rappeler qu'elle avait mentionné, avant même que ne commencent les enquêtes complémentaires de la Défense, qu'il était envisageable de recourir à des moyens de déposition autres que la comparution physique en salle d'audience3487. À cette occasion, elle avait également précisé que, « si la comparution d'un témoin ne pouvait d'évidence pas intervenir dans un délai compatible avec l'exigence de célérité à laquelle est tenue la Chambre, cette dernière s'interrogera sur le point de savoir s'il y a lieu de recourir aux dispositions de la Règle 68-a du Règlement ». Si la Défense a elle-même évoqué les témoignages par vidéo link, elle a toutefois fait le choix de ne pas y recourir en l'espèce". (*Prosecutor v Katanga and Ngudjolo Chui* (Jugement rendu en application de l'article 74 du Statut) ICC-01/04-01/07-3436, T Ch II (7 March 2014) para. 1571).

133 *Prosecutor v Katanga and Ngudjolo Chui*, Transcript ICC-01/04-01/07-T-211-RED2-ENG, T Ch II (2 November 2010).

134 *Prosecutor v Katanga and Ngudjolo Chui* (Corrigendum – Directions for the conduct of the proceedings and testimony in accordance with rule) ICC-01/04-01/07-1665-Corr, T Ch II (1 December 2009) para. 92.

135 *Prosecutor v Katanga and Ngudjolo Chui* (Decision on Request to admit prior recorded testimony of P-30 as well as related video excerpts) ICC-01/04-01/07-2233, T Ch II (30 June 2010).

teams further submitted that the video excerpts were unnecessarily graphic, and could prejudice the accused.[136] While not denying that video testimony could be admissible under Rule 68, the Chamber found that, although a party requesting the admission of parts of prior recorded testimony shall attach any other material to which reference is made in the statement, in the case at hand the statement of the witness was primarily descriptive of what shown in the videos, thus being it meaningless in the absence of the video excerpts. Therefore, in the view of the Chamber, the request appeared to be more for the admission of the 22 video excerpts without going through a witness, rather than a request to allow the introduction of the prior recorded testimony of the witness. The Chamber largely rejected the Prosecution's request, despite noting that the Prosecution could still seek to present some of the video excerpts during the examination of the witness, with admissibility to be decided at that stage.

The Prosecution claimed that it would later tender other video excerpts into evidence through the witness, but that the excerpts which were the subject of this request did not require further comments from the witness; moreover, according to the Prosecution, their admission under Rule 68 was not prejudicial to the accused, as the witness would later be available for cross-examination.[137]

The Defense for Mr Katanga partly opposed the motion, submitting that Rule 68(b) was not designed to facilitate the admission of exhibits. In this regard, it argued that the determination of the reliability and relevance of the video excerpts depends on the testimony of the witness; therefore, it would be prejudicial to the rights of the accused to make such a determination before the witness is questioned on their reliability and relevance in court.[138] The Defense for Mr Ngudjolo Chui also opposed the motion. In particular, it submitted that Rule 68(b) governs the modality of the presentation of evidence through documentary or audio/video recording of testimony provided by a neutral person who saw or heard a fact and could testify to the truth of such fact. It further argued that the principle of orality means that witnesses called before a court must be directly questioned and respond orally, and that Rule 68 allows the admission of written statements in limited circumstances.[139]

The Chamber noted that the *Lubanga Dyilo* Trial Chamber had previously ruled that the term 'previously recorded testimony' under Rule 68 included

---

136   Ibid.
137   *Prosecutor v Katanga and Ngudjolo Chui* (Corrigendum to the Decision on the Prosecution Motion for admission of prior recorded testimony of Witness P-02 and accompanying video excerpts) ICC-01/04-01/07-2289-Corr-Red, T Ch II (27 August 2010).
138   Ibid para. 6.
139   Ibid para. 9.

written statements provided by a witness.[140] The Chamber affirmed that as with any other material tendered into evidence, prior recorded testimony and any accompanying material must satisfy the criteria for the admissibility of evidence, namely (i) whether they are relevant to the charges in the present case, (ii) whether they are of probative value, (iii) and whether their probative value is not overweighed by their prejudicial effect, with probative value comprising two factors, namely the materiality of the information contained in a piece of evidence and the reliability of the piece of evidence.[141] It further agreed with the *Lubanga Dyilo* Trial Chamber 'that "fact-specific decisions" need to be taken in determining whether a previously recorded testimony may be introduced in place of "live" evidence pursuant to Rule 68(b)' and that the factors in favour of allowing the introduction of previously recorded testimony include, but are not limited to, '(i) that the testimony relates to issues which are not materially in dispute; (ii) that it is not central to core issues in the case, but rather provides relevant background information; and (iii) that it is corroborative of other evidence' and that the use of Rule 68(b) must not be prejudicial to or inconsistent with the rights of the accused. An important factor in making this assessment would be, even if the entirety of their evidence would not be *viva voce*, whether or not the witness would appear before the Court and be available for cross-examination by the Defense. In the present case, applying the criteria it had enumerated, the Chamber partially accepted the motion in that parts of the witness statement were provisionally admitted on the condition the witness later testified in person, and provided that the relevance and probative value of the admitted video-excerpts remain intact after cross-examination of the witness.[142]

In a request from the Prosecution to allow prior recorded testimony in the form of written statements, both Defense teams argued that written declarations did not constitute prior recorded testimony within the meaning of Rule 68, and that prior recorded testimony violated the principle of orality.[143] Specifically, Defense Counsel for Mr Katanga raised the point that, when prior

---

140　*Prosecutor v Lubanga Dyilo* (Decision on the prosecution's application for the admission of the prior recorded statements of two witnesses) ICC-01/04-01/06-1603, T Ch I (15 January 2009) paras 18–19.

141　*Prosecutor v Katanga and Ngudjolo Chui* (Corrigendum to the Decision on the Prosecution Motion for admission of prior recorded testimony of Witness P-02 and accompanying video excerpts) ICC-01/04-01/07-2289-Corr-Red, T Ch II (27 August 2010) para. 13.

142　*Ibid* paras 22–23.

143　*Prosecutor v Katanga and Ngudjolo Chui* (Decision on Prosecutor's request to allow the introduction into evidence of the prior recorded testimony of P-166 and P-219) ICC-01/04-01/07-2362, T Ch II (3 September 2010).

recorded statements are admitted as evidence and witnesses are then questioned on the statements, this raises issues regarding the principle of equality of arms. The Defense argued that the massive resources available to the Prosecution mean that witness statements recorded by the Prosecution are considerably more detailed than those taken by Defense investigators. Thus, the Prosecution witness statements would provide a considerably greater wealth of material from which to draw out information and highlight inconsistencies.

The Chamber in *Katanga* noted the importance of the distinction between out-of-court statements – which qualify as prior recorded testimony under Rule 68 – and statements that do not. In this regard, it affirmed that, generally speaking, statements provided to representatives of the Office of the Prosecutor, which at the time the witness knew might be used in proceedings before the Court, will be considered as testimonies. In that instance, the Chamber concluded that as the makers of both statements would be available for examination by the parties and the Chamber, their prior recorded testimony could, in principle, be admitted under the exception contained in Rule 68(b).[144]

Regarding whether statements could be admitted in full or only in part through excerpts, the Chamber recalled its Direction on the conduct of the proceedings, where it clarified that 'the application shall be accompanied by a copy of the prior recorded statement indicating precisely which passages the party calling the witness wishes to enter into evidence'[145] and affirmed that this unambiguously implied that prior recorded testimony may be admitted only in part.[146]

Always during the proceedings in *Katanga and Ngudjolo Chui*, the Prosecution questioned a witness on a prior recorded statement, with the intention of pointing out an alleged inconsistency between the prior recorded testimony and the one given in Court. To this end, the witness was provided with copies of his prior recorded statements to read before questioning. After that, the extract was admitted as evidence. The Katanga Defense sought to have the entirety of the statement admitted.[147] However, the Trial Chamber rejected

---

144　*Ibid* paras 12–13.
145　*Prosecutor v Katanga and Ngudjolo Chui* (Corrigendum – Directions for the conduct of the proceedings and testimony in accordance with rule) ICC-01/04-01/07-1665-Corr, T Ch II (1 December 2009).
146　*Prosecutor v Katanga and Ngudjolo Chui* (Decision on Prosecutor's request to allow the introduction into evidence of the prior recorded testimony of P-166 and P-219) ICC-01/04-01/07-2362, T Ch II (3 September 2010) para. 16.
147　*Prosecutor v Katanga and Ngudjolo Chui* (Corrigendum to Defense Request to Admit into Evidence Entirety of Document DRC-OTP-1017-0572) ICC-01/04-01/07-2839-Corr, T Ch II (18 April 2011).

the request, clarifying that the excerpt was admitted because the witness had read it silently and not out loud in the courtroom. The Chamber considered that even where the grounds for compliance with Rule 68(b) were met, this did not of itself create sufficient ground to deviate from the principle of orality. In particular, the Chamber specified that an assertion that the written statement of a witness could provide broader context or corroborate oral testimony at trial 'does not qualify as a sufficient reason for admitting it into evidence'.[148]

A later request from the Defense to admit a witness statement under Rule 68(b) was also rejected by the Trial Chamber, which affirmed the principle of orality and explained that recourse to Rule 68 should be undertaken with caution so as to not 'prejudice the rights of the accused or the fairness of the trial. The Chamber observed that its approach to Rule 68 was moderate, and 'drew attention to the fact that the rule requires the witness to consent to the admission into evidence and that the parties and the Chamber have an opportunity to examine the witness'.[149]

6.4.2.3 Ruto and Sang

In submissions on the conduct of the proceedings in 2013, both Prosecution and Defense accepted the possibility of the recourse to Rule 68 – although the submissions were based on the original Rule 68 and not on the version adopted later that year (which incorporated the option of statements from witnesses without cross-examination). The Prosecution argued that 'in certain circumstances, recourse to Rule 68 could be beneficial to the interests of justice, as it aids the judicial economy of the proceedings by allowing for the introduction of evidence in an efficient yet fair manner'.[150] The Sang Defense cautioned that excessive resort to Rule 68 'would deny the triers of facts the opportunity to fully assess the witnesses' credibility', but conceded that there may be situations where the use of Rule 68 is indeed appropriate. The Sang Defense suggested that this be handled by way of written application, with sufficient time before the witness's anticipated testimony and for the opposing party to respond, as per the modalities set out in *Katanga*.[151] Similarly, the

---

148 *Prosecutor v Katanga and Ngudjolo Chui* (Decision on Defense Request to Admit into Evidence Entirety of Document DRC-OTP-1017-0572) ICC-01/04-01/07-2954, T Ch II (25 May 2011).

149 *Prosecutor v Katanga and Ngudjolo Chui* (Decision on Request to admit prior recorded testimony of P-30 as well as related video excerpts) ICC-01/04-01/07-2233, T Ch II (30 June 2010) paras 5–7.

150 *Prosecutor v Ruto and Sang* (Sang Defense Submissions on the Conduct of the Proceedings) ICC-01/09-01/11-796, Defense (3 July 2013) para. 28.

151 *Ibid* para. 20.

Ruto Defense aknowledged that Rule 68 provides an exception to the principle of orality and that recourse may be made to it during the trial. However, it also submitted that this should be only in exceptional circumstances or with the agreement of the parties.[152]

6.4.2.4 Bemba Gombo

Rule 68 was also used throughout the trial in *Bemba Gombo*. Generally, relevant decisions were adopted by majority, with Judge Ozaki dissenting and particularly expressing concerns about the impact of prior recorded testimony on the fair trial rights of the Defense. She also reiterated the concerns expressed in *Lubanga Dyilo* about the potential lack of neutrality of prior recorded witness statements when taken by a party to the proceedings.

6.4.2.4.1 *Rule 68 Only for Exceptional Circumstances*

In *Bemba Gombo*, following an application by the Prosecution to submit prior recorded testimony of three witnesses,[153] the Trial Chamber discussed the principle of the primacy of orality and its statutory exceptions. The Chamber stated that the general principle is that evidence should be given in person and that this could be departed from only when not prejudicial to, or inconsistent with, the rights of the accused. Therefore, the option of introducing prior-recorded testimony should be adopted only in specific and exceptional circumstances. In the present case, the Chamber rejected the application on the ground that the Prosecution had not shown exceptional circumstances justifying any derogation from the general principle of the *viva voce* evidence.[154]

6.4.2.4.2 *'Cautious Item-by-Item Analysis' Required*

In another *Bemba Gombo* decision a few weeks later, the majority of the Chamber was less equivocal – although the decision was later overturned in Appeal. In *prima facie* admitting all items on the Prosecution's list of evidence, including witness statements,[155] the majority stated that 'the Statute only envisages a presumption in favour of oral testimony, but no prevalence of orality of

---

152   *Ibid* paras 42 and 43.
153   *Prosecutor v Bemba Gombo* (Decision on the "Prosecution Application for Leave to Submit in Writing Prior-Recorded Testimonies by CAR-OTP-WWWW-0032, CAR-OTP-WWWW-0080, and CAR-OTP-WWWW-0108") ICC-01/05-01/08-886, T Ch III (16 September 2010) paras 7 and 15.
154   *Ibid* para. 7.
155   *Prosecutor v Bemba Gombo* (Decision on the admission into evidence of materials contained in the prosecution's list of evidence) ICC-01/05-01/08-1022, T Ch III (19 November 2010).

the procedures as a whole'.[156] Dissenting, Judge Ozaki said that the principle of orality was a cornerstone of proceedings under the Rome Statute and that: "trials which have so far taken place before international criminal tribunals in principle have relied on oral testimonies of witnesses, with written statements being exceptionally admitted on a specific case-by-case basis. In fact, in-court, live testimony is arguably the best way for a Chamber to evaluate the credibility of a witness, through his/her demeanour, hesitations, facial expressions, etc and thus to gauge the reliability of his/her testimony. This is especially true in cases before this Court, where most witnesses come from remote areas, have completely different cultural backgrounds and are testifying in a criminal case of extreme complexity. It is therefore unsurprising that the principle of primacy of orality has also been systematically applied by Trial Chambers of the Court, including this Chamber, which has consistently treated the admission into evidence of witness statements and other prior recorded testimonies as an exception to the rule, and has considered such requests for admission on a case-by-case basis".[157]

Regarding prior recorded witness statements, Judge Ozaki noted that witness statements at the ICC are not taken in neutral, impartial circumstances, but by a party "mainly in order to gather evidence to mount a case against an accused, and without the supervision of any impartial arbiter". Hence, in her view, their admission 'must remain the exception' in specific, limited circumstances.[158]

The Appeals Chamber reversed the Trial Chamber's decision,[159] affirming that "admission into evidence of the witnesses' written statements without a cautious item-by-item analysis and without satisfying Rule 68 of the Rules of Procedure and Evidence is incompatible with the principle of orality as set out in Article 69 (2) of the Statute".[160]

In contrast to *Katanga and Ngudjolo Chui* (see above), where the admission of parts of prior recorded testimony was expressly allowed, in *Bemba Gombo* the majority of the Trial Chamber (Judge Ozaki dissenting) favoured

---

156   *Ibid* para. 14.
157   *Prosecutor v Bemba Gombo* (Dissenting Opinion of Judge Kuniko Ozaki on the Decision on the admission into evidence of materials contained in the prosecution's list of evidence) ICC-01/05-01/08-1028, T Ch III (23 November 2010) para. 7.
158   *Ibid* para. 11.
159   *Prosecutor v Bemba Gombo* (Judgment on the appeals of Mr Jean-Pierre Bemba Gombo and the Prosecutor against the decision of Trial Chamber III entitled "Decision on the admission into evidence of materials contained in the prosecution's list of evidence") ICC-01/05-01/08-1386, A Ch (3 May 2011).
160   *Ibid* para. 3.

the admission of the entirety of a witness statement, as opposed to excerpts, "when considered necessary for the determination of the truth in accordance with Article 69(3) of the Statute and to ensure that information is not taken out of context".[161]

6.4.2.4.3   Witness Consent

Another *Bemba Gombo* decision concerning the admission under Rule 68(b) of three witness statements (one tendered by the Prosecution and two by the Defense) highlighted the importance of witness consent. The Chamber had initially deferred consideration of the three statements in light of the fact that, while the other requirements of Rule 68(b) were met, the witnesses had not expressly consented to the submission of their statements into evidence.[162] Once the Registry had filed a report confirming that the three witnesses had no objection to the admission of their statements as evidence, the Chamber proceeded to consider their admission in accordance with Rule 68.[163] The Chamber admitted all three statements.[164]

6.4.2.4.4   Witness CHM-01 – Retroactive Application

At a more advanced stage in *Bemba Gombo*, the Chamber itself decided to call a witness for questioning just days prior to the amendment of Rule 68.[165] The

---

161   *Prosecutor v Bemba Gombo* (Order on the procedure relating to the submission of evidence) ICC-01/05-01/08-1470, T Ch III (31 May 2011) para. 11.

162   *Prosecutor v Bemba Gombo* (Public redacted version of the First decision on the prosecution and Defense requests for the admission of evidence, dated 15 December 2011) ICC-01/05-01/08-2012-Red, T Ch III (9 February 2012), as cited, for example, in *Prosecutor v Bemba Gombo* (Decision on the admission into evidence of items deferred in the Chamber's "First decision on the prosecution and Defense requests for the admission of evidence" (ICC-01/05-01/08-2012)) ICC-01/05-01/08-2793, T Ch III (03 September 2013) footnote 11.

163   As cited, for example, in *Prosecutor v Bemba Gombo* (Decision on the admission into evidence of items deferred in the Chamber's "First decision on the prosecution and Defense requests for the admission of evidence" (ICC-01/05-01/08-2012)) ICC-01/05-01/08-2793, T Ch III (03 September 2013) footnote 16.

164   *Prosecutor v Bemba Gombo* (Decision on the admission into evidence of items deferred in the Chamber's "First decision on the prosecution and Defense requests for the admission of evidence" (ICC-01/05-01/08-2012)) ICC-01/05-01/08-2793, T Ch III (03 September 2013).

165   *Prosecutor v Bemba Gombo* (Public redacted version of Decision on the presentation of additional testimony pursuant to Articles 64(6)(b) and (d) and 69(3) of the Rome Statute) ICC-01/05-01/08-2863, T Ch III (6 November 2011) para. 5.

   Witness CHM-01 appeared before the Chamber and provided testimony from 18 to 22 November 2013; cf. *Prosecutor v Bemba Gombo* (Order seeking observations on the admission into evidence of written statement of Witness CHM-01) ICC-01/05-01/08-2923, T Ch III (13 December 2013).

witness was questioned on, among other things, a statement he had previously provided to the OTP.

On 13 December 2013, post-amendment, the Chamber sought views from the parties and participants as to whether the statement should be admitted as evidence.[166] In January 2014 submissions, both Prosecution and Defense opposed such admission. In particular, the Prosecution was of the view that the exceptional nature of judges' discretion "derives from a general acceptance that witness testimony is primarily evaluated on the basis of the oral testimony in court and documentary evidence apart from prior statements. The decision to admit a prior statement under Rule 68 should therefore only be made in exceptional circumstances, where good reasons exist".[167]

The Defense was concerned about the late nature of the proposed admission of a 67 page statement, and referred to the rights of the accused to be tried without undue delay pursuant to Article 67(1)(c), to examine, or have examined, the witnesses against him or her under Article 67(1)(e) as well as to the primacy of orality at the ICC under Article 69(2). The Defense further recalled issues with the recording of Prosecution witness statements, where witnesses later claimed under oath that the recordings of their interviews were inaccurate, and eventually considered that the prejudicial effect of the admission of the statement outweighed any probative value or relevance it may have.[168]

Neither party nor the Chamber made any reference to the fact that Rule 68 had been amended in the interval between the witness testifying and the Chamber seeking views on whether it should use the rule to admit a prior statement of the witness. This is perhaps due to the fact that the amendments were only of marginal relevance in that situation, given that the testimony in question did not fall under one of the new sub-rules (for unavailable witnesses or interference with witnesses).

The final decision on the admissibility into evidence of the statement was released together with decisions on various other forms of evidence, some of which also being considered under Rule 68. In relation to the witness statement that the Chamber itself had proposed, it said that "in order for the Chamber to properly discharge its statutory truth-finding mandate" it should be able to have access to the entirety of the prior recorded statements

---

166 *Prosecutor v Bemba Gombo* (Order seeking observations on the admission into evidence of written statement of Witness CHM-01) ICC-01/05-01/08-2923, T Ch III (13 December 2013).

167 *Prosecutor v Bemba Gombo* (Prosecution's Observations on the admission into evidence of the written statement of witness CHM-01) ICC-01/05-01/08-2930, T Ch III (10 January 2014) para. 10.

168 *Prosecutor v Bemba Gombo* (Defence submissions on the proposed admission of Witness CHM-01's statement) ICC-01/05-01/08-2936, Defense (13 January 2014) para. 21.

rather than being limited to assessing the testimony of a witness against only "those excerpts of their prior interviews or statements that the parties decide to refer to in court in the limited time available to them".[169] Thus, the Chamber again expressed a preference for the entirety of prior recorded testimonies as opposed to excerpts.[170] However, the Chamber noted that the parties had opposed the admission of the statement and decided that it was unnecessary to consider the issue further.[171]

6.4.2.4.5   *Consideration of a Document for Admission under Rule 68(a)*

Another matter decided in the same decision related to a document[172] proposed for admission in confidential filings by the Prosecution, but which had been deferred from earlier decisions on admissibility of evidence in late 2013.[173] The document was a written statement from a witness not present before the Chamber and, thus, related to Rule 68(a). The Majority (Judge Steiner dissenting) found that Rule 68(a), in accordance with Art. 69(2) RS, only allowed the admission of a non-present witness's written statement if both the Prosecution and the Defense had the opportunity to examine the witness during the recording of the statement. As the Defense had not had such opportunity in this case, the Majority found that the requirements of Rule 68(a) were not met and rejected the admission of the document.[174] At present, there is no publicly available version of Judge Steiner's dissenting opinion.

6.4.2.4.6   *Retroactive Application of Rule 68?*

Although the admission of the document was ultimately rejected, the decision of the majority shows that such admission was considered under the old

---

169 *Prosecutor v Bemba Gombo* (Public Redacted Version of "Decision on the admission into evidence of items deferred in the Chamber's previous decisions, items related to the testimony of Witness CHM-01 and written statements of witnesses who provided testimony before the Chamber") ICC-01/05-01/08-3019-Red, T Ch III (26 August 2014) para. 87.

170 Like in *Prosecutor v Bemba Gombo* (Order on the procedure relating to the submission of evidence) ICC-01/05-01/08-1470, T Ch III (31 May 2011) para. 11.

171 *Prosecutor v Bemba Gombo* (Public Redacted Version of "Decision on the admission into evidence of items deferred in the Chamber's previous decisions, items related to the testimony of Witness CHM-01 and written statements of witnesses who provided testimony before the Chamber") ICC-01/05-01/08-3019-Red, T Ch III (26 August 2014) para. 87.

172 CAR-OTP-0069-0083_R01.

173 *Prosecutor v Bemba Gombo* (Public Redacted Version of "Decision on the admission into evidence of items deferred in the Chamber's previous decisions, items related to the testimony of Witness CHM-01 and written statements of witnesses who provided testimony before the Chamber") ICC-01/05-01/08-3019-Red, T Ch III (26 August 2014).

174 *Ibid* para. 34.

version of Rule 68. Indeed, despite the fact that there is no discussion of the matter in the body of the decision, in two foot notes the Chamber made it very clear that it was required to decide the motion under the original Rule.

In particular, the Chamber acknowledged that Rule 68 had been amended, but it also noted that the amended rule cannot be applied retroactively to the detriment of the person who is being investigated or prosecuted. Consequently in the case at hand, the Chamber applied the unamended Rule 68.[175] This issue will be further explored below.

6.4.3   ICC Practice: Amended Rule 68

In accordance with Article 51(1)RS, amendments to the ICC RPE enter into force upon adoption by a two-thirds majority of the members of the ASP.[176] The amendments to Rule 68 were adopted on 27 November 2013, and are in force as of that date. Whether or not the amended rule can be applied to an ongoing case is unclear and will depend on the circumstances of the case, as will be explained below.

This section will consider the practice on the amended Rule 68 at the ICC. In this regard and where appropriate, it will provide comments and suggestions on its use.

6.4.3.1   Ntaganda

6.4.3.1.1   Rule 68(2)(c) – Deceased Witnesses

New Rule 68(2)(c) – concerning deceased witnesses and based on ICTY Rule 92*quater* – was discussed during the confirmation of charges in *Ntaganda*. In a Defense request of 6 February 2014, it was claimed that it would be unfair to refer a case to trial on the basis of elements that could not be used in the continuation of the proceedings – namely the prior recorded testimonies of four now-deceased witnesses. The Defense referred to the jurisprudence of the ICTY (*Šešelj*),[177] arguing that in the case of deceased witnesses whose state-

---

175   *Ibid* footnote 88 and 111.
176   The ASP is the management oversight and legislative body of the International Criminal Court. It is composed of representatives of the States that are party to the Rome Statute. According to article 112 (7), each State Party has one vote and every effort has to be made to reach decisions by consensus both in the Assembly and the Bureau. If consensus cannot be reached, decisions are taken by vote.
177   *Prosecutor v Šešelj* (Redacted version of the "Decision on the prosecution's consolidated motion pursuant to Rules 89 (F), 92 bis, 92 ter and 92 quater of the Rules of Procedure and Evidence" filed confidentially on 7 January 2008) IT-03-67-T, T Ch III (21 February 2008) para. 41, as cited in *Prosecutor v Ntaganda* (Prosecution's Response to the « Requête de la Défense relative à l'admissibilité de certains éléments de preuve que le Procureur entend présenter à l'audience de confirmation des charges et en radiation de certaines parties

ment directly implicates the responsibility of the accused, it is in the interests of justice not to allow applications by the Prosecution for admissibility of written statements.[178]

The Prosecution's response took a different interpretation, recalling that in *Šešelj*, 'the Trial Chamber had held that retroactive application of rule 92quater (similar to rule 68) was permissible and did not prejudice the accused. In that case, rule 92quater came into effect on 13 September 2006, while the trial began in December 2007; therefore, the accused was on notice of the new rule'.[179] The Prosecution argued that the evidence in question was relevant and probative to the issues in the case at hand, and that its admission would not unfairly prejudice the Defense. Regarding the applicability of Rule 68, the Prosecution argued that it would be applicable: "the recent amendment to rule 68, which took effect on 27 November 2013, specifically provides for the admission of the prior statements of deceased individuals at trial, which is equally applicable at the confirmation hearing stage. Pursuant to article 51(2) of the Statute, amendments to the Rules of Procedure and Evidence enter into force immediately upon their adoption by the Assembly of States Parties. This new amendment came into effect prior to the presentation of the evidence to the Pre-Trial Chamber and the Defense was on notice of the new rule and not prejudiced by it".[180]

The decision of the single judge on evidence from deceased witnesses was that the fact of not being able to examine these witnesses at trial does not 'in and of itself warrant the exclusion of the evidence concerned for the purposes of the article 61(7) decision'.[181] The Judge noted that Article 61(5) RS allows the Prosecution to present at the pre-trial stage documentary or summary evidence, and that this may include statements and material pertaining to

---

　　　du Document contenant les charges ») ICC-01/04-02/06-269, Prosecution (3 March 2014) footnote 11.
178　*Prosecutor v Ntaganda* (Prosecution's Response to the « Requête de la Défense relative à l'admissibilité de certains éléments de preuve que le Procureur entend présenter à l'audience de confirmation des charges et en radiation de certaines parties du Document contenant les charges ») ICC-01/04-02/06-269, Prosecution (3 March 2014) para. 27 : « Or, il serait inéquitable de renvoyer à procès une affaire sur la base d'éléments qui ne pourraient être utilisés au procès. À cet égard, la Défense se réfère à la jurisprudence du TPIY qui dispose que s'agissant des témoins décédés dont la déclaration met directement en cause la responsabilité de l'Accusé, il est dans l'intérêt de la justice de ne pas faire droit aux demandes d'admission de déclarations écrites de l'Accusation ».
179　*Ibid* footnote 69 (refering to Prosecutor v *Šešelj*, paras 33–37).
180　*Ibid* paras 48–49.
181　*Prosecutor v Ntaganda* (Decision on Admissibility of Evidence and Other Procedural Matters) ICC-01/04-02/06-308, PT Ch II (8 June 2014).

deceased persons. Furthermore, the Judge noted that Article 61(5) RS does not make the presentation of such evidence contingent upon the availability of the witnesses at trial and affirmed that 'while it would be ideal if the Prosecutor's evidentiary basis of the case stays the same throughout the stages of the proceedings, the Statute does not establish such a stringent requisite'. Finally, the Single Judge agreed with the Prosecution 'that the rights of the Defense are not infringed, as it could still have challenged the evidence in question during the Hearing through other means'.[182]

6.4.3.2 Lubanga Dyilo
6.4.3.2.1 Rule 68(2)(c) – Unavailable Witnesses

At around the same time in the first half of 2014, Rule 68(2)(c) was also under discussion in the *Lubanga Dyilo* appeal, although this time it was the Defense seeking the admission of evidence from an unavailable witness. The Defense had sought to maintain contact with a witness, who had informed that he would soon leave its place of habitual residence to find a job in a remote location where it would be difficult to contact him. The Defense had also been informed that the witness was working in a gold mining quarry in a locality difficult to access and outside of cell phone coverage. The Defense had attempted to regain contact with the witness through his family and friends and had attempted physically to locate the witness in the field, but unsuccessfully. Thus, the Defense renounced the request to call the witness to testify and instead sought to invoke Rule 68(2)(c) for the admission of the witness's signed written statement and its elector card, on the grounds that they had made every effort to locate the witness who was, in spite of all attempts, unavailable to testify.[183]

The Prosecution opposed the admission under Rule 68(2)(c),[184] arguing that the documents lacked the sufficient indicia of reliability needed to meet the requirements of Rule 68(2)(c). The Prosecution claimed that Rule 68 presumes a minimum probative value and quality for documents before they are admitted as evidence, but that this witness's statement was "cursory and lacks detail, and only makes bald assertions with little or no verifiable independent support. The statement fails to address fundamental questions such as: how he obtained his electoral card and in particular how he proved his age at that time to the electoral officials – including whether he had any other documentation

---

182 *Ibid* para. 31.
183 *Prosecutor v Lubanga Dyilo* (Requête de la Défense aux fins d'admission en preuve des éléments relatifs à D-0041) ICC-01/04-01/06-3088, Defense (12 May 2014) para. 31.
184 *Prosecutor v Lubanga Dyilo* (Prosecution's Response to « Requête de la Défense aux fins d'admission en preuve des éléments relatifs à D-0041 ») ICC-01/04-01/06-3091, Prosecution (14 May 2014).

(which has not been tendered by the Defense) or whether he simply provided his own verbal confirmation of his purported age; and what, if any, additional support he can provide as to his age; the dates and manner in which he joined the UPC/FPLC; his role in that armed group; what he was doing in the location where the video was shot and additional questions aimed at establishing that he is indeed the person portrayed in the video. In relation to the electoral card itself, there is no information on the nature of the corroborating evidence, if any, that was provided to obtain it".[185]

6.4.4 ICC Current Position on Rule 68(2)(c)

6.4.4.1 Al Hassan

In 2021 in the case of *Al Hassan*, Trial Chamber X clarified that three requirements must be met for the introduction of the previously recorded testimony of a witness who is not present before such Chamber to be allowed pursuant to Rule 68(2)(c).[186] These requirements are that (i) the prior recorded testimony comes from a person who has died, must be presumed dead, or is, due to obstacles that cannot be overcome with reasonable diligence, unavailable to testify orally; (ii) the necessity of measures under Article 56 of the Statute could not have been anticipated; and (iii) the prior recorded testimony has sufficient indicia of reliability.[187]

ICC Chambers have taken a rather broad approach to the last requirement, retaining discretion to consider those factors that may be relevant to its determination on a case-by-case basis.[188] This requirement is also the most interesting for Defense Council. In this regard, Judge Henderson expressed concerns about the practice of "admitting prior recorded testimony, especially if no

---

185 *Ibid* para. 14.
186 *Prosecutor v Al Hassan* (Public redacted version of "Decision on the introduction into evidence of P-0570's prior recorded testimony pursuant to Rule 68(2)(c) of the Rules") ICC-01/12-01/18-1588-Red, T Ch X (11 August 2021); *Prosecutor v Al Hassan* (Decision on the introduction into evidence of P-0125's prior recorded testimony pursuant to Rule 68(2)(c) of the Rules) ICC-01/12-01/18-1413-Conf, T Ch X (14 April 2014).
187 *Prosecutor v Al Hassan* (Public redacted version of "Decision on the introduction into evidence of P-0570's prior recorded testimony pursuant to Rule 68(2)(c) of the Rules") ICC-01/12-01/18-1588-Red, T Ch X (11 August 2021); *Prosecutor v Al Hassan* (Decision on the introduction into evidence of P-0125's prior recorded testimony pursuant to Rule 68(2)(c) of the Rules) ICC-01/12-01/18-1413-Conf, T Ch X (14 April 2014).
188 *Prosecutor v Gbagbo and Blé Goudé* (Judgment on the appeals of Mr Laurent Gbagbo and Mr Charles Blé Goudé against the decision of Trial Chamber I of 9 June 2016 entitled "Decision on the Prosecutor's application to introduce prior recorded testimony under Rules 68(2)(b) and 68(3)", 1 November 2016) ICC-02/11-01/15-744, A Ch (1 November 2016) para. 103.

effort is made to filter out statements that do not provide minimum indicia of trustworthiness".[189] In his view, one should be very careful when examining prior recorded testimony under Rule 68(2)-(3) and, thus, there should be no presumption of reliability and credibility, as witnesses may change their testimony more or less significantly when examined by the Defense.[190] Judge Henderson also stressed that, in relation to prior recorded testimony under Rule 68(2), factors that deserve particular attention are the extent to which the examiner probed the witness's account and his or her interest in the case, as well as "whether or not the examiner made a genuine effort to ensure that the witness provided all relevant information and not only the facts that may have been supportive of the examining party's case. Where the evidence relates to contested facts, if certain critical questions that might have cast the testimony in a different light were not asked".[191]

In a Decision from April 2021, after recalling the *Gbagbo and Ble Goudé* Appeal judgment that trial chambers are not obliged to consider factors beyond formal requirements pursuant to Rule 68(2)(b)(i) when assessing indicia of reliability,[192] the *Al Hassan* Trial Chamber established that a statement taken in the ordinary course of the OTP investigations, given voluntarily and in the presence of a qualified interpreter, and declared to be accurate by the witness, bore "sufficient indicia of reliability of formal nature and was not so manifestly unbelievable or incoherent so as to make it unsuitable for introduction under Rule 68(2)(c)".[193]

---

189 *Prosecutor v Gbagbo and Blé Goudé* (Public Redacted Version of Reasons of Judge Geoffrey Henderson) ICC-02/11-01/15-1263-AnxB-Red, T Ch I (16 July 2019) para. 39.
190 *Ibid.*
191 *Ibid* para. 40.
192 *Prosecutor v Gbagbo and Blé Goudé* (Judgment on the appeals of Mr Laurent Gbagbo and Mr Charles Blé Goudé against the decision of Trial Chamber I of 9 June 2016 entitled "Decision on the Prosecutor's application to introduce prior recorded testimony under Rules 68(2)(b) and 68(3)", 1 November 2016) ICC-02/11-01/15-744, A Ch (1 November 2016) paras 3, 103–104; *Prosecutor v Al Hassan* (Public redacted version of "Decision on the introduction into evidence of P-0570's prior recorded testimony pursuant to Rule 68(2)(c) of the Rules") ICC-01/12-01/18-1588-Red, T Ch X (11 August 2021), where the Chamber expressly endorsed the view that this finding "equally applies to the assessment of indicia of reliability for prior recorded testimony sought to be introduced under Rule 68(2)(c)". Cf. Also *Prosecutor v Yekatom and Ngaïssona* (First Decision on the Prosecution Requests for Formal Submission of Prior Recorded Testimonies pursuant to Rule 68(2)(c) of the Rules) ICC-01/14-01/18-1975-Red, T Ch V (12 July 2023) paras 33–34.
193 *Prosecutor v Al Hassan* (Decision on the introduction into evidence of P-0125's prior recorded testimony pursuant to Rule 68(2)(c) of the Rules) ICC-01/12-01/18-1413-Conf, T Ch X (14 April 2014).

According to the Appeals Chamber in *Gbagbo and Ble Goudé*, the reason why the assessment of indicia of reliability can be more cursory in nature is because factors like the internal consistency of the statement or its consistency with other evidence contained in the record may still be considered when assessing the probative value of the evidence.[194] In this regard, the Trial Chamber in *Al Hassan* – also endorsing the submission model to the admission of evidence[195] – recalled that "the full consideration of the standard evidentiary criteria for material introduced into evidence, in particular in terms of its relevance and probative value, is deferred to its eventual deliberation for its judgment".[196] In this regard, the absence of cross-examination is a factor to be considered "in the Chamber's ultimate assessment of the probative value and weight, if any, to be attributed to the material, especially where inconsistencies are identified. Similarly, the extent to which a prior statement is corroborated by other evidence is also important in determining the weight to be accorded to it in the final judgment".[197]

Identical considerations apply to the associated material that the Prosecution seek to introduce such as handwritten notes, video excerpts, and photographs. In a Decision from April 2021 in *Al Hassan*, the associated material had been presented to and discussed by the witness, at least to a certain extent; accordingly, the Chamber considered that "the associated material identified by the Prosecution can be introduced into evidence via this witness pursuant to Rule 68(2)(c). The absence of cross-examination, which is due to the witness's unavailability, is a factor which will be considered by the Chamber in its

---

194 *Prosecutor v Gbagbo and Blé Goudé* (Judgment on the appeals of Mr Laurent Gbagbo and Mr Charles Blé Goudé against the decision of Trial Chamber I of 9 June 2016 entitled "Decision on the Prosecutor's application to introduce prior recorded testimony under Rules 68(2)(b) and 68(3)", 1 November 2016) ICC-02/11-01/15-744, A Ch (1 November 2016) paras 3 and 104.

195 *Prosecutor v Al Hassan* (Annex A to the Decision on the conduct of proceedings) ICC-01/12-01/18-789-AnxA, T Ch X (6 May 2020) para. 34.

196 *Prosecutor v Al Hassan* (Public redacted version of "Decision on the introduction into evidence of P-0570's prior recorded testimony pursuant to Rule 68(2)(c) of the Rules") ICC-01/12-01/18-1588-Red, T Ch X (11 August 2021).

197 *Ibid*; *Prosecutor v Al Hassan* (Decision on the introduction into evidence of P-0125's prior recorded testimony pursuant to Rule 68(2)(c) of the Rules) ICC-01/12-01/18-1413-Conf, T Ch X (14 April 2014); *Prosecutor v Ntaganda* (Public redacted version of Judgment on the appeals of Mr Bosco Ntaganda and the Prosecutor against the decision of Trial Chamber VI of 8 July 2019 entitled 'Judgment') ICC-01/04-02/06-2666-Red, A Ch (30 March 2021) para. 630.

ultimate assessment of the probative value and weight, if any, to be attributed to this evidence".[198]

Furthermore, the *Al Hassan and Said* Trial Chambers noted that under Rule 68(1) the introduction of prior recorded testimony must not be prejudicial to or inconsistent with the rights of the accused.[199] In this regard, the Appeals Chamber had previously held that 'a cautious assessment' is required in assessing prejudice, and that a chamber may take into account 'a number of factors, including the following: (i) whether the evidence relates to issues that are not materially in dispute; (ii) whether that evidence is not central to core issues in the case, but only provides relevant background information; and (iii) whether the evidence is corroborative of other evidence'".[200]

In a Decision from August 2021, the *Al Hassan* Trial Chamber noted that the fact that a testimony concerned matters which were materially in dispute did not bar its introduction under Rule 68(2)(c).[201] By contrast, this was merely one of the factors to be taken into account in the exercise of its discretion. In addition to this, the statement did not go to the acts and conduct of the accused,

---

198   *Prosecutor v Al Hassan* (Decision on the introduction into evidence of P-0125's prior recorded testimony pursuant to Rule 68(2)(c) of the Rules) ICC-01/12-01/18-1413-Conf, T Ch X (14 April 2014).

199   *Prosecutor v Al Hassan* (Public redacted version of "Decision on the introduction into evidence of P-0570's prior recorded testimony pursuant to Rule 68(2)(c) of the Rules") ICC-01/12-01/18-1588-Red, T Ch X (11 August 2021); *Prosecutor v Said* (Public Redacted Version of Decision on the Prosecution's Request under Rule 68(2)(c) to Introduce the Prior Recorded Testimony of Six Witnesses) ICC-01-14-01-21-506-RED, T Ch VI (26 October 2022) para. 22. Cf. Also *Prosecutor v Yekatom and Ngaïssona* (First Decision on the Prosecution Requests for Formal Submission of Prior Recorded Testimonies pursuant to Rule 68(2)(c) of the Rules) ICC-01/14-01/18-1975-Red, T Ch V (12 July 2023) para. 35.

200   *Prosecutor v Said* (Public Redacted Version of Decision on the Prosecution's Request under Rule 68(2)(c) to Introduce the Prior Recorded Testimony of Six Witnesses) ICC-01-14-01-21-506-RED, T Ch VI (26 October 2022) para. 22; *Prosecutor v Bemba Gombo* (Judgment on the appeals of Mr Jean-Pierre Bemba Gombo and the Prosecutor against the decision of Trial Chamber III entitled "Decision on the admission into evidence of materials contained in the prosecution's list of evidence") ICC-01/05-01/08-1386, A Ch (3 May 2011) para. 78; *Prosecutor v Al Hassan* (Public redacted version of "Decision on the introduction into evidence of P-0570's prior recorded testimony pursuant to Rule 68(2)(c) of the Rules") ICC-01/12-01/18-1588-Red, T Ch X (11 August 2021). Cf. Also *Prosecutor v Yekatom and Ngaïssona* (First Decision on the Prosecution Requests for Formal Submission of Prior Recorded Testimonies pursuant to Rule 68(2)(c) of the Rules) ICC-01/14-01/18-1975-Red, T Ch V (12 July 2023) para. 36.

201   *Prosecutor v Al Hassan* (Public redacted version of "Decision on the introduction into evidence of P-0570's prior recorded testimony pursuant to Rule 68(2)(c) of the Rules") ICC-01/12-01/18-1588-Red, T Ch X (11 August 2021).

and most of it was of a cumulative or corroborative nature.[202] On the other hand, in a Decision from October 2022 in *Said*, the statement did go to proof of acts and conduct of the accused as the witness provided information regarding his interactions with the accused, as well as his role and activities.[203] Moreover, "the witness also provides information related to the accused's usual attire, the vehicle he drove and his place of residence, which, in the view of the Chamber, could be relevant to establishing the 'acts and conduct' of the accused".[204]

In this regard, in February 2021 in *Abd-Al-Rahman*, the Trial Chamber had observed that "Rule 68(2)(c)(ii) also provides that the fact that the prior recorded testimony goes to proof of acts and conduct of the accused may be a factor against its introduction, or part of it".[205] As to the concept of 'acts and conduct', the Trial Chamber in *Ntaganda* affirmed that "refers to the personal actions and omissions of the accused, which are described in the charges against him or her or which are otherwise relied upon to establish his or her criminal responsibility for the crimes charged".[206] Nevertheless, in *Said*, the Chamber noted that the amount of information that may directly relate to the criminal responsibility of the accused was extremely limited, as well as cumulative and corroborative in nature.[207] Indeed, "in line with the Appeals Chamber's pronouncement on the assessment of prejudice to the accused under rule 68(1) of the Rules, the Chamber may have regard to whether the prior recorded testimony is corroborated by other evidence, but also more

---

202   *Ibid.*
203   *Prosecutor v Said* (Public Redacted Version of Decision on the Prosecution's Request under Rule 68(2)(c) to Introduce the Prior Recorded Testimony of Six Witnesses) ICC-01-14-01-21-506-RED, T Ch VI (26 October 2022) para. 46.
204   *Ibid.*
205   *Prosecutor v Abd-Al-Rahman* (Public redacted version of the Decision on the Prosecution's request to introduce prior recorded testimonies under Rule 68(2)(c)) ICC-02/05-01/20-603-Red, T Ch I (21 February 2022) para. 7; *Prosecutor v Yekatom and Ngaïssona* (First Decision on the Prosecution Requests for Formal Submission of Prior Recorded Testimonies pursuant to Rule 68(2)(c) of the Rules) ICC-01/14-01/18-1975-Red, T Ch V (12 July 2023) para. 38.
206   *Prosecutor v Ntaganda* (Public redacted version of 'Decision on admission of prior recorded testimony of Witness P-0773 under Rule 68', 2 December 2016, ICC-01/04-02/06-1667-Conf) ICC-01/04-02/06-1667-Red, T Ch VI (27 February 2017) para. 11; *Prosecutor v Ongwen* (Decision on the Prosecution's Applications for Introduction of Prior Recorded Testimony under Rule 68(2)(b) of the Rules) ICC-02/04-01/15-596-Red, T Ch IX (18 November 2016) paras 11–12; *Prosecutor v Yekatom and Ngaïssona* (First Decision on the Prosecution Requests for Formal Submission of Prior Recorded Testimonies pursuant to Rule 68(2)(c) of the Rules) ICC-01/14-01/18-1975-Red, T Ch V (12 July 2023) para. 39.
207   *Prosecutor v Said* (Public Redacted Version of Decision on the Prosecution's Request under Rule 68(2)(c) to Introduce the Prior Recorded Testimony of Six Witnesses) ICC-01-14-01-21-506-RED, T Ch VI (26 October 2022) para. 46.

broadly whether the testimony is cumulative of other evidence of similar facts. The purpose of the assessment is to inform the Chamber's exercise of discretion in determining whether prior recorded testimony should be introduced under rule 68(2)(c) of the Rules. In light of this purpose and at this stage in the proceedings, the Chamber considers that this assessment is possible only at a general level in relation to broad themes discussed by the witness. The Chamber underlines that this assessment does not predetermine or inform the manner in which this evidence may subsequently be weighed and used for the purposes of its decision under article 74 of the Statute".[208]

Therefore, for evidence to be introduced pursuant to Rule 68(2)(c), the *prima facie* probative value of the material must outweigh potential prejudice that the admission may cause to the fair trial rights of the accused.

The court may also allow a party to recall its witness. However, recall is only granted in the most compelling circumstances, where the evidence is of significant probative value and not of a cumulative nature.[209]

In the *Al Hassan* case, the court decided that Rule 68(2)(1) of the ICC RPE shall not be transformed into a loophole to circumvent the procedural requirements under Rule 68(2)(b) (i.e. certification of prior recorded statement).[210] Further, it holds that a witness's simple unwillingness to testify, or refusal to provide the declaration required under Rule 68(2)(b)(ii), is not sufficient to conclude that a witness is 'unavailable' under Rule 68(2)(c).

6.4.4.2 Ruto and Sang
6.4.4.2.1 *Rule 68(2)(d) – Witnesses Subject to Interference*

Since the amendments to Rule 68 ICC RPE, the possibility of using the provisions of new Rule 68(2)(d) (based on ICTY's Rule 92*quinquies* and concerning witnesses who have been subjected to interference) has been discussed in cases related to the Situation in Kenya. During a Status conference in *Ruto and Sang*, the Prosecution argued in favour of the ICC having the power to subpoena witnesses, claiming that it had a good-faith basis for its belief that

---

208 *Ibid* para. 25; *Prosecutor v Al Hassan* (Public redacted version of "Decision on the introduction into evidence of P-0570's prior recorded testimony pursuant to Rule 68(2)(c) of the Rules") ICC-01/12-01/18-1588-Red, T Ch X (11 August 2021).

209 *Prosecutor v Al Hassan* (Public Redacted Version of 'Decision on Defence application to exclude the evidence of or recall P-0547') ICC-01/12-01/18-2344-Red, T Ch X (21 September 2022) para. 34.

210 *Prosecutor v Al Hassan* (Decision on the Defence's request for variation of the time limit related to the accompanying declarations of Rule 68(2)(b) witnesses and the introduction into evidence of the prior recorded testimony of D-0002 and D-0146 pursuant to Rule 68(2)(c) of the Rules) ICC-01/12-01/18-2445-Red, T Ch X (16 December 2022) paras 22–23.

the original statements deposed to by these witnesses represented truthful accounts and that any subsequent denials or recantations would be false and caused by '*intimidation, bribery or other improper influence*'.

Rule 68(2)(d) might most commonly be expected to be used to admit prior recorded testimony of a witness who does not later testify due to interference. However in this case, the Prosecution seemed to envisage also using the rule to admit prior recorded testimony of a witness who does testify in person but who 'fails to give evidence with respect to material aspects included in his or her prior recorded testimony'. This would not be known until after the actual testimony, meaning that a motion to admit the prior recorded testimony would follow the testimony in person. As the Prosecution referred to interrogating the witness on the discrepancy, this would presumably require recalling the witness for further questioning. This may well assist the Court in its truth-seeking mandate, but is hardly in line with the aim of using Rule 68 to streamline evidence.

In its written submissions on the same issue of witness compellability, the Prosecution stated: "moreover, the Prosecution has informed the Court and the Defense in advance of the probability that some of the witnesses are likely to testify to the contrary of a prior statement, therefore enabling the Court to satisfy itself of the absence of any improper motive and to intervene if necessary. Moreover, rule 68(2) of the ICC Rules, as with ICTY rule 92*quinquies* adopted after the *Popovic* Appeals Decision, specifically permits the admission of the prior recorded testimony of a witness who has been subjected to interference".[211]

On 10 June 2014, a decision was released by the *Ruto and Sang* Trial Chamber that tangentially referred to Rule 68, although without mentioning whether the reference was either to the original or to the amended version of the rule.[212] The decision followed a Prosecution's request for admission of documentary evidence, initially filed on 19 July 2013 as a bar table application under Article 64(9) to tender 49 items into evidence without introducing them through a witness.[213] Following a direction from the Chamber, the Prosecution re-filed its application on 2 December 2013 – namely after the

---

211   *Prosecutor v Ruto and Sang* (Prosecution's further submissions pursuant to the Prosecution's request under article 64(6)(b) and article 93 to summon witnesses) ICC-01/09-01/11-1202, Prosecution (4 March 2014) para. 34.

212   *Prosecutor v Ruto and Sang* (Decision on the Prosecution's Request for Admission of Documentary Evidence) ICC-01/09-01/11-1353, T Ch V(A) (10 June 2014).

213   *Prosecutor v Ruto and Sang* (Prosecution's Application for Admission of Documents from the Bar Table Pursuant to Article 64(9)) ICC-01/09-01/11-819, Prosecution (19 July 2013).

Rule 68 amendment.[214] Neither Prosecution application makes reference to Rule 68.

Nonetheless, the Chamber took the opportunity in its decision[215] to discuss both the general rules of admissibility and to make some comments relevant to Rule 68. The Chamber considered that the general rule of admissibility may be simply stated as follows: "all prima facie relevant evidence is admissible subject to the Chamber's discretion to exclude relevant evidence by operation of the provisions of the Statute or the Rules or by virtue of general principles of national or international law pursuant to Article 21 of the Statute".[216]

Specifically on Rule 68, the Chamber noted that this Rule, together with Article 69(2)RS, set out a distinct regime in respect of the 'testimony' of a witness and stated that it would consider whether the material the Prosecution sought to admit may more properly be considered as potentially falling within that regime.[217] The Chamber reiterated that a 'bar table' motion should not be used in a manner which would be duplicative of the Rule 68 and considered that some of the material tendered by the Prosecution for admission was testimonial in nature. With regard to three of the documents, the Chamber rejected them on the grounds that they should have been submitted under Rule 68. Unlike the aforementioned ICTY Chamber in *Tolimir*, the Chamber did not proceed to consider admission under Rule 68, but merely denied the admission under the provision by which its admission had been sought (Article 64(9)).

Among other conditions, Rule 68(2)(d) requires the Chamber to be satisfied that i) the person has failed to attend as a witness or, having attended, has failed to give evidence with respect to a material aspect included in his or her prior recorded testimony; and that ii) the failure of the person to attend or to give evidence has been materially influenced by improper interference, including threats, intimidation, or coercion.[218] In this regard, the question that arises is whether in-Court testimony which deviates from prior recorded testimony may fall within the scope of Rule 68(2)(d).

Based on the drafting history of the Rule and the jurisprudence of the ICC, the answer to this question should be in the negative, as such an interpretation would defeat the object and purpose of Rule 68(2)(d). This conclusion can

---

214 *Ibid.*
215 *Prosecutor v Ruto and Sang* (Decision on the Prosecution's Request for Admission of Documentary Evidence) ICC-01/09-01/11-1353, T Ch V(A) (10 June 2014).
216 *Ibid* para. 15.
217 *Ibid* para. 25.
218 'Working Group on Lessons Learnt: Second Report of the Court to the Assembly of States Parties' (International Criminal Court 2013) ICC-ASP/12/37/Add.1, para. 26.

be drawn from the Second Report of the Working Group on Lessons Learned, which explains that the amendments to Rule 68 are intended to reduce the length of ICC proceedings and to streamline the presentation of evidence.[219] Thus, to endorse the view that 68(2)(d) could apply to cases in which the witness is present before the Chamber, but the in-Court testimony deviates from the previously recorded one, would render the Trial more complex and time-consuming, contrary to the recommendations expressed by the Working Group in the Report. Moreover, this would mean that in the record different versions of one witness evidence would appear.

As recalled in the Report of the Working Group, Article 69(2) RS provides: "The testimony of a witness at trial shall be given in person, except to the extent provided by the measures set forth in article 68 or in the Rules of Procedure and Evidence."[220] Furthermore, "In rule 68(2)(c) and rule 68(2)(d), the introduction of prior recorded testimony that goes to the proof of the acts or conduct of the accused is discouraged, although it is not prohibited. This distinction is justified by the fact that it is not possible to call a witness to provide testimony regarding acts and conduct of the accused under rules 68(2)(c) and 68(2)(d), given that those sub-rules apply to unavailable and intimidated witnesses respectively. In contrast, a rule 68(2)(b) witness could potentially be called to the seat of the Court".[221]

As a result, where the witness is present to give testimony before the Chamber, there is no reason why Rule 68(2)(d) should apply, contrary to what the Prosecution submitted in *Ruto and Sang*. Indeed, in this case several witnesses recanted the contents of the statements made to the Prosecution, which the latter had intended to use at trial.[222] Therefore, the Prosecution argued that the Chamber should admit the prior recorded statements of prior interviews of missing and recanting witnesses who succumbed to improper influences.[223] In this regard, the Prosecution stated: "Each of the [REDACTED] Witnesses recanted material portions of [REDACTED] Prior Recorded Testimony and was declared hostile by the Chamber. There is sufficient evidence to satisfy the Chamber that these witnesses were subjected to improper influence and that this materially affected [REDACTED] decision to withdraw as a witness

---

219   *Ibid* para. 8.
220   *Ibid* para. 4 (footnote 4).
221   *Ibid* para. 15.
222   *Prosecutor v Ruto and Sang* (Public redacted version of "Prosecution's request for the admission of prior recorded testimony of [REDACTED] witnesses", 29 April 2015, ICC-01/09-01/11-1866-Conf + Annexes) ICC-01/09-01/11-1866-Red, Prosecution (21 May 2015) para. 10.
223   *Ibid* para. 3.

and, [REDACTED], to fail to give evidence with respect to material aspects of [REDACTED] Prior Recorded Testimony".[224]

The majority of the Trial Chamber admitted the evidence under 68(2)(c)-(d) on the ground, inter alia, that "the witness was the subject of improper interference and that this interference materially influenced the evidence provided by [REDACTED], including, in particular, the explanation given by the witness for diverging from the prior recorded testimony".[225] In reaching its conclusion, the Chamber noted that "although the Defense has contested the motivations, truthfulness and overall reliability of these, it has not contested either the relevance or authenticity of the testimonies and accompanying annexes sought to be admitted. Moreover, as noted above in the analysis related to the indicia of reliability of the prior recorded testimonies, the Chamber is of the view that these have prima facie probative value. Given that reliability is a component of probative value, the Chamber does not consider it necessary to re-conduct that assessment once the requirements of Rule 68 of the Rules have been met.

Moreover, as discussed above, the Chamber considers that their prima facie probative value outweighs any prejudicial effect caused to the accused. In this regard, the Chamber emphasises that 'its assessment of evidence for the purpose of admissibility is a distinct question from the evidentiary weight which the Chamber may ultimately attach to admitted evidence in its final assessment once the entire case record is before it, for the purpose of the verdict in the case'. Accordingly, the objections and considerations made by the Defense to the Request, may be taken into account by the Chamber in the ultimate assessment as to the weight of the admitted prior recorded testimonies".[226]

Judge Eboe-Osuji appended a Separate, partly concurring opinion to the Decision of the majority, where he stated: "I am not convinced that r 68 (old or new) is applicable for purposes of admissibility of the out-of-court statements for the truth of their contents. There are two main reasons why, and neither has much to do with considerations of retroactivity of the new rule 68.2 First, it seems to me that the overall intendment of r 68 is to make trials simpler and

---

224   *Ibid* para. 5. For the position of the Defense, *Prosecutor v Ruto and Sang* (Public redacted version of "Corrigendum of Ruto Defense response to the 'Prosecution's request for the admission of prior recorded testimony of [REDACTED] witnesses'", 12 June 2015, ICC-01/0901/11-1908-Conf) ICC-01/09-01/11-1908-Corr-Red, Defense (23 June 2015); *Prosecutor v Ruto and Sang* (Public Redacted Version of Corrigendum to Sang Defense Response to Prosecution's Request for the Admission of Prior Recorded Testimony of [Redacted] Witnesses, filed on 12 June 2015) ICC-01/09-01/11-1911-Corr-Red, Defense (30 June 2015).

225   *Prosecutor v Ruto and Sang* (Public redacted version of Decision on Prosecution Request for Admission of Prior Recorded Testimony) ICC-01/09-01/11-1938-Corr-Red, T Ch v(A) (19 August 2015) para. 79.

226   *Ibid* para. 151.

shorter, not longer and more complicated. The intendment, as it appears to me, is that to admit into the trial record materials that meet the test of 'testimony' will hopefully make proceedings simpler and shorter, by avoiding reasonable disagreements as to admissibility and forensic value. It is for that reason that the drafters of the new rule went to great lengths to circumscribe the circumstances under which prior recorded 'testimony' is admissible into trials. To a similar effect may be noted the repeated indication that '[t]he fact that the prior recorded testimony goes to proof of acts and conduct of an accused may be a factor against its introduction, or part of it.'4 In my view, there is great salutary potential for r 68 in circumstances other than those implicated in the present litigation".[227]

Regarding the second reason, Judge Eboe-Osuji explained: "I am aware that the new r 68(2)(b)(ii) provides that 'prior recorded testimony falling under sub-rule (b) may only be introduced if it is accompanied by a declaration by the testifying person that the contents of the prior recorded testimony are true and correct to the best of that person's knowledge and belief.

Accompanying declarations may not contain any new information and must be made reasonably close in time to when the prior recorded testimony is being submitted.' It will be tempting to hold this provision up as suggesting that 'testimony' need not be sworn (so to speak), except for purposes of r 68(2)(b). It is an understandable – and reasonable – view. But it is not a conclusive view on the matter, capable of removing all doubts to the effect of diminishing 'testimony' out of its traditional usage. This is why: (i) r 68 does not make sufficiently clear that, for its own purposes, the ordinary meaning of 'testimony' (requiring the element of oath or affirmation) no longer applies; (ii) while r 68 of the Rules of Procedure and Evidence consistently employs the term 'testimony' and not 'statement' in its provisions, there are other provisions in the same the Rules of Procedure and Evidence, specifically r 76, where the term 'statements' has been consistently employed in the usual manner that does not require the element of oath or affirmation; (iii) article 69 of the Rome Statute speaks of the verb 'testifying' and its derivative noun 'testimony', providing that 'before testifying, each witness shall, in accordance with the Rules of Procedure and Evidence, give an undertaking as to the truthfulness of the evidence to be given by that witness', and r 66 specifically provides for the undertaking that each witness must give 'before testifying'—i.e. before giving

---

[227] *Prosecutor v Ruto and Sang* (Separate, Partly Concurring Opinion of Judge Eboe-Osuji on the "Decision on Prosecution Request for Admission of Prior Recorded Testimony") ICC-01/09-01/11-1938-Anx-Red, T Ch v(A) (19 August 2015) para. 18.

their 'testimony'. [Emphases added].[228] Therefore, Judge Eboe-Osuji concluded: "(...) In that context, is not a trifling for the average defendant when the Prosecution seeks to resort to r 68 for purposes of putting incriminatory out-of-court statements into the record. Thus, any reasonable doubt as to what r 68 imports for the average defendant is more acceptably resolved in his or her favour, according to a trite rule".[229]

On 10 September 2015, the Trial Chamber granted the Defense teams of Mr Ruto and Mr Sang leave to appeal on the ground, inter alia, that the Decision erred in its assessment of the concept of 'failure to give evidence with respect to a material aspect' pursuant to Rule 68(2)(d)(i) of the Rules.[230] However, the Appeal Chamber never addressed this issue specifically, as the conclusion reached by such Chamber in relation to the first ground on whether the amended Rule 68 could be applied without offending Articles 24(2) and 51(4) RS absorbed the remaining issues.[231] In this regard, the Appeal Chamber found that "the application of the amended rule resulted in (i) additional exceptions to the principle of orality and restrictions on the right to cross-examine witnesses, and (ii) as a consequence, the admission of evidence, not previously admissible in that form under former rule 68 of the Rules or article 69 (2) and (4) of the Statute which could be used against the accused in an article 74 decision. Considering these disadvantages, the Appeals Chamber finds that the application of this rule negatively affected the overall position of Mr Sang and Mr Ruto in the proceedings at hand. Accordingly, the Appeals Chamber holds that the Trial Chamber applied amended rule 68 of the Rules retroactively to the detriment of the accused".[232]

In conclusion, based on the current normative framework and in light of the Working Group Report in which the drafting history of Rule 68 is outlined, there are arguments to say that Subrule 2(d), through a prior recorded statement, should not apply to the case where the testimony given in court diverges from that previously given; in such a situation, the former should take precedence, even in view of the fact that often only a summary of the previously given testimony is provided without the possibility of verifying the manner in which that testimony was taken. Therefore, caution should be exercised in

---

228   *Ibid* para. 20.
229   *Ibid* para. 21.
230   *Prosecutor v Ruto and Sang* (Judgment on the appeals of Mr William Samoei Ruto and Mr Joshua Arap Sang against the decision of Trial Chamber v(A) of 19 August 2015 entitled "Decision on Prosecution Request for Admission of Prior Recorded Testimony") ICC-01/09-01/11-2024, A Ch (12 February 2016) para. 9.
231   *Ibid* paras 9 and 97.
232   *Ibid* para. 95.

admitting such out-of-court statements. For Defense counsel, it remains relevant to challenge the applicability of rule.68(2)(d) in the event of discrepancies between the trial testimony and the prior recorded statement.

6.4.4.2.2 Admission of Non-ICC Transcripts into Evidence

The Prosecution sought to tender into evidence transcripts from the Commission of Inquiry into the Post-Election Violence (CIPEV). The latter submitted that even though 'some information in these items is "testimonial in nature, it is not 'prior recorded testimony' of a Prosecution witness", pursuant to Rule 68 of the Rules. Rather, the admission of these documents is governed by Articles 64(9) and 69(4) of the Statute'.[233]

The Chamber reiterated its previous Admission Decision holding that 'there is an obvious interest on the part of the accused person to confront any person whose testimony (on the stand or through a document) would implicate an accused in criminal conduct, either directly or indirectly'.[234] Therefore, Trial Chamber V(a) denied the Prosecution's request on the ground that these CIPEV transcripts, 'clearly testimonial in nature, should more appropriately be considered pursuant to Rule 68 of the Rules'.[235]

6.4.4.2.3 Kenyatta

In the *Kenyatta* case, the Legal Representative for Victims (LRV) did not miss the opportunity to express the view that Rule 68(2)(d) should be used in that case. While responding to the Prosecution's application to adjourn the trial date, the LRV stated that in light of the recent rule changes, the Prosecution had a tool at its disposal to deal with the situation of intimidated witnesses who no longer wished to testify and noted that the Prosecution had not disclosed whether or not this avenue was under consideration:

> The Application does not disclose whether the Prosecution has given due consideration to seeking the admission, pursuant to Rule 68(2) of the

---

[233] *Prosecutor v Ruto and Sang* (Public redacted version of "Corrected Version of Prosecution's Application for Admission of Documentary Evidence Related to the Testimony of Witness P-0013",28 October 2014, ICC-01/09-01l11-1619-Conf-Corr) ICC-01/09-01/11-1619, Prosecution (12 November 2014), paras. 2, 6, 9–11.

[234] *Prosecutor v Ruto and Sang* (Decision on the Prosecution's Application for Admission of Documentary Evidence Related to the Testimony of Witness 13) ICC-01/09-01/11-1804, T Ch V(A) (4 February 2015), para. 27; *Prosecutor v Ruto and Sang* (Decision on the Prosecution's Request for Admission of Documentary Evidence) ICC-01/09-01/11-1353, T Ch V(A) (10 June 2014), para. 25.

[235] *Prosecutor v Ruto and Sang* (Decision on the Prosecution's Application for Admission of Documentary Evidence Related to the Testimony of Witness 13) ICC-01/09-01/11-1804, T Ch V(A) (4 February 2015), para. 27.

Rules of Procedure and Evidence ("RPE"), of the evidence of *all* witnesses who have decided not to testify, where their action appears to have been motivated, directly or indirectly, by intimidation. Rule 68 was amended recently by the Assembly of States Parties ("ASP"), in the aftermath of what the Prosecution has described as "unprecedented levels of tampering and anti-witness activity" in the Kenya cases. The high rate of withdrawal of prosecution witnesses in both Kenya cases is not unrelated to that climate of fear: in respect of witness withdrawals in the present case, the Prosecution has frequently referred to fears held by the witnesses. The Application does not clarify the precise nature of the reasons for the withdrawal of P-0011, a key witness. But in the light of the general climate which appears to have influenced many in this case, it appears likely that it might have been influenced, at least in part, by a form of intimidation. It is clearly in the interest of justice for the Prosecution to seek the admission of this witness's evidence under Rule 68(2). It is to be presumed that the ASP did not act in vain, and amended Rule 68 with the intention that it be used in precisely such a situation. The Prosecution has not fully explained its reluctance to use it.[236]

This issue was followed up several weeks later during the status conference:

At the ASP in November 2013, the large Kenyan delegation, including the Attorney General, the Director of Public Prosecutions, the Minister for Foreign Affairs, and the Permanent Representative of Kenya to the United Nations used their status as State representatives to promote those amendments which were favourable to the accused and to oppose amendments to Rule 68, which aims to permit the admission at trial of evidence of a witness who has been bribed, intimidated, or who has disappeared. Why, one might ask, did the Kenyan delegation oppose the new Rule 68 and indeed try to inoculate the two Kenya cases from its effect? Surely the new Rule 68 is a wise response to widespread witness intimidation. Why to oppose it? Instead of acting to secure justice for the victims at the ASP, the accused instead took steps to frustrate their search for the truth. Instead of championing the interests of the victims, he has worked against them.[237]

---

236 *Prosecutor v Kenyatta and Ali* (Victims' response to Prosecution's application for an adjournment of the provisional trial date) ICC-01/09-02/11-879-Red, Victim (13 January 2014), paras 25–28.
237 *Prosecutor v Kenyatta, Muthaura and Ali*, Transcript ICC-01/09-02/11-T-27-ENG, T Ch V(B) (5 February 2014), 22 (lines 9–16).

In the Trial Chamber's decision on the Prosecution's request, a footnote referred to a series of confidential filings where the issue was possibly further addressed.[238] The Trial Chamber, however, merely noted the LRV's statements on Rule 68(2) without addressing them.[239]

6.4.4.3 New Developments on Rule 68(2)(c)

In a Decision of 20 May 2024, the Appeals Chamber in the case of the *Prosecutor v Yekatom and Ngaïssona* rendered a conclusion on Rule 68(2)(c) that might have an adverse effect on the rights of the accused.

In particular, after recalling the Trial Chamber's finding that "the term "unavailable" in rule 68(2)(c) of the Rules "must be interpreted broadly",[240] the Appeals Chamber considered that this notion should be assessed on a case-by-case basis, as it may cover different situations. "In this respect, the Appeals Chamber notes that, as highlighted in the Working Group Report, the reference to "insurmountable obstacles" in a previous draft version of rule 68(2)(c) of the Rules was considered to "import too high a standard", and subsequently replaced with "obstacles that cannot be overcome with reasonable diligence", which may cover not only "the examples that are explicitly" mentioned in the corresponding ICTY Rules of Procedure and Evidence provision, but also "other potential situations that may arise in the course of the Court's work as a permanent institution"".[241] From a practical point of view, this includes, for example, situations in which "a witness cannot be located after numerous attempts and efforts".[242] Moreover, the Appeals Chamber affirmed that the fact that the witness is initially unwilling to testify is not determinative for the interpretation of this Rule. "Instead, the Trial Chamber took into account other factors,

---

[238] *Prosecutor v Kenyatta* (Decision on Prosecution's applications for a finding of non-compliance pursuant to Article 87(7) and for an adjournment of the provisional trial date) ICC-01/09-02/11-908, T Ch V(B) (31 March 2014), Fn. 170; *Prosecutor v Kenyatta and Ali* (Annex: Victims' response to Prosecution's application for an adjournment of the provisional trial date) ICC-01/09-02/11-879-Anx-Red, Victim (13 January 2014).

[239] *Prosecutor v Kenyatta* (Decision on Prosecution's applications for a finding of non-compliance pursuant to Article 87(7) and for an adjournment of the provisional trial date) ICC-01/09-02/11-908, T Ch V(B) (31 March 2014), para. 73: "*The LRV queried whether the Prosecution has given 'due consideration' to using additional powers to address the difficulties encountered, including those under [...] Rule 68(2) of the Rules (prior recorded testimony)...*".

[240] *Prosecutor v Yekatom and Ngaïssona* (Public redacted Judgment on the appeal of Mr Patrice Edouard Ngaïssona against the decision of Trial Chamber V of 6 October 2023 entitled "Third Decision on the Prosecution Requests for Formal Submission of Prior Recorded Testimonies pursuant to Rule 68(2)(c) of the Rules") ICC-01/14-01/18-2502-Red, A Ch (20 May 2024) para. 25.

[241] *Ibid* para. 38.

[242] *Ibid* para. 39.

such as the subsequent inability to locate the witnesses and the absence of any further available information on their potential whereabouts, and concluded that those factors amounted to "obstacles that cannot be overcome with reasonable diligence" within the meaning of rule 68(2)(c) of the Rules".[243] Thus, according to the Chamber, a witness's reluctance or unwillingness to testify does not preclude a finding that the witness is unavailable to testify orally, if it is established that there are other circumstances that cannot be overcome with reasonable diligence.[244]

This interpretation of Rule 68(2)(c) creates a tension from the perspective of the fair trial rights of the accused. Indeed, the unwillingness of a crucial witness for the parties might be legally remedied by a finding that the witness cannot be located after numerous attempts. Therefore, the notion of unwillingness can be easily disguised by the sheer observation that the witness cannot be found. For this reason, the Defense should be very cautious when this situation arises and should be mindful of the criterion of the appeals chamber that unavailability can only be accepted if objective circumstances appear to prevent the witness from testifying, which circumstances cannot be overcome with reasonable diligence.

6.4.4.4 New Developments on Rule 68(2)(d)

In the interlocutory appeal of Prosecutor *v* Patrice Edouard Ngaïssona, the Appeals Chamber addressed significant issues concerning the submission of prior recorded testimonies under Rule 68(2)(d) of the Rules of Procedure and Evidence.[245] This appeal specifically challenges a decision rendered by Trial Chamber V on 6 October 2023. The Trial Chamber had authorized the formal submission of prior recorded testimony of witness P-1847 under Rule 68(2)(d), which allows for the admission of such testimonies when witnesses are unavailable due to circumstances such as death, illness, or other insurmountable obstacles that cannot be overcome with reasonable diligence.[246]

The Defence advanced six grounds of appeal against this decision,[247] asserting that the conditions mandated by Rule 68(2)(d) were not satisfied and that

---

243   *Ibid* para. 40.
244   *Ibid* para. 41.
245   *Prosecutor v Yekatom and Ngaïssona* (Judgment on the appeal of Mr Patrice Edouard Ngaïssona against the decision of Trial Chamber V of 6 October 2023 entitled "Decision on the Prosecution Request for Formal Submission of Prior Recorded Testimony pursuant to Rule 68(2)(d) of the Rules") ICC-01/14-01/18-2501-Conf 20-05-2024, A Ch (20 May 2024).
246   *Prosecutor v Yekatom and Ngaïssona* (Decision on the Prosecution Request for Formal Submission of Prior Recorded Testimony pursuant to Rule 68(2)(d) of the Rules) ICC-01/14-01/18-2126-Red, T Ch V (31 October 2023).
247   *Ibid* (n 1) paras 26, 45, 64, 80, 105, 118.

the admission of these testimonies compromised Mr. Ngaïssona's right to a fair trial. The Defence argued that the testimonies were prejudicial and that the efforts to secure the witness's presence for cross-examination were insufficient, namely in regard to the timing of the Prosecution's request.

The Appeals Chamber, composed of Judges Solomy Balungi Bossa, Luz del Carmen Ibáñez Carranza, Gocha Lordkipanidze, Kimberly Prost, and Erdenebalsuren Damdin, unanimously rejected the Defence's arguments on all six grounds.[248] After thorough examination, the Appeals Chamber upheld the Trial Chamber's decision, confirming that the application of Rule 68(2)(d) was appropriate and that the admission of the prior recorded testimony did not violate the rights of the accused. Indeed, the Appeal Chamber confirmed that Rule 68(2)(d) does not exclude testimony related to the accused's actions and conduct, a pivotal contention raised by the Defence.[249] The Appeals Chamber underscored that the Trial Chamber had acted within its discretion, having sufficiently evaluated the unavailability of the witness and the relevance and probative value of the testimony.

The balance the ICC must maintain between upholding the rights of the accused and addressing the practical challenges of obtaining witness testimony in international criminal proceedings is extremely delicate, as this decision highlights. It underscores the pivotal role of the Trial Chamber's discretion in interpreting procedural rules and emphasizes the necessity for defense counsel to meticulously scrutinize the application of these rules to protect the fair trial rights of their clients. This ruling serves as a critical reference for defense counsel, emphasizing that de facto the burden of proof is indirectly placed on the defense to show that all efforts on part of the prosecution to secure a witness's presence were insufficient. Again, this decision illustrates that the mere reference by defense counsel to the burden of proof resting upon the prosecution in the context of Rule 68(2)(d) is no longer sufficient under the interpretation by the ICC Appeals Chamber.

6.5   Analysis and Future Issues

6.5.1   *Challenges to the Applicability of Rule 68*

The two rules allowing for the admission of prior recorded testimony going to proof of acts and conduct of an accused, without any possibility of cross-examination, (Rule 68(2)(c) and Rule 68(2)(d), based on ICTY Rules 92*quater* and *quinquies*) are, predictably, the most controversial at the ICC.

---

248   *Ibid* (n 1) para. 126.
249   *Ibid* (n 1) paras 3, 80–81.

Obviously, there are many possibilities as to what the potential challenges to the use of Rule 68 are likely to involve. They may be grouped into two broad categories.

The first consists of challenges to the effect that Rule 68 should not be used in a given case because a relevant factor contained in the rule itself is not satisfied, such as the consent of the witness as required under 68(3), or that reasonable efforts were not made to secure the attendance of the person before relying on 68(2)(d)(i).

The second category comprises challenges to the applicability of Rule 68 *in toto* in a given case, based on another provision of the Statute. Accordingly, this section will also consider the grounds whereby, even where the constitutive requirements were otherwise met, Rule 68 might be opposed as inapplicable through Articles 24(2), 51(4) and 69(4) RS.

6.5.1.1 Challenges to the Applicability of Rule 68 When Its Requirements Are Not Satisfied

When facing such challenges, the jurisprudence of the ICTY as outlined above may help in interpreting the elements of Rule 68 which are common to ICTY Rule 92; for example, 'proof of a matter other than the acts and conduct of the accused' under 68(2)(b) or 68(2)(c)(ii), or 'unavailability' under 68(2)(c)(i). Similarly, the relevant ICC jurisprudence may be of assistance.

For ease of reading, the following table sets out the key features of each sub-rule of the new Rule 68 and cross-references back to the relevant jurisprudence in the sections above:

ICC rule	Key term	Link to other relevant rule	Link to relevant jurisprudence
Rule 68(2)(a) + Rule 68(3)	'opportunity to examine the witness'	ICC (previous) Rule 68(a) ICC (previous) Rule 68(b)	*Lubanga Dyilo* *Bemba Gombo*
Rule 68(2)(b) + Rule 68(2)(c)(ii) + Rule 68(2)(d)(iv)	'acts and conduct of the accused'	ICTY Rule 92*bis*(A) ICTY Rule 92*ter*(B) ICTY Rule 92*quater*(B) ICTY Rule 92*quinquies*(B)	*Galić* *Milošević*
Rule 68(2)(b)(i)	'cumulative or corroborative nature'	ICTY Rule 92*bis*(A)(i)(a)	*Blagojević and Jokić*

(cont.)

ICC rule	Key term	Link to other relevant rule	Link to relevant jurisprudence
Rule 68(2)(b)(i) + Rule 68(2)(c)(i) + Rule 68(2)(d)(i)	'indicia of reliability'	The term 'indicia of reliability' was not present in the ICTY Rules or in previous Rule 68, but has been a feature of ICTY jurisprudence since the first trial.[250]	See footnote 201.
Rule 68(2)(c)	'unavailable'	ICTY Rule 92*quater*	*Popović* *Tolimir* *Naletilić and Martinović* *Lubanga Dyilo*
Rule 68(2)(d)(i)	'interference'	ICTY Rule 92*quinquies*	*Haradinaj* *Ruto and Sang*
Rule 68(2)(c) + Rule 68(2)(d)(i)	'reasonable efforts/diligence'	ICTY Rule 92*quater*(A) ICTY Rule 92*quinquies*(A)(iii)	
Rule 68(3)	'does not object to the submission of the previously recorded testimony'	ICC (previous) Rule 68(b)	*Bemba Gombo*

---

250 The term 'indicia of reliability' contained in Rule 68(2)(b)(i), Rule 68(2)(c)(i) and Rule 68(2)(d)(i) was not present in the ICTY Rules nor in previous Rule 68, but has been a feature of ICTY jurisprudence since the first case. In a decision on a Defense motion on hearsay, the Trial Chamber stated that reliability is '*a component of admissibility*' and that a Trial Chamber must pay special attention to '*indicia of reliability*' in evaluating the probative value of hearsay evidence. (cf. *Prosecutor v Tadić* (Decision on the Defense Motion on Hearsay) IT-94-1-T, T Ch I (5 August 1996), paras 15 and 16.) In *Delalić*, the Appeals Chamber quoted a statement of the Trial Chamber to the effect that giving due consideration to indicia of reliability when assessing the relevance and probative value of evidence at the stage of determining its admissibility was '[...]*an implicit requirement of the Rules*'. (Cf. *Prosecutor v Delalić et al.* (Decision on Application of Defendant Zejnil Delalic for Leave to Appeal Against the Decision of the Trial Chamber of 19 January 1998 for the Admissibility of Evidence) IT-96-21-AR73.2, A Ch (4 March 1998), paras 19–21).

6.5.1.2 Challenges to the Applicability of Rule 68 in Toto: Three Possible Provisions of the Rome Statute

In addition to the argument that the requirements of Rule 68 were not fulfilled in a given case, under the RS three further grounds may be identified whereby, regardless of whether its constitutive elements are satisfied, the applicability of Rule 68 could be denied: (i) Article 51(4) – when, in an ongoing case, there would be detriment to the person who is being investigated or prosecuted; (ii) Article 24(2) – when, in an ongoing case and prior to final conviction, its use would be less favourable to the person being investigated, prosecuted or convicted; or (iii) Article 69(2)/Rule 68(1) – in any case, ongoing or otherwise, where its use would be prejudicial to or inconsistent with the rights of the accused.

This section will discuss each of those options in turn and address what 'detriment', 'less favourable' or 'prejudicial to or inconsistent with the rights of the accused' entail, as well as consider any differences between the three standards.

6.5.1.2.1 *Article 51(4) – Retroactivity and Detriment to the Person Being Investigated or Prosecuted*

Operative paragraph 2 of the resolution by which the new Rule 68 was adopted at the ASP reads (emphasis added):

> *Further decides* that the following shall replace rule 68 of the Rules of Procedure and Evidence, *emphasizing* article 51, paragraph 4, of the Rome Statute according to which amendments to the Rules of Procedure and Evidence *shall not be applied retroactively to the detriment of the person who is being investigated or prosecuted*, with the understanding that the rule as amended is without prejudice to article 67 of the Rome Statute related to the rights of the accused, and to article 68, paragraph 3, of the Rome Statute related to the protection of the victims and witnesses and their participation in the proceedings.[251]

As to whether reliability was a component of admissibility, later decisions took a different approach to *Tadić*, finding that reliability was not an inherent but rather a separate component of admissibility. A third 'alternative approach' put forward by May and Wierda and later adopted by the *Katanga* Trial Chamber is 'to consider reliability as a component of the evidence when determining its weight', that is to assess the totality of the evidence at the conclusion of the trial and determine then the weight accorded to each separate piece. Cf. May and Wierda (n 7).

251 Resolution ICC-ASP/12/Res.7, operative paragraph 2, internal citations omitted.

At the ASP, Kenya's delegation – after unsuccessfully lobbying against the amendment – then managed to get the phrase 'shall not be applied retroactively to the detriment of the person who is being investigated or prosecuted' added to the text in order to join consensus on the resolution.

The language 'shall not be applied retroactively to the detriment of the person who is being investigated or prosecuted' that was inserted into the resolution is drawn from Article 51(4) RS. This may be seen as a political compromise to enable consensus on the resolution that in legal terms adds nothing to the application of the amended Rule 68. Indeed, Article 51(4) stands whether or not emphasised in the resolution. Moreover, it may be the case that, while Kenya saw this addition as a "face-saving" measure, other State Parties assessed it as adding nothing new to the previously agreed language. The key point lies in the fact that the provision does not prohibit retroactive applications as such, but only retroactive applications that are detrimental to the accused.[252] Thus, whether it is politically advisable for the Prosecution to seek to use the amended Rule 68 in ongoing cases is a separate question, as legally speaking, there is no bar under Article 51(4) to retroactive applications unless there is detriment to the accused.

As discussed above in section 4.2.4 of this chapter, in *Bemba Gombo*, the Chamber considered the admission of an item under Rule 68 in early 2014, a few months after the amendment of the Rule. Using the same language as the resolution, the Chamber noted that 'the amended rule cannot be applied retroactively to the detriment of the person who is being investigated or prosecuted' and concluded that it was 'bound to apply the unamended Rule 68'.[253]

However, the Chamber missed the opportunity to discuss in more detail the reasons why it considered itself bound, and particularly whether by 'bound', the Chamber meant that it considered itself to be obligated by law. Nevertheless, this case is interesting as the only decision thus far taken on a Rule 68 admission that overlaps with the time when the rule was amended. In future, other Chambers may endorse the same approach. Conversely, it may also be the case that they choose to take into consideration factors such as the exact time when

---

252   Similar to ICTY Rule 6(D) which reads: "An amendment shall enter into force seven days after the date of issue of an official Tribunal document containing the amendment, but shall not operate to prejudice the rights of the accused or of a convicted or acquitted person in any pending case".

253   *Prosecutor v Bemba Gombo* (Public Redacted Version of "Decision on the admission into evidence of items deferred in the Chamber's previous decisions, items related to the testimony of Witness CHM-01 and written statements of witnesses who provided testimony before the Chamber") ICC-01/05-01/08-3019-Red, T Ch III (26 August 2014), footnotes 88 and 111.

the trial commenced, the exact moment the motion to admit prior recorded testimony was admitted, and the time the testimony was produced in order to determine whether there is any prejudice to the rights of the accused.

Furthermore, although this *Bemba Gombo* decision overlapped with the amendment of Rule 68, in fact the admission of the document in question was sought by the Prosecution in April 2013, alongside other materials – thus under the original Rule 68.[254] In November 2013, the Chamber ruled on the admissibility of the majority of those materials, as well as on others tendered by the Defense – thus again under the original Rule 68. However, it postponed the consideration of a small number of documents which were related to and/or mentioned in a separate motion that the Prosecution had previously filed, seeking to reject allegedly fraudulent documents.[255] Rather than a case of the original Rule 68 being used to avoid retroactive application because this was an ongoing case, this particular document had actually been before the Chamber for many months prior to the amendment of the Rule, but its consideration had been deferred due to its relation with another ongoing motion. These circumstances may explain why the judges felt bound to have recourse to the original Rule 68 and may reduce the novelty of this ruling in the sense of a general proposition that the new Rule cannot be applied in ongoing cases. Obviously, the situation may be different where a new motion to use Rule 68 in an ongoing case would be submitted, especially a motion to use one of the new sub-rules that were not covered by former Rule 68(a) or (b).

The only situation before the ICC where Article 51(4) RS has been discussed thus far does not elucidate what 'detriment' entails. This took place in relation to the new Rule 134*quater* on Excusal from presence at trial due to extraordinary public duties; the Defense for Mr. Sang argued for the application of the new rule 134quater (also adopted at ASP12) on the grounds, *inter alia*, that it was not detrimental to the accused.[256]

The only ICTY precedent on this issue is the case of *Šešelj* discussed in section 3.3.2 of this chapter. In that case, the Defense unsuccessfully argued for the retroactive application of ICTY Rule 92*quater*, which had been adopted some three and a half years after the indictment but more than one year before the commencement of the trial. The relevant ICTY Rule 6(D) provides that amendments 'shall not operate to prejudice the rights of the accused […]

---

254   *Ibid* footnote 10.
255   *Ibid* para. 3.
256   *Prosecutor v Ruto and Sang* (Sang Defense response to the request pursuant to article 63(1) of the Rome Statute and rule 134quarter of the Rules of Procedure and Evidence to excuse Mr. William Samoei Ruto from attendance at trial, and the Office of the Prosecutor's Application […]) ICC-01/09-01/11-1127, Defense (19 December 2013), para. 3.

in any pending case'. In particular, the Defense had argued that the by-then adopted Rome Statute's Article 51(4) codified customary international law, claiming that retroactive application of Rule 92*quater* would be prejudicial.[257] The Trial Chamber was not persuaded by this argument and concluded that there was no prejudice, even though in the case the Prosecution had filed to use 92*quater* only two weeks before the Pre-Trial Conference. The Chamber's reasoning for finding no prejudice was that it was also open to the Defense to make use of the new rules for prior recorded testimony. Accordingly, the outcome of the only directly relevant jurisprudence on whether application of the new rule might be prejudicial was not in favour of the accused.

Although *Šešelj* is the only Rule 6(D) precedent directly related to Rule 92, given the number of changes to the ICTY RPE, there are Rule 6(D) decisions involving other ICTY rules. These other decisions suggest that the strongest challenge to the use of ICC Rule 68 on the ground of 'prejudice' under Art. 51(4), would be one that could show prejudice to an actual right of the accused, rather than to any procedural entitlement or broader interests of the Defense.

In *Ljubicic*, it was held that it did not prejudice the accused to transfer his or her case to a domestic jurisdiction pursuant to Rule 11bis when that Rule was enacted after the accused's surrender.[258] In *Mejakić*, the Defense claimed that the referral prejudiced the rights of the accused because the version of Rule 11*bis* that existed at the time of the accused's surrender granted them the assurance that they could not be referred to another jurisdiction.[259] The Appeals Chamber, distinguished between 'procedural' provisions of the RPE and those rights to which a defendant has a legal entitlement, holding that an examination of whether a defendant would be prejudiced under Rule 6(D) did not "extend to that wide variety of advantages or benefits which are frequently described as rights [...], but to which there is no legal entitlement". In this case, the Appeals Chamber found that there was no 'right' to be tried by the ICTY rather than by a national jurisdiction. Therefore, the accused was not prejudiced in the sense of Rule 6(D) by the application of the new rule 11*bis*.

---

257 *Prosecutor v Šešelj* (Redacted version of the "Decision on the prosecution's consolidated motion pursuant to Rules 89 (F), 92 bis, 92 ter and 92 quater of the Rules of Procedure and Evidence" filed confidentially on 7 January 2008) IT-03-67-T, T Ch III (21 February 2008), para. 19.

258 *Prosecutor v Ljubičić* (Decision on Appeal Against Decision on Referral Under Rule 11 bis) IT-00-41-AR11bis.1, A Ch (4 July 2006), para. 9.

259 *Prosecutor v Mejakić et al.* (Decision on Joint Defense Appeal Against Decision on Referral under Rule 11bis) IT-02-65-AR11bis.1, A Ch (7 April 2006), para. 83.

6.5.1.2.2　*Article 24(2) – Less Favourable to the Person Being Investigated, Prosecuted or Convicted*

Article 24(2) RS provides: '*In the event of a change in the law applicable to a given case prior to a final judgment, the law more favourable to the person being investigated, prosecuted or convicted shall apply*'.

This statement of the general principle of non-retroactivity of criminal law is a codification of customary international law, the *raison d'être* being that one shall not be found guilty for conduct that did not constitute a crime at the time it was committed. It also means that a convicted person must be subject to the application of the penalty in effect at the relevant time, and not of a harsher one that came into effect at a later stage (*nullum crimen, nulla poena sine praevia lege poenali*).

Given that this principle relates to crime and penalty, views in the legal doctrine are inconclusive as to whether its scope extends to changes in the RPE: one authority states that Article 24(2) applies '*at least to all substantive provisions*' of the Rome Statute (and thus arguably to procedural provisions);[260] another claims that Article 24(2) '*appears to concern also changes to RPE*',[261] while a third affirms that the question of applicability to '*criminal procedural provisions*' is '*more problematic*'.[262] Thus the argument could be made that Article 24, which is concerned with protecting individuals from arbitrary abuses (*nullum crimen, nulla poena sine lege*), does not apply to changes to the RPE as they are too far removed from the object and purpose of the principle of non-retroactivity in criminal law.

On the other hand, Article 21 RS outlines the sources of applicable law at the ICC as, in the first place, the Statute, the Elements of Crimes (EC), and the RPE.[263] By virtue of this provision, it could be argued that '*law*' in Article 24(2) RS included the RPE; as a result, Article 24(2) RS would cover the amendments to Rule 68. Therefore, in seeking to rely on Article 24(2) RS to oppose

---

[260] Mark Klamberg, comment on article 24(2) in the ICL Database & Commentary (available at www.iclklamberg.com): "As Article 24(2) refers to "the law" as opposed to "(definitions of) crimes", this provision applies not only to Articles 5–8, but also at least to all substantive provisions, i.e. also to the definitions of forms of participation (Article 25 and 28), grounds for excluding criminal responsibility etc".

[261] Machteld Boot, Genocide, Crimes Against Humanity, War Crimes: Nullum Crimen Sine Lege and the Subject Matter Jurisdiction of the International Criminal Court (Intersentia 2002) 374.

[262] Stefano Manacorda, "Non-Retroactivity", in Antonio Cassese et al., *The Oxford Companion to International Criminal Justice*, (Oxford University Press 2009) 438.

[263] Article 21(1)(a) RS reads: "The Court shall apply: in the first place, this Statute, Elements of Crimes and its Rules of Procedure and Evidence".

application of Rule 68 in an ongoing case, it would be necessary to demonstrate that the new rule is less favourable than the original version.

Although only applicable to cases already pending as of 27 November 2013, when the new Rule 68 was adopted, and assuming that the aforementioned argument were accepted, Article 24(2) RS would seem to be the least stringent of the three possibilities under consideration in this section. Indeed, it does not require actual detriment or prejudice, but simply that it be demonstrated the original Rule would be more favourable to the accused. Regarding the new sub-rules not existing under former Rule 68, this may imply that a non-cross examined statement going to the acts and conduct of an accused, even if not a violation of an accused's rights or actually detrimental, were less favourable to an accused than the previous regime where such testimony would not be allowed. As it has not yet been discussed in the case law of the ICC, it remains to be seen what factors might be used to determine what constitutes 'more favourable'.

Cases alleging breaches of human rights law in a criminal law context where 'no less favourable' treatment have been considered relate to the principle of *nullum crimen, nulla poena sine lege*. These cases tend to involve changes in law or penalty, not the procedure by which the trial was conducted.[264] However, it could be argued that the same logic applies. Analogies from other fields of law may also be useful. The concept of 'less favourable treatment' or 'treatment no less favourable' is also known in fields such as trade law or labour law, where the meaning to be attributed is the literal one, namely that treatment placing the applicant in a worse position is less favourable.

6.5.1.2.3 Article 69(2)/Rule 68(1) – Prejudicial to or Inconsistent with the Rights of the Accused

Rule 68(1), reflecting the language in the related Article 69(2) of the Rome Statute, includes the provision that the introduction of prior recorded testimony may be allowed 'provided that this would not be prejudicial to or inconsistent with the rights of the accused'. Unlike the two previous bars to the application of Rule 68, this option not only applies to ongoing cases, but to any case where the Rule is invoked. On a plain reading of its terms, 'prejudicial or inconsistent' may result in a more stringent bar to the use of Rule 68 than showing its use is 'detrimental' to the accused or that the use of the original Rule 68 would be 'more favourable'. Regardless of whether it was restated in the new Rule 68(1), the fact that measures shall not be 'prejudicial to or inconsistent with the rights of the accused' not only applies to Rule 68 but

---

264   I.e. *Del Rio Prada v Spain* App no 42750/09 (ECtHR, 21 October 2013).

also to the proceedings as a whole by virtue of the Statute.[265] For example, even if the requirements of Rule 68 were met, a judge may determine that the probative value outweighs any prejudice to the accused already when admitting evidence.

As the above discussed jurisprudence of the Court demonstrates, this requirement was present under the original Rule 68 already, although not expressly stated. Therefore, jurisprudence on human rights may be useful in determining where the use of Rule 68 could contravene Article 69(2).

6.5.2   *Human Rights*

Under any scenario, but particularly when considering whether the use of Rule 68 would be prejudicial to or inconsistent with the rights of the accused, Article 21(3) RS is also relevant in that the application of law (including, by virtue of Article 21(1), the RPE) must be consistent with internationally recognised human rights.

6.5.2.1   'Sole or Decisive' Rule: Al-Khawaja and Tahery

A number of significant international human rights law cases before the ECtHR have considered the introduction of written testimony from witnesses.[266] In general, the position of the ECtHR has been that written testimonial evidence does not contravene the rights of the accused provided that either there has been an opportunity to challenge the material[267] or, in the alternative, that the

---

[265] For example, in addition to Article 69(2) related to evidence, cf. Article 69(4): "The Court may rule on the relevance or admissibility of any evidence, taking into account, inter alia, the probative value of the evidence and any prejudice that such evidence may cause to a fair trial or to a fair evaluation of the testimony of a witness, in accordance with the Rules of Procedure and Evidence,"; cf., in particular, Article 64(2): "The Trial Chamber shall ensure that a trial is fair and expeditious and is conducted with full respect for the rights of the accused and due regard for the protection of victims and witnesses".

[266] Cf, inter alia, *Unterpertinger v Austria* App no 9120/80 (ECtHR, 24 November 1986); *Kostovski v the Netherlands* App no 11454/85 (ECtHR, 20 November 1989); *Saïdi v France* App no 14647/89 (ECtHR, 20 September 1993); *Doorson v the Netherlands* App no 20524/92 (ECtHR, 26 March 1996); *Van Mechelen and Others v the Netherlands* App nos. 21363/93, 21364/93, 21427/93 and 22056/93 (ECtHR, 23 April 1997); *Lucà v Italy* App no 33354/96 (ECtHR, 27 February 2001).

[267] E.g. *Saïdi v France* App no 14647/89 (ECtHR, 20 September 1993), paras 43 and 44: "The Court reiterates that the taking of evidence is governed primarily by the rules of domestic law and that it is in principle for the national courts to assess the evidence before them. The Court's task under the Convention is to ascertain whether the proceedings in their entirety, including the way in which evidence was taken, were fair. All the evidence must normally be produced in the presence of the accused at a public hearing with a view to adversarial argument. However, the use as evidence of statements obtained at

conviction is not based solely on such material – the so-called 'sole or decisive rule'.[268] Whatever the reason for the defendant's inability to examine a witness, whether absence, anonymity or both, the ECtHR starting point for the assessment of whether there has been a breach of the fair trial rights of the defendant was, as set out in the case *Lucà v Italy*:

> If the defendant has been given an adequate and proper opportunity to challenge the depositions either when made or at a later stage, their admission in evidence will not in itself contravene Article 6 §§ 1 and 3(d). The corollary of that, however, is that where a conviction is based solely or to a decisive degree on depositions that have been made by a person whom the accused has had no opportunity to examine or to have examined, whether during the investigation or at the trial, the rights of the Defense are restricted to an extent that is incompatible with the guarantees provided by Article 6 [references omitted].[269]

In this regard, leading case is *Al-Khawaja and Tahery v The United Kingdom*, where the ECtHR Grand Chamber departed from this previous position and held that even where a hearsay statement is the sole or decisive evidence against a defendant, its admission as evidence will not automatically result in

---

the stage of the police inquiry and the judicial investigation is not in itself inconsistent with paragraphs 3 (d) and 1 of Article 6 (art. 6-3-d, art. 6-1), provided that the rights of the Defense have been respected. As a rule these rights require that the defendant be given an adequate and proper opportunity to challenge and question a witness against him either when he was making his statements or at a later stage of the proceedings".

268 The 1997 case of *Van Mechelen v The Netherlands*, for example, stated in the context of non-cross examined statements for reasons of witness anonymity that: "[...] if the anonymity of prosecution witnesses is maintained, the Defense will be faced with difficulties which criminal proceedings should not normally involve. Accordingly, the Court has recognised that in such cases Article 6 para. 1 taken together with Article 6 para. 3 (d) of the Convention (art. 6-1+6-3-d) requires that the handicaps under which the Defense labours be sufficiently counterbalanced by the procedures followed by the judicial authorities. [...] a conviction should not be based either solely or to a decisive extent on anonymous statements." (*Van Mechelen and Others v the Netherlands* App nos. 21363/93, 21364/93, 21427/93 and 22056/93 (ECtHR, 23 April 1997), paras 54 and 55). Similarly, Kostovski v the Netherlands related to a conviction based to a decisive extent on anonymous testimony due to witnesses being afraid to testify. The Chamber found unanimously that the use of such evidence 'involved limitations on the rights of the Defense which were irreconcilable with the guarantees' contained in the European Convention and stated that the 'right to a fair administration of justice holds so prominent a place in a democratic society that it cannot be sacrificed to expediency." (*Kostovski v the Netherlands* App no 11454/85 (ECtHR, 20 November 1989), para. 44).

269 Lucà v Italy App no 33354/96 (ECtHR, 27 February 2001), para. 40.

a breach of the accused's rights under the European Convention on Human Rights, provided that sufficient counterbalancing factors are in place.[270]

Responding to an alleged lack of precision of the "sole or decisive" rule, the Court noted that the word "sole", in the sense of the only evidence against an accused[271] does not appear to have given rise to difficulties. In contrast, the word "decisive' has been more challenging. In this context, the ECtHR stated that decisive means more than 'probative' and more than the fact that without the evidence, the chances of a conviction would recede, while the chances of an acquittal would advance. Instead, the word "decisive" should be narrowly construed as indicating evidence of such significance or importance as is likely to be determinative of the outcome of the case. Where the untested evidence of a witness is supported by other corroborative evidence, the assessment of whether it is decisive will depend on the strength of the supportive evidence; the stronger the corroborative evidence, the less likely that the evidence of the absent witness will be treated as decisive.[272]

This joined case involved the admission of written statements of absent witnesses: in *Al-Khawaja* because the witness was deceased, while in *Tahery* because the witness was afraid to testify. The Court found that evidence must generally be produced at a public hearing with a view to examination. Exceptions to this principle were possible, provided that the rights of the Defense would not be infringed. As a rule, this required that the accused should be given an adequate and proper opportunity to challenge and question a witness against him either when the statement was made or at a later stage of the proceedings. Two consequences followed from this general principle:

(i) There must be a good reason for the admission of evidence of an absent witness. Good reason existed, *inter alia*, when a witness is deceased or is absent owing to fear attributable to the defendant or to someone acting

---

270 *Al-Khawaja and Tahery v the United Kingdom* App nos. 26766/05 and 22228/06 (ECtHR, 15 December 2011).

Articles 6(1) and 6(3)(d) of the European Convention on Human Rights read as follows: "1. In the determination of his civil rights and obligations or of any criminal charge against him, everyone is entitled to a fair and public hearing within a reasonable time by an independent and impartial tribunal established by law [...] 3. Everyone charged with a criminal offence has the following minimum rights: [...] (d) to examine or have examined witnesses against him and to obtain the attendance and examination of witnesses on his behalf under the same conditions as witnesses against him".

271 *Al-Khawaja and Tahery v the United Kingdom* App nos. 26766/05 and 22228/06 (ECtHR, 15 December 2011), para. 131; cf., for example, Saïdi v France App no 14647/89 (ECtHR, 20 September 1993).

272 *Al-Khawaja and Tahery v the United Kingdom* App nos. 26766/05 and 22228/06 (ECtHR, 15 December 2011), para. 131.

on behalf of the defendant. However, before a witness could be excused from testifying on grounds of fear, the court needed to be satisfied that all available alternatives, such as witness anonymity and other special measures, would be inappropriate or impracticable.[273]

(ii) A conviction based solely or to a decisive degree on the statement of an absent witness whom the accused has had no opportunity to examine or to have examined, whether during the investigation or at trial, would generally be considered incompatible with the requirements of fairness under Article 6 ("sole or decisive rule"), however, this was not an absolute rule to be applied in an inflexible way.[274]

While *Al-Khawaja and Tahery* held that the "sole or decisive rule" was not absolute, where a conviction is based solely or decisively on the evidence of absent witnesses, the Court must subject the proceedings to '*the most searching scrutiny*' of whether there are sufficient counterbalancing factors in place, including measures that allow a fair and proper assessment of the reliability of that evidence.[275]

Accordingly, the ECtHR jurisprudence concluded that even a conviction that is solely or decisively based on hearsay testimonial evidence will not necessarily breach the defendant's right to a fair trial, provided that sufficient counterbalancing factors are in place. As the joined case resulted in one finding of violation and one of no violation, the Court's reasoning is useful in highlighting what is a sufficient safeguard to be considered a counterbalancing factor.

On the one hand, in the case of Mr Al-Khawaja, it was sufficient that the evidence of the deceased witness's was corroborated by the other complainant in that trial (whom the deceased had never met) as well as by two other witnesses (friends of the deceased, to whom she had given details of what had happened to her). Thus the statement was sufficiently reliable to outweigh any potential prejudice arising from Mr Al-Khawaja not being able to cross-examine her.

On the other hand, Mr Tahery was convicted on the basis of a statement from a witness too afraid of retribution to testify due to the nature of the close-knit Iranian community in London, where the crime had occurred. The witness's statement was decisive and uncorroborated, and the ECtHR found a violation because the procedural safeguard, namely the trial judge's warning to the jury, was insufficient to counterbalance the unfairness to Mr Tahery.[276]

---

273   *Ibid* paras 120–125.
274   *Ibid* para. 146.
275   *Ibid* para. 147.
276   Where corroboration is a '*counterbalancing factor*' to test reliability, this raises the question of what other kind of evidence is sufficient to corroborate non-cross examined evidence? If, for example, other hearsay evidence can be considered sufficiently

6.5.2.2 What Does the ECtHR Jurisprudence Mean for the ICC?

While *Al-Khawaja and Tahery* clearly watered down the ECtHR position, there are a number of features which reduce the relevance of this judgment to the ICC. Firstly, given the different nature and scope of international criminal trials compared to European ones, it is unlikely that the ICC will be faced with the possibility of a conviction on the basis of non-cross examined sole or decisive testimonies under Rule 68 ICC RPE.

Secondly, the case was based on the criminal procedural law of the United Kingdom.[277] This consideration is important with regard to the reliability of the evidence: while in common law or adversarial systems, where juries decide criminal law trials, relevant evidence may be inadmissible if it falls under an exclusionary evidential rule, in civil law or inquisitorial systems a professional judge may admit all relevant evidence, leaving the determination of the weight to be attributed to each piece to a later stage of the proceedings. As Kevin Jon Heller put it:

> The hearsay rule at the international tribunals reflects the influence of the civil-law tradition, in which lay jurors are not asked to assess the reliability and probative value of hearsay. Indeed, the ICTY specifically held in *Blaskic* that the Tribunal's liberal hearsay rule was justified because, to quote the authors of the leading treatise on international criminal evidence, "the proceedings were conducted by professional judges, who, due to their training and experience, could give appropriate weight to testimony declared admissible in light of its reliability.[278]

No legal system purely fits into either model; the ICC is truly a *sui generis* blend of a hybrid nature, and its evidentiary model reflects features of both the adversarial and inquisitorial systems. It was so created both to meet the unique needs of an international court and to overcome the inconsistencies

---

corroborative, then it is hard to see how this could be a counterbalancing safeguard for the rights of the accused.

277 The ECtHR has frequently reiterated that the admissibility of evidence is primarily a matter for regulation by national law and as a general rule it is for the national courts to assess the evidence before them. The Court's task under the Convention is not to give a ruling as to whether statements of witnesses were properly admitted as evidence, but rather to ascertain whether the proceedings as a whole, including the way in which the evidence was taken, were fair.

278 Kevin Heller, 'Not All Hearsay Rules Are Created Equal' (*OpinioJuris.org*, 29 July 2008) <http://opiniojuris.org/2008/07/29/not-all-hearsay-rules-are-created-equal/> accessed 14 June 2023.

that resulted from the multilateral negotiating process of the Rome Statute.[279] Hence, while the UK's common law system may be considered in *Al-Khawaja and Tahery* to have 'sufficient counterbalancing factors in place, including measures that allow a fair and proper assessment of the reliability of the evidence', this doesn't necessarily apply to the ICC system.

6.5.2.3 Taylor

This issue was later addressed by the SCSL Appeals Chamber in *Taylor*, albeit not entirely persuasively.[280] The Appeals Chamber may have misinterpreted the Al-Khawaja and Tahery decision as more permissive than it actually was, since it upheld the general rule that evidence must be produced at a public hearing for examination, allowing only the possibility of limited exceptions where the rights of the Defense were not violated due to sufficient counterbalancing factors.[281] The SCSL was unconvincing in holding that it had complied with Al-Khawaja and Tahery: it appears to have assumed that the presence of provisions on the rights of the accused in its framework were sufficient countervailing factors, without examining the implementation of those provisions in Taylor's case, as the ECtHR did in Al-Khawaja and Tahery.[282]

6.5.3 Right to Examine Witnesses under Same Conditions as Those against You

In the Rome Statute, the right to examine witnesses is set out in essentially the same terms as in the ICCPR and other instruments, as follows: 'To examine, or have examined, the witnesses against him or her and to obtain the attendance and examination of witnesses on his or her behalf under the same conditions as witnesses against him or her'.[283] As discussed above, this is not an absolute

---

[279] Cf., for example, Klamberg (n 50) 47; Robert Cryer, Darryl Robinson and Sergey Vasiliev, *An Introduction to International Criminal Law and Procedure* (4th edn, Cambridge University Press 2019) <https://www.cambridge.org/core/books/an-introduction-to-international-criminal-law-and-procedure/7A2068BB50AE8386A5D8C689F140C37C, 428.

[280] *Prosecutor v Taylor* (Appeal judgment) SCSL-03-01-A, A Ch (26 September 2013).

[281] Recalling that the ECtHR found such counterbalancing factors to be in place in the UK criminal procedure system in the case of Mr Al-Khawaja, where no violation was found, but not in the case of Mr Tahery, where the safeguards were found insufficient to counter the prejudice against him.

[282] The *Al-Khawaja and Tahery* judgment is also interesting in that the court looked at how hearsay is dealt with in other jurisdictions: Australia, Canada, Hong Kong, Ireland, New Zealand, Scotland, South Africa and the United States.

[283] Cf. Article 67(2)(e)RS, Article 21(4)(e) ICTY Statute, Article 14(2)(e) ICCPR and Article 6(3)(d) ECHR.

right, and sometimes has to be balanced against the rights and interests of others, such as in the case of protected witnesses.[284]

Of interest to the present book is the notion of equality of arms inherent in the words '*under the same conditions*'. The Prosecution seems to make considerably more use of ICTY Rule 92*bis et seq.* and ICC Rule 68 procedures than the Defense does.[285] This raises concerns not only about the different conditions under which witness testimony is examined but also with respect to the equality of arms, given the disparity of resources available to the Prosecution compared to the Defense. As the *Katanga* Defense noted above: 'We simply don't have the same resources as the Prosecution to produce the elaborate, detailed statements that they have produced for their witnesses'.[286]

This position was echoed at the ICTR in *Munyakazi*, where it was held that it would be a breach of equality of arms if the majority of Prosecution witnesses were heard in person, while the majority of Defense witnesses testified by video-link. The ICTR declined to transfer the case to Rwanda on the grounds that 'the Accused's fair trial right to obtain the attendance of, and to examine, Defense witnesses under the same conditions as witnesses called by the Prosecution' could not be guaranteed at that time in Rwanda.[287] One of the factors the ICTR considered in reaching this decision was that the majority of Defense witnesses resided outside Rwanda: 'this places the Defense in a disadvantageous position with regard to the right to obtain the attendance and examination of witnesses'.[288] The Chamber noted that, if transferred to Rwanda, the accused would no longer be able to rely on the benefit of Article 28 of the Tribunal's Statute to obtain the cooperation of States with regard to securing the attendance and/or the evidence of witnesses. Even if Rwanda were able to secure the attendance, and/or evidence, of witnesses from abroad by video-link testimony, the Chamber considered that:

---

284   It also does not imply a guarantee of confrontation, as opposed to other jurisdictions – like the U.S., where such right is accorded by virtue of the 6th Amendment.
285   Yvonne Mcdermott, 'The Admissibility and Weight of Written Witness Testimony in International Criminal Law: A Socio-Legal Analysis' (2013) 26 Leiden Journal of International Law 971, 971–989.
286   *Prosecutor v Katanga and Ngudjolo Chui*, Transcript ICC-01/04-01/07-T-97-Red-ENG, T Ch II (8 February 2010), 28–29.
287   *Prosecutor v Munyakazi* (Decision on the Prosecutor's Request for Referral of Case to the Republic of Rwanda) ICTR-97-36-R11*bis*, T Ch III (28 May 2008) para. 66.
288   *Ibid* para. 63.

the availability of video-link facilities is not a complete solution to obtaining the testimony of witnesses residing outside Rwanda. The Chamber notes that it is preferable to hear direct witness testimony unless the interests of justice require otherwise. In the Chamber's view, if the majority of Defense witnesses are heard via video-link, while the majority of those for the Prosecution are heard in person, the right to examine witnesses under the same conditions, and consequently the principle of equality of arms, is undermined.[289]

The relevance of this is that a case where a significant proportion of Prosecution witness testimony is presented through Rule 68 could violate an accused's right to examine witnesses called by both parties under the same conditions.

6.6 Conclusion

There is no doubt that some changes to ICC practice were needed and that some elements of the changes to Rule 68 will be both useful and necessary in meeting the aim of fair and expeditious trials. However, the wholesale change adopted at the ICC would likely not have been accepted at the ICTY had it been presented simultaneously rather than over many years.

This can be evidenced by analysing the arguments used at various points to defend the changes: for example, in defending Rule 92*bis*, the arguments made were generally that the safeguards in place were sufficient to ensure respect for the rights of the Defense. Successively, these safeguards (such as only admitting evidence that goes to proof of matters other than the acts and conduct of the accused, or ensuring that there be an opportunity either while taking the statement or later during the trial to examine the maker of the statement), were repealed through the enactment of subsequent rules. Similarly at ICC, the rule 68 package was presented as being the practice of the ICTY – undoubtedly facilitating its adoption – regardless of the fact that there is no published practice on one of the sub-rules and that elements of the others have been controversial.

Considering the totality of these amendments calls to mind the word of Lord Bingham, speaking about the rise in the use of anonymous witnesses in criminal trials, 'By a series of small steps, largely unobjectionable on their own facts, the courts have arrived at a position which is irreconcilable with long-standing

---

289   The Admissibility and Weight of Written Witness Testimony para. 65.

principle'.[290] This 'series of small steps' evinces a gradual chipping away of the rights of the Defense; it raises real questions about the equality of arms at the ICC and has the potential to imperil the delicate balance between fairness and expeditiousness.

This tension can be expected to play out in challenges to the use of Rule 68. We have seen above that Rule 68 might be inapplicable in a given case because one of its constitutive elements is not met; the jurisprudence on ICTY Rule 92bis et seq and ICC previous Rule 68 can assist in determining when this is the case. We have also seen three possible grounds under the Rome Statute where the use of Rule 68 could be denied *in toto*, even if the elements of the rule are otherwise met. While the circumstances of a given case will dictate which combination of these options is most persuasive for that case, in general it may be expected that as the Rule 68 amendments were proposed by the judges then they are perhaps unlikely to accept that the use of the rule *in and of itself* is harmful to the accused. This may render arguments based on the three *in toto* prohibitions unconvincing for a chamber, as was the case at the ICTY in *Šešelj*, where retroactive application was not considered to be detrimental *per se* to the accused. As shown, if one of the three is to be accepted, on a plain reading of its terms then an argument based on Article 24(2) may be easier to fulfil than one based on either of the other two possibilities.

Relevant human rights law has also been considered, suggesting that for the use of Rules 69(2)(c) and (d) (deceased or intimidated witnesses) to be consistent with ECtHR jurisprudence, reliance on such evidence would require that it be with 'sufficient counterbalancing factors', such as safeguards to test reliability and that its overall weight take into account the circumstances in which it was produced. Regarding the circumstances in which prior recorded witness testimony is taken, we have seen in the ICTY and ICC jurisprudence above two key problems from a Defense perspective with prior recorded testimony: (i) that it poses equality of arms problems given the Prosecution's greater capacity and resources to obtain it, and (ii) that it is not taken in neutral circumstances, limiting its reliability.

In the same way that a strategy to challenge the application of Rule 68 will likely rely on a combination of the options outlined in this Chapter, the jurisprudence shows that a party unsuccessful in seeking to tender prior recorded testimony in this manner may try again under another sub-rule until it finds one that will work. A challenge inherent in this is how the ICC will treat such applications: either the procedure in *Tolimir* where the ICTY proceeded to consider under what they thought was most appropriate, or as in *Ruto and*

---

290   *R v Davis* [2008] UKHL 36, para. 29.

Sang where the Chamber denied an application submitted under one provision on grounds it did not satisfy the criteria and should have been submitted under another.[291]

Aside from any of these challenges to the use of Rule 68, the general framework on the admission of evidence remains. In a given case, the judges may thus consider that Rule 68 is applicable and that its elements are met. Then, in applying the three-part test of relevance, probative value, and potential prejudice, it may be concluded that the probative value of the evidence does not outweigh the prejudice to the accused and the material is not admissible.[292] Or that, even where such material were admissible, this is not determinative of the overall weight it may be given later when the judges will consider the totality of the evidence. Furthermore, Rule 68 is not the only provision of the Court's legal framework under which the admissibility of written statements may be assessed.[293]

In this light, considerations over the use of Rule 68 are not so much new debates at the ICC but situated within broader debates about the fair trial rights of the accused, and the balance between those rights and the so-called efficiency of the Court. In deciding on challenges under Rule 68, as with

---

291 Note that the circumstances of these two cases were different in that the first was an application under Rule 92*bis* that the Chamber thought should have been under 92*quater* and considered on that basis. The second included a motion to introduce three documents as bar table evidence under Article 64(9), the Chamber rejected them on the grounds that they should have been submitted under Rule 68.
   Cf. *Prosecutor v Tolimir* (Partial Decision on Prosecution's Rule 92bis and Rule 92ter Motion for Five Witnesses) IT-05-88/2-T, T Ch II (27 August 2010); *Prosecutor v Ruto and Sang* (Decision on the Prosecution's Request for Admission of Documentary Evidence) ICC-01/09-01/11-1353, T Ch V(A) (10 June 2014).

292 In *Bemba Gombo*, the Trial Chamber said that after determining if the conditions of Rule 68 are met, the Chamber will proceed to analyse the relevance and probative value of the witness' statements, together with the potential prejudice that their admission may cause, in line with the three-prong test, and that this procedure would comply with the "cautious item-by-item analysis" mandated by the *Bemba Gombo* Appeals Chamber. Cf. *Prosecutor v Bemba Gombo* (Decision on the admission into evidence of items deferred in the Chamber's "First decision on the prosecution and Defense requests for the admission of evidence" (ICC-01/05-01/08-2012)) ICC-01/05-01/08-2793, T Ch III (03 September 2013), paras 134–136.

293 When Rule 68 of the Rules is not applicable, the Chamber is not precluded from considering that written statements may be admissible under other provisions. In particular, Articles 69(4) and 64(9) RS and Rule 63(2) of the Rules give the Chamber the authority and discretion to freely assess all evidence submitted – including written statements – and rule on their relevance and admissibility, taking into account, inter alia, any prejudice that the admission of such evidence may cause to a fair trial or to a fair evaluation of the testimony of a witness.

other questions, the Court will have to decide where the line should be drawn between the rights of the accused and more efficient trials. The judges taking such decisions are of course elected by the states parties who fund the Court and constantly call for it to be more efficient, which is often a euphemism meaning to operate more quickly and at lower cost. The experience of the ICTY in this regard has been criticised, suggesting too much may be being asked of the judges:

> it is not unfair to say that far too often there have been serious failures on the part of the judges to fulfil their obligation to be the guardians and guarantor of the rights of the accused. The judges stand in a unique position as both the legislative and judicial powers of the Tribunal. [...] It has proven dangerously easy for the judges to seriously infringe into the right of an accused to effectively challenge evidence against him through cross-examination. There has been a lack of judicial robustness in ensuring that the right to fair trial is not compromised.[294]

On a final note, a study by Yvette McDermott makes a number of conclusions relevant to Rule 68, even though it was published in December 2013 and did not take the new Rule 68 into account.[295] The study analyses nine judgements from the ICTY, ICTR and SCSL handed down in 2011 and 2012. Overall, the author finds that the rules such as 92*quater* have been used relatively infrequently; that the ICTY uses the new rules more than the other tribunals and (as noted above) that the rules are far more frequently used by the Prosecution than by the Defense.

The study cautions both against alarmism and reliance on assurances of increased efficiency. McDermott finds that the relatively infrequent use of some of the rules, suggests that some of the criticisms of them may have been premature. Nonetheless, the author concludes that the broad admissibility rules for prior recorded testimony may not in fact meet aims of expediency, given that their use is so frequently challenged on grounds of 'whether the evidence goes to the acts and conduct of the accused, whether the witness is truly unavailable, and so on'.

Specifically regarding 92*bis*, replicated at the ICC now as Rule 68(2), McDermott notes that the frequent argument that because it does not require cross-examination, Rule 92*bis* 'has the potential to open a Pandora's Box', especially in trials involving extended forms of liability. However, the author finds

---

294 O'Sullivan and Montgomery (n 14) 511, 511–538.
295 McDermott (n 275) 971–989.

that of the more than 200 92*bis* witnesses across the nine judgments in the three tribunals studied, more than one third were actually called for cross-examination, makes it more akin to Rule 92*ter* testimony than to the form originally envisioned for Rule 92*bis*.

Whether the ICC will adopt also these practices of the ICTY or only its Rules remains to be seen but in its drive towards greater efficiency, the legacy of the ICC depends on it finding the appropriate balance with fairness. Trials like these are difficult and complex matters, both from a legal and evidentiary point of view. Moreover, they are challenging on the human level. Sympathy for the victims' plight and an urgent awareness that this Court is called upon to "end impunity" are powerful stimuli. Yet, the Court's success or failure cannot be measured just in terms of "bad guys" being convicted and innocent victims receiving reparation. Success or failure is determined first and foremost by whether or not the proceedings, as a whole, are fair and just.[296]

---

[296] *Prosecutor v Katanga and Ngudjolo Chui* (Annex I – Minority Opinion of Judge Christine Van den Wyngaert) ICC-01/04-01/07-3436-AnxI, T Ch II (7 March 2014), paras 310–311.

CHAPTER 7

Using Witness Preparation at the ICC

7.1 Introduction

This chapter will elaborate on the question whether witness preparation at the level of the International Criminal Court is accepted by the various Trial chambers. 'Witness preparation' or sometimes also referred to as 'witness proofing', can be defined as the practice of preparing a witness for his or her testimony by the calling party. This practice serves two purposes: "i) 'to assist the witness who will be giving evidence during the proceedings'; as well as ii) 'for the calling party to assess and clarify the witness's evidence in order to facilitate the focused, efficient and effective questioning of the witness during the proceedings.'"[1] It can involve having the witness review documents, such as his or her written statement, potential exhibits, records, and other written documents.[2]

Witness preparation is not to be confused with 'witness coaching', which is the idea of "preparing the witness in a manner that involves improper influence upon the witness, intentionally exerted by counsel, with the view to rendering false evidence into testimony."[3] It must also be differentiated from the process of investigations, which aims to *obtain* evidence, whereas witness preparation aims to *review* and *clarify* the witness' evidence.[4]

---

1 *Prosecutor v Al Hassan* (Decision on witness preparation and familiarisation) ICC-01/12-01/18-666, T Ch X (17 March 2020) para. 11; *Prosecutor v Al Hassan* (Annex A tot he Decision on witness preparation and familiarisation) ICC-01/12-01/18-666, T Ch X (17 March 2020) para. 1.
2 Thomas A. Mauet, *Trials: Strategy, Skills, and the New Powers of Persuasion* (Aspen Publishers, New York 2005) 151; *Prosecutor v Lubanga Dyilo* (Decision Regarding the Practices Used to Prepare and Familiarise Witnesses for Giving Testimony at Trial) ICC-01/04-01/06-1049, T Ch I (30 November 2007) para. 47.
3 *Prosecutor v Ruto and Sang* (Decision on witness preparation: Partly Dissenting Opinion of Judge Eboe-Osuji) ICC-01/09-01/11-524, T Ch V (3 January 2013) para. 27.
4 *Prosecutor v Ruto and Sang* (Decision on witness preparation) ICC-01/09-01/11-524, T Ch V (2 January 2013) para. 41.

7.2 Statutory Law

The practice of witness preparation is not provided for explicitly in the ICC's statutory framework, nor is it considered a general principle of law pursuant to Article 21(1)(c) of the RS.[5] However, this practice is frequently used in common law systems and has been accepted before other international courts, including the ICC.

Trial chambers have the broad discretion of adopting the necessary procedures to ensure fair and expeditious proceedings, under Article 64(2) and (3)(a) of the Statute. Article 68(1) of the Statute also provides that "the Court shall take appropriate measures to protect the safety, physical and psychological well-being, dignity and privacy of (...) witnesses." The purpose of this chapter will be to demonstrate how this translates to witnesses appearing before the Court and the different Trial Chambers' approach to the question of witness preparation.

7.3 Witness Preparation in Other Common Law Jurisdictions

Witness preparation is unique to adversarial systems of law, notably in common law jurisdictions, where in-court testimonies play a key role in the assessment the evidence, such as the United States of America and Canada.[6] It is a commonly used tool for the calling party to prepare witnesses to examination-in-chiefs, as well as cross-examinations. Tribunals depend on the witnesses being properly prepared in order for their evidence to be presented in a well organised and efficient manner.[7] However, factors regarding the way these preparation sessions are conducted, their duration, the questions or discussions that are permitted, the individuals who are allowed to conduct these meetings or the obligations concerning the disclosure of new information or material, differ

---

5 *Prosecutor v Bemba Gombo et al.* (Decision on Witness Preparation and Familiarisation) ICC-01/05-01/13-1252, T Ch VII (15 September 2015) para. 20; *Prosecutor v Lubanga Dyilo* (Decision on the Practices of Witness Familiarisation and Witness Proofing) ICC-01/04-01/06-679, PT Ch I (9 November 2006) paras 11 and 42; *Prosecutor v Ruto and Sang* (Decision on Witness Preparation) ICC-01/09-01/11-524, T Ch V (2 January 2013) para. 26; *Prosecutor v Lubanga Dyilo* (Decision Regarding the Practices Used to Prepare and Familiarise Witnesses for Giving Testimony at Trial) ICC-01/04-01/06-1049, T Ch I (30 November 2007) para. 36.
6 Earl J. Levy, *Examination of Witnesses in Criminal Cases*, (Carswell, 2004) 22.
7 Bryan Finlay, Thomas A. Cromwell and Nikiforos Iatrou, *Witness Preparation – A Practical Guide Aurora*, (Law Book, 2010), p. 6.

from one jurisdiction to another. Defense counsel is to abstain from coaching the witness for his or her testimony, as it is prohibited in these jurisdictions.[8]

An example of the application of this practice in common law can be found in the American Law Institute's *Restatement (Third) of the Law Governing Lawyers*, where paragraph 116(1) recognises the legitimacy of witness preparation and provides that 'a lawyer may interview a witness for the purpose of preparing the witness to testify.' The Supreme Court of North Carolina established in *State v McCormick* the following:

> It is not improper for an attorney to prepare his witness for trial, to explain the applicable law in any given situation and to go over before trial the attorney's questions and the witness' answers so that the witness will be ready for his appearance in court, will be more at ease because he knows what to expect, and will give his testimony in the most effective manner that he can. Such preparation is the mark of a good trial lawyer (...) and is to be commended because it promotes a more efficient administration of justice and saves court time.[9]

Finlay, Cromwell and Latrou raises an important idea in the following way: "The goal of "winning the case" argues in favour of witnesses being properly prepared and centred on relevant materials before the commencement of the hearing."[10] In the same vein, John S. Applegate in his article on witness preparation expresses that:

> One may deduce from the lawyer-as-champion position that trials are not essentially exercises in fact finding or truth seeking. Instead, they are social and political mechanisms for resolving disputes. Truth is valued, but its importance is only a part of the larger adversarial framework. "[F]ar more than a search for truth," a trial is a vindication of the rights of the individual and a ritual for the peaceful resolution of disputes among members of society.[11]

---

8   Levy (n 6) 23.
9   *State v McCormick* 259 S.E. 2d 880 (1979) at pp 882; See also *Hamdi & Ibrahim Mango Co v Fire Association of Philadelphia*, 20 FRD 181 (SONY, 1957) at pp 182–183.
10   Finlay, Cromwell and Latrou (n 7) 7.
11   John S. Applegate, "Witness Preparation" *Texas Law Review*, Maurer School of Law: Indiana University, 1989, p. 326

Witness preparation makes evident the tension within adversarial systems between the goals of truth seeking and partisan representation.[12] It is for this reason that the common law adversarial system differentiates from the ICC's purpose, which is to establish the truth. Therefore, the ICC will evaluate the specific case before the court in order to determine if witness preparation is a favourable procedure to engage in and if it will be favourable to its truth seeking function, considering the potential risks it entails.

7.4 Witness Preparation at the ad hoc Tribunals

In order to fully understand the extent to which witness preparation is applicable in the International Criminal Court, one must consider its common usage at the *ad hoc* tribunals, whose statutes and rules of procedure are also silent on the matter. The ICTR's Appeals Chamber has ruled that:

> The Tribunal's Statute and Rules do not directly address the issue of witness preparation. In the absence of express provisions. Rule 89(B) of the Rules generally confers discretion on the Trial Chamber to apply "rules of evidence which will best favour a fair determination of the matter before it and are consonant with the spirit of the Statute and the general principles of law.[13]

Although the statutory provisions and the jurisprudence of these tribunals are in no sense binding for the ICC,[14] they are relevant to the analysis of the applicability of witness preparation at the ICC. At both the ICTY and the ICTR a practice of witness preparation has developed and has been consistently allowed. The following sections will focus on the different decisions that were ruled in these *ad hoc* tribunals and the reasoning that supports the ruling.

7.4.1   ICTY
The Trial Chamber III in the *Milutinovic* case granted the witness preparation request. The Chamber considered that when the discussions are focused on clarifying the witness's testimony, this practice can enhance the fairness and

---

12   Ibid.
13   *Prosecutor v Karemara et al.* (Decision on Interlocutory Appeal Regarding Witness Proofing) ICTR-98-44-AR73.8, A Ch (11 May 2007) para. 8.
14   *Prosecutor v Ruto and Sang* (Decision on the appeals of Mr William Samoei Ruto and Mr Joshua Arap Sang against the decision of Pre-Trial Chamber II of 23 January 2012 entitled "Decision on the Confirmation of Charges Pursuant to Article 61(7)(a) and (b) of the Rome Statute"), ICC-01/09-01/11-414, A Ch (24 May 2012), para. 3.

expeditiousness of the proceedings.[15] The Chamber established that witness preparation assists "(a) in providing a "detailed review [of relevant and irrelevant facts] in light of the precise charges to be tried"; (b) in aiding "the process of human recollection"; (c) in "enabling the more accurate, complete, orderly and efficient presentation of the evidence of a witness in the trial"; and (d) in identifying and putting the Defence on notice of differences in recollection thereby preventing undue surprise".[16] In regards to the issue of delayed disclosure, the Chamber found that the issue is caused by the *late proofing* of witness, as oppose to the practice in and of itself. Thus, earlier preparation sessions would resolve this issue.[17]

The *Limaj* Trial Chamber considered witness proofing to be an appropriate and useful practice because it guarantees efficient use of court time and a faire determination of the cases before the court, considering the depts of the investigations and the length of the cases before the ICTY.[18] The Chamber found that witness preparation would contribute to a more complete and structured testimony from the witness. In the event that the proofing sessions would result in the late notice of new material, measures were available to overcome the potential difficulties the Defense may face.

7.4.2 ICTR

Witness proofing is coherent with the Appeals Chamber's findings that each party has the right to interview a potential witness.[19] Trial Chamber III in the *Karemera et al.* case is of the opinion that this practice does not cause an undue prejudice to the rights of the accused, but is rather a useful and permissible practice.[20] This practice is allowed to encompass : "preparing and familiarizing a witness with the proceedings before the Tribunal, comparing prior statements made by a witness, detecting differences and inconsistencies in recollection of the witness, allowing a witness to refresh his or her memory in respect of the evidence he or she will give, and inquiring and disclosing to the

---

15   *Prosecutor v Milutinović* (Decision on Ojdanic Motion to Prohibit Witness Proofing) IT-05-87-T, T Ch III (12 December 2006) para. 16.
16   *Ibid* para. 20.
17   *Ibid*.
18   *Prosecutor v Limaj et al.* (Decision on Defence Motion on Prosecution Practice of 'Proofing' Witnesses) IT-03-66-T, T Ch II (10 December 2004).
19   *Prosecutor v Mrkšić* (Decision on Defence Interlocutory Appeal on Communication with Potential Witnesses of the Opposite Party) IT-95-1311-AR73, A Ch (30 July 2003); see also; *Prosecutor v Halilović* (Decision on the Issuance of Subpoenas) IT-01-48-AR73, A Ch (21 June 2004) para. 12–15.
20   *Prosecutor v Karemera et al.* (Decision on Defence Motions to Prohibit Witness Proofing, Rule 73 of the Rules of Procedure and Evidence) ICTR-98-44-T, T Ch III (15 December 2006) para. 10.

Defence additional information and or evidence of incriminatory or exculpatory nature in sufficient time prior to the witness' testimony."[21] The Chamber recalls that witness preparation is not an opportunity for a party to train, coach or tamper a witness.[22]

As for the evidence emanating from these meetings, should there be admission of evidence outside the scope of indictment, the appropriate remedies will be granted to the Defense as well as, if need be, the exclusion of the evidence.[23] The Appeals Chamber observes that cross-examination is a tool to diminish the witness's credibility and to put into question the impacts of witness preparation. In addition, if there is proof of witness interference, a Trial Chamber can undertake proceedings under Rule 77 of the Rules of procedure and evidence and exclude tampered evidence under Rule 95 of the Rules of procedure and evidence.[24]

7.5 Witness Preparation at the ICC

The remainder of this chapter will address the various ICC cases that have delt with the issue of witness preparation. In more recent cases, Trial Chambers have allowed the practice of witness preparation namely because of the singularity and complexity of the specific case,[25] the time elapsed since the occurrence of the alleged events,[26] and in whole to favour the expeditiousness of the proceedings.[27]

---

21 *Ibid* para. 15.
22 *Ibid* para. 12.
23 *Ibid* para. 20.
24 *Prosecutor v Karemara et al.* (Decision on Interlocutory Appeal Regarding Witness Proofing) ICTR-98-44-AR73.8, A Ch (11 May 2007) para. 13.
25 *Prosecutor v Kenyatta* (Decision on witness preparation) ICC-01/09-02/11-588, T Ch V (2 January 2013) para. 41; *Prosecutor v Ntaganda* (Decision on witness preparation) ICC-01/04-02/06-652, T Ch VI (16 June 2015) para. 18; *Prosecutor v Ruto and Sang* (Decision on witness preparation) ICC-01/09-01/11-524, T Ch V (2 January 2013) para. 33; *Prosecutor v Bemba et al.* (Decision on Witness Preparation and Familiarisation) ICC-01/05-01/13-1252, T Ch VII (15 September 2015) para. 23.
26 *Prosecutor v Al Hassan* (Decision on witness preparation and familiarisation) ICC-01/12-01/18-666, T Ch X (17 March 2020) para. 12; *Prosecutor v Ntaganda* (Decision on witness preparation) ICC-01/04-02/06-652, T Ch VI (16 June 2015) para. 18.
27 *Prosecutor v Ntaganda* (Decision on witness preparation) ICC-01/04-02/06-652, T Ch VI (16 June 2015) para. 18; *Prosecutor v Al Hassan* (Decision on witness preparation and familiarisation) ICC-01/12-01/18-666, T Ch X (17 March 2020) para. 15; *Prosecutor v Ruto and Sang* (Decision on witness preparation) ICC-01/09-01/11-524, T Ch V (2 January 2013) paras

However, most trial chambers have explicitly refused witness preparation[28] on the grounds that it would affect the truth seeking purpose of the court.[29] The reason for this conclusion can be resumed by the fact that, as previously mentioned, the ICC bears a greater focus on its truth finding purpose, as oppose to a purely adversarial system, such as common law.

Though, Judge Jeffrey Henderson argues that the independence and party control over trial preparation is intrinsic to adversarial (criminal) proceedings and is necessary when the parties are responsible to further the case. Before the ICC, not only does the Defense has to rely on the Prosecution's information and disclosure, but it also has to face the reluctant collaboration from foreign territory authorities, which makes it difficult to effectively conduct investigations and therefore diminishes party control. This 'lesser' version of a true adversarial system therefore demands of a replacement of party dependency to external actors with an increase of party control over evidence. That being said, witness preparation before the ICC is not a necessity compared to a purely common law system, nor a completely foreign practice to the ICC trial system's components.[30]

7.5.1   *Merits of Witness Preparation*

The Chamber considers that witness preparation can, in principle, contribute to the fairness and expeditiousness of the proceedings, however any decision regarding this issue must be taken in consideration of the specific circumstances prevailing in each case at the Court.[31] There are certain cases for which Trial Chambers have authorised parties to conduct preparation sessions with the witnesses they intend to call at trial, done so in respect of the adopted witness preparation protocol.[32] The main factors in favour of witness preparation are elucidated here below.

        31, 34, 36; *Prosecutor v Kenyatta* (Decision on witness preparation) ICC-01/09-02/11-588, T Ch V (2 January 2013) para. 39.

28   Trial Chamber I (in both the Lubanga Dyilo and Gbagbo and Blé Goudé cases), III (by majority, Judge Ozaki dissenting), VII, VIII, and IX. Trial Chambers II and IV did not pronounce on this issue.

29   *Prosecutor v Ntaganda* (Decision on witness preparation) ICC-01/04-02/06-652, T Ch VI (16 June 2015) para. 18.

30   Kai O. Schüttpelz, *Witness Preparation in International and Domestic Legal Proceedings*, (Nomos, 2014) 176.

31   *Prosecutor v Ntaganda* (Decision on witness preparation) ICC-01/04-02/06-652, T Ch VI (16 June 2015) para. 17.

32   See for example *Prosecutor v Bemba Gombo*, (Victims and Witnesses Unit's Unified Protocol on the practices used to prepare and familiarise witnesses for giving testimony at trial) ICC-01/05-01/08-972, Registrar (22 October 2010).

7.5.1.1 Lapse of Time since the Occurrence of the Alleged Events

The time lapse between the allegations and the trial has been considered as a significant factor by Trial Chambers. In fact, in the *Al Hassan* case, the Chamber found that eight years justified the authorisation of a witness preparation session in order for the witness to review his or her statement and understand the subjects on which they will be questioned.[33] This was also the case in the *Ntaganda* case, where the Trial Chamber VI considered that witness preparation would allow the calling party to engage with the witness with the aim of establishing the most effective way to uncover the truth during the trial considering that the alleged events took place more than twelve years before.[34]

7.5.1.2 Protection of the Well-Being of Witnesses

The Chamber considers that witness preparation ensures that the witness – whom may be unfamiliar with the judicial process and appearing before a court for the first time in a foreign country – is more comfortable and confident during his or her testimony.[35] It also adds that it is especially useful for crime-based witnesses who are called to testify on alleged traumatic events and mistreatment. These witnesses are placed in a very vulnerable position whilst testifying and would benefit from meeting with the counsel beforehand.[36] Witness preparation helps reduce the stress and anxiety a witness can have due to his or her upcoming testimony before a court.[37]

In the *Ruto and Sang* case, the Chamber considered that "limiting pre-testimony contact between counsel and witnesses to the ten minute "courtesy meeting" provided for in the Familiarisation Protocol does not best serve the Chamber's Article 68(1) duty to take appropriate measures to protect the

---

33   *Prosecutor v Al Hassan* (Decision on witness preparation and familiarisation) ICC-01/12-01/18-666, T Ch X (17 March 2020) para. 12.

34   *Prosecutor v Ntaganda* (Decision on witness preparation) ICC-01/04-02/06-652, T Ch VI (16 June 2015) para. 18.

35   *Prosecutor v Al Hassan* (Decision on witness preparation and familiarisation) ICC-01/12-01/18-666, T Ch X (17 March 2020) para. 13; *Ibid*; *Prosecutor v Ruto and Sang* (Decision on witness preparation) ICC-01/09-01/11-524, T Ch V (2 January 2013) para. 36; *Prosecutor v Ruto and Sang* (Decision on witness preparation: Partly Dissenting Opinion of Judge Eboe-Osuji) ICC-01/09-01/11-524, T Ch V (3 January 2013), para. 8; *Prosecutor v Kenyatta* (Decision on witness preparation) ICC-01/09-02/11-588, T Ch V (2 January 2013) para. 40.

36   *Prosecutor v Al Hassan* (Decision on witness preparation and familiarisation) ICC-01/12-01/18-666, T Ch X (17 March 2020) para. 13.

37   *Prosecutor v Ruto and Sang* (Decision on witness preparation) ICC-01/09-01/11-524, T Ch V (2 January 2013) para. 37; *Prosecutor v Ruto and Sang* (Decision on witness preparation: Partly Dissenting Opinion of Judge Eboe-Osuji) ICC-01/09-01/11-524, T Ch V (3 January 2013), paras 7–9; *Prosecutor v Kenyatta* (Decision on witness preparation) ICC-01/09-02/11-588, T Ch V (2 January 2013) para. 41.

well-being and dignity of witnesses."[38] In the same vein, witness preparation also contributes to witness protection; this practice reduces risks in regards to the security situation on the field, by allowing the parties to engage in less meetings and interviews with the witnesses on the field.[39]

7.5.1.3 Facilitation of a Fair and Expeditious Trial

The Court finds that witness preparation can contribute to the fair and expeditiousness of the trial proceedings.[40] These sessions allow the witnesses to recollect the alleged events and to thoroughly understand what they will be questioned on, thus leading to more efficient, focused and better structured witness examinations. A witness whom testifies in an incomplete and unstructured matter does not assist the Chamber in its truth-finding function.[41] Furthermore, as for the introduction of previously recorded testimonies under Rule 68(3) of the Rules, the Chamber found that witness preparation sessions are ideal, as they give the opportunity to the witness to confirm the veracity of their statements and to make the appropriate modifications, if need be.[42]

Relatedly, witnesses who are presented a document on stand for the first time may not have enough time to fully consider what they know of the document, nor its relevance to their testimony. In these circumstances, the witness may be incapable of providing the Chamber with the relevant information, if not. Therefore, in cases where there are a high number of potential exhibits, the Chamber considered it favourable for the witness to be shown the potential exhibits ahead of time to ensure a complete testimony and efficiency in the conduct of proceedings.[43]

---

38   Ibid.
39   *Prosecutor v Al Hassan* (Decision on witness preparation and familiarisation) ICC-01/12-01/18-666, T Ch X (17 March 2020) para. 14.
40   *Prosecutor v Ntaganda* (Decision on witness preparation) ICC-01/04-02/06-652, T Ch VI (16 June 2015) para. 18; *Ibid* para. 15; *Prosecutor v Ruto and Sang* (Decision on witness preparation) ICC-01/09-01/11-524, T Ch V (2 January 2013) paras 31, 34, 36; *Prosecutor v Kenyatta* (Decision on witness preparation) ICC-01/09-02/11-588, T Ch V (2 January 2013) para. 39.
41   *Prosecutor v Ruto and Sang* (Decision on witness preparation) ICC-01/09-01/11-524, T Ch V (2 January 2013) para. 31; *Prosecutor v Kenyatta* (Decision on witness preparation) ICC-01/09-02/11-588, T Ch V (2 January 2013) para. 35; *Prosecutor v Bemba Gombo* (Partly Dissenting Opinion of Judge Kuniko Ozaki on the Decision on the Unified Protocol on the practices used to prepare and familiarise witnesses for giving testimony at trial) ICC-01/05-01/08-1039, T Ch III (24 November 2010) para. 21.
42   *Prosecutor v Al Hassan* (Decision on witness preparation and familiarisation) ICC-01/12-01/18-666, T Ch X (17 March 2020) para. 16.
43   *Prosecutor v Ntaganda* (Decision on witness preparation) ICC-01/04-02/06-652, T Ch VI (16 June 2015) para. 18; *Prosecutor v Ruto and Sang* (Decision on witness preparation) ICC-01/09-01/11-524, T Ch V (2 January 2013) para. 33; *Prosecutor v Kenyatta* (Decision on

In Judge Jeffrey Henderson's Partially Dissenting Opinion regarding paragraphs 13 to 19 of the *Decision on witness preparation and familiarisation*,[44] in which the Majority reject the requests for a protocol to prepare witnesses for trial, she elaborates on the different benefits – namely providing the Chamber with the best evidence possible in regards to issues relating to language barriers, time that has elapsed between the moment of the investigations and the testimony and efficient and effective questioning of the witnesses during the proceedings – of witness preparation and how it is in line with the practice and procedure of an adversarial trial, that of which the ICC abides by.[45] In the present system, the parties conduct investigations, involving the interviewing of witnesses, as well as taking of witness statements. Judge Henderson also notes that the adversarial system is intrinsically dependant on the ability of the calling parties to guarantee that the evidence presented to the Court through its witnesses is relevant and efficiently delivered in a way that is clear, complete and understood by the Chamber.[46]

7.5.2   *Risks of Witness Preparation*

Some Pre-Trial and Trial Chambers at the ICC have however ruled against witness preparation. Trial Chamber VII clearly states:

> that the principles of orality and immediacy that govern trial proceedings require that evidence is brought before the Chamber in a genuine and undistorted manner, leaving it for the Judges to assess any inconsistencies or additional evidence which are, in any case, better tested in the courtroom before the Chamber.[47]

---

witness preparation) ICC-01/09-02/11-588, T Ch V (2 January 2013) para. 37; *Prosecutor v Bemba et al.* (Decision on Witness Preparation and Familiarisation) ICC-01/05-01/13-1252, T Ch VII (15 September 2015) para. 23; *Prosecutor v Bemba Gombo* (Partly Dissenting Opinion of Judge Kuniko Ozaki on the Decision on the Unified Protocol on the practices used to prepare and familiarise witnesses for giving testimony at trial) ICC-01/05-01/08-1039, T Ch III (24 November 2010) para. 22.

44   *Prosecutor v Gbagbo and Blé Goudé* (Decision on witness preparation and familiarisation) ICC-02/11-01/15-355, T Ch I (2 December 2015).
45   *Prosecutor v Gbagbo and Blé Goudé* (Partially Dissenting Opinion of Judge Henderson) ICC-02/11-01/15-355-Anx1, T Ch I (3 December 2015).
46   *Ibid* para. 5.
47   *Prosecutor v Bemba et al.* (Decision on Witness Preparation and Familiarisation) ICC-01/05-01/13-1252, T Ch VII (15 September 2015) para. 25; *Prosecutor v Gbagbo and Blé Goudé* (Decision on witness preparation and familiarisation) ICC-02/11-01/15-355, T Ch I (2 December 2015) para. 16; Article 69(2) of the Statute

The Chambers that are confronted to a request to authorize witness preparation have to evaluate and balance the risks that this practice entails and its potential benefits, in the specific circumstances of the respective case presented before the Chamber.[48] The following sections will look at the main reasons that mitigate against witness preparation.

7.5.2.1 Impermissible Conduct, i.e. Tailoring of Evidence

Witness preparation inevitably results in inherent risks of interference and truth distortion.[49] Simply partaking in the exercise of systematically scanning through inconsistencies in a witness' statement may lead to impermissible conduct, namely rehearsal, practice and coaching. This practice could influence the true extent of an account and disregard what would have been considered as helpful spontaneity during the witness' live testimony.[50] The *Lubanga Dyilo* Trial Chamber I held that regarding the subject matters to be raised in court or the potential exhibits to be presented in court, "it is the opinion of the Chamber that this could lead to a distortion of the truth and may come dangerously close to constituting a rehearsal of in-court testimony."[51]

That being said, according to the professional standards of the Court, counsel is, in principle, bound to act in good faith and is prohibited to interfere intentionally with a witness's evidence.[52] In Judge Henderson's point of view, the existing risks of 'impermissible conduct' should be included in the balance of evaluating whether witness preparation should be authorised.[53] However, to conclude that the said risks automatically outweigh any other factor would

---

48 *Prosecutor v Bemba et al.* (Decision on Witness Preparation and Familiarisation) ICC-01/05-01/13-1252, T Ch VII (15 September 2015) paras 22, 25.
49 See also *Prosecutor v Bemba Gombo* (Partly Dissenting Opinion of Judge Kuniko Ozaki on the Decision on the Unified Protocol on the practices used to prepare and familiarise witnesses for giving testimony at trial) ICC-01/05-01/08-1039, T Ch III (24 November 2010) para. 25.
50 *Prosecutor v Gbagbo and Blé Goudé* (Decision on witness preparation and familiarisation) ICC-02/11-01/15-355, T Ch I (2 December 2015) para. 17; *Prosecutor v Bemba et al.* (Decision on Witness Preparation and Familiarisation) ICC-01/05-01/13-1252, T Ch VII (15 September 2015) para. 22.
51 *Prosecutor v Lubanga Dyilo* (Decision regarding the Practices used to Prepare and Familiarise Witnesses for Giving Testimony at Trial) ICC-01/04-01/06-1049, T Ch I (30 November 2007) para. 51; See also *Prosecutor v Lubanga Dyilo* (Decision on the Practices of Witness Familiarisation and Witness Proofing) ICC-01/04-01/06-679, PT Ch I (9 November 2006).
52 *Prosecutor v Ruto and Sang* (Decision on witness preparation) ICC-01/09-01/11-524, T Ch V (2 January 2013) para. 46.
53 *Prosecutor v Gbagbo and Blé Goudé* (Partially Dissenting Opinion of Judge Henderson) ICC-02/11-01/15-355-Anx1, T Ch I (3 December 2015) para. 10.

be to disregard the complexities of the complex system which emanates of the Rome Statute.

7.5.2.2   Alteration of the Reliability of the Evidence

Notwithstanding that Trial Chamber V in the *Ruto and Sang* case ruled favourably for witness preparation, the Chamber held that:

> The Chamber is mindful of the concern that witness preparation could become an improper rehearsal of in-court testimony which may negatively affect the reliability of the evidence adduced at trial.[54]

Witness preparation directly, yet superficially, enhances the witness' appearance of confidence before the Court. The addition of (i) the evidence being altered and thus not reliable, and (ii) the artificial 'upgrade' in its impact can only result in negatively influencing the fact finding capacities of a trial, and ultimately on the truth seeking role of the Court.[55]

Furthermore, the idea of spontaneity in witness testimony mitigates against witness preparation.[56] The Trial Chamber in the *Lubanga Dyilo* case held that the preparation of the witnesses prior to their testimonies may impact the spontaneity a witness would have had during the giving of evidence, which assists the Chamber in its truth seeking role.[57] The *Bemba et al.* Trial Chamber VII, echoing these conclusions, found that the risks of the reliability and the spontaneity of the testimonies being tainted by witness preparation outweighed the potential benefits of the practice.[58]

7.5.2.3   Delayed Disclosure

A crucial factor to take into account is the fact that new evidence, which was not previously included in the witness's statement, may emerge from the witness

---

[54] *Prosecutor v Ruto and Sang* (Decision on witness preparation) ICC-01/09-01/11-524, T Ch V (2 January 2013) para. 44.

[55] Kai O. Schuttpelz, *Witness Preparation in International and Domestic Legal Proceedings*, (Nomos, 2014) 166.

[56] *Prosecutor v Bemba et al.* (Decision on Witness Preparation and Familiarisation) ICC-01/05-01/13-1252, T Ch VII (15 September 2015) para. 22.

[57] *Prosecutor v Lubanga Dyilo* (Decision regarding the Practices used to Prepare and Familiarise Witnesses for Giving Testimony at Trial) ICC-01/04-01/06-1049, T Ch I (30 November 2007) paras 52, 57; See also *Prosecutor v Ruto and Sang* (Decision on witness preparation: Partly Dissenting Opinion of Judge Eboe-Osuji) ICC-01/09-01/11-524, T Ch V (3 January 2013) paras 13–19.

[58] *Prosecutor v Bemba et al.* (Decision on Witness Preparation and Familiarisation) ICC-01/05-01/13-1252, T Ch VII (15 September 2015) paras 22–23.

preparation session. The said evidence thus falls under the Prosecution's disclosure obligations, pursuant to the Statue and the Rules, and may be disclosed to the Defense before the witness testifies.[59] However, as set forth by Trial Chamber I in the *Laurent Gbagbo and Blé Goudé* case, this delayed disclosure can cause unwarranted delays in the proceedings.[60]

7.5.3   *Witness Preparation Protocol and Witness Familiarisation*

Chambers that have accepted witness preparation, through the adopting of Protocols,[61] have applied certain safeguards to guarantee the practice's efficiency and the fairness of proceedings, whilst protecting the accused's rights.

Firstly, the use of cross-examination, as well as questioning by the Chamber, regarding the scope of a witness's preparation can allow the Court to verify and avoid improper conduct.[62]

Secondly, the Chamber adopts guidelines as to what conduct is permissible and what is prohibited, in order to eradicate the risks of witness coaching during the witness preparation.[63] For instance, the calling-party may need to require authorisation to communicate with the witness within the 24 hours preceding the witness's testimony[64] and the calling-party may be prohibited to make the witness *practice* his or her testimony.[65] *Thirdly*, the video recording of the preparation sessions may be required as an additional safeguard measure. Should there be any allegations concerning witness coaching or any other

---

59   *Prosecutor v Ruto and Sang* (Decision on witness preparation) ICC-01/09-01/11-524, T Ch V (2 January 2013) para. 42.
60   *Prosecutor v Gbagbo and Blé Goudé* (Decision on witness preparation and familiarisation) ICC-02/11-01/15-355, T Ch I (2 December 2015) para. 17.
61   *Prosecutor v Ntaganda* (Annex to Decision on witness preparation) ICC-01/04-02/06-652-Anx, T Ch VI (16 June 2015); See also *Prosecutor v Ntaganda* (Annex A Protocol on the practices to be used to familiarise witnesses for giving testimony at trial) ICC-01/04-02/06-656-AnxA, T Ch VI (17 June 2015) and *Prosecutor v Ntaganda* (Annex B Protocol on the practices to be used to familiarise witnesses for giving testimony at trial) ICC-01/04-02/06-656-AnxB, T Ch VI (17 June 2015); *Prosecutor v Ruto and Sang* (Annex: Decision on witness preparation) ICC-01/09-01/11-524-Anx, T Ch V (7 February 2013);
62   *Prosecutor v Ruto and Sang* (Decision on witness preparation) ICC-01/09-01/11-524, T Ch V (2 January 2013) para. 45.
63   *Ibid* para. 46; See also *Prosecutor v Ruto and Sang* (Annex: Decision on witness preparation) ICC-01/09-01/11-524-Anx, T Ch V (7 February 2013); *Prosecutor v Ruto and Sang* (Decision on witness preparation: Partly Dissenting Opinion of Judge Eboe-Osuji) ICC-01/09-01/11-524, T Ch V (3 January 2013) paras 38–39.
64   *Prosecutor v Al Hassan* (Decision on witness preparation and familiarisation) ICC-01/12-01/18-666, T Ch X (17 March 2020) para. 57.
65   *Prosecutor v Ruto and Sang* (Annex: Decision on witness preparation) ICC-01/09-01/11-524-Anx, T Ch V (7 February 2013).

witness interference, the Chamber may order the disclosure of the said video following a request to that effect from the non-calling party.[66]

Finally, one of the components of witness preparation that has been put into place by many Trial Chambers is 'witness familiarisation', which consists of a series of arrangements to familiarise the witness with the court proceedings, falling under the functions of the VWU.[67] Technically, this does not amount to witness preparation. The Chamber found that this practice is supported by the Rome Statute and the Rules of Procedure and Evidence.[68] The witness is informed of the different responsibilities and roles of the various participants at the hearing and will namely be given the opportunity to meet the questioning party.[69] When comparing the risks of content-wise witness preparation and the benefits of both preparation and familiarisation, it becomes evident that the severe risks of preparation are not present in familiarisation, still all the benefits preparation provides to the witness and the court are contained in familiarisation.[70] This is the approach adopted by many Trial Chambers.

7.6 Conclusion

To conclude, this chapter has shown that even though witness preparation is a prevalent practice in common law jurisdictions and has previously been accepted by *ad hoc* international tribunals, the majority of the ICC Trial Chambers have explicitly refused this practice by way of decision, or implicitly, by allowing Unified Protocols for witnesses' familiarisation, in which no margin for witness preparation or proofing have been given to the parties.[71]

In light of the above, whilst this practice may remain an advantage in regards to the conduct of proceedings, from the perspective of Defense counsel, it might strategically be beneficial to oppose witness preparation if such

---

66 *Prosecutor v Ruto and Sang* (Decision on witness preparation) ICC-01/09-01/11-524, T Ch V (2 January 2013) para. 47.
67 *Prosecutor v Lubanga Dyilo* (Decision on the Practices of Witness Familiarisation and Witness Proofing) ICC-01/04-01/06-679, PT Ch I (9 November 2006) para. 15; *Prosecutor v Ntaganda* (Decision on the protocol on witness familiarisation) ICC-01/04-02/06-656, T Ch VI (17 June 2015).
68 *Prosecutor v Lubanga Dyilo* (Decision on the Practices of Witness Familiarisation and Witness Proofing) ICC-01/04-01/06-679, PT Ch I (9 November 2006) para. 15.
69 *Ibid*.
70 Schuttpelz (n 55) 177.
71 *Prosecutor v Bemba et al.* (Decision on the Unified Protocol on the practices used to prepare and familiarise witnesses for giving testimony at trial) ICC-01/05-01/08-1016, T Ch III (18 November 2010), para. 34.

practice were to be requested by the Prosecution. For the Prosecution, its case might otherwise be strengthened through the direct examination of witnesses which are prepared. Consequently distancing the Court from its truth seeking function. Since the emphasis at the ICC (and in fact at any trial) lies on whether the Prosecution has met its burden of proof, the advantage of not having witness preparation for Prosecution witnesses in place outweighs the potential benefits of Defense preparation for Defense witnesses.

In addition, Defense counsel may suffer a prejudice from the late disclosure of relevant evidence to the case, resulting in short delays, if any, to conduct the appropriate investigations and analysis. The spontaneity of the witnesses' answers and reactions during examinations outweigh can be extremely beneficial to the assessment of a witness's credibility and reliability.

CHAPTER 8

(Crosss-)Examining Witnesses at the ICC

8.1 Types of Cross-examination

Cross-examination, at the ICC also referred to as 'examination by the non-calling party', is a powerful tool for the Prosecution or the Defense to challenge the testimony of a witness of the opposing party in order to discredit the evidentiary value of a certain witness testimony.[1] Additionally, it is a similar powerful instrument to elicit evidence from the witness of the opposing party to adduce support for the case theory of the cross-examining party.

The question as to the most effective technique of cross-examination depends on the specific case at hand. Yet, there are in general two types of cross-examination which can be effective also before the ICC, or a combination thereof.[2]

(i) First, the constructive cross-examination. This technique aims at obtaining from the witness information or answers which corroborate the Defense narrative (in case the Defense is the cross-examining party;[3]

(ii) Second, the destructive cross-examination. This technique is meant to damage and challenge the credibility of the particular witness, and to treat this witness as 'hostile'.[4]

Both techniques can best be applied by using 'leading questions', a type of questioning in which the form of the question suggests the answer.[5] In the U.S. Federal system,[6] while leading questions are generally not allowed during the direct examination of a witness, they are instead allowed on the cross-examination.[7] In 2001 in the case of *Akayesu*, the ICTR Appeals Chamber recalled that "the Rules of the Tribunal have never contained any specific

---

1 'Cross Examination', *Legal Information Institut* (Cornell University insignia) <https://www.law.cornell.edu/wex/cross_examination#content> accessed 23 August 2023.
2 'Five Steps to an Effective Cross-examination' (*LexisNexis*, 31 January 2023) <https://www.lexisnexis.com/community/insights/legal/b/thought-leadership/posts/five-steps-to-an-effective-cross-examination> accessed 23 August 2023.
3 Ibid.
4 Ibid.
5 'Leading Question', *Legal Information Institut* (Cornell University insignia) <https://www.law.cornell.edu/wex/leading_question#content> accessed 23 August 2023.
6 Rule 611(c) of the Federal Rules of Evidence.
7 'Leading Question', *Legal Information Institut* (Cornell University insignia) <https://www.law.cornell.edu/wex/leading_question#content> accessed 23 August 2023.

provision on the issue of leading questions. However, they do lay down general rules on examination and cross-examination of witnesses, which appear to be patterned on the United States Federal Rules of Evidence. True, under this system, leading questions are allowed and used during cross-examination whereas they are not permitted during examination-in-chief. Still in the opinion of the Appeals Chamber, the Rules take on a life of their own upon adoption. Interpretation of the provisions thereof may be guided by the domestic system it is patterned after, but under no circumstance can it be subordinated to it".[8]

8.2   ICTY Jurisprudence on Cross-examination of Witnesses

Although the ICTY had envisaged proceedings of a more adversarial nature than the ICC system, its jurisprudence affirms that the right to cross-examination is not an absolute right, especially with reference to the question of victim and witness protection. In 2006 in the case of *Martic*, the Appeals Chamber stated:

> [T]he right of an accused to cross-examine a witness is not absolute. The Appeals Chamber recalls that the right to cross-examination may, for instance, be limited in accordance with Rule 92bis and that its exercise remains subject to the control of the Trial Chamber pursuant to Rule 90(F).[9] In this regard, the Appeals Chamber rejected the Appellant's claim that the fairness of a trial is uniquely predicated on the fairness accorded to the Accused, recalling how it had previously observed that "the application of a fair trial in favour of both parties is understandable because the Prosecution acts on behalf of and in the interests of the community, including the victims of the offences charged (in cases before the Tribunal the Prosecutor acts on behalf of the international community) [...] Seen in this way, it is difficult to see how a trial could ever be considered fair where the accused is favoured at the expense of the Prosecution beyond a strict compliance with those fundamental protections. Although proceedings must be conducted with full respect for the rights enumerated in Article 21 of the Statute, restrictions on the right to cross-examination will not necessarily entail a violation of that

---

8   *Prosecutor v Akayesu* (Appeal judgment) ICTR-96-4-A, A Ch (1 June 2001) para. 323.
9   *Prosecutor v Martić* (Decision on Appeal Against the Trial Chamber's Decision on the Evidence of Witness Milan Babić) IT-95-11-AR73.2, A Ch (14 September 2006) para. 12.

provision or be inconsistent with a fair trial".[10] Moreover, the Chamber agreed with the Trial Chamber that "[...] the right to cross-examination is subject to the duty of the Trial Chamber to ensure the fairness and expeditiousness of the proceedings [...]".[11] It further affirmed that "[...] In such a case [when neither the Statute nor the Rules envisage a situation]. Rule 89(B) provides that 'a Chamber shall apply rules of evidence which will best favour a fair determination of the matter before it and are consonant with the spirit of the Statute and the general principles of law.' The Appeals Chamber therefore considers that, to the extent that the Trial Chamber relies on the jurisprudence of the ECHR, its reliance is entirely appropriate in the circumstances.[12] In this regard, the Appeals Chamber further recalled that "the right to cross-examination in Article 21(4)(e) of the Statute is in pari materia with Article 6(3)(d) of the European Convention on Human Rights and its importance has been repeatedly stressed and its violation sanctioned by the ECHR. The Appeals Chamber considers that the jurisprudence of the ECHR provides a useful source of guidance for the interpretation of the right to cross-examination and the scope of its permissible limitations.[13] Conclusively, the Appeals Chamber observed that, in any event, "the two principles that the Trial Chamber derived from the jurisprudence of the ECHR, namely that (1) a complete absence of, or deficiency in, the cross-examination of a witness will not automatically lead to exclusion of the evidence, and (2) evidence which has not been cross-examined and goes to the acts and conduct of the Accused or is pivotal to the Prosecution case will require corroboration if used to establish a conviction, are consistent with the jurisprudence of the International Tribunal as well as that of national jurisdictions.[14]

8.3 Applying Cross-examination Techniques in Trials before the ICC

Several main guidelines are of paramount importance for Defense counsel operating in criminal trials, including in trials before the ICC:

(i) Firstly, prior to deciding to cross-examine a Prosecution witness at the ICC, the main purpose or goal to cross-examine the particular witness should be clear to Defense counsel. This requires that Defense counsel assess three questions:

---

10   *Ibid* para. 13.
11   *Ibid* para. 14.
12   *Ibid* para. 18.
13   *Ibid* para. 19.
14   *Ibid* para. 20.

a. Is the purpose of the cross-examination to have the witness confirm the Defense case theory?
b. Is the purpose to undermine the Prosecution case theory?
c. Is the purpose to damage the credibility of the Prosecution witness?

The purposes sub (b) and (c) are not necessarily similar; indeed, in the course of cross-examination, one could undermine the Prosecution case theory without damaging the credibility of the witness. The purposes sub (b) and (c) could also be jointly applied, provided that this happens in the right sequence. In deciding upon which purpose is most helpful and achievable, the review of the prior statements of the witness is instrumental.

(ii) Secondly, once the main purpose of the cross-examination has been decided upon, the second step for Defense counsel is to create the most effective strategy to achieve this goal by:

a. Creating a clear structure of topics starting with general subjects and ultimately moving to more specific items.
b. Formulating concise leading questions which fit this scheme and focus on the specific fact that the Defense seeks to establish. These questions should prevent the witness from being tempted to provide mere opinions.

(iii) Thirdly, as outlined in the previous paragraph, two different cross-examination techniques are possible: the constructive and the destructive ones. Each of them requires a specific approach.

a. The constructive cross-examination, aimed at obtaining exculpatory information from the witness, requires to transform the cross-examination into a non-hostile examination of the witness. The question should be framed in such a way that the witness has only to confirm certain facts which are put before them.
b. The destructive cross-examination, aimed at discrediting the (Prosecution) witness, involves challenging the witness' knowledge underlining their assertions. This requires that Defense counsel have a thorough knowledge of the witness personal and political backgrounds, which provides the Defense with ammunition to raise doubt as to the witness' motives.

In ICC trials, this factor is very important, as most witnesses appearing before the ICC have held a certain political position within an armed conflict. Challenging the credibility of a particular witness should therefore be based on a detailed analysis of their background, including their criminal records and social media contacts.[15]

---

15 Cf. further chapter XVII.

It is important to save the most damaging evidence to discredit the witness until the end of the cross-examination: This will provide the best resonance in the minds of the judges.

    c. There are some witnesses who can be subjected to a combination of the techniques sub (a) and (b). In the event that the Defense opts for such a combination, it is of paramount importance to cross-examine the witness first on the basis of the technique sub (a) and only when the Defense has received the exculpatory information from the witness, to invoke the technique sub (b).[16]

(iv) Fourthly, as anticipated, Defense counsel should be well aware of any prior statements and exhibits produced by the witness. Indeed, this information may constitute the bases for deciding which cross-examination technique and strategy to adopt. There can – and there will be – instances in which the testimony deviates from his or her prior statement(s). Therefore, it is vital to have detailed knowledge of these prior statements and to confront the witness with such contradictions. This could create a situation where Defense counsel may have to adjust their strategy during the course of the trial, switching from a constructive technique to a more destructive one.

(v) Fifthly, one of the 'golden' cross-examination rules is to never enter into a discussion or argument with the (Prosecution) witness. Even when a witness of the Prosecution turns out to be non-cooperative with the Defense at trial, Defense counsel should not show their resentment but instead remain in control of the questions and remind the witness of the question at hand. Ultimately, Defense counsel can ask the chamber to instruct the witness to answer the question.[17]

(vi) Sixthly, the primary aim of cross-examination, also at the ICC, is to put the defense case to the Prosecution witness in order to test the witness' response to the defendant's version of the events. By doing so, it enables the Prosecution witness to react to the Defense case by either agreeing or disagreeing. In case Defense counsel fails to put the Defense case to the Prosecution witness, particularly with respect to an element which is in dispute, the Defense counsel risks that the Court might conclude that the allegations of the Prosecution witness have been accepted. Failure to do so, also creates the risks that Defense counsel forfeited the possibility to

---

16   'Five Steps to an Effective Cross-Examination' (*LexisNexis*, 31 January 2023) <https://www.lexisnexis.com/community/insights/legal/b/thought-leadership/posts/five-steps-to-an-effective-cross-examination> accessed 23 August 2023.

17   *Ibid.*

raise this specific point in the closing submissions. For all these reasons, it is paramount that the Defense case is put to the Prosecution witness. This view also follows from an important ruling from a UK Court in the case *R v Farooqi*:

> Now that is a considerable accusation to make, and one which if it was to be made, should have been put to Detective Chief Inspector Richardson, the senior investigating officer when he was in the witness box, so that he could deal with it. He has had no opportunity of dealing with what is a very grave allegation ... Counsel simply cannot wait until his closing speech to make such an allegation because the Crown have no way of answering it or dealing with it.[18]

One can say that this view embodies a general principle of criminal evidence and is therefore also applicable at the ICC.

In conclusion, the most important six cross-examination guidelines are:

(i) To determine the primary goal for the witness to be cross-examined;
(ii) To formulate the cross-examination (leading) questions accordingly;
(iii) To apply this structure within the overall technique (either constructive or destructive);
(iv) To get acquainted with all prior statements of the witness (including his or her background);
(v) To master the cross-examination even when dealing with a non-cooperative witness;[19]
(vi) To put the Defense case to the Prosecution witness.

---

18 *R v Farooqi* [2013] EWCA Crim 1649.
19 'Five Steps to an Effective Cross-examination' (*LexisNexis*, 31 January 2023) <https://www.lexisnexis.com/community/insights/legal/b/thought-leadership/posts/five-steps-to-an-effective-cross-examination> accessed 23 August 2023.

CHAPTER 9

The Defendant as Witness at His or Her Own Trial

In common law jurisdictions, the defendant can opt to testify as witness in his or her own case. A similar possibility exists at the ICC. In the ICC case of *Prosecutor v Ongwen*, this happened at the sentencing phase.

Former president of Liberia, Charles Taylor, testified in his own case before the Special Court for Sierra Leone. He was charged with war crimes and crimes against humanity committed from 30 november 1996 to January 18, 2002 during the course of the civil war in Sierra Leon. From 14 July 2009 until 19 February 2010, for seven months, Taylor testified in his own Defense case, denying all charges against him. At the end of the examination by the Defense, Taylor was asked the following question: 'Did you, Charles Taylor, between November 1996 and January 2002 provide assistance, support or any kind of help with war-like materials to either the AFRC or the RUF?' Taylor responded: 'No, never.'[1]

This procedural move of the Defense was to no avail. On 26 April 2012, the Trial Chamber of the Special Court for Sierra Leone found Taylor guilty on all eleven counts on the modes of liability of planning of crimes and for aiding and abetting of crimes by rebel forces in Sierra Leone. On 30 May 2012, Taylor was given a sentence of fifty years imprisonment, which conviction and sentence was upheld in appeal.

A question of perennial concern for Defense counsel is to determine when the defendant should testify in his or her own case. Multiple factors may contribute to such a decision. Some factors can be the following:

(i) The lack of a Defense witness to refute a specific element of the charges, while the defendant is the only person who can enlighten the Court or jury to on this point.
(ii) To substantiate a certain Defense such as that of necessity, duress, Defense or mental disease. The explanation by the defendant itself as to the circumstances he or she committed the offense while acting under one of these Defenses, can be essential to persuade the Court or jury.

---

1 See Alpha Sesay, 'Charles Taylor Concludes His Testimony: Prosecutors Have Not Proven Their Case, He Says' (International Justice Monitor, 19 February 2010) <https://www.ijmonitor.org/2010/02/charles-taylor-concludes-his-testimony-prosecutors-have-not-proven-their-case-he-says/> accessed 27 June 2024.

(iii) The personality of the defendant, especially his or her charisma, integrity and credibility which will make his version of the events more probable than the Prosecution theory.
(iv) The ability of the defendant to withstand an invasive cross-examination by the Prosecution.
(v) The assessment whether a 'personalization' of the Defense case makes the chances for an acquittal more likely.

In the event the Defense decides to have their defendant testify in his or her own case, it is of crucial importance that all the incriminatory evidence which was presented by the Prosecution in the case file and at trial, is being put by Defense counsel to the defendant – while of course having prepared this beforehand with the defendant in order to countervail the cross-examination on these points by the Prosecution.

Needless to say that such a Defense strategy requires a detailed preparation, preferably with a thorough rehearsal of such an examination with the defendant. However, if there is any doubt whether the defendant can withstand the rigors of a thorough cross-examination by the Prosecution, it might be better for Defense counsel to advise this client not to take the stand as a witness in their own case: the potential damage might be far greater than any possible benefits.

PART 3

Indirect Evidence

∴

CHAPTER 10

Circumstantial Evidence at the ICC

10.1 Introduction

The Prosecution before the ICC, in most cases whereby direct evidence is absent, has to resort to circumstantial evidence. This type of evidence is frequently, but not exclusively, used to establish *mens rea*, whether the requirement is one of general or specific intent, incoherent crimes such as conspiracy and superior responsibility or other indirect forms of participation.[1] This type of evidence is admissible, albeit that the jurisprudence of the International Criminal Tribunals has set forth some parameters for such admissibility.

The inherent legal danger of circumstantial evidence is that it is subject to a rather subjective interpretation by a Trial Chamber, based on so-called inferences. A Trial Chamber has to draw conclusions from different indicia, taken and weighed in conjunction with one another, but which in themselves do not constitute direct proof.[2]

The problem with circumstantial evidence is the absence of any clear definition of what it is or should be and the lack of a transparent legal threshold. This issue makes it quite difficult for Defense counsel to challenge this type of evidence. The present chapter intends to determine the jurisprudential contours of circumstantial evidence which could assist Defense counsel.

10.2 Jurisprudential Denominations for Circumstantial Evidence

The concept of circumstantial evidence has been of relevance since 1872 when James Stephen wrote:

> Facts relevant to the issue are facts from the existence of which inferences as to the existence of the facts in issue may be drawn. A fact is relevant to another fact when the existence of the one fact can be shown to

---

1 Richard May and Marieke Wierda, *International Criminal Evidence*, vol 9 (Brill 2021) 112–113 <https://brill.com/display/title/13900#navigation> accessed 14 June 2023; cf. Also *Prosecutor v Blaškić* (Trial judgment) IT-95-14-T, T Ch (3 March 2000) para. 281; The fact that an order was given can also be proven by circumstantial evidence, cf. *Prosecutor v Galić* (Trial judgment) IT-98-29-T, T Ch I (5 December 2003) para. 171.
2 May and Wierda (n 1) 114.

be the cause or one of the causes, or the effect or one of the effects, of the existence of the other, or when the existence of the one, either alone or together with other facts, renders the existence of the other highly probable, or improbable, according to the common course of events.[3]

The Chamberlain judgment of 1983 of the British High Court is one of the judgments in which the parameters of circumstantial evidence are to be found, as Judge Brennan held:

> The prosecution case rested on circumstantial evidence. Circumstantial evidence can, and often does, clearly prove the commission of a criminal offence, but two conditions must be met. First, the primary facts from which the inference of guilt is to be drawn must be proven beyond reasonable doubt. No greater cogency can be attributed to an inference based upon particular facts. Secondly, the inference of guilt must be the only inference which is reasonably open on all the primary facts which the jury finds. The drawing of the inference is not a matter of evidence: it is solely a function of the jury's critical judgment of men and affairs, their experience and their reason. An inference of guilt can safely be drawn if it is based upon primary facts which are found beyond reasonable doubt and if it is the only inference which is reasonably open upon the whole body of primary facts.[4]

The first condition is particularly not to be overlooked in the law practice.

One of the first rulings on the parameters of circumstantial evidence can be found in the Appeal Judgment of the ICTY of 20 February 2001 in *Prosecutor v Mucić et al.*:

> A circumstantial case consists of evidence of a number of different circumstances which, taken in combination, point to the guilt of the accused person because they would usually exist in combination only because the accused did what is alleged against him – here that the participated in the second beating of Gotovac. Such a conclusion must be established beyond reasonable doubt. It is not sufficient that it is a

---

3   Ian Barker, 'Circumstantial Evidence in Criminal Cases' [2011] Bar News: The Journal of the NSW Bar Association 32, 32; James Stephen, *Digest of the Law of Evidence Shaw* (Macmillan 1907) 14 (introduction).
4   Barker (n 3) 35.

reasonable conclusion available from that evidence. It must be the only reasonable conclusion available. If there is another conclusion which is also reasonably open from that evidence, and which is consistent with the innocence of the accused he must be acquitted.[5]

At the ICC, this approach has been applied in several cases. One of the first judgments rendered by the ICC which allowed the introduction of circumstantial evidence was the Trial Judgment pursuant to article 74 of the ICC Statute in *Prosecutor v Lubanga Dyilo* of 14 March 2012.[6] Trial Chamber I held in this regard:

> 111. Nothing in the Rome Statute framework prevents the Chamber from relying on circumstantial evidence. When, based on the evidence, there is only one reasonable conclusion to be drawn from particular facts, the Chamber has concluded that they have been established beyond reasonable doubt.

Yet, Judge Henderson writing the majority opinion in the article 74 decision of Trial Chamber I of the ICC in *Prosecutor v Gbagbo and Blé Goudé* d.d. 16 July 2019, alluded to the potential risk of the use of circumstantial evidence. In paragraph 51 of his opinion Judge Henderson noted

> Proof of the charges against the accused in this trial, depends in part on circumstantial evidence and it has been settled in the Court's jurisprudence that this is permissible. It is also well accepted that circumstantial evidence can be as strong as direct evidence. However, the potential weakness of this type of evidence is that wrong inferences may be drawn from a set of entirely true circumstantial facts or from facts which may have been mischaracterized. It is for this reason that the Chamber is required to narrowly evaluate the evidence for the underlying primary facts submitted to ensure not only that they are accurately portrayed but also before drawing the inferences invited by the prosecutor, to be sure that there are no other co-existing circumstances which would weaken or destroy that inference. In order to convict, the beyond a reasonable

---

5 *Prosecutor v Mucić et al.* (Appeal judgment) IT-96-21-A, A Ch (20 February 2001) para. 458.
6 *Prosecutor v Lubanga Dyilo* (Trial judgment) ICC-01/04-01/06-2842, T Ch 1 (14 March 2012) para. 111.

doubt standard requires that the inference must be the only reasonable inference that can be drawn from the primary fact.[7]

10.3   Circumstantial Evidence within ad hoc Tribunals

As stated previously, the *Prosecutor v Mucić et al.* case established the standard of proof applicable to circumstantial evidence applied at the ICTY,[8] as well as at the ICRC. This standard has been applied in numerous cases before the ICTY, namely in the *Vasiljević, Krstić* and *Kvocka et al.* Appeal Judgments in the context of the establishment of the accused state of mind by inference[9] and the *Stakić* Appeal Judgment.[10]

Echoing this standard of proof, in response to the Prosecution's claim that the Trial Chamber erroneously failed to the draw the only reasonable conclusion from the circumstantial evidence, the *Ntagerura et al.* Appeals Chamber held that:

> It is settled jurisprudence that the conclusion of guilt can be inferred from circumstantial evidence only if it is the only reasonable conclusion available on the evidence. Whether a Trial Chamber infers the existence of a particular fact upon which the guilt of the accused depends from direct or circumstantial evidence, it must reach such a conclusion beyond reasonable doubt. If there is another conclusion which is also reasonably open from that evidence, and which is consistent with the non-existence of that fact, the conclusion of guilt beyond reasonable doubt cannot be drawn.[11] (…) The same requirement must apply in inferring from the available evidence that there is an act upon which the accused's

---

[7] *Prosecutor v Gbagbo and Blé Goudé* (Public Redacted Version of Reasons of Judge Geoffrey Henderson) ICC-02/11-01/15-1263-AnxB-Red, T Ch I (16 July 2019) para. 51, also referring to *Prosecutor v Bemba Gombo* (Trial judgment) ICC-01/05-01/08-3343, T Ch III (21 March 2016) para. 239.

[8] *Prosecutor v Mucić et al.* (Appeal judgment) IT-96-21-A, A Ch (20 February 2001) para. 458.

[9] *Prosecutor v Vasiljević* (Appeal judgment) IT-98-32-A, A Ch (25 February 2004) para. 120; *Prosecutor v Krstić* (Appeal judgment) IT-98-33-A, A Ch (19 April 2004) para. 41; *Prosecutor v Kvočka et al.* (Appeal judgment) IT-98-30/1-A, A Ch (28 February 2005) para. 237.

[10] *Prosecutor v Stakić* (Appeal judgment) IT-97-24-A, A Ch (22 March 2006) para. 219.

[11] *Prosecutor v Ntagerura et al.* (Appeal judgment) ICTR-99-46-A, A Ch (7 July 2006) paras 304–306.

guilt depends and in inferring a finding upon which the accused's guilt depends from several distinct factual findings.[12]

10.4 Challenging Circumstantial Evidence at Trial

For Defense counsel to challenge circumstantial evidence in court, it means that he or she has to show the Court that a certain piece of evidence could be interpreted otherwise than the Prosecution submits and which contradicts the incriminatory nature of such a piece of evidence. Cross-examination techniques can be a useful tool to achieve this goal.

An example may illustrate this Defense approach. A defendant is charged with aiding and abetting war crimes through the financing of weapons. The Prosecution introduces a witness who testifies at trial that he knows that defendant provided money to certain armed groups, albeit that he does not know for what exact purposes. The Court might infer from this testimony that the defendant indeed financed the purchase of weapons for this armed group. During cross-examination, Defense counsel questions the witness on the social-economic conditions during the particular conflict and hears the witness saying that everyone was struggling at that time for food and medication. Defense counsel then raises the possibility that the defendant could have provided money for the latter purpose. Although the witness does not know the exact purpose of the alleged financial support, he admits to know that the defendant helped some poor families during the civil war in question. This type of cross-examination creates a fruitful ground to present to the Court an alternative inference, which makes the Prosecution's inference not the only reasonable one.

It is important to note that the criterion of the 'only reasonable conclusion available' applies to both the *actus reus* as the *mens rea* element of the charges. The mental element of a certain crime, in the absence of a confession, is mostly based on inferences and deductions. It is therefore also for the Defense to show that a certain requisite *mens rea*, in terms of a guilty mind, is not the only reasonable conclusion. In the example mentioned above, the Defense could argue that, apart from the *actus reus*, the intent of the defendant was not to facilitate the war but simply to prevent the armed group from plundering property of civilians to obtain food.

---

12   *Ibid* para. 399.

10.5 Evidentiary Value and Requirements for Circumstantial Evidence

The consequence of the analysis made in the preceding paragraphs is that when the Prosecution case would substantially rest on circumstantial evidence, a Trial Chamber should not rule a guilty verdict unless the Prosecution would have excluded all reasonable hypotheses consistent with the innocence of the accused.[13] This implies the following evidentiary consequences:

(i) For an inference to be reasonable, it must rest upon elements which are more than a mere conjecture.[14]

(ii) The burden does not rest on the Defense either to establish that some inference other than guilt should be drawn from the evidence or to prove particular facts which might support such an inference.[15]

(iii) To refuse a Prosecution case which rests on circumstantial evidence, it is sufficient that the Defense's alternative hypothesis consistent with innocence can be derived reasonably from the evidence available in the Prosecution case.[16]

(iv) When assessing the evidentiary value of circumstantial evidence, all the circumstances which arise from the Prosecution evidence must be taken into account and weighed to determine if there exists an inference consistent with innocence which is reasonably open in light of the evidence.[17]

(v) According to common law jurisprudence, the evidence must be weighed as a whole and '(…) not by a piecemeal approach to each particular circumstance', which means that individual items of evidence which on their own are not sufficient to justify a conviction '(…) may take strength from other items'.[18]

---

13 The Queen v Baden-Clay (2016) 258 CLR 308, paras 46–50; Barca v The Queen (1975) 133 CLR 82, para. 104.
14 The Queen v Baden-Clay, para. 47, quoting Peacock v The King (1911) 13 CLR 619, para. 661; Gwilliam v R [2019] NSWCCA 5, paras 101 and 104.
15 The Queen v Baden-Clay (2016) 258 CLR 308, para. 62, citing Barca v The Queen (1975) 133 CLR 82, para. 105.
16 Wiggins v R [2020] NSWCCA 256, para. 65.
17 The Queen v Baden-Clay (2016) 258 CLR 308, para. 47.
18 Davidson v R (2009), 75 NSWLR 150, para. 61.

10.6 Increasing the Evidentiary Burden: the 'Shepherd Direction' Doctrine's Broad Application within the ICC

Within common law, a specific approach has been developed which increases the evidentiary burden for the Prosecution when relying on circumstantial evidence. This approach has been known as the 'Shepherd direction'.

As mentioned, if a component of a case rests upon circumstantial evidence, the particular circumstances of that said component, in their individuality, do not need to be proven beyond reasonable doubt.[19] Yet, there may be instances where within a case built on circumstantial evidence, one or more facts which are relied upon by the Prosecution are '(...) so fundamental to the process of reasoning to the guilt of the accused that the fact or facts must be proved beyond reasonable doubt.'[20] In common law, such facts are referred to as 'intermediate facts', meaning that they are 'an indispensable limb in a chain of reasoning toward an inference of guilt.'[21]

This evidentiary exception is derived from the UK judgement in *Shepherd v The Queen*.[22] The following question emerges: what constitutes such an 'indispensable, intermediate fact'? In the judgment of *Davidson v R* of 2009, Judge Simpson tried to solve this question by introducing the test whether in the absence of evidence of that fact, there '(...) would nonetheless be a case to go to the jury'.[23]

One can also formulate the 'Shepherd direction' for the purposes of ICC proceedings as follows. If without a certain fact, the Court could not arrive at the unavoidable conclusion that the Prosecution did establish the guilt of the accused, that particular fact on its own has to be proven beyond reasonable doubt. If this is not the case, the Court should have to 'return a verdict of not guilty'.[24]

---

19   "Shepherd direction" paras 2–510.
20   *Ibid*.
21   *Ibid*.
22   Shepherd v The Queen (1990), 170 CLR 573.
23   *Ibid*, also referring to the fact that this exception is often mentioned as a 'link in a chain case'.
24   *Ibid* paras 2–530; The *Stakić* Appeals Chamber formulates it as such: "The question for the Appeals Chamber is whether it was reasonable for the Trial Chamber to exclude or ignore other inferences that lead to the conclusion that an element of the crime was not proven.", see *Prosecutor v Stakić* (Appeal judgment) IT-97-24-A, A Ch (22 March 2006) para. 219.

10.7 Conclusion

This chapter sought to further elucidate the concept of circumstantial evidence, how it is applied in common law jurisdictions, as well as in *ad hoc* international tribunals, how it can be challenged and how it may be applied in the course of ICC proceedings. In short, Defense counsel may present to the court evidence from which it can draw different inferences leading to alternative conclusions than those suggested by the Prosecution.

CHAPTER 11

Evidentiary Principles of Corroboration at the ICC

11.1   Introduction

The purpose of this chapter is to address the application, relevance and challenges of corroborative evidence at the ICC. Foremost, the principle in relation to evidentiary corroboration is namely that it is not formally required in international criminal law.

Corroborative evidence refers to evidence that aims to strengthen or confirm already existing evidence.[1] It is often used in court to confirm a witness's testimony. An overly broad definition, thus application, of corroboration may lead to causing prejudice to the accused.[2] Nevertheless, Trial Chambers have the full discretion as to the weigh, *if* any, that should be attributed to a given piece of evidence, whether that said evidence is corroborated or not.[3]

11.2   The Purpose of Corroboration in Criminal Law

To fully assess the application of corroborative evidence at the ICC, one must first understand its role in the broad scope of criminal law. Although no general prohibition exists against conviction being based on the uncorroborated evidence of a single witness or an uncorroborated other type of evidence,[4] the question as to whether this view makes the criminal justice system vulnerable to miscarriages of justice arises.

In English criminal law, no formal corroboration requirement exists.[5] However, some common law jurisdictions such as Scotland's and some U.S. states' penal codes, do provide for such requirement. Similarly, various civil law jurisdictions such as the Kingdom of the Netherlands have codified the principle

---

1   *R v Aksidan*, 2006 BCCA 258, para. 44.
2   *Prosecutor v Gbagbo and Blé Goudé* (Corrigendum of Party Dissenting Opinion of Judge Henderson) ICC-02/11-01/15-950-Anx-Red-Corr, T Ch I (23 June 2017) para. 7.
3   *Prosecutor v Setako* (Appeal judgment) ICTR-04-81-A, A Ch (28 September 2011) para. 222.
4   Nicola Laver, 'Corroboration in Criminal Cases' (*claims.co.uk*) <https://www.claims.co.uk/knowledge-base/court-proceedings/corroboration> accessed 27 November 2023.
5   Paul Roberts and Adrian Zuckerman, *Criminal Evidence* (3rd edn, Oxford University Press 2022) 752–753.

of *'unus testis nullus testis'*, i.e. one cannot convict merely on the basis of one witness, literally 'one piece of evidence is no evidence'.[6]

By focusing, in common law, predominantly on the quality of evidence, i.e. the rules of admissibility of evidence as an evidentiary threshold, rather than the quantity of the evidence, and by allowing conviction purely based on circumstantial evidence, one may increase the risk for miscarriages of justice.[7] That being so, requiring evidentiary corroboration in criminal cases raises the question as to whether this could create injustice for the victims of crime and also make it more difficult for the Prosecution to prove its case.[8]

The reason why societies have a criminal justice apparatus in the first place is to protect society from crime. However, the reason for subsequently strictly regulating said apparatus is to defend the accused from government overreach. One should thus bear in mind that the criminal justice system not only arose from a desire to protect society, but also to shield its citizens from abuse of power by governmental institutions, and accordingly to protect citizens against frivolous criminal prosecutions.[9]

The criminal law principle of the requirement of corroborative evidence should therefore be positioned within this perspective, namely to evade miscarriages of justice and as a result, this principle contributes to the protection of the citizen against the unfettered power of the state.

Within common law, in practice, there are some categories of cases whereby, due to the potential pitfalls of the particular type of evidence, a form of corroboration is required in order to avoid a wrongful conviction. These cases are when:

(i) A co-accused who testifies on behalf of the Prosecution against the accused;
(ii) Purported victims in sexual assault cases testify against the accused;
(iii) Testimony of children;
(iv) Evidence provided by witnesses with a mental impairment.[10]

The purpose of evidentiary corroboration is, as mentioned, to prevent wrongful convictions. Hence, corroborating evidence is meant to strengthen or confirm already available evidence.[11] In essence, corroboration does not imply adducing evidence of any particular fact as such which is already in evidence,

---

6　*Ibid*, referring to art. 342 paragraph 2 of the Dutch Code of Criminal Procedure.
7　*Ibid*.
8　Roberts and Zuckerman (n 5) 754–755.
9　*Ibid*.
10　*Ibid* 761–764; Laver (n 4) 2023.
11　'Corroborate', *Legal Information Institute* (Cornell University insignia) <https://www.law.cornell.edu/wex/corroborate#> accessed 27 November 2023.

produced by a certain witness. Rather, corroboration means producing evidence to reinforce the probative incriminating implication of said witness testimony.[12]

For this reason, the California Penal Code section 1111 proclaims that:

> A conviction cannot be had upon the testimony of an accomplice unless it be corroborated by such other evidence as shall tend to connect the defendant with the commission of the offense; and the corroboration is not sufficient if it merely shows the commission of the offense or the circumstances thereof.[13]

The reasoning behind this principle is that accomplices are more likely to have an incentive to incriminate the accused in order to mitigate his or her own conduct.[14]

In the aforementioned four common law instances where evidence corroboration is required, the trial judge is obliged to issue an instruction to the jury specifying that he or she disseminates a corroboration writing.[15] The essence of this warning is to make a jury aware that it is risky to render a guilty verdict solely on the uncorroborated testimony of an accomplice, an alleged victim of sexual assault, or that of a child.[16]

The implication of the abovementioned is that corroborative evidence may be of the same nature as circumstantial evidence, such that it may not be sufficient to prove all the elements of the charged offense or to cover all the allegations to which the accomplice testified.[17] This comparison will be further clarified below.

11.3 An Example of the Corroboration Principle Applied in Criminal Law

The approach to the corroboration principle differs from one law system to another. In some law systems, the requirement for corroboration has been part of its principles of law for many years. Indeed, the criminal law system of Scotland, having embraced this principle for hundreds of years, illustrates the

---

12   Ibid.
13   California Penal Code section 1111.
14   Roberts and Zuckerman (n 5) 764.
15   Ibid 761.
16   Ibid.
17   Ibid.

practical application of the corroboration principle.[18] The Scottish law system is not strictly common law *per se*, as it does integrate Roman law principles. Within Scottish criminal law, the implication of the corroboration principle is that an accused cannot be convicted of a crime '(...) unless the essential facts of the crime are able to be established by evidence from at least two independent sources'.[19] The 'essential facts' within this context are:

(i) The fact that the crime charged was committed; and
(ii) The fact that the accused was the person who committed the crime.

In this context, the Prosecution has quite some leniency as to how it may comply with the corroboration rule. Actually, there are three alternatives regarding the presentation of evidence that can feature:

(A) Two eyewitnesses testifying about the two main facts sub (i) and (ii) as mentioned above;
(B) One eyewitness whose testimony is supported by one source of indirect or circumstantial evidence, for instance a hearsay witness.
(C) Circumstantial evidence from two or more sources which, each on their own, don't have sufficient evidentiary value and on which the Prosecution case is entirely built upon.[20]

Following the logic of these three evidentiary constructions, a confession made by the accused is not in itself sufficient evidence for a conviction, but needs to be corroborated as well. There is however one exception to this rule, namely when the confession contains 'special inside knowledge' which only the perpetrator could know.[21] Otherwise, if the corroboration principle is not met, the Court cannot render a not guilty verdict at the end of the Prosecution's case – even before the case is brought before a jury.[22]

Should the trial judge decide to put the case in the hands of a jury, he or she is obliged to provide the jurors with proper instructions on how to apply the corroboration rule. In the event that this application has not been properly explained to the jury, a successful appeal may follow.[23]

In conclusion, the corroboration rule is to be considered as an integral part of criminal law and should thus be attributed an important role in international criminal proceedings.

---

18   Scottish Government, 'The not proven verdict and related reforms: consultation' (13 December 2021) <www.gov.scot/publications/not-proven-verdict-related-reforms-consultation> accessed 21 September 2023.
19   Ibid.
20   Ibid.
21   Ibid.
22   Ibid.
23   Ibid.

EVIDENTIARY PRINCIPLES OF CORROBORATION 179

11.4 Corroboration under the ICC Framework

This section seeks to dive into the application of corroboration in ICC proceedings. To do so, one must also incorporate in its analysis the statutory framework around this concept and how the said concept has been used before other international criminal courts.

11.4.1 *Statutory Law*

Evidentiary corroboration is mentioned twice in the court's statutory framework. Rule 63 of the ICC's Rules of Procedure and Evidence provides that "a Chamber shall not impose a legal requirement that corroboration is required in order to prove any crime within the jurisdiction of the Court, in particular, crimes of sexual violence."

As for the submission of prior recorded testimonies, Rule 68(2)(b)(i) ICC RPE states that the Chamber shall consider it admissibility on the basis of, notable if other witnesses have or will testify in corroboration to the facts alleged in the targeted prior recorded testimony. However, this Rule does not solely refer to corroborative evidence, but also to evidence of cumulative nature.[24] Following this reasoning, corroboration is not a requirement for the introduction of prior recorded testimonies.

11.4.2 *Corroboration at ad hoc Tribunals*

When it concerns the meaning of 'corroboration' in the jurisprudence of international criminal tribunals, a first attempt to delineate this legal term was made by the ICTR, ruling:

> that two testimonies corroborate one another when one *prima facie* credible testimony is compatible with the other *prima facie* credible testimony regarding the same fact or a sequence of linked facts.[25]

The same interpretation can be found in ICTY case law, as recently as November 2017 in the Appeal Judgment in *The Prosecutor v Prlić et al.* case where the

---

24   *Prosecutor v Said* (Decision on the Prosecution's First, Second and Fourth Requests Pursuant to Rule 68(2)(b) of the Rules, filed on 20 October 2022 (ICC-01/14-01/21-507-Conf)) ICC-01/14-01/21-507-Red, T Ch VI (21 October 2022) para. 28.

25   *Prosecutor v Nahimana et al.* (Appeal judgment) ICTR-99-52-A, A Ch (28 November 2007) para. 428; cf. also *Prosecutor v Gatete* (Appeal judgment) ICTR-00-61-A, A Ch (9 October 2012) para. 125; *Prosecutor v Karera* (Appeal judgment) ICTR-01-74-A, A Ch (2 February 2009) para. 173; *Prosecutor v Rukundo* (Appeal judgment) ICTR-2001-70-A, A Ch (20 October 2010) para. 76.

Appeals Chamber cited as authority on corroboration the ICTR precedent quoted above.[26] The issue is whether evidence is corroborative when it is compatible with a 'sequence of linked facts'. Unfortunately, the ICTY in *Prlić* did not define what is a 'sequence of linked facts' when determining whether there is corroboration. It appears that a 'sequence of linked facts' is determined on a case-by-case basis.

Concerning the legal principle that underlies a correct interpretation of 'a sequence of linked facts', it is helpful to recall Judge Henderson's dissenting opinion in *Prosecutor v Blé Goudé* to the 'Decision on the "Prosecution's consolidated application to conditionally admit the prior recorded statements and related documents of various witnesses under rule 68 and Prosecution's application for the introduction of documentary evidence under paragraph 43 of the directions on the conduct of proceedings relating to the evidence of Witnesses P-0087 and P-0088".[27] In his dissenting opinion, Judge Henderson rejected a broad interpretation of the term 'corroboration', holding that it is not because two statements "deal roughly with the same topic" that they corroborate one another.[28] As an example, Judge Henderson referred to the Rule 68(2)(b) statements of certain witnesses and found that "a statement giving details about the death of one particular victim during the women's march does not corroborate a statement by another witness concerning the death of a different person who died in that incident, unless they were both killed by the same explosion."[29]

Thus, an interpretation of the 'sequence of linked facts' can be for example that is as such that evidence relating to an uncharged act A may corroborate evidence relevant to charged or uncharged act B, if the evidence relates to the same pattern.[30] The full reading of the ICTR ruling in this regard reads:

> two testimonies corroborate one another when one prima facie credible testimony is compatible with the other prima facie credible testimony regarding the same fact or a sequence of linked facts. *It is not necessary that both testimonies be identical in all aspects or describe the same fact in*

---

26 *Prosecutor v Prlić et al.* (Appeal judgment) IT-04-74-A, A Ch (29 November 2017) para. 210.
27 *Prosecutor v Gbagbo and Blé Goudé* (Corrigendum of Party Dissenting Opinion of Judge Henderson) ICC-02/11-01/15-950-Anx-Red-Corr, T Ch I (23 June 2017).
28 Ibid para. 7.
29 Ibid.
30 *Prosecutor v Gbagbo and Blé Goudé* (Second public redacted version of "Annex 1 – Prosecution's Consolidated Response to the Defense No Case to Answer", 10 September 2018, ICC-02/11-01/15-1207-Conf-Anx1) ICC-02/11-01/15-1207-Conf-Anx1, T Ch I (8 November 2018) para. 198.

the same way. Every witness presents what he has seen from his own point of view at the time of the events, or according to how he understood the events recounted by others [emphasis added]. It follows that corroboration may exist even when some details differ between testimonies, provided that no credible testimony describes the facts in question in a way which is not compatible with the description given in another credible testimony.[31]

From this full citation, it appears that 'sequence of linked facts' would mean sequence of facts that are observed at the same time within a certain geographic scope. This interpretation seems consistent with the plain meaning of the word "sequence." The Cambridge English dictionary defines sequence as "a series of related things or events, or the order in which they follow each other."[32] The facts therefore must follow each other either temporally, geographically, or with respect to some other concrete feature. Indeed, the Prosecution must first prove how the linked facts make up a sequence before stating that these facts corroborate one another.

In *Prosecutor v Rukundo*, the Appeals Chamber in determining whether there was corroboration with respect to the same fact or a sequence of linked facts, the Court found no error in the Trial Chamber's finding that a series of witnesses corroborated each other on the sequence of events that transpired at Saint Joseph's College.[33] Indeed, the Appeals Chamber held that the Trial Chamber noted that there were discrepancies between the different testimonies, but that all the testimonies gave evidence as to the accused involvement in the kidnapping of Madame Rudahunga at St. Joseph's college.[34] While one witness saw the accused interacting with the soldiers and another just heard that his car was within the vicinity of the attack in which Madame Rudahunga was kidnapped, the two different testimonies were found to be corroborative of the fact that the accused was involved in the kidnapping.[35] Thus, the Appeals Chamber interpreted a "sequence of linked facts" to mean a sequence of events in relation to one specific crime, at a specific locality with respect to a specific individual who was abducted.

---

31 *Prosecutor v Rukundo* (Appeal judgment) ICTR-2001-70-A, A Ch (20 October 2010) para. 76 (*citing Prosecutor v Nahimana et al.* (Appeal judgment) ICTR-99-52-A, A Ch (28 November 2007)).
32 'Sequence' <https://dictionary.cambridge.org/dictionary/learner-english/sequence> accessed 27 November 2023.
33 *Prosecutor v Rukundo* (Appeal judgment) ICTR-2001-70-A, A Ch (20 October 2010) para. 77.
34 Ibid.
35 Ibid.

Similarly, in *Prosecutor v Gatete* – which is also the case cited by the Prosecution in support of its interpretation of corroboration explained above – the Appeals Chamber found that, with respect to the accused Gatete, "it was not necessary that all witnesses describe the same visit by Gatete."[36] Indeed, testimonies do not need to be identical in all aspects or detail the same fact the exact same way.[37] Although the witnesses may have described different visits, it did not undermine the conclusion that each of their testimonies were compatible with the fact that Gatete was seen at the parish before 11 April 1994.[38] Unlike the *Rukundo* case, the facts here concerned different visits, yet the Appeals Chamber found corroboration. However, one should note that the facts in the present case concern one event, namely the visit to the parish.

In *Prlić et al.*, the Appeals Chamber of the ICTY also found that corroboration can refer to the same fact or a "sequence of linked facts."[39] With respect to the accused Stojic, the Chamber found that he was personally involved in organising and conducting an eviction campaign in Mostar.[40] In support of this fact, the Trial Chamber relied on the testimony of Witness DZ who was told that Stojic was in charge of implementing the plan to cleanse Mostar and that he had heard that Stojic ordered the evictions, destruction and burning of homes. The Appeals Chamber dismissed the Defense's argument that Witness DZ's evidence was uncorroborated, given the three facts mentioned hereafter.[41] The Appeals Chamber noted the following evidence: (1) Stojic presented himself as an "HVO military chief who control over West Mostar in May 1993," (2) he received reports from HVO officials regarding events that occurred during the eviction campaigns, and (3) he informed international representatives of the HVO strategies and objectives regarding Mostar. However, the Appeals Chamber did note that Witness DZ's evidence was not relied upon to establish Stojic's responsibility for the ordering of homes to be burned, but rather his active involvement in organising and conducting the eviction campaign.

In the same vein, it has been ruled by many Chambers at the ICTR that "corroboration may exist even when some details differ between testimonies,

---

36   *Prosecutor v Gatete* (Appeal judgment) ICTR-00-61-A, A Ch (9 October 2012) para. 126.
37   *Ibid* para. 125; cf. also *Prosecutor v Munyakazi* (Appeal judgment) ICTR-97-36A-A, A Ch (28 September 2011) para. 103; *Prosecutor v Kanyarukiga* (Appeal judgment) ICTR-02-78-A, A Ch (8 May 2012) para. 220; *Prosecutor v Bikindi* (Appeal judgment) ICTR-01-72-A, A Ch (18 March 2010) para. 81; *Prosecutor v Nahimana et al.* (Appeal judgment) ICTR-99-52-A, A Ch (28 November 2007) para. 428.
38   *Prosecutor v Gatete* (Appeal judgment) ICTR-00-61-A, A Ch (9 October 2012) para. 126.
39   *Prosecutor v Prlić et al.* (Appeal judgment) IT-04-74-A, A Ch (29 November 2017) para. 1647.
40   *Ibid*.
41   *Ibid*.

provided that no credible testimony describes the facts in question in a way which is not compatible with the description given in another credible testimony."[42] This further demonstrates the idea that corroboration is used as a tool to strengthen a said fact.

11.4.3   ICC Rulings regarding Corroboration

In the *Gbagbo and Blé Goudé* case, in his *Reasons*, Judge Henderson stated the following on the subject of corroborative evidence:

> While there is no requirement for corroboration, it makes good sense that evidence should never be assessed in isolation. Corroboration or corroborative evidence is evidence which tends to confirm the truth or accuracy of certain other evidence by supporting it in some material particular. To fulfil this function, it must itself be relevant and credible, and it must come from a source independent of any evidence which is to be supported by it. (…) Corroboration only occurs when two pieces of evidence independently confirm the same fact. When exhibits relate to similar but different facts; for example, a number of killings that took place at different times and locations, even at close proximity, such evidence does not necessarily provide corroboration. It is equally not possible to argue in such a scenario that there is necessarily corroboration for a pattern of events, because the patterns do not exist independently from the individual instances that constitute it.[43]

In regards to the introduction of prior recorded testimonies pursuant to Rule 68(2)(b) of the Rules, Trial Chamber V in the *Yekatom and Ngaïssona* case considered:

> it necessary to further define the factors of whether the prior recorded testimony 'is of cumulative or corroborative nature, in that other witnesses will give or have given oral testimony of similar facts' or 'relates to background information'. In this regard, the Chamber also notes that,

---

42   *Prosecutor v Setako* (Appeal judgment) ICTR-04-81-A, A Ch (28 September 2011) para. 31; *Prosecutor v Munyakazi* (Appeal judgment) ICTR-97-36A-A, A Ch (28 September 2011) para. 71; *Prosecutor v Rukundo* (Appeal judgment) ICTR-2001-70-A, A Ch (20 October 2010) para. 201; *Prosecutor v Karera* (Appeal judgment) ICTR-01-74-A, A Ch (2 February 2009) para. 173; *Prosecutor v Nahimana et al.* (Appeal judgment) ICTR-99-52-A, A Ch (28 November 2007) para. 428.

43   *Prosecutor v Gbagbo and Blé Goudé* (Public Redacted Version of Reasons of Judge Geoffrey Henderson) ICC-02/11-01/15-1263-AnxB-Red, T Ch I (16 July 2019) paras 46–47.

based on the wording of the rule, the prior recorded testimony does not need to be of cumulative or corroborative nature to oral testimony of the *same* events or facts, but it is sufficient that the oral testimony concerns *similar* facts.[44]

11.5 Elements of Corroboration in International Criminal Law

11.5.1 *Direct Evidence Implicating the Accused*

In *Prlić et al.*, the Appeals Chamber found it important that the Trial Chamber did not rely on Witness DZ's evidence to establish Stojic's responsibility for burning homes. While the Appeals Chamber did not explicitly say so, it is a well-established principle that certain categories of uncorroborated evidence, such as evidence directly implicating the accused, must be scrutinized by Chambers "with great care before accepting it as sufficient to make a finding of guilt."[45] Indeed, the Appeals Chamber at the ICTY determined that Trial Chambers could not rely on Rule 92bis statements – which is the equivalent of Rule 68(2)(b) at the ICC – to convict the accused, unless there is other evidence which corroborates the statement.[46]

The same reasoning which compels Trial Chambers to not consider prior recorded testimony to convict the accused, unless there is corroborative (or cumulative) evidence, should also be applied to hearsay evidence even when elicited by a witness testifying *viva voce*. In both situations, the Chamber is not in a position to assess the credibility of such evidence and the Defense is not able to cross-examine the witness. Hearsay should not be considered by the Chamber unless there is independent evidence to corroborate it.

Judge Eboe-Osuji echoed this idea in his Partly Concurring Opinion, stating that:

> It will be going too far in the erosion of the rights of the accused, if the 'discrete factual findings' that a trial chamber makes are those that

---

44 *Prosecutor v Yekatom and Ngaïssona* (First Decision on the Prosecution Requests for Formal Submission of Prior Recorded Testimonies pursuant to Rule 68(2)(b) of the Rules) ICC-01/14-01/18-1833-Corr-Red, T Ch V (17 April 2023) para. 66.
45 *Prosecutor v Krnojelac* (Trial Judgment) IT-97-25-T, T Ch II (15 March 2002). para. 71; *Prosecutor v Brđanin* (Trial Judgment) IT-99-36-T, T Ch II (1 September 2004) para. 27
46 *Blagojević and Jokić* (Trial judgment) IT-02-60-T, T Ch I(A) (17 January 2005) para. 26 citing *Prosecutor v Galić* (Decision on Interlocutory Appeal concerning Rule 92 bis(C)) IT-98-29-AR73.2, A Ch (7 June 2002) fn. 34, referring to Judgements of the European Court of Human Rights.

directly address acts and omissions of the accused; and they are made on the basis of rule 68 material. That, in [his] view, would be a violation of the minimum right guaranteed in article 67(1)(e). This is the case, notwithstanding that those 'discrete factual findings' are only corroborative rather the 'sole or decisive' evidential basis for findings as to the acts and omissions of the defendant. Whenever it is needed, *the value of corroboration is to strengthen the backbone of conviction* [emphasis added]. To derive that strengthening from evidence of acts and conduct of the accused is to violate what article 67(1)(e) guarantees for the accused as a minimum right.[47]

11.5.2 Witness Reliability

In the case of the *Prosecutor v Ngudjolo Chui*, in its judgement on the Prosecution's appeal against the acquittal decision of the Trial Chamber, the Appeals Chamber found that "the evidence of a witness in relation to whose credibility the trial chamber has some reservations may be relied upon to the extent that it is corroborated by other reliable evidence."[48] However, the fact that some parts of the witness' testimony were corroborated was not sufficient for the Chamber to find that the witness is in fact credible and reliable.[49] Indeed, the Appeals Chamber found that there are "some witnesses whose credibility is impugned to such an extent that he or she cannot be relied upon even if other evidence appears to corroborate parts of his or her testimony."[50]

11.6 Conclusion

As Roberts and Zuckerman in their seminal work, *Criminal Evidence*, express:

> Corroboration has a somewhat different relationship to the fairness of trials in the Article 6 jurisprudence of the European Court of Human Rights (ECtHR). Most of the Strasbourg judges were schooled in the civilian legal tradition (or its post-Soviet variations) and can be expected to be comfortable with the non-technical concept of corroboration, meaning

---

47 *Prosecutor v Ntaganda* (Judgment – Annex 5: Partly Concurring Opinion of Judge Eboe-Osuji) ICC-01/04-02/06-2666-Anx5-Corr, A Ch (31 March 2021) para. 10.
48 *Prosecutor v Ngudjolo Chui* (Judgment on the Prosecutor's appeal against the decision of Trial Chamber II entitled "Judgment pursuant to article 74 of the Statute") ICC-01/04-02/12-271-Corr, A Ch (7 April 2015) para. 168.
49 *Ibid* paras 168–169.
50 *Ibid* para. 168.

simply 'supporting evidence'. Sure enough, the ECtHR frequently refers to the existence or non- existence of supporting evidence when assessing overall fairness in the light of potential violations of Article 6's specifically enumerated rights. The Strasbourg judges have never said (translating into common lawyers' terminology) that hearsay evidence is inadmissible in a fair trial, only that untested hearsay evidence would require support from other evidence in order to generate a Convention-compliant conviction. Hearsay evidence from anonymous witnesses has been especially frowned upon.[51]

Considering the tension of the concept of corroboration with the fairness of trials, in terms of the 'decisive evidence'-concept, Defense counsel should therefore be aware to raise the question whether a criminal case built on corroboration can pass the test of reliability and whether the purported evidentiary items of corroboration would indeed, in isolation or taken in combination, pass the test of confirming the Prosecution case based upon the standard of proof. The overriding duty of the trial chambers to ensure the fairness of trials, also justify the utmost scrutiny of a criminal case built on corroborative evidence.[52]

---

51   Roberts and Zuckerman (n 5) 783–784.
52   *Ibid.*

CHAPTER 12

The Admissibility of 'Patterns of Conduct' as Evidence in (International) Criminal Cases

12.1 The Pendergrass Jurisprudence

One of the most sensitive evidentiary issues in criminal law relates to the admissibility of 'patterns of conduct' or 'pattern evidence' which is not the same as 'propensity evidence'. In several legal systems of both common law and civil law, the Prosecution can introduce evidence of a certain specific pattern of criminal conduct – sometimes referred to as *'modus operandi'* – to have the accused convicted.

An example from common law may illustrate the role of 'pattern evidence' in criminal cases. The example relates to a U.S. federal case, namely that of *United States v Pendergrass* which was brought before the U.S. 11th Circuit Court of Appeals.[1] In this case, the accused was charged with committing a series of five armed robberies in Georgia between November 2016 and January 2017.

In first instance, a jury found the defendant guilty of all five robberies. On appeal, the Defense of the accused advocated that there was insufficient evidence to sustain a conviction for three out of the five robberies. The Judges of the 11th Circuit rejected this argument and upheld the verdict of the jury. The Circuit Court of Appeals observed that for two of the robberies there was an abundance of evidence, which the Defense did not challenge on appeal. It additionally held that there was sufficient, '(...) evidence of the modus operandi and other evidentiary patterns' for the jury to infer from this pattern that the accused committed all five robberies. Importantly, the Appeals judges came to the conclusion that there was 'a pattern of evidence' on the basis of the following observations:

(i) First, all of the five robberies targeted 'mom-and-pop establishments', including two stores located in the same strip mall;
(ii) Second, all robberies occurred at or after closing time;
(iii) Thirdly, during each robbery, the robbers (...) covered their faces and brandished guns in the same way

---

1 *United States v Pendergrass*, 991 F.3d 1327 (11th Cir. 2021).

(iv) Fourthly, in four of the five robberies, the same robber – which was according to the Prosecution the accused – wore a red shirt and white gloves.
(v) Fifthly, the appeals judges noted the robber's left-handed use of a black-and-silver pistol, while bullets of their casings cycled through the same 40-caliber pistol in three of the five robberies and clothing and accessories with unique designs.[2]

The Appeals Court included in its judgement a summary of the evidence to demonstrate the many similarities among the five robberies:

Characteristic	China Star	Polo's Taqueria	Discount Grocery	Bonita Coin Laundry	Best Wings
Occurred at closing or later at night	X	X	X	X	X
Mom-and-Pop-type shop	X	X	X	X	X
Taller robber	X	X	X	X	X
Who was left-handed	X	X	X	X	X
Who brandished silver-and-black pistol	X	X	X	X	X
And who covered his face	X	X	X	X	X
And who wore a black shirt with a distinctive white design (like one recovered at Pendergrass's residence and which he admitted he owned)	X	X			
And wore red under- or outer-shirt layer	X	X		X	X
And wore a single-strap, cross-body backpack (like one recovered at Pendergrass's residence)		X	X		
And wore white gloves		X	X	X	X
Shot or shots fired		X	X		X
Casings or bullets recovered from Smith & Wesson .40-caliber gun		X	X		X
Casings recovered matched other casings recovered at other charged robberies		X	X		X

---

2 *Ibid.*

THE ADMISSIBILITY OF 'PATTERNS OF CONDUCT' 189

(cont.)

Characteristic	China Star	Polo's Taqueria	Discount Grocery	Bonita Coin Laundry	Best Wings
Cell-tower dump data showed phone associated with Pendergrass in the area		X	X		X
Rifle with distinctive chrome barrel and scope (like one recovered at Pendergrass's residence and which he admitted he owned), used by another robber		X			
Pendergrass's DNA recovered from scene			X		

Based on those similarities, the Court opined that "(...) a reasonable jury could (and did) find beyond a reasonable doubt that these patterns were not coincidence but rather evidence that the same person committed all five robberies."[3] Additionally, the judges took into account that Pendergrass was also 'firmly linked to the string of robberies in significant ways' since his DNA was found at one scene; cell tower evidence connected Pendergrass with three of the crimes, while at his residence, the police found a black shirt with a distinctive white pattern like the piece of clothing a robber wore at two of the five robberies.

12.2 'Pattern Evidence' at the ICC

At the ICC, there exists no clear jurisprudence or guidance under which conditions 'pattern evidence' is admissible. It is difficult to apprehend that without direct evidence and solely on the argument of pattern evidence, someone could be convicted for war crimes or crimes against humanity. For instance, someone who at the ICC is accused of aiding and abetting the commission of war crimes by giving financial support to armed groups and procurement of weapons at a certain date for which there is proof in terms of a money transfer,

---

3 *Ibid.*

cannot be held accountable for similar incidents for which there is no forensic proof simply on the argument of 'pattern evidence' i.e. the argument that it is reasonable to infer that the same accused was involved in those other money transfers. Similarly, if an accused at the ICC is charged with superior responsibility for his group's alleged attacks on five villages, during which civilians were killed and for which the Prosecution can only adduce evidence for two of those attacks, it remains doubtful that a war crimes charge for all the five villages can be supported by a reasoning based on 'pattern evidence'.

To find 'pattern evidence' in such a case admissible, there has to be at the least proof in regards to the identity of the same armed groups who would have attacked those five villages; in this case, the Prosecution might compensate the lack of evidence proving the presence of the accused at the location of those five attacks with 'pattern' evidence.

For the Defense to refute such an evidentiary approach, it is necessary to establish that within the specific time frame of the charges, mere armed groups led by other individuals were in the vicinity of these other villages. Furthermore, during cross-examination Defense counsel can question the Prosecution witnesses as to how they were able to differentiate the various fighting groups from one another, within that context.

It is also interesting to analyse how *ad hoc* tribunals deals with this type of evidence. Trial Chamber in the *Ayyash et al.* case at the Special Tribunal for Lebanon considered that the telecommunications evidence presented by the Prosecution was almost fully circumstantial and the relevant information needed to be assessed in its entirety in order for a chamber to detect patterns that are so prevalent that they surpass coincidence.[4] The Chamber adds that:

> when each circumstantial piece of evidence is viewed in the totality of all the other pieces of evidence, patterns could emerge that could collectively elevate individual pieces of evidence to a point that mere coincidence cannot explain, to equate to proof beyond reasonable doubt. This could occur even where each circumstantial piece of evidence appears insufficient on its face.[5]

The Trial Chambers of the ICC have been occasionally confronted with 'pattern evidence'. Indeed, it is the case when dealing with article 6 of the Elements of Crimes which defines the count of genocide, referring to a 'conduct [that] took

---

[4] *Prosecutor v Ayyash et al.* (Trial judgment) STL-11-01/T/TC, T Ch (18 August 2020) para. 253.
[5] *Ibid* para. 273.

place in the context of a manifest pattern of similar conduct'.[6] In this context and in accordance with the *Vienna Convention on the Law of Treaties*, Pre-Trial Chamber I in *Prosecutor v Al Bashir* considered the expression "manifest pattern" to mean "a systematic, clear pattern of conduct in which the alleged genocidal conduct occurs."[7] The Chamber considered this element to be met because there were reasonable grounds to believe that there was a systematic and widespread attack on members of certain populations.[8]

Furthermore, pattern evidence can also be considered in regards to the commissions of act referred to in Article 7of the Statute. Pre-Trial Chamber I in *Prosecutor v Gbagbo* stated that expression 'course of conduct' implies the presence of a certain pattern "as the 'attack' refers to a 'campaign or operation carried out against the civilian population', which involves the multiple commission of acts referred to in article 7(1) of the Statute directed against any group distinguishable by nationality, ethnicity or other distinguishing features, including (perceived) political affiliation."[9] Thus, even though a course of conduct incorporates multiple acts, its existence is not proven by the sole fact that its repeated. In fact, as the course of conduct necessitates a certain "pattern of behaviour, the Chamber considered that "evidence relevant to proving the degree of planning, direction or organisation by a group or organisation is also relevant to assessing the links and commonality of features between individual acts" that illustrate the existence of a "course of conduct", pursuant to Article 7(2)(a) of the Statute.[10]

In this regard, in their Separate opinion, Judge Christine Van den Wyngaert and Judge Howard Morrison pointed out that a 'course of conduct' does not exist apart from the individual criminal acts, rather it equivalates the sum of these acts.[11] To consider the opposite would mean that one could prove a pattern of killing, without however proving a single specific death. The judges were of the opinion that the Prosecution had to prove to the relevant standard, therefore providing sufficient evidence for each of individual criminal conduct that they alleged to be included in the said 'course of conduct'. Concrete

---

6   Elements of Crimes, Article 6.
7   *Prosecutor v Al Bashir* (Decision on the Prosecution's Application for a Warrant of Arrest against Omar Hassan Ahmad Al Bashir) ICC-02/05-01/09-3, PT Ch I (4 March 2009) para. 19.
8   *Ibid.*, para. 20.
9   *Prosecutor v Gbagbo* (Decision on the confirmation of charges) ICC-02/11-01/11-656-Red, PTC I (12 June 2014) para. 209.
10 *Ibid.*, para. 210.
11 *Prosecutor v Bemba Gombo* (Separate opinion of Judge Christine Van den Wyngaert and Judge Howard Morrison) ICC-01/05-01/08-3636-Anx2, A Ch (8 June 2018) para. 66.

material facts must support these allegations, such as a time and place, identified victims and perpetrators, and so on.[12]

12.3 Conclusion

In light of the above, Defense counsel must be vigilant when confronted to 'pattern evidence' presented by the Prosecution. Defence counsel must ensure that the facts have been individually proven to the applicable threshold, for their admission may lead to unfairness in the trial proceedings. By cross-examining the Prosecution's witnesses and by presenting evidence that suggest a different perspective on the alleged pattern are tools for Defense counsel to use in order to counter the credibility of the Prosecution's evidence.

---

12 *Ibid.*

CHAPTER 13

The Evidentiary Value and Admissibility of 'Bad Character Evidence' and 'Propensity Evidence'

13.1 Introduction

In common law, to use 'bad character evidence' and 'propensity evidence' in regards to an accused to prove the commission of a criminal offence is an admissible evidentiary tool for the Prosecution albeit under certain circumstances. Within the ICC RPE, one cannot find an equivalent of this principle. Yet, most ICC Trial Chambers allow that the Prosecution introduces evidence relating to the behaviour of an accused prior to or after the time frame of the charges, as long as the evidence is used to prove the contextual elements of the crimes charged or the *mens rea* of the accused.[1]

This section addresses the common law requirements for the admissibility of 'bad character' evidence and its potential application in ICC proceedings.

13.2 Common Law Parameters of 'Bad Character Evidence'

The introduction of 'bad character' evidence under common law is not unlimited. The general principle is as such that the character of an accused is inadmissible if its sole purpose is to demonstrate his or her propensity to act in conformity therewith. This principle had been adopted by the ICTY[2] as well as the ICTR. Trial Chamber I in the *Bagosora et al.* case interpreted the said principle as such:

> "This means that prior criminal offences by the accused – even of precisely the same offence with which the accused is charged – are not admissible if the only purpose for their introduction is to establish that the accused was capable of committing the offence, is inclined to commit the offence,

---

1 *Prosecutor v Yekatom and Ngaïssona* (Decision on Motions on the Scope of the Charges and the Scope of the Evidence at Trial) ICC-01/14-01/18-703-Red, T Ch V (30 October 2020) para. 51 *referring to Prosecutor v Dominic Ongwen*, transcript of hearing, ICC-02/04-01/15-T-147-Red2-ENG, T Ch IX (24 January 2018) p. 7, lines 3–12.
2 *Prosecutor v Kupreškić et al.* (Decision on evidence of the good character of the accused and the defence of *Tu quoque*) IT-95-16-T, T Ch (17 February 1999).

or on some prior occasion actually did have the intent to commit the criminal offence. Such evidence is excluded because the evidence may so severely blacken the reputation of the accused as to make acquittal virtually impossible, even though the direct evidence of the commission of the offence is weak."[3]

Under UK law 'bad character' evidence is defined in the Criminal Justice Act 2003 (Sections 98–113), namely in section 98, as "evidence of, or of a disposition towards, misconduct on his part, other than evidence which (a) has to do with the alleged facts of the offence with which the defendant is charged or (b) is evidence of misconduct in connection with the investigation or prosecution of that offense."[4]

One of the challenging parts of this definition is the interpretation of the criterion 'has to do' with the alleged facts of an offense. Case law in common law has predominantly explained this criterion to require a temporal nexus between the misconduct and the offense charges such that "(…) at any rate they were reasonably contemporaneous and closely associated with its alleged facts"[5]

Even when no temporal nexus is to be established, the 'has to do' requirement can be met if the bad character evidence aims to prove motive.[6] Evidence of motive is, under common law, admissible to establish the higher probability that the accused was the individual who committed the offense.[7]

There exists a second type of 'bad character' evidence within common law; hence, 'bad character' evidence that falls outside the legal definition of 'bad character evidence' mentioned above. For the admissibility of this type of 'bad character' evidence, the UK law prescribes that seven conditions are to be fulfilled:

1. All the parties to the proceedings agree that the evidence be admissible;
2. The evidence is adduced or elicited by the defendant;

---

3 *Prosecutor v Bagosora et al.* (Decision on Admissibility of Proposed Testimony of Witness DBY) ICTR-98-41-T, T Ch I (18 September 2003) para. 12.
4 The Crown Prosecutor Service, 'Bad character evidence' (*Legal Guidance,* updated 10 September 2021) <https://www.cps.gov.uk/legal-guidance/bad-character-evidence> accessed 25 September 2023.
5 *Ibid, referring to R v McNeill* [2007] EWCA Crim 2927. In this case the nexus was established based on a statement of a threat to kill someone, made two days after an alleged offense of a threat to kill.
6 *Ibid, referring to R v Sule* [2012] EWCA Crim 1130 and *R v Ditta* [2016] EWCA Crim 8.
7 The Crown Prosecutor Service, 'Bad character evidence' (*Legal Guidance,* updated 10 September 2021) <https://www.cps.gov.uk/legal-guidance/bad-character-evidence> accessed 25 September 2023.

3. The defendant's bad character provides important explanatory evidence;
4. The evidence is relevant to an important matter in issue between the prosecution and defence and can be used to rebut, for example, the assertion of coincidence or to rebut a defence of innocent association;
5. The evidence should have substantial probative value in relation to sub (4);
6. It relates to evidence to correct a false impression given by the defendant during the proceedings or by a witness called by the defendant; or
7. The defendant has made an attack on another person's character. However, a mere denial of the prosecution case is not sufficient to have 'bad character' evidence introduced via this gateway.[8]

In regards to these two types of 'bad character' evidence, it is important to stress that the prosecution's application to adduce and introduce bad character evidence into a criminal case should be assessed with circumspection. Even when the defendant has prior convictions, or otherwise would have a 'bad character', he or she can still be innocent of the charged crimes. For this reason, UK law stipulates that "an application [for bad character evidence] should never be made to bolster a weak case."[9]

This tenet similarly applies to the use of evidence at the ICC which lies outside the scope of the charges and is meant to prove certain contextual elements of the charged crimes or the *mens rea* of the accused.

13.3 Counterbalancing 'Bad Character Evidence'

In the event that the prosecution introduces 'bad character' evidence, there are several arguments available to the defence to challenge the said evidence.

First, defence counsel can contest the relevance of the proposed admission of this type of evidence. For instance, the introduction by the prosecution of a criminal conviction of the accused for fraud or theft several years before a criminal charge at the ICC regarding war crimes does not at its face seem relevant to prove such charges. At the least, there has to be a reasonable factual nexus between a prior offense and the charges at hand.[10] As stressed within UK law, "(…) prosecutors must not lose sight of the need to focus on the important issues in the case and should never seek to adduce bad character evidence

---

8 *Ibid.*
9 *Ibid.*
10 *Ibid.*

as probative of peripheral or relatively unimportant issues in the context of the case as a whole."[11]

Second, the prior 'bad behaviour' should be positioned in a reasonable relation in terms of time with the criminal charges. In other words, between the events leading to the bad behaviour of the accused and the charges at hand, the time elapsed should not be of unreasonable length. This element is also featured in UK law, specifically in Section 103(3) of the Criminal Justice Act 2003. This provision promulgates that propensity evidence will not be applied "(...) in the case of a particular defendant if the court is satisfied, by reason of the length of time since the conviction or for any other reason, that it would be unjust for it to apply in his case."[12] A similar provision which introduces the element of time elapse as a countervailing factor in regard to reliance on bad character features in Section 101(4) of the Criminal Justic Act. This provision states that confronted with an application to exclude bad character evidence, the court must have regard, in particular, to the length of time between the matters to which that evidence relates and the matters which form the subject of the offence charged. The length of time elapsed is therefore a relevant argument that contravenes the acceptance of 'bad character' evidence.

Third, the defence can challenge the admissibility of 'bad character evidence' or propensity evidence on the basis that the prosecution failed to provide sufficient detail and accurate information in order for the Court to properly assess the evidence's admissibility.[13] In fact, in order to introduce this evidence and thereby demonstrate the propensity to commit the charged crimes, the underlying facts and details of a specific prior conviction or conduct on which the prosecution intends to rely upon are required.[14] Should the prosecution not be able to provide to the Court accurate and detailed information about the accused's prior conduct to suggest propensity to commit the crimes charged, such evidence should be dismissed.

Fourth, if 'bad character' evidence would be related to uncharged crimes, the defence can argue that such alleged misconduct cannot be introduced by the prosecution in the absence of a formal charge and proper opportunity for the accused to defend him or herself against such allegations. If 'bad character' evidence were to relate to previous convictions, the defence could invoke the 'double jeopardy' prohibition, stating that the admission of such

---

11   *Ibid, referring to* Section 112 of the CJA.
12   The Crown Prosecutor Service, 'Bad character evidence' (*Legal Guidance*, updated 10 September 2021) <https://www.cps.gov.uk/legal-guidance/bad-character-evidence> accessed 25 September 2023.
13   *Ibid.*
14   *R v M* [2012] EWCA Crim 1588.

previous convictions is misused, namely because it leads *de facto* to a double punishment. This argument merits special attention in the event the prosecution case is weak and the previous convictions evidence is used as a means to compensate for the evidentiary weakness in the prosecution case.[15]

Fifth, it is also possible for defence counsel to call so-called 'Character Witnesses'. These witnesses may be favourable to the defence's case for they present evidence of the accused's good character. This was the case of the Kilolo Defence in the *Bemba et al.* case. The Defence argued that the character, professionalism and ethics of the accused were put into question by the prosecution. For that reason, the said witnesses would be used to "rebut such challenges and to highlight the exemplary character and professional practices of Mr Kilolo over the course of his professional career"."[16] Although the Chamber had reserves as to the relevance of this type of evidence, considering the seriousness of the charges and the fact that these witnesses constituted more than half of the accused's list of evidence, the Chamber allowed the Defence to present this evidence, insofar as it is presented in a manner compliant with Rule 68(2)(b) of the Rules.[17]

13.4 The Admissibility of 'Propensity Evidence' at Trial

Closely related to 'bad character' evidence features the phenomenon, in common law, of 'propensity evidence'. This type of evidence pertains to the question whether the defendant has a propensity to commit the offenses of the kind with which he or she is charged. At the ICC, the prosecution in some cases uses certain acts of the accused which were performed outside the scope of the charges, to establish propensity of the accused to prove its case.

Within UK law, the admissibility of propensity evidence is framed within the following five guidelines:

1. Does the history of conviction(s) establish a propensity to commit offenses of the kind with which the accused is charged?
2. If so, does the propensity make it more likely that the defendant committed the crime?

---

15 Paul Roberts and Adrian Zuckerman, *Criminal Evidence* (3rd edn, Oxford University Press 2022) 673–677.
16 *Prosecutor v Bemba et al.* (Decision on Relevance and Propriety of Certain Kilolo Defence Witnesses) ICC-01/05-01/13-1600, T Ch VII (4 February 2016) para. 12.
17 *Ibid* para. 17.

3. Although there exists no minimum number of events necessary to demonstrate such a propensity, the fewer the number of convictions, the weaker the evidence of propensity. A single previous conviction for an offense of the same description or category would not often show propensity unless the *modus operandi* would be quite similar.
4. The strength of the prosecution case must be taken into account; in the event the evidence against an accused is weak, it is unjust to admit his or her previous convictions.
5. It is important to assess each individual conviction and underlying facts instead of just looking at the legal qualification of the offense.[18]

Concerning the establishment of *mens rea* for war crimes or crimes against humanity at the ICC, it is not without a legal risk in view of the guidelines sub (2) and (5) to extrapolate the requisite *mens rea* for these crimes from certain actions of the accused prior to the time frame of the charges. For instance, the fact that an accused of war crimes before the ICC participated in certain meetings with a purpose to discuss a potential resistance against an invasion of his or her country, while several months later such a resistance emerged by means of armed groups which ultimately resorted to violence, does not necessarily determine any concrete relevant information about the propensity of this person to commit violence, i.e. the *mens rea* to commit war crimes.

It can therefore be quite relevant for defence counsel to use the character of the accused in the near past in order to challenge the charges in terms of the *mens rea* component. In their work on bad character evidence, Roberts and Zuckerman warn of the dangerous consequences of over-reliance on such evidence:

> Over-reliance on bad character evidence would also risk further repercussions for criminal proceedings. If bad character were an acceptable make-weight for evidentially weak prosecution cases, police officers might be disinclined to look for more reliable evidence and prosecutors might be prepared to bring weaker cases to trial. Indeed, citizens with previous convictions might be targeted by law enforcement (even more than they are at present), since their criminal records would in themselves already constitute partial proof of guilt. In this way, the law of criminal evidence would be in danger of generating mutually reinforcing perverse

---

18 The Crown Prosecutor Service, 'Bad character evidence' (*Legal Guidance,* updated 10 September 2021) <https://www.cps.gov.uk/legal-guidance/bad-character-evidence> accessed 26 September 2023; *referring to R v Hanson* [2005] EWCA Crim 824 and *R. v Gilmour* [2005] EWCA Crim 824.

incentives in the administration of criminal justice, with predictably bad outcomes, including: more wrongful convictions; misplaced focus of law enforcement efforts, possibly allowing more serious offenders to escape detection; and a pervasive corruption of the processes of proof, allowing citizens (guilty and innocent) to be condemned on an evidential basis that, objectively considered [...], is insufficiently robust to support the burden of criminal censure and punishment.[19]

Trial Chamber VII points out that it does not require any evidence regarding the accused's character, ruling that evidence on good or bad character does not have much, if any, relevance to the Chamber's Article 74 decision.[20] In respect to the accused Mr Kilolo, the Chamber even considered the presentation of this type of evidence as 'inefficient' in regards to the assessment of the accused guilt or innocence.[21] Therefore, there is always a reserve that defence counsel must have when wanting to present this type of evidence or when being confronted to it.

Finally, character evidence can also be used as factor to assess an accused's risk of absconding. This assessment takes into consideration the personal and professional situation of the suspect, such as the individual's character, values, home, occupation, and so on.[22] Although these factors may be relevant to the question whether or not a suspect will appear before the Court, still the Appeals Chamber remains of the view that decisions on interim release need to be taken according to the circumstances of the specific case it has at hand.

13.5 Conclusion

To conclude, this chapter has presented the extent to which 'bad character evidence' and 'propensity evidence' is used in common law. Evidently, the use of

---

[19] Paul Roberts and Adrian Zuckerman, *Criminal Evidence* (3rd edn, Oxford University Press 2022) 676.

[20] *Prosecutor v Bemba et al.* (Decision on Narcisse Arido's Request to Preclude the Prosecution from Using Private Communications) ICC-01/05-01/13-1711, T Ch VII (10 March 2016) para. 8; *Prosecutor v Bemba et al.* (Decision on Relevance and Propriety of Certain Kilolo Defence Witnesses) ICC-01/05-01/13-1600, T Ch VII (4 February 2016) para. 12.

[21] *Prosecutor v Bemba et al.* (Decision on Relevance and Propriety of Certain Kilolo Defence Witnesses) ICC-01/05-01/13-1600, T Ch VII (4 February 2016) paras 14–15.

[22] *Prosecutor v Bemba et al.* (Judgment on the appeal of Mr Jean-Jacques Mangenda Kabongo against the decision of Pre-Trial Chamber II of 17 March 2014 entitled "Decision on the 'Requete de mise en liberte' submitted by the Defence for Jean-Jacques Mangenda") ICC-01/05-01/13-560, A Ch (11 July 2014) para. 119.

these types of evidence has been more prevalent in criminal law of common law jurisdictions, whereas the jurisprudence of international criminal tribunals on this particular question is limited. However, it is important for defence counsel to know the potential role of bad character evidence within the ICC system, if this ever would arise, and how to counter its negative effects.

PART 4

The Admissibility of Expert Evidence

CHAPTER 14

The Admissibility and Evidentiary Value of Expert Evidence

14.1 Introduction

Expert evidence has been called upon by the various international criminal tribunals over the last two decades to determine factual issues.[1] At the ICC, experts are often called as witnesses to assist the Trial Chambers with the assessment of certain factual phenomena, such as demographical or geopolitical topics, but also in regards to more discrete topics such as the subject matter of child soldiers. Chambers have described an expert witness as an individual who "'by virtue of some specialized knowledge, skill or training can assist the Chamber in understanding or determining an issue of a technical nature that is in dispute.'"[2]

The judicial stance at the ICC to the admissibility of expert evidence is not one of considerable flexibility in favour of admissibility. No clear admissibility test is to be detected in regards to the admission of expert evidence. In particular, no consistent and transparent legal test to safeguard the reliability of expert evidence including the underlying methodology and data, can be found in the case law of the ICC.

In order to ensure the objective and unbiased nature of expert evidence, it is important that the ICC Trial Chambers endorse more concise admissibility criteria. This chapter intends to promulgate some of the most relevant elements which could be applied within ICC proceedings.

14.2 Upcoming Role of Forensic Sciences at the ICC

At the international level, given the scarce statutory framework with respect to the admission of evidence, international criminal judges have been given

---

1 For an overview of this role at the ICTY and ICTR, Richard May and Marieke Wierda, *International Criminal Evidence*, vol 9 (Brill 2021) 198–204 <https://brill.com/display/title/13900#navigation> accessed 14 June 2023.
2 *Prosecutor v Al Hassan* (Decision on Prosecution's proposed expert witness) ICC-01/12-01/18-989-Red, T Ch X (21 October 2020) para. 14 and jurisprudence cited therein.

a broad discretion in matters of admissibility of (forensic) evidence. Regulation 44(5) of the ICC Regulations of the Court gives the power to the Chamber to, inter alia, issue any order as to "(...) the manner in which the evidence is to be presented".[3] This latitude appears to be at odds with the epistemic nature of expert evidence, as distinct from general factual or crime-based evidence.[4] The way in which forensic experts should present expert evidence can actually not be dictated by the judiciary since it largely depends on an interpretation of a certain issue based on specific knowledge.

Generally, before the international criminal tribunals, the assessment of admissibility of expert (forensic) evidence follows a two-step test which includes the assessment of relevance and probative value – including reliability and credibility – followed by a fairness or 'rights test', which may bar the consideration of otherwise admissible evidence.[5] Reliability 'speaks to the fact to which the testimony is directed', whereas credibility 'refers to the truthfulness of a witness' testimony; although, the former may be seen as encompassing the latter.[6] Such assessment is made on a case-by-case basis[7] and ICC Chambers have favoured an approach whereby the final decision on evidentiary weight is made at the end of trial. The second step requires a weighing of the probative value of the evidence against its prejudicial effect,[8] in other words, whether the prejudicial effect of otherwise probative evidence will adversely affect the fairness or expeditiousness of the proceedings, for instance if it was obtained by means of a violation of internationally recognized human rights.[9]

Although international criminal chambers have considerable flexibility and discretion in assessing the admissibility of evidence, they are somewhat more limited with respect to expert evidence, such as forensic expertise, which requires adherence to stricter criteria, as discussed below. For example, a certain degree of specificity regarding an expert witness' sources and methods

---

3   This power may be limited by Article 69(2) of the Statute, which states that [t]he testimony of a witness at trial shall be given in person, except to the extent provided by the measures set forth in Article 68 of the Statute or the Rules of Procedure and Evidence.
4   Artur Appazov, *Expert Evidence and International Criminal Justice* (1st edn, Springer Cham 2016) 5–10.
5   Kai Ambos, *Treatise on International Criminal Law: International Criminal Procedure*, vol 3 (Oxford University Press 2016) 448–449, 485.
6   *Ibid.*, 472.
7   *Ibid* 459, 472.
8   *Prosecutor v Lubanga Dyilo* (Corrigendum to Decision on the admissibility of four documents) ICC-01/04-01/06-1399, T Ch I (20 January 2011) para. 31.
9   Kai Ambos, *Treatise on International Criminal Law: International Criminal Procedure*, vol 3 (Oxford University Press 2016) 513–520; Rome Statute of the International Criminal Court, Article 69(7).

is required for effective cross-examination by opposing counsel,[10] and could be a consideration upon assessing whether such evidence is admissible or not. When one deals with the interpretative challenges of forensic sciences for defence counsel operating at international criminal tribunals, one touches upon its interpretative scope and the avenues forensic sciences offer to the bench and trial parties. It is intriguing to observe that in the case against *Jean-Pierre Bemba Gombo*, the ICC seemed to take an evidentiary position that was rather lenient to the prosecution when it came to proving its case forensically. The Court stated that:

> in case of mass crimes it may be impractical to insist on a high degree of specificity. In this respect, it is not necessary for the Prosecutor to demonstrate, for each individual killing, the identity of the victim and the direct perpetrator. Nor is it necessary that the precise number of victims be known.[11]

The question is really whether this assumption could be accepted; at the very least, it triggers the question whether the said assumption impedes on the defence counsel challenging the forensic evidence presented by the prosecution in such cases. From the analysis in this chapter, it follows that the view as endorsed in the *Jean-Pierre Bemba* case is contentious. A prerequisite question, which is decisive for both prosecution and defence counsel, pertains to the scope of the forensic expertise at trial. In essence this question comes down to determining to what extent a forensic scientist may offer "(...) an interpretation of the findings in the context of the case (...) and deal with matters beyond ordinary knowledge and experience."[12]

Within forensic sciences, three interpretative levels of examination can be identified, for the defence counsel, but also for the bench and prosecution. The first and second level merit specific attention. The third level, the establishment

---

10   *Ibid* 485; *Prosecutor v Lubanga Dyilo* (Judgment pursuant to Article 74 of the Statute) ICC-01/04-01/06-2842, T Ch I (14 March 2012) para. 112; *Prosecutor v Ngudjolo Chui* (Judgment pursuant to Article 74 of the Statute) ICC-01/04-02/12-3-tENG, T Ch II (18 December 2012) para. 60; *Prosecutor v Katanga* (Judgment pursuant to Article 74 of the Statute) ICC-01/04-01/07-3436-tENG, T Ch II (7 March 2014) para. 94.

11   *Prosecutor v Bemba Gombo* (Decision pursuant to article 61(7)(a) and (b) of the Rome Statute on the charges of the prosecutor against Jean-Pierre Bemba Gombo) ICC-01/05-01/08-424, PTC II (15 June 2009) para. 133.

12   X. Laroche and E. Baccard, 'International Courts and Forensic Sciences', *Encyclopaedia of Forensic Sciences* (vol 3, 2013) 491.

of criminal guilt, does not pertain to the task of a forensic expert, who solely operates to assist the court on the first and second level.

After all, a forensic expert may not usurp the role of the bench, being prohibited from invading the competence of the judge by virtue of the ultimate issue rule.[13] This implies for instance that a military expert testifying on behalf of the prosecution cannot expound on a legal theme such as command responsibility, in order to give an opinion on which commander is to be held criminally responsible for certain crimes. The ultimate issue rule dictates that an expert is prevented from giving an opinion on the ultimate issue of the case, which is the very issue that the court has to decide.[14] An example from the practice of the ICTY is the case against *Kordic and Cerkez*, in which the prosecution sought to introduce a report written by a military analyst on the conflict in Bosnia-Herzegovina. This report, based on prosecution witness statements rather than on the expert's own observations, alluded to the alleged superior responsibility of the accused as military commander. The Trial Chamber ultimately excluded this evidence pursuant to the ultimate issue rule, considering that the expert was in fact invading the province of the court.[15]

Similarly, the ICC Chambers have concluded that an expert report or testimony may touch upon facts contested by the parties as long as they relate to the expert's expertise and does not usurp the role of the Chamber as the ultimate arbiter of fact and law.[16] In the case of *Ruto and Sang*, the Chamber found that anticipated expert testimony which would qualify as usurping the functions of the Chamber by going into the 'ultimate issues' at trial include, for instance, "opinions as to an accused guilt or innocence, or whether the contextual, material or mental elements of the crimes charged are satisfied".[17]

---

13   Richard May and Marieke Wierda, *International Criminal Evidence*, vol 9 (Brill 2021) 200 <https://brill.com/display/title/13900#navigation> accessed 14 June 2023.

14   *Prosecutor v Ruto and Sang* (Decision on Sang Defence Application to Exclude Expert Report of Mr Herve' Maupeu,) ICC-01/09-01/11-844, T Ch V(A) (7 August 2013) paras 12–13; *Prosecutor v Ntaganda* (Decision on Defence Preliminary Challenges to Prosecution's Expert Witnesses) ICC-01/04-02/06-1159, T Ch VI (9 February 2016) para. 8; *Prosecutor v Ongwen* (Decision on the Defence Request to Order a Medical Examination of Dominic Ongwen) ICC-02/04-01/15-637-Red, T Ch IX (16 February 2016) para. 19; *Prosecutor v Nahimana et al.* (Judgment) ICTR-99-52-A, A Ch (28 November 2007) para. 212.

15   *Prosecutor v Kordić & Čerkez* (Public Transcripts) IT-95-14/2-T, T Ch II (28 January 2000) pp. 13289–13306.

16   *Prosecutor v Ruto and Sang* (Decision on Sang Defence Application to Exclude Expert Report of Mr Herve' Maupeu,) ICC-01/09-01/11-844, T Ch V(A) (7 August 2013) para. 23; *Prosecutor v Ntaganda* (Decision on Defence Preliminary Challenges to Prosecution's Expert Witnesses) ICC-01/04-02/06-1159, T Ch VI (9 February 2016) para. 8.

17   *Prosecutor v Ruto and Sang* (Decision on Sang Defence Application to Exclude Expert Report of Mr Herve' Maupeu,) ICC-01/09-01/11-844, T Ch V(A) (7 August 2013) para. 13.

The Chamber noted that anticipated testimony should not, directly or indirectly, address the role of the accused, or other key members of the alleged Network in the post electoral violence in Kenya.[18] The Chamber further determined that it would be unduly restrictive to prohibit an expert from testifying about facts regarding the historical or political background of a case and that expert evidence relating to background issues – which do not touch upon ultimate issues – is therefore appropriate.[19]

For the prosecution and defence counsel, the most interesting level is the second interpretative level: the activity level. Here, the forensic expert is asked to discern what type of physical activity or process is likely to have caused the traces he or she has found at the first level. Yet, a (second) prerequisite question is on what basis a forensic expert is to introduce and provide 'an interpretation of the findings' on this second level of examination? Essential to such determination are three conditions:

i.   The availability of two opposite hypotheses; one prosecution and one defence hypothesis;
ii. The availability of the requisite and balanced context-information from the case-file to enable the forensic expert to weigh the respective probabilities of these two hypotheses;
iii. The assurance that the chain of custody of the first level is not compromised (see Section IV).

For the defence counsel it will be vital to question a forensic expert in court about which hypotheses were at the basis of their opinion. In the event they were merely provided with one (the prosecutor's) hypothesis, the expert should, *proprio motu* examine any alternative theory which is permissible pursuant to the evidence. In this regard, Laroche and Baccard, forensic consultants at the Office of the Prosecutor at the ICC, make the following observation:

> The prosecution expert builds the forensic action plan according to international scientific standards; he shall verify, confirm, or exclude investigation's working hypothesis while exploring all other possibilities or explanations than the one put forward by the prosecution, including any alternative theory consistent with the scientifically demonstrated facts.[20]

---

18   *Ibid* para. 24.
19   *Ibid*.
20   X. Laroche and E. Baccard, 'International Courts and Forensic Sciences', *Encyclopaedia of Forensic Sciences* (vol 3, 2013) 492.

The emphasis should be put on the verification with the experts whether they, explored "(...) any alternative theory consistent with the scientifically demonstrated facts."[21] For instance, if a (forensic) expert, on behalf of the prosecutor, has analysed a video allegedly depicting an armoured vehicle belonging to a certain armed group firing a grenade in a densely populated area, and is asked the question whether this footage is authentic, it is relevant that this expert is questioned in court on any other viable hypothesis. For example, whether the alleged grenade could have been fired from another source. This would also raise questions as to the foundation of the expert's opinion that credence should be given to the prosecution's hypothesis and not so much the defence hypothesis or vice versa.

A scientifically based opinion on the probabilities of two hypotheses requires a statistical calculation or foundation. To this end, the theory and formula of the 18th century Englishman Thomas Bayes is to be used. This theory presumes that the probability of two hypotheses can be translated into a likelihood ratio (LR). This is the ratio of two evidentiary probabilities that are evaluated under different hypotheses.[22] For instance, the prosecution's hypothesis is that a suspect is the source of a DNA trace and the defence hypothesis is that another, unknown person is the source of this DNA trace.

14.3 Towards a Uniform Admissibility Framework

14.3.1 *Four Level Test*
In order to set forth a potential admissibility framework for expert evidence, recourse can be had to the experience in common law, which established a four level test. First and foremost, the test can only be applied once the Chamber has decided that the proposed witness is in fact an expert.[23]

---

21 Ibid.
22 Peter Gill, *Misleading DNA Evidence: Reasons for Miscarriages of Justice* (Elsevier Inc. 2014) 17; S. de Smet, 'The International Criminal Standard of Proof at the ICC – Beyond Reasonable Doubt or Beyond Reason?', in C. Stahn, The Law and Practice of the International Criminal Court, Oxford University Press (2015), pp. 872–873; on the merits, demerits and consequences of applying Bayesian reasoning in forensic science for both experts and legal decision-makers, see M. Sjerps, 'Pros and Cons of Bayesian Reasoning in Forensic Science', in J.F. Nijboer and W.J.J.M. Sprangers (eds.), Harmonisation in Forensic Expertise, Amsterdam: Thela Thesis (2000), pp. 566–582.
23 *Prosecutor v Ntaganda* (Decision on Defence Preliminary Challenges to Prosecution's Expert Witnesses) ICC-01/04-02/06-1159, T Ch VI (9 February 2016) para. 8.

1. Does the evidence assist the Court?

The first test is whether the proposed expert evidence would be (potentially) of assistance to the Trial Chamber, that is to say that:
(i) It must adduce evidence which is at first sight to be outside the Trial Chamber's knowledge; and
(ii) The purported expert evidence must be such that it can reasonably assist the Trial Chamber in its truth-finding mandate.[24]

2. Does the evidence usurp the role of a trial judge?

From this first criterion, a second test arises. If the expert is seeking to advance an opinion on the very issue the Trial Chamber has to decide, i.e. the content of the charges and the determination of guilt of the accused, then the opinion should be found inadmissible. As previously stated, this admissibility concept has been known as the 'ultimate issue rule'.[25] The rationale of this rule is that an expert witness never could or should usurp the role of a trial judge and thus should abstain from giving opinions which trespass the domain of the Trial Chamber.

There are however some 'grey areas' which make it difficult to sometimes ascertain if the expert opinion enters the domain of a trial judge. One of these grey areas touches the assessment of whether someone gave a false confession. In several jurisdictions, courts have previously accepted expert evidence from forensic psychologists to serve the argument that confessions in criminal cases were false due to undue pressure or coercive interrogation techniques.[26]

3. Is the evidence based on an academically recognized scientifical methodology?

A third important test pertains to the scientific basis of the expert evidence. This means that the expert's opinion must be given on the basis of expert evidence with an underlying identifiable and academically accepted methodology.[27]

---

[24] The Crown Prosecutor Service, 'Expert evidence' (*Legal Guidance*, updated 5 August 2022) <www.cps.gov.uk/legal-guidance/expert-evidence> accessed 26 September 2023.

[25] Richard May and Marieke Wierda, *International Criminal Evidence*, vol 9 (Brill 2021) 200 <https://brill.com/display/title/13900#navigation> accessed 14 June 2023.

[26] See for examples on this topic: Saul Kassin, DUPED: *Why Innocent People Confess – and Why We Believe Their Confessions* (Prometheus 2022).

[27] The Crown Prosecutor Service, 'Expert evidence' (*Legal Guidance*, updated 5 August 2022) <www.cps.gov.uk/legal-guidance/expert-evidence> accessed 26 September 2023.

This also implies that the expert should be able to give account of the methods applied, for instance which forensic techniques are scientifically recognised within his or her field.

Part of this test involves that the expert must give access to the Court of the data which was used. At the ICC, UN or NGO reports are most often submitted based on interviews with (anonymous) witnesses without the underlying interview notes or even the identity of these interviewees being disclosed.[28]

4. Is the evidence reliable?

The question as to how a Trial Chamber could verify if a sufficiently reliable foundation exists for expert evidence to be admitted still remains. A quite relevant example and checklist can be taken from the UK Criminal Practice Directions Evidence, which includes at section 7.1.2:

a. the extent and quality of the data on which the expert opinion is based;
b. the validity of the methodology employed by the expert;
c. if the expert's opinion relies on an inference from any findings, whether the opinion properly explains how safe or unsafe the inference is (whether by reference to statistical significance or in other appropriate terms);
d. if the expert's opinion relies on the results of the use of any method (for instance, a test, measurement or survey), whether the opinion takes proper account of matters, such as the degree of precision or margin of uncertainty, affecting the accuracy or reliability of those results;
e. the extent to which any material upon which the expert's opinion is based has been reviewed by others with relevant expertise (for instance, in peer-reviewed publications), and the views of those others on that material;
f. the extent to which the expert's opinion is based on material falling outside the expert's own field of expertise;[29]
g. the completeness of the information which was available to the expert, and whether the expert took account of all relevant information in arriving at the opinion (including information as to the context of any facts to which the opinion relates);

---

28   See Chapter XVI.
29   The Chamber in *Prosecutor v Ntaganda* (Decision on Defence Preliminary Challenges to Prosecution's Expert Witnesses) ICC-01/04-02/06-1159, T Ch VI (9 February 2016) para. 8 considered that one of the criterias for the admissibility of the expert's evidence is whether the content of the expert's report and/or anticipated testimony falls within the scope of the witness' expertise.

h. if there is a range of expert opinion on the matter in question, where in the range the expert's own opinion lies and whether the expert's preference has been properly explained; and
i. whether the expert's methods followed established practice in the field and, if they did not, whether the reason for the divergence has been properly explained.[30]

The said text adds at section 7.1.3 that the expert opinion's reliability can be diminished by certain flaws identified by the court, including:

a. being based on a hypothesis which has not been subjected to sufficient scrutiny (including, where appropriate, experimental or other testing), or which has failed to stand up to scrutiny;
b. being based on an unjustifiable assumption;
c. being based on flawed data;
d. relying on an examination, technique, method or process which was not properly carried out or applied, or was not appropriate for use in the particular case; or
e. relying on an inference or conclusion which has not been properly reached.[31]

The criterion sub 7a) of section 7.1.2, the extent and quality of the data on which the expert opinion is based, touches upon the precious observation that most of the UN or NGO reports submitted within the ICC proceedings do not provide for verifiable data.

The jurisprudence at the ICC does not reflect much decisions excluding expert evidence based on admissibility. One of the rare examples is the ruling of Trial Chamber I of the ICC in the *Gbagbo and Blé Goudé* case, which is described in Chapter 11. The solution contemplated by the judges of Trial Chamber I was probably from a practical perspective a more efficient one; that is, not to exclude the report in its entirety but rather to exclude certain portions or to instruct the expert to not testify about certain elements contained in the report which do not comply with factors sub (a) and (c) of Section 7.1.2. or factors sub (b) and (c) of Section 7.1.3. When it concerns deficiencies in the methodology (sub (d)(g)(i) of Section 7.1.2 and sub (d) and (e) of Section 7.1.3), it is more likely that the expert evidence in its totality will be rejected.

14.3.2 *Admissibility at the ICC*

Recent jurisprudence reveals that the ICC Chambers have relied on certain criteria – which integrate the common law analysis as elucidated above – to

---

30 Criminal Practice Directions 2023, Section 7.1.2 Admissibility Generally.
31 Criminal Practice Directions 2023, Section 7.1.3 Admissibility Generally.

decide on the admission of a witness' evidence as expert evidence. The criteria are the following:
  (i) the witness is an expert as defined above [see definition in the Introduction of the present Chapter];
  (ii) the testimony in the subject area of expertise would be of assistance to the Chamber;
  (iii) the content of the report and/or the anticipated testimony falls within the area of expertise of the witness; and
  (iv) the content of the report and/or the anticipated testimony does not usurp the functions of the Chamber as the ultimate arbiter of fact and law.[32]

14.4 Substantive Requirements of Expert Evidence

After having set forth four important admissibility tests to be applied within the ICC legal framework, this paragraph will delve into several substantive requirements for expert evidence. The Rules of Procedure and Evidence, nor the case law of the ICC govern such requirements.

Common law practice might be of assistance to develop a more coherent test. The UK Criminal Procedure Rules, Rule 19.4 does indicate that an expert's report must:
(a) give details of the expert's qualifications, relevant experience and accreditation;
(b) give details of any literature or other information which the expert has relied on in making the report;
(c) contain a statement setting out the substance of all facts given to the expert which are material to the opinions expressed in the report, or upon which those opinions are based;
(d) make clear which of the facts stated in the report are within the expert's own knowledge;

---

[32] *Prosecutor v Al Hassan* (Decision on Defence's proposed expert witnesses and related applications seeking to introduce their prior recorded testimony under Rule 68(3) of the Rules) ICC-01/12-01/18-2206 (1 June 2022) para. 9; *See also Prosecutor v Al Hassan* (Decision on Prosecution's proposed expert witness) ICC-01/12-01/18-989-Red, T Ch X (21 October 2020) para. 16; *Prosecutor v Ntaganda* (Decision on Defence Preliminary Challenges to Prosecution's Expert Witnesses) ICC-01/04-02/06-1159, T Ch VI (9 February 2016) para. 8; *Prosecutor v Bemba et al.* (Decision on Prosecution Request to Exclude Defence Witness D22-0004) ICC-01/05-01/13-1653, T Ch VII (24 February 2016) para. 11.

(e) where the expert has based an opinion or inference on a representation of fact or opinion made by another person for the purposes of criminal proceedings (for example, as to the outcome of an examination, measurement, test or experiment) –
  (i) identify the person who made that representation to the expert,
  (ii) give the qualifications, relevant experience and any accreditation of that person, and
  (iii) certify that that person had personal knowledge of the matters stated in that representation;
(f) where there is a range of opinion on the matters dealt with in the report –
  (i) summarise the range of opinion, and
  (ii) give reasons for the expert's own opinion;
(g) if the expert is not able to give an opinion without qualification, state the qualification;
(h) include such information as the court may need to decide whether the expert's opinion is sufficiently reliable to be admissible as evidence;
(i) contain a summary of the conclusions reached;
(j) contain a statement that the expert understands an expert's duty to the court, and has complied and will continue to comply with that duty; and
(k) contain the same declaration of truth as a witness statement.[33]

The particular factor sub (h) deserves attention. The requirement that the expert report must incorporate the necessary information, as the Trial Chamber may need to determine the reliability of the expert evidence, is closely connected to the abovementioned admissibility criteria.[34] In addition to the explicitly mentioned elements, sub (h) adds that part of the requisite information should be the applied methodology of the underlying research and the data used.

The problem with most of the ICC proceedings is that, as oppose to ordinary domestic criminal trials in which the Prosecution Service relies on forensic DNA, ballistic or facial recognition techniques to build its case, such proceedings are meant to prove the evidence of legal-political concepts such as: armed conflicts, war crimes, crimes against humanity, military structures and chains of command. These types of concepts are subject not to forensic-mathematical expert evidence, but rather to more subjective opinions of individuals who are called experts, oftentimes related to an international organisation. How such an expert can present his or her conclusions with a certain degree of support, similarly to for instance the degree of certainty offered by DNA-evidence,

---

33 Criminal Procedure Rules 2020, Rule 19.4 Content of expert's report
34 The Crown Prosecutor Service, 'Expert evidence' (*Legal Guidance*, updated 5 August 2022) <www.cps.gov.uk/legal-guidance/expert-evidence> accessed 27 September 2023.

remains questionable. This observation is of relevance in regards to the possibilities for defence counsel to challenge such findings.

14.5 Testing Forensic Sciences in Court by Defense Counsel[35]

14.5.1 Generally Accepted Criteria to Test Forensic Sciences in International Criminal Law

When it concerns the qualification of forensic experts and the testing of the reliability of this type of evidence, this section aims to identify in more depth the main criteria used to test forensic sciences in criminal cases. These criteria are derived from US law and now seem to constitute a consensus within the forensic community and transpire into international criminal cases.

As to the first element, the competence of forensic experts, resort should be had to the landmark ruling of the U.S. Supreme Court in 1993 in *Daubert vs. Merrell Dow Pharmaceuticals, Inc.*[36] The claimants in this case, two minor children and their parents, filed a law suit against Merrell Dow Pharmaceuticals, saying that the children's' serious birth defects had been caused by the mothers' prenatal ingestion of Bendectin, a prescription drug marketed by Merrell Dow. The California District Court refused this claim, basing its ruling on the opinion of an expert who, having reviewed the extensive published scientific literature on the subject, came to the conclusion that maternal use of Bendectin had not been shown to be a risk factor for human birth defects. Yet, the claimants presented their case based upon the testimony of eight other well-credentialed experts, who did conclude that Bendectin could cause birth defects. Their findings relied on animal studies, chemical structure analyses, and the unpublished 'reanalysis' of previously published human statistical studies. However, the court held that this evidence did not meet the applicable general acceptance' standard for the admission of expert testimony. The Court of Appeals upheld this ruling. It opined, citing *Frye v United States*,[37] that expert opinion based on a scientific technique is inadmissible unless the technique is 'generally accepted' as reliable in the relevant scientific community.[38]

In the pioneering Daubert judgment, which lies at the foundation of contemporary forensic norms in regard to the admissibility of forensic evidence,

---

[35] A more extensive version of this section appeared in Geert-Jan Alexander Knoops, 'The proliferation of forensic sciences and evidence before international criminal tribunals from a defence perspective' (2019) 30 Criminal Law Forum 33.
[36] *Daubert v Merrell Dow Pharmaceuticals, Inc.*, 509 U.S. 579 (1993).
[37] *Frye v United States*, 293 F. 1013 (D.C. Cir. 1923).
[38] *Daubert v Merrell Dow Pharmaceuticals, Inc.*, 509 U.S. 579 (1993).

the US Supreme Court justices set forth the criteria according to which the reliability and credibility of forensic evidence produced by a forensic expert should be assessed. These criteria are the following:
- Has the theory of technique used been tested?
- Was it subject to peer review?
- What is the error rate?
- Do scientific standards exist and were they maintained?
- Was this standard widely accepted in scientific community?
- Does an internationally accepted norm exist?
- Was the norm applied properly?[39]

This list of criteria, which has been adapted and applied by various domestic and international jurisdictions and evolved into widely accepted contemporary forensic norms as to the qualification of a forensic expert,[40] can also serve as a checklist for defence counsel appearing before international criminal tribunals. Yet, the way the admissibility and reliability of forensic sciences is to be determined may vary depending on the underlying law system.

14.5.2 Admissibility and Reliability Tests in a Comparative Perspective

In the UK, the Law Commission has proposed measures for reform in the English and Welsh courts' current approach to expert evidence; based on an extensive study, the Law Commission postulated that the safeguards for testing the reliability and weight of expert evidence common to most common law jurisdictions – cross-examination, adduction of contrary expert evidence and judicial guidance at the end of a jury trial,– particularly with respect to more scientific and technical fields, are insufficient. It recommended special rules to test the admissibility of expert evidence, in light of the particular nature of expert evidence, including the fact that experts can provide opinion evidence on matters outside of most judges' or jurors' knowledge and expertise.[41]

---

39   X. Laroche and E. Baccard, 'International Courts and Forensic Sciences', *Encyclopaedia of Forensic Sciences* (vol 3, 2013) 491; Artur Appazov, *Expert Evidence and International Criminal Justice* (Springer 2016) 123–132; William A. Schabas, *The UN International Criminal Tribunals: The Former Yugoslavia, Rwanda and Sierra Leone* (Cambridge University Press: Cambridge 2006) 480.

40   See inter alia Judgment Supreme Court of the Netherlands, ECLI:HR:1998:ZD0917, 27/01/1998; drawing from the *Daubert* criteria; Judgment of the Supreme Court of Canada, *R. v J.-L.J.*, 2000 SCC 51, para. 33; *R. v Trochym*, 2007 SCC 6, para. 26; *Prosecutor v Sesay et al.* (Judgment) SCSL-04-15-T, T Ch I (25 February 2009) para. 27.

41   UK Law Reform Commission, Expert Evidence in Criminal Proceedings in England and Wales, Law Com No 325 (21 March 2011), presented to Parliament pursuant to section 3(2) of the Law Commissions Act 1965, <www.lawcom.gov.uk/app/uploads/2015/03/lc325_Expert_Evidence_Report.pdf>, pdf.

In the French legal system, the reliability of expert witnesses tends to be more implicit, as he or she is typically appointed by the instructing judge or the court and chosen from a list.[42] Expert reports are typically examined at the pre-trial stage and the expert's qualifications are established at the time of his or her registration in the Court of Cassation's list of experts.[43] The German system presents similar characteristics in that experts are appointed and instructed by the court, drawing from a register of accredited experts.[44]

14.5.3 Admissibility and Reliability Tests at the International Criminal Court

At the international *ad hoc* tribunals and the ICC, expert evidence is judge-driven and therefore more akin to the civil law traditions.[45] The Statute of the International Criminal Court, its Rules of Procedure and Evidence, and even the Regulations of the court are silent on delineating what the term 'expert witness' entails, and what scientific standards ought to be applicable at the ICC. The only modest exception to this silence is ICC Regulation 44, which obliges the Registrar to compile and maintain a list of experts accessible to all organs and participants of the court proceedings. Regulation 56 of the Regulations of the Registry provides that for the purposes of Regulation 44 of the Court, candidates applying for inclusion on the list of experts must provide a detailed curriculum vitae, proof of qualifications, indication of expertise in a relevant field, and where applicable, a statement of whether he or she is included in any list of experts acting before any national court. The Trial Chamber in *Lubanga* provided further clarifications with respect to Regulation 44 by indicating that the list should include a wide selection of experts, all of whom will have had their qualifications verified; moreover, they will have undertaken to uphold the interests of justice when admitted to the list'.[46] The Chamber also reminded the Registrar that the list should have regard to equitable geographical representation and a fair representation of female and male experts, as well as experts with expertise in trauma, including trauma related to crimes of sexual and gender violence, children, elderly, and persons with disabilities among others.[47]

---

42   Avi Singh, 'Expert Evidence' in Karim A. A. Khan, Caroline Buisman and Chris Gosnell (eds), *Principles of Evidence in International Criminal Justice* (Oxford University Press 2010) 601; Artur Appazov, *Expert Evidence and International Criminal Justice* (Springer 2016) 157.
43   Artur Appazov, *Expert Evidence and International Criminal Justice* (Springer 2016) 157.
44   Ibid 161–162.
45   Ibid 602.
46   *Prosecutor v Lubanga Dyilo* (Decision on the procedures to be adopted for instructing expert witnesses) ICC-01/04-01/06-1069, T Ch I (10 December 2007) para. 24.
47   Ibid.

In this regard, in the Judgement of the *Ngudjolo Chui* case, the Chamber stated at paragraph 60 that:

> In assessing the testimony of expert witnesses, the Chamber considered factors such as the established competence of the particular witness in his or her field of expertise, the methodology used, the extent to which the expert's findings were consistent with other evidence in the case and the general reliability of the expert's evidence. On this last point, the Chamber considered scientific evidence to be objective, even if the expert was appointed by only one party or by the Court in accordance with regulation 44 of the Regulations of the Court.[48]

The Court has also favoured the joint instruction of expert witnesses by parties, as "through the exercise of identifying with precision the real areas of disagreement between the parties, the expert will be placed in the best possible position to achieve a balanced and comprehensive analysis".[49] In such cases, by appointing a jointly or judicially instructed expert, the Trial Chamber would appear to be making an assessment on the expert's qualifications and impartiality.[50]

It is therefore of paramount importance that defence counsel, confronted with expert witnesses derived from the mentioned list, test the competence of each expert, led by the aforegoing *Daubert* criteria. The same counts for experts not appearing on this list, as the list as such is not imperative to appear in court as an expert.[51] Even if though Regulation 44 provides an invaluable safeguard as to the quality of experts at the ICC, it does not promulgate much clarity as to what actually defines an expert witness.[52] Even the definition of an expert

---

48 *Prosecutor v Ngudjolo Chui* (Judgment pursuant to article 74 of the Statute) ICC-01/04-02/12-3-tENG, T Ch II (18 December 2012) para. 60; *See also Prosecutor v Katanga* (Judgment pursuant to article 74 of the Statute) ICC-01/04-01/07-3436-tENG, T Ch II (7 March 2014) para. 94.

49 *Prosecutor v Bemba* (Decision on the procedures to be adopted for instructing expert witnesses) ICC-01/05-01/08-695, T Ch III (12 February 2010) paras. 11–12, citing *Prosecutor v Lubanga Dyilo* (Decision on the procedures to be adopted for instructing expert witnesses) ICC-01/04-01/06-1069, T Ch I (10 December 2007) paras. 14–23.

50 Avi Singh, 'Expert Evidence' in Karim A. A. Khan, Caroline Buisman and Chris Gosnell (eds), *Principles of Evidence in International Criminal Justice* (Oxford University Press 2010) 608.

51 X. Laroche and E. Baccard, 'International Courts and Forensic Sciences', *Encyclopaedia of Forensic Sciences* (vol 3, 2013) 491.

52 *Prosecutor v Lubanga Dyilo* (Decision on the procedures to be adopted for instructing expert witnesses) ICC-01/04-01/06-1069, T Ch I (10 December 2007) para. 25; see

witness as formulated by the ICTY being a "(...)person who by virtue of some specialized knowledge, skill or training can assist the trier of fact(...)"[53] does not enlighten the practical implications of how to deal with the competence of expert witnesses at trial. It is for this reason that the *Daubert* criteria could substitute for this substantial hiatus.

As evidenced by the Pre-Trial Chamber's approach in *Bemba*, above, judges have not only taken a flexible approach to the admission of evidence but have applied a seemingly low forensic evidentiary threshold, particularly with respect to crime-based evidence.[54] Trial Chamber X in *Al Hassan* has ruled on "the expertise of witnesses on the basis of reports and not witness statements."[55] The Chamber continues with stating that the scope and nature of the evidence proposed, i.e. the expert's report or testimony, is what is considered to decide on a witness' expertise. Furthermore, even if the evidence found in the expert's report for example goes beyond the timeframe of the charged accounts, the Court may still find the information to be relevant to the case it has at hand.[56]

14.6   Challenging Expert Evidence: Strategic Guidelines

A topic of practical value to prepare for proceedings before the ICC pertains to the approach one may take to challenge expert evidence. For defence counsel, it matters whether the prosecution's expert provides evidence on DNA or on the contours of an international armed conflict. Several recommendations can be put forward:

X. Laroche and E. Baccard, 'International Courts and Forensic Sciences', *Encyclopaedia of Forensic Sciences* (vol 3, 2013) 491.

53   *Prosecutor v Galić* (Decision Concerning the Expert Witnesses Ewa Tableau and Richard Philipps) IT-98-29-T, T Ch I (3 July 2002); *Prosecutor v Ntaganda* (Decision on Defence Preliminary Challenges to Prosecution's Expert Witnesses) ICC-01/04-02/06-1159, T Ch VI (9 February 2016) para. 7.

54   Richard May and Marieke Wierda, *International Criminal Evidence*, vol 9 (Brill 2021) 52 <https://brill.com/display/title/13900#navigation> accessed 14 June 2023; Melanie Klinker, 'Forensic Science Expertise for International Criminal Proceedings: an old Problem, a new Context and a Pragmatic Resolution' (2009) 13 The International Journal of Evidence and Proof 102, 127.

55   *Prosecutor v Al Hassan* (Decision on the introduction of evidence of witness P-0643) ICC-01/12-01/18-1409-Red, T Ch X (12 April 2021) para. 18.

56   *Prosecutor v Ntaganda* (Decision on Defence Preliminary Challenges to Prosecution's Expert Witnesses) ICC-01/04-02/06-1159, T Ch VI (9 February 2016) para. 26.

1. *Firstly*, if the prosecution expert testifies on a more forensic-mathematical subject, such as ballistics or DNA, the defence could beforehand analyse the prosecution's expert evidence with the help of its own expert in order to find discrepancies or flaws in the purported evidence.

2. *Secondly*, it is crucial to undertake a thorough background check of the prosecution's expert. In the event the prosecution intends to introduce a report of an expert who, for instance did research on the socio-political implications in a given conflict for purposes of illuminating the origins of that said conflict, defence counsel must verify if the background of such an expert might reveal any potential conflict of interest and accordingly a bias. In particular, past publications issued by the expert on the very same conflict could disclose a certain predisposition against the accused's role within the conflict. An example of the importance of this recommendation follows from the recusal of Judge Geoffrey Robertson as presiding Judge of the Appeals Chamber of the Special Court for Sierra Leone; this Court was mandated with the trials against accused persons responsible for war crimes committed during the civil war in Sierra Leone between 1991 and 2002. His recusal was based on a book publication Judge Robertson authored in 1999 titled 'Crimes Against Humanity'. In this book, Mr. Robertson gave, inter alia, an account of his views of what happened during the mentioned civil war and the entities and individuals he considered responsible. It happens to be that one of the armed factions he mentioned and (dis)qualified in his book faced trial at the Special Court for Sierra Leone. As a result, the position of Judge Robertson within the Appeals Chamber created for the specific accused persons an appearance of bias and lack of independence. The removal decision details the response of the Prosecution, which aptly describes the situation:

> having carefully reviewed the facts as alleged by the Defence and elsewhere, to include a careful reading of the book in question, the Prosecution concedes that there could be a valid argument that there is an appearance of bias on the part of Judge Robertson. The material could lead a reasonable observer, properly informed, to apprehend bias.[57]

3. *Thirdly*, an additional recommendation can be extracted from the previous one. The defence should investigate the admissibility of expert

---

57 *Prosecutor v Sesay et al.* (Decision on Defence Motion Seeking the Disqualification of Judge Robertson from the Appeals Chamber) SCSL-2004-AR15-15, T Ch I (13 March 2003).

evidence on the basis of the absence of the requisite expertise, qualification, lack of methodology or even lack of independence, in a timely manner, before the scheduled hearing of the expert.[58]

Raising these arguments as soon as feasible enables the Trial Chamber to fully digest the defence counsel's arguments and provide a reasoned decision, rather than waiting to raise this argument at the hearing of the expert itself. In the latter situation, one puts the Trial Chamber in the position of having to 'rush to a decision', which increases the risk that the said decision will not be in the defence's favour.

14.7 Defense Strategies to Challenge Expert Witnesses before Trial

The approach that the defence counsel will take to challenge expert evidence prior to the hearing will greatly depend on the legal-strategic choice made according to the specific case that it at its hand.

(i) A first strategy to challenge expert evidence is to pursue an application to the Trial Chamber requesting the exclusion of the report in its entirety. This can be granted only if the defence is able to make probable that the evidence which underlies the report is unreliable. The defence therefore has the burden to demonstrate that practically all of the sources or data which form the basis of the report, are tainted or obtained by unethical methods.

(ii) A second strategy to challenge expert evidence is to argue before the Trial Chamber, by means of an application, that certain provisions of the expert report be removed or deleted, on the basis that these documents fail to comply with either the admissibility tests (see above) or with factor sub (h) of the abovementioned substantive requirements. Additionally, the defence, in its application, could also seek from the Trial Chamber to issue the order to prohibit the prosecution from examining the expert on specific aspects of his or her report, as they fall outside the scope of the expert's expertise, which would violate the 'ultimate issue rule' or would lead to the introduction of non-verifiable data such as anonymous sources.

This occurred in the mentioned ICC case of *Prosecutor v Laurent Gbagbo and Charles Blé Goudé* in regard to a witness, a human rights worker, who was called to testify about his research during the conflict in Ivory Coast. Trial Chamber I

---

[58] The Crown Prosecutor Service, 'Expert evidence' (*Legal Guidance*, updated 5 August 2022) <www.cps.gov.uk/legal-guidance/expert-evidence> accessed 28 September 2023.

of the ICC ruled that this witness was prohibited from testifying about his personal opinions and the information he gathered from unknown sources.

14.8   Guidelines to (Cross-)examine and Test Forensic Experts at Trial

Based upon the leading *Daubert* criteria, which have been adopted in various domestic jurisdictions,[59] the following four main guidelines for defence counsel can be set forth when testing an expert witness regarding his qualifications:
i.   What is the knowledge and skill of the person of the expert?
ii. What is the validity and reliability of the applied method?
iii. Did the expert have experience with this method?
iv. What was the manner in which the method was applied by the expert in the present case to the acquired data?

A fifth criterion relates to verifying the way the forensic evidence was collected. The collection is contingent upon the chain of custody. Although neither the ICC Statute nor the statutes of the *ad hoc* tribunals refer to the requirement of the preservation of the chain of custody, not even in their respective Rules of Procedure and Evidence, the Regulations on the ICC Prosecutor oblige the prosecutor to secure the (forensic) evidence by way of an "(…) uninterrupted chain of custody of documents and all other types of evidence. All evidence shall constantly be in the possession of the collector or the individual authorised to have possession of the item. The maintenance of the chain of custody shall be recorded and managed in accordance with regulation 23".[60]

Typically, domestic legal systems impose various possible legal consequences in case the chain of custody is compromised, such as exclusion of inculpatory evidence. An example of this can be found in the case of the murder of *Meredith Kercher* in Perugia (Italy) in 2007. The case became widely known for one of the defendants, Amanda Knox, an American national. In the course of the criminal proceedings, which lasted from 2007 to 2015, experts found that multiple pieces of evidence had not been handled properly by police investigators,

---

59   See inter alia Judgment Supreme Court of the Netherlands, ECLI:HR:1998:ZD0917, 27/01/1998; drawing from the *Daubert* criteria; Judgment of the Supreme Court of Canada, *R. v J.-L.J.*, 2000 SCC 51, para. 33; *R. v Trochym*, 2007 SCC 6, para. 26; *Prosecutor v Sesay et al.* (Judgment) SCSL-04-15-T, T Ch I (25 February 2009) para. 27.

60   Regulations of the Office of the Prosecutor (2009), ICC-BD-05/01/09, Regulation 22; P. Amann and M. P. Dillon, 'Electronic Evidence Management at the ICC: Legal, Technical, Investigative and Organizational Considerations', in A. Babington-Ashaye, A. Comrie and A. Adeniran, *International Criminal Investigations* (Eleven international publishing 2018), 237–248.

in disregard of standard principles on the correct approach of a crime scene; several omissions by investigators in this respect, which amounted to an interruption of the chain of custody, entailed the contamination of crucial forensic materials.[61] These expert findings, amongst other factors, eventually led the Italian Court of Cassation to find the evidence to be unreliable, which necessitated the exoneration of the convicts.[62] This example emphasizes the importance of compliance with the chain of custody in handling forensic evidence.

The question arises as to what could be the legal consequences of the chain of custody being interrupted and not recorded within ICC proceedings. The ICC Chambers have found that in order to assess documentary evidence the Chamber must examine its "provenance, source or author, as well as their role in the relevant events, the chain of custody from the time of the item's creation until its submission to the Chamber, and any other relevant information."[63] To date, no clear precedent thereto exists at the ICC with respect to the interruption of the chain of custody even though no viable reason can be found why such interruption should not incur a consequence similar to the one which was adopted in the *Amanda Knox* case, as the underlying forensic issues remain the same. By contrast to the domestic legal systems, exclusion of evidence is infrequent before international criminal jurisdictions, where judges have favoured admitting an item of evidence and making a determination on admissibility at the time of the judgment.[64] However, as recently noted by Lindsay Freeman, there has, in recent years, "been a notable increase in the exclusion of evidence, particularly for items of new media that have not been properly sourced", which is a partial reflection of the challenges posed by new types of evidence.[65] A forensic scientist who is not assured of a preserved chain of custody should refrain from providing an opinion about the probabilities of the hypothesis, or at the least should implement this factor in his statistical

---

61   Peter Gill, *Misleading DNA Evidence: Reasons for Miscarriages of Justice* (Elsevier Inc. 2014) 136–158.
62   Corte di Cassazione, 36080/15, Judgment 27/03/2015 (the Italian text of the judgment can be found here: http://www.giurisprudenzapenale.com/wp-content/uploads/2015/09/cass-pen-2015-36080.pdf).
63   *Prosecutor v Bemba Gombo* (Judgment pursuant to Article 74 of the Statute) ICC-01/05-01/08-3343, T Ch III, (21 March 2016) para. 247.
64   Lindsay Freeman, 'Digital Evidence and War Crimes Prosecutions: The Impact of Digital Technologies on International Criminal Investigations and Trials' (2018) 41 Fordham Int'l L.J. 283 <https://ir.lawnet.fordham.edu/ilj/vol41/iss2/1> accessed 27 September 2023, 293.
65   *Ibid*, citing *Prosecutor v Bemba Gombo* (Decision on the Admission into Evidence of Items Deferred in the Chamber's «Decision of the Prosecution's Application for Admission of Materials into Evidence Pursuant to Article 64(9) of the Rome Statute») ICC-01/05-01/08-2721, T Ch III (27 June 2013).

calculation. Therefore, this aspect needs to be further developed at the ICC to meet the challenges forensic sciences create.

A verification by defence counsel operating at international criminal tribunals of the chain of custody is even more relevant in light of the fact that in most instances crime scene investigations within these trials "(...) take place well after the crime has been committed (...), which (...) exacerbates the intrinsic limitations of forensic science".[66] One important question for cross-examination of a forensic expert is therefore whether he or she was able to ascertain the chain of custody of the piece of evidence he or she examined.

Furthermore, regulation 24 of the ICC OTP Regulations merits attention. This regulation entails three important forensic guidelines for the Prosecution:

i. To develop and apply a consistent and objective method for the evaluation of sources and (forensic) evidence;
ii. To take into account the credibility and reliability of such sources and evidence;
iii. To examine this evidence "from multiple sources as a means of bias control".

These three elements can also serve as fundamentals for defence counsel cross examination. Also here, the regulation is silent as to what potential legal consequences an infringement thereof would encompass. Yet, especially the obligation to evade 'bias' should be a topic for cross-examination for defence counsel. This last element of regulation 24 coincides with the forensic professional obligation of an expert to ascertain alternative theories which do not conflict with the evidence.[67]

By digesting the subject-matter of the expert opinion and getting familiarized with the literature and state of the art of the discipline in question, defence counsel can also uncover the areas and methods the expert has not touched upon. This especially accounts for the performance of certain psychological tests. For instance, if the prosecution was to call a psychologist at trial to persuade the Trial judges that a certain witness suffered from a trauma due to

---

66 X. Laroche and E. Baccard, 'International Courts and Forensic Sciences', *Encyclopaedia of Forensic Sciences* (vol 3, 2013) 491; on the limits of international criminal investigations, see Nancy Amoury Combs, 'Grave Crimes and Weak Evidence: Fact-Finding Evolution in International Criminal Law' (2017) 58 Harvard International Law Journal 47 <https://scholarship.law.wm.edu/facpubs/1867/> accessed on 27 September 2023, 48–49; Robert Cryer and Hakan Friman, *An Introduction to International Criminal Law and Procedure* (Cambridge University Press 2016) 449–450.

67 X. Laroche and E. Baccard, 'International Courts and Forensic Sciences', *Encyclopaedia of Forensic Sciences* (vol 3, 2013) 493.

the consequences of certain war crimes with which the accused is charged;[68] in the same vein, defence counsel could benefit from researching in particular the underlying data of the expert report and the information embedded in the footnotes of the said report.[69] In the ICC case of *Prosecutor v Yekatom and Ngaïssona*, the prosecution in 2023 called an anthropologist as expert on the topic of child soldiers. This expert produced two reports, one of which was co-authored by another expert. The reports contained some conclusions as to the involvement of a certain group of (young) individuals in an armed attack on the capital city of the Central African Republic and the alleged 'galvanization' by the former president of this country of a number of youth and children. This assertion referred to a footnote which comprised a reference to an article in a journal. Upon studying this article, the defence was able to demonstrate that the expert's assertion in the report was not supported by this referred footnote. Needless to say that such examination at trial may affect the veracity of the expert's report.

As an overall conclusion of this section, it can be said that defence counsel should be mindful to examine the forensic expert as to whether he or she was instructed to assess the evidence based upon different theories and which sources were made available to him or her by the prosecution.

14.9 Defense Preparations to (Cross-)examine Experts at Trial

As mentioned in the preceding paragraphs, at the ICC, recourse is often made by the prosecution to expert evidence on for instance, the socio-political or military background of a certain armed conflict. Some of these experts are academics and some are affiliated with the UN or an NGO.[70] This observation already triggers the relevance for defence counsel to enter into a thorough background check of the expert who is called by the prosecution:

(i) The first and most important part of preparing a (cross-)examination of a prosecution expert is to delve into the professional history of this expert. This should exceed merely reading his or her resume, but it should rather

---

68 See further for this topic: Thomas Mauet, *Trials: Strategy, Skills, And the New Powers of Persuasion* (1st edn, Aspen Publishers 2005) 443.

69 Thomas Mauet, *Trials: Strategy, Skills, And the New Powers of Persuasion* (1st edn, Aspen Publishers 2005) 440–441.

70 See for instance, the cases of *Prosecutor v Gbagbo and Blé Goudé* and *Prosecutor v Yekatom and Ngaissona*.

encompass an inquiry into the publications of the expert, as mentioned in the previous paragraphs.[71]

(ii) The second important defence strategy pertains to finding reports and (academic) articles which can refute the content of the report of the prosecution's expert. This type of information can be quite useful to cross-examine the expert and to challenge his or her findings.

(iii) A third aspect of defence preparation that may be helpful to mount an effective cross-examination of the expert, is to consult another expert of the relevant field and ask him or her review the prosecution expert's report. This type of preparation can provide for valuable information and questions to examine the prosecution expert. The expert defence counsel decides to consult is to be distinguished from a defence expert who will testify at trial.[72]

(iv) Finally, defence counsel must acquaintance him- or herself with the subject matter of the expert's report. For instance, examining the prosecution expert on ballistic evidence cannot be done without beforehand having knowledge of this forensic discipline.

These four steps constitute the basis to building a cross-examination plan and choice to treat the expert as potentially a 'hostile one'.

14.10 Joint Instructions to Forensic Experts

According to Article 56 of the Rome Statute, the ICC Pre-Trial Chamber decides on the engagement of an expert during the proceedings. However, it is possible for the defence to engage in 'joint instructions' with the prosecution, which implies that the prosecution and the defence both agree on the formulation of specific questions that are to be provided to an expert.

Strategically, in the defence counsel's point of view, such 'joint instructions' may backfire if the expert report is not favourable to the defence. In such a situation it is quite difficult for the defence to challenge at trial the expert's report in light of its previous consent to the said joint instructions.

A similar strategic disadvantage for the defence may arise in the event it provides separate instructions beforehand to the prosecution expert. In this scenario, the defence already discloses its strategy, that is the way it intends to challenge the prosecution expert at trial, before the examination of the said

---

71   See the example of the book of Judge Geoffrey Robinson
72   Thomas Mauet, *Trials: Strategy, Skills, And the New Powers of Persuasion* (1st edn, Aspen Publishers 2005) 435.

expert. Should the defence have specific questions it intends to ask the expert, which are meant to undermine his or her potential report, it may be preferable to save these questions for the examination during the trial hearings; as a result, the expert is not given the opportunity to anticipate the questions and therefore his or her answers. This approach – not entering in joint or separate instructions to a prosecution expert – is even more preferable if the defence counsel has reasons to believe that the prosecution expert, in light of his or her background, is most likely not going to produce a favourable opinion for the accused. In cases where the evidence is disputed by the defence and where it is to be expected that an expert's opinion will be called for by the prosecution to support its case, one can assume – by way of presumption – that the expert opinion will not be favourable to the accused, bearing in mind the psychological phenomenon of 'confirmation bias' which can also be applied to experts.[73]

'Confirmation bias' implies that a researcher who has been assigned by one of the parties and has been asked to investigate a certain hypothesis has a tendency to be led by one's existing beliefs or perceptions, which may be fuelled by mostly one-sided information given to the expert by the prosecution or the defence. Therefore, disclosure of all the preceding correspondence between the expert and the prosecutor is of paramount importance in order to verify the potential existence of such a confirmation bias.

14.11   Disclosure Requirements

Another relevant topic in regards to expert evidence is the disclosure of all the material accumulated by the expert witness in the course of his or her inquiry. In this context, what type of material should be disclosed? It can be argued that at the least the following information should be disclosed to the defence and the Trial Chamber:

i.   In principle, the prosecution is under duty to disclose to the defence the materials used and unused by the expert, if the unused material assists the defence case or undermines the prosecution's case.[74]
ii. Material that has a bearing on the competence and/or credibility of an expert witness.[75]

---

73   Claire A J van den Eeden, Christianne J de Poot and Peter J van Koppen, 'The Forensic Confirmation Bias: A Comparison Between Experts and Novices' (2019) 64,1 Journal of forensic sciences <doi:10.1111/1556-4029.13817> accessed 2 October 2023.

74   The Crown Prosecutor Service, 'Expert evidence' (*Legal Guidance*, updated 5 August 2022) <www.cps.gov.uk/legal-guidance/expert-evidence> accessed 2 October 2023.

75   *Ibid.*

iii. Material that has been accumulated by the expert in the course of his or her analysis or investigation and that could have an effect on the assessment of the veracity of the expert evidence. This might also include the underlying tests performed by an expert in a laboratory in the event forensic techniques are applied, such as DNA evidence.[76]
iv. A record, if available, of all investigatory steps and contacts the expert undertook in the course of his research.[77] Such a record could also be relevant for a potential contra-expertise (second-opinion) which enables another expert to review the foundation of submitted expert evidence.

Also, the crux of the disclosure test that is to be applied here is that any material that might cast doubt on the safety of a potential conviction should be disclosed to the defence. This test should thus also be pursued in regards to expert evidence.[78]

14.12 Cross-examination of Expert Witnesses

Another important tool to challenge expert evidence is the cross-examination. When cross-examining an expert witness, the following questions should at the least be part of the examination plan:
(i) What was the expert's specific research question?
(ii) Did the expert have meetings or informal contacts with the prosecution and what was the information he or she received during these contacts?
(iii) What documents did the expert receive?
(iv) Did the documents received by the expert include comments written by the prosecution?
(v) What is the underlying foundation of his or her opinion and in how far is this opinion based on a personal judgement made by the expert?[79]

14.13 Examining Expert Evidence at Trial: the ECtHR Perspective

International criminal trials are predominantly conducted on the basis of documentary and witness evidence.[80] The role of expert evidence is in most cases

---

76 *Ibid.*
77 *Ibid.*
78 *Ibid.*
79 *Ibid.*
80 Richard May and Marieke Wierda, *International Criminal Evidence*, vol 9 (Brill 2021) 143.

limited to political, historical and military subject matters, in order to inform the court of the background of a particular international or internal armed conflict. As mentioned above, in *Prosecutor v Yekatom and Ngaïssona*, the ICC Trial Chamber allowed the admission of an expert report on child soldiers, drafted by an anthropologist. In its decision of 10 March 2021, the Chamber recalled in this regard in paragraph 64: "It is possible to call an expert on issues that to not go specifically to the facts *sub judice*, but to necessary contextual information."[81]

Still, contextual information provided by an expert witness can be of incriminating nature for an accused in that a Trial Chamber could use that type of information to provide for instance the contextual elements of crimes against humanity, such as the 'policy element'. For this reason, the defence should have an adequate opportunity to (cross-)examine an expert in court.

One particular decision of the ECtHR draws attention and could be relevant for defence counsel to invoke when advocating an adequate possibility to challenge such type of evidence in court. The ECtHR case of *Danilov v Russia*, resulting in decision of 1 December 2020, related to Mr. Danilov, a physician who was convicted for treason by Russian courts because he allegedly shared information about a space-simulation system, held by the university, with his Chinese colleagues. Eight out of the ten expert reports submitted in his trial, qualified this information as 'state secret': Danilov complained that he was not enabled to question the experts nor was he able to call his own experts. The Court however ruled that it was necessary to call these reports at trial as the reports were clear, while the request of Danilov was not particularly detailed and only referred to his rights under article 6(3)(d) of the Convention for the

---

81   *Prosecutor v Yekatom and Ngaïssona* (Decision on the Prosecution Requests for Formal Submission of Prior Recorded Testimonies under Rule 68(3) of the Rules concerning Witnesses P-1962, P-0925, P-2193, P-2926, P-2927, P-1577 and P 0287, and the Ngaïssona Defence Motion to Limit the Scope) ICC-01/14-01/18-907-Red, T Ch V (1 April 2021) para. 64; *See also Prosecutor v Yekatom and Ngaïssona* (Decision on the Yekatom Defence Request to Exclude Expert Witness P-2926) ICC-01/14-01/18-881, T Ch V (11 February 2021) para. 9; *Prosecutor v Bemba et al.* (Decision on the Prosecution Request to Exclude Defence Witness D22–0004) ICC-01/05-01/13-165324, T Ch VIII (February 2016) para. 11, *referring to Prosecutor v Ntaganda* (Decision on Defence preliminary challenges to Prosecution's expert witnesses) ICC-01/04-02/06-1159, T Ch VI (9 February 2016) para. 21; *Prosecutor v Ruto and Sang* (Decision on Sang Defence Application to Exclude Expert Report of Mr Hervé Maupeu,) ICC-01/09-01/11-844, T Ch V(A) (7 August 2013); *Prosecutor v Bemba Gombo* (Decision on "Prosecution's Motion to Exclude Defence Political-Military Strategy Expert") ICC-01/05-01/08-2273, T Ch III (21 August 2012); *Prosecutor v Yekatom and Ngaïssona* (Initial Directions on the Conduct of Proceedings) ICC-01/14-01/18-631, T Ch V (26 August 2020) para. 53.

Protection of Human Rights and Fundamental Freedoms ("the Convention"). In appeal, the defence argued that the experts necessarily had to be examined in order to show the court that these they lacked the required expertise. The Appeals Court held that these experts did have the proper expertise to answer questions on the subject matter of 'state secrecy'. At the end of its decision of 1 December 2020, the ECtHR held that:

> One of the requirements of a fair trial is the possibility for the accused to confront the witnesses in the presence of the judge who must ultimately decide the case, because the judge's observations on the demeanour and credibility of a certain witness may have consequences for the accused (see *Matytsina v Russia*, no. 58428/10, § 153, 27 March 2014, with further references; *Avagyan*, cited above, § 43; and *Khodorkovskiy and Lebedev* (no. 2), cited above, § 482). The same also applies to expert witnesses (see *Gregačević v Croatia*, no. 58331/09, § 67, 10 July 2012, and *Constantinides v Greece*, no. 76438/12, § 39, 6 October 2016): the defence must have the right to study and challenge not only an expert report as such, but also the credibility of those who prepared it, by direct questioning (see, among other authorities, *Brandstetter v Austria*, 28 August 1991, § 42, Series A no. 211; *Matytsina*, cited above, § 177; *Avagyan*, cited above, § 43, and *Khodorkovskiy and Lebedev* (no. 2), cited above, § 482).[82]

Based on these observations, the ECtHR contemplates that the mentioned eight reports were drafted for the prosecution and constituted an important part of the prosecution case against Danilov to prove the charge of treason.

In paragraphs 113–114 of the Danilov ruling, the expert reports are qualified by the European Court Judges as 'of crucial relevance' for the outcome of the case. Moreover, the Court stipulates that even in the event these reports did not contain inconsistencies, the examination of these experts at trial was still relevant for purposes of detecting potential deficiencies in these reports and conflicts of interest.[83] To conclude to the violation of Article 6 of the Convention, the Court assesses:

> To sum up, the applicant's conviction for high treason by disclosure of a State secret was based on the opinions of experts who were neither cross-examined during the trial (see *Avagyan v Armenia*, cited above, § 46, and

---

82 *Danilov v Russia* App no 88/05 (ECtHR, 1 March 2021) para. 111.
83 *Danilov v Russia* App no 88/05 (ECtHR, 1 March 2021) paras 116–117.

Khodorkovskiy and Lebedev (no. 2), cited above, § 484), nor during the investigation stage.[84]

It is therefore the view of the ECtHR that Article 6 could be infringed upon in the event expert evidence is admitted before a Trial Chamber without the defence having had an adequate opportunity to challenge, by direct questioning, such experts. These findings of the ECtHR underline the importance for the defence at the ICC to use cross-examination to not only demonstrate potential flaws in expert reports, but also to extract exculpatory information.

The following example can illustrate this idea: an expert on child soldiers is called by the prosecution and testifies that during an armed conflict several armed groups did recruit themselves child soldiers. The accused is charged with superior responsibility for recruitment of child soldiers. During cross-examination the defence counsel is able to retrieve the acknowledgement from the expert that there was no centralized system for such recruitment. This evidence might then contravene the thesis of 'superior responsibility'.

14.14 Conclusion

The role of expert evidence at the level of international criminal tribunals and especially the ICC, as demonstrated in this chapter, is not to be underestimated. Adequate knowledge of the basics of the common law admissibility criteria of expert evidence, the possible ways to challenge this evidence and the forensic sciences and the principles which underpin this discipline enables defence counsel to elicit potential exculpatory information during cross-examination of an expert. Also, understanding the basics of contemporary methodologies for forensic examination can create an advantage for such defence counsel.

It is important that more uniform and objective criteria are promulgated by the Trial Chambers which will set out the procedural and substantive requirements for the presentation of expert evidence both in written form and in court. For defence counsel, attention should be paid to the admissibility of the expert evidence prior to the expert giving testimony at trial. To this end, several procedural-strategical avenues arise which should be discerned on a case-by-case basis.

Based upon the findings in this chapter, the following main conclusions and recommendations can be discerned for defence counsel appearing before the ICC:

---

84 *Ibid* paras 119–120.

i. The chain of custody needs to be properly recorded so it can be assessed by judges and lawyers in court;
ii. The expert independence needs to be guaranteed and tested in court;
iii. The defence needs to have access to original material/crime scene when possible in order to be able to have alternative theories tested by forensic experts as well as to verify 'scientific bias';
iv. Verification and testing of the applied scientific methodology is essential;
v. The defence needs to have knowledge of basic and new forensic technology/developments.

For the future of defence counsel operating at the ICC, it could be beneficial to have special training programmes for defence counsel in place in order to further familiarize with the influx of forensic science, such as call data records and DNA evidence, at these courts from a defence perspective. Only this way defence counsel can optimize its task to ensure the fair trial rights of the defendants.

Challenging and applying forensic sciences in court is nowadays, as this chapter shows, part and parcel of these fair trial obligations. As Laroche and Baccard observe, "(...) the value of forensic science to international criminal tribunals is unquestionable but its use needs to mature in a systematic way in the coming years in order to con- solidate its crucial evidentiary role".[85] Within this process towards 'maturity' the supervisory role of defence counsel in court, in order to merge the proliferation of forensic sciences within the scheme of fair trial rights of the accused, has to be a prominent one. To this end, the said recommendations are yet to be seen as a first step.

---

85 X. Laroche and E. Baccard, 'International Courts and Forensic Sciences', Encyclopaedia of Forensic Sciences (vol 3, 2013) 494.

PART 5

Documentary Evidence

∴

CHAPTER 15

Challenging Documentary Evidence at the ICC

15.1 Submission or Admission of Documentary Evidence at Trial

Trials before international criminal tribunals rest upon three evidentiary pillars: documentary, testimonial, and forensic evidence. This chapter will first delve into the documentary evidentiary system at international criminal tribunals.

15.1.1 *ICC Jurisprudence*
In most criminal law systems, an argument pertaining to the relevance or the admissibility of a certain document must be directly raised at the time that a particular document is submitted by either the prosecution or defence to the court, or, as soon as possible after the potential deficiency of the document has been discovered.

This is also the view of the ICC. In the case of *Prosecutor v Laurent Gbagbo and Charles Blé Goudé*, Trial Chamber I in its important Decision on the submission and admission of evidence of 29 January 2016, in paragraph 7 held:

> Pursuant to Rule 64(1) of the Rules, an issue relating to relevance or admissibility must be raised at the time when the evidence is submitted to the Chamber, or, exceptionally, immediately after the issue has become known. Whilst the Chamber retains the discretion ("may") to request that the issue be raised in writing, it is the Chamber's view that, as regards evidence presented during a hearing, issues of this nature should be immediately raised orally at the same hearing.[1]

In this case, the question arose as to whether the admissibility of evidence, in particular documents, should be established directly at the time the said item is shown to a witness or should rather be determined at the end of the trial. Both the prosecution and defence argued in favour of the first option. The defence's argumentation was based on the idea that since the issue of the probative value or weight which one has to attribute to a certain evidentiary item only arises once that the item has been found admissible by a court of law,

---

1 *Prosecutor v Gbagbo and Blé Goudé* (Decision on the submission and admission of evidence) ICC-02/11-01/15-405, T Ch I (January 2016) para. 7.

the discussion on the admissibility should be resolved beforehand, i.e. at the moment this item is served to the judges. Such an admissibility system would avoid uncertainty and the use of unnecessary human and court resources.

The Bench of Trial Chamber I decided otherwise; it held that any decision on the admissibility and relevance of evidence submitted "(...) will be deferred to the final judgment, except when an intermediate ruling is required (...)."[2] It resumed that the ICC-system attributes to a Trial Chamber a broad discretion at which ever point in time a ruling on the admissibility or relevance of evidence shall occur.[3]

To this end, it referred to Article 64(9)(a) of the Rome Statute and Article 69(4) thereof which provisions, dealing with the admissibility or relevance of evidence, say that Trial Chambers "shall have (...) the power (...) to rule on the admissibility or relevance of evidence" and "(...) the Court may rule on (...)" these subjects.[4] In paragraphs 10–16, Trial Chamber I contemplated that it had to weigh two principles: first, ensuring a fair and expeditious trial and, second, its duty to not omit the consideration of "the relevance, probative value and potential prejudice to the accused of each item of evidence at some point in the proceedings".[5]

When balancing these two interests, it rejected the defence's view, holding that several factors militated in favour of a system "(...) whereby, as a matter of principle, the assessment of both the admissibility and the relevance or probative value of evidence is deferred until the moment when the Chamber will be deliberating its judgment (...)."[6]

On this topic, the Court differentiated a bench-system of professional judges from a jury-system. The latter system may require a different approach in order to prevent criminal proceedings to "(...) be compromised by irrelevant or prejudicial material."[7] Precisely, the judges of Trial Chamber I set forth three arguments in favour of a submission-system. The said arguments conclude that:

(i) Only at the end of the trial, once submission of evidence has been completed, the Chamber will be in the best position to make determinations in regards to each individual item of evidence in light of the totality of all items.

---

2 *Prosecutor v Gbagbo and Blé Goudé* (Decision on the submission and admission of evidence) ICC-02/11-01/15-405, T Ch I (January 2016) 10.
3 *Ibid* para. 9.
4 *Ibid* para. 8.
5 *Ibid* para. 10.
6 *Ibid* para. 12; Judge G. Henderson appended a dissenting opinion.
7 *Ibid* para. 16.

(ii) To defer this decision to the end of the trial will prevent multiple determinations on one and the same item and will thereby avoid the creation of unnecessary interlocutory litigation, resulting in the disruption of the proceedings.
(iii) A submission-system will also ensure that all the evidence will be treated uniformly and secure overall certainty of the proceedings.[8]

The Court emphasised that this submission-regime would not prevent the parties to raise admissibility objections upon submission of the relevant item. Indeed, the Chamber, in the exercise of its discretion, may continue to rule on the admissibility of an item in order to preserve the fairness of the proceedings.[9]

As mentioned, the Appeals Chamber in its decision of 24 July 2017 confirmed the rating of Trial Chamber I, stating in paragraph 52 that:

> It is clear that, depending on the circumstances, the authenticity of a given document may be further elucidated by other evidence, be it evidence specifically adduced for that purpose of evidence otherwise submitted in the course of the trial.[10]

The Appeals Chamber thus created the option that the tendering party can remedy any admissibility objections from the non-tendering party by the later submission of other material that was submitted at a later stage of the trial. The Appeals Chamber also held that failure by the tendering party to submit sufficient information in order to enable the parties and judges to formulate uniformed responses as to admissibility-issues, does not mean that Article 64(1) of the Rules of Procedure and Evidence is violated.[11]

As for the relevance of the documentary evidence, the Chamber in the *Katanga* case considered that an authentic documentary evidence is not necessarily reliable.[12] The same Chamber stated that:

> If a party has tendered an item of evidence as proof of a particular proposition, the Chamber will in principle admit it only for that purpose, even

---

8 *Ibid* paras 13–15.
9 *Ibid* para. 17.
10 *Prosecutor v Gbagbo and Blé Goudé* (Judgment on the appeals of Mr Laurent Gbagbo and Mr Charles Blé Goudé against Trial Chamber I's decision on the submission of documentary evidence) ICC-02/11-01/15-995, A Ch (24 July 2017) para. 54.
11 *Ibid* paras 55–56.
12 *Prosecutor v Katanga* (Judgment pursuant to article 74 of the Statute) ICC-01/04-01/07-3436-tENG, T Ch II (7 March 2014) para. 91.

if the entire exhibit is admitted into evidence. Accordingly, if the same item of evidence could also prove another proposition than the one(s) for which it was tendered, the Chamber will not consider the evidence in relation to that additional proposition, unless the parties were given an opportunity to address this aspect of the evidence.[13]

The conclusion of this section regarding the ICC jurisprudence is that the Chambers of the Court have chosen the adoption of a modified submission-regime when it concerns the tendering of evidence.

15.1.2 Types of Documentary Evidence at the ICC

Documentary evidence surfaces at the ICC in many forms, such as birth certificates of victims, military reports, minutes of governmental meetings, Facebook records, email correspondence, diary notes, logbooks press communiques[14] and payment receipts. For instance, in the case of *Prosecutor v Gbagbo and Blé Goudé*, the Prosecution submitted over 4610 items of documentary and other non-oral items of evidence.[15] In the majority opinion to the ICC judgment of acquittal in the *Gbagbo and Blé Goudé* case, Judge Geoffrey Henderson set forth the requirements when treating documentary evidence.

(i) The first requirement Judge Henderson describes is the condition that the relevance and authenticity of the particular exhibit 'must be duly established';[16]

(ii) It is therefore the tendering party that bears the burden, unless the origin and genuineness are apparent from the document itself, to introduce evidence to prove both the authorship and integrity of the document;[17]

In the ICC case of *Katanga and Ngudjolo Chui*, The Court held in this regard:

> The first issue the Chamber must consider, in this respect, is whether the item of evidence is authenticated. In the absence of authentication, there can be no guarantee that a document is what the party tendering it purports it to be. Under no circumstances can the Chamber admit

---

13 *Prosecutor v Katanga and Ngudjolo Chui* (Decision on the Prosecutor's Bar Table Motions) ICC-01/04-01/07-2635, T Ch II (17 December 2010) para. 17.

14 *Prosecutor v Ongwen* (Decision on Prosecution Request to Submit Interception Related Evidence) ICC-02/04-01/15-615, T Ch IX (1 December 2016).

15 *Prosecutor v Gbagbo and Blé Goudé* (Reasons of Judge Henderson) ICC-02/11-01/15-1263-AnxB-Red, T Ch I (16 July 2019) para. 32.

16 *Ibid.*

17 *Ibid*, referring to *Prosecutor v Katanga and Ngudjolo Chui* (Decision on Prosecutor's Bar Table Motions) ICC-01/04-01/07-2635, T Ch II (17 December 2010) paras 22–23.

unauthenticated documentary evidence since, by definition, such evidence has no probative value. The Prosecution's assertion that 'there is no legal basis in the jurisprudence of the tribunals that proof of authenticity is a threshold requirement for the admissibility of documentary evidence', irrespective of its accuracy, is misconceived in the context of proceedings before this Court. To admit unauthenticated evidence would unjustifiably burden the record of the trial with non-probative material and serve no purpose in the determination of the truth.

Accordingly, unless an item of evidence is self-authenticating, or the parties agree that it is authentic, it is for the party tendering the item to provide admissible evidence demonstrating its authenticity. Such evidence may be direct or circumstantial but must provide reasonable grounds to believe that the exhibit is authentic, which, although not a particularly high standard, does impose a burden of proof on the party tendering the evidence. If no authenticating evidence is provided whatsoever, the documentary evidence will be found inadmissible. It is insufficient merely to state that "the information provided satisfies the required indicia of reliability and each document presents an intrinsic coherence and prima facie probative value, in light of the whole body of evidence introduced in this case". A mere general reference to the record of the trial is unsatisfactory since it is not for the Chamber to start its own investigations into material which may prove a document's authenticity and reliability.[18]

This requirement particularly counts for social media exhibits such as Facebook entries. In light of the risk that Facebook messages might not be authentic, the admissibility of this type of documentary evidence should depend on the purported author's in court testimony on the relevant Facebook page, in order to establish its authenticity.[19]

(iii) A third requirement pertains to the preservation of the chain of custody or chain of evidence. An example is to be found, in para 35 of the aforementioned Reasons of Judge Henderson. In that case, the prosecution investigators found in February 2012 at the Presidential residence several hundred documents which were used in court to prove the existence of a pattern of crimes committed against civilians by individuals loyal to the accused, i.e. the former president Gbagbo.

---

18 *Prosecutor v Katanga and Ngudjolo Chui* (Decision on Prosecutor's Bar Table Motions) ICC-01/04-01/07-2635, T Ch II (17 December 2010) paras 22–23.

19 See Chapter XVII for further on this topic.

The investigator's report mentioned that the Ivorian authorities had informed the ICC prosecution that the Presidential Palace had been left untouched since the arrest of the former president. However, as Judge Henderson observed, "(...) no evidence has been presented by the Prosecutor showing that no one entered the Presidential Palace in the period between the arrest of the former president and the prosecution's site visit."[20] As a result, Judge Henderson held that "it is thus far from certain that the documents that were found there ten months later were also present on the day of the arrest and that they were not tampered with."[21] In this regard, interestingly enough, Judge Henderson also took into account that "(...) much of the evidence was essentially provided by the current government, which is headed by political opponents of the accused."[22] Under these circumstances, as was reasoned by Judge Henderson, "(...) the Chamber would have expected the Prosecutor to take further steps to ensure that important documentary evidence was properly and demonstrably authenticated before being submitted for the Chamber's consideration."[23]

These three criteria illustrate that documentary evidence never should be accepted on its face value. Defence counsel should be aware of these principles in order to challenge this type of evidence. For defence counsel, it is important to raise such authentication arguments as early as possible at trial so that the Chamber can properly and timely digest them in the context of other pieces of evidence. Yet, for the assessment of the veracity of the particular documentary evidence it does not make "(...) a difference whether the Chamber considers its authenticity, for the purpose of assessing admissibility or whether it is considered at the end of the trial, when the weight of the evidence is assessed."[24]

15.2 Foundation Conditions for Documentary Evidence and Exhibits at Trial

An exponent of documentary evidence is the use of exhibits at trial. It is an important principle of criminal procedural law that exhibits must have a proper foundation before they can be admitted into evidence.[25] A second

---

[20] *Prosecutor v Gbagbo and Blé Goudé* (Reasons of Judge Henderson) ICC-02/11-01/15-1263-AnxB-Red, T Ch I (16 July 2019) para. 35.
[21] *Ibid*.
[22] *Ibid* para. 36.
[23] *Ibid*.
[24] *Ibid* para. 37.
[25] Thomas Mauet, TRIALS *Strategy, Skills, and the New Powers of Persuasion* (1st edn, Aspen Publishers 2005) 295.

principle for such admission is that the exhibit is relevant and reliable.[26] What does this mean for the criminal law practice?

(i) When it concerns the establishment of a proper foundation, an instructive guideline could be the standard as set forth by the US Federal Rules of Procedure and Evidence. In particular, Rule 901 can be applied as a standard saying: "The requirement of authentication or identification as a condition precedent to admissibility is satisfied by evidence sufficient to support a finding that the matter in question is what its proponent claims". This standard implies that the prosecution or defence, when relying on a specific exhibit, has first to present to the Court 'authentication' evidence, i.e. that the exhibit is what it purports to be. Thomas Mauet describes this requirement as enhancing two things: (i) a competent foundation witness who has first-hand knowledge of the required foundation facts (unless the exhibit is self-authenticating) and (ii) testimony from the foundation witness (or witnesses) that establishes the required foundation facts for that type of evidence (unless the exhibit is, again, self-authenticating).[27] When one is dealing with exhibits stemming from forensic investigations, such as drugs, blood, bullets, DNA and saliva, another authentication element arises, namely the preservation of the chain of custody. Forensically speaking, the chain of custody raises two important questions for defence counsel: (1) was the sample in question in the exclusive possession of one or more individuals and if so, who? (2) was the sample properly sealed and stored to protect against contamination?[28] An example which could arise before the ICC pertains to a situation where the prosecution intends to submit various emails with the aim to connect the accused to these messages. Yet, before forensically investigating such emails, a forensic copy should be made of the original e-mails before the forensic experts analyse the authenticity of the email chain. In the event the forensic experts start working on the original email chain, and not on a forensic copy, this work methodology can raise questions as to whether the said emails were manipulated.

(ii) Once the foundation to admit an exhibit has been established, it is not automatically relevant to a case.[29] 'Relevance' implies that the exhibit in question is able to make a certain fact in dispute 'more probable or

---

26   *Ibid* 296.
27   *Ibid* 296–300.
28   Thomas A. Mauet, TRIALS *Strategy, Skills, and the New Powers of Persuasion* (Aspen Publishers, New York 2005) 300–301.
29   For another opinion, Thomas A. Mauet, TRIALS *Strategy, Skills, and the New Powers of Persuasion* (Aspen Publishers, New York 2005) 290.

less probable', or 'prove or disprove something in issue in the case'.[30] However, this criterion is not to be applied restrictively, as the defence is not obliged to disclose its full strategy beforehand.

For defence counsel, it is pertinent to anticipate potential objections to the introduction of a certain exhibits in relation to the abovementioned requirements sub (i) and (ii). This means that the defence, prior to such introduction, should inquire from its source as much inf3ormation as possible about the origin and veracity of the exhibit including its context.[31] When it concerns prosecution exhibits, defence counsel preparation should include an inquiry into the conditions (i) and (ii) above and, if needed, defence counsel should file timely disclosure requests to the Office of the Prosecutor as to the origin of certain documents or exhibits and the necessary information to verify the chain of custody.

15.3 Conclusion

To conclude, the ICC's adoption of a modified submission-regime regarding the admissibility and relevance of documentary evidence reflects a careful balance between ensuring a fair and expeditious trial and considering the relevance, probative value, and potential prejudice to the accused. The decision to defer determinations until the final judgment aims to avoid unnecessary interlocutory litigation and ensure uniform treatment of all evidence. Defence counsel should be attuned to authentication challenges, particularly for social media exhibits, and promptly raise objections to ensure a thorough evaluation by the Chamber.

Furthermore, foundation conditions for documentary evidence must meet standards of authentication, relevance, and reliability, emphasizing the importance of a proper foundation before admission. In navigating these principles, defence counsel should anticipate objections, inquire into the origin and veracity of exhibits, and proactively address chain of custody concerns to contribute to a robust trial process at the ICC.

---

30   Thomas A. Mauet, *TRIALS Strategy, Skills, and the New Powers of Persuasion* (Aspen Publishers, New York 2005) 289; referring to Rule 401 and 302 of the RPE).
31   Thomas A. Mauet, *TRIALS Strategy, Skills, and the New Powers of Persuasion* (Aspen Publishers, New York 2005) 296.

CHAPTER 16

The Evidentiary Value of NGO and IO Reports at the ICC

16.1 Introduction[1]

The use of reports issued by non-governmental organizations (NGOs) and international organizations (IOs) on conflict situations is prevalent in international criminal trials, including before the International Criminal Court (ICC). Yet, such reports, which are at times drafted on the basis of short-term fact-finding missions, should be received with considerable circumspection in the context of international criminal proceedings. Given the identity of sources are most often not provided in such reports, information contained therein often amounts to anonymous hearsay. The use of NGO/IO reports has significant repercussions on a suspect or accused' basic fair trial rights, given that the anonymous hearsay information is effectively subtracted from testimonial scrutiny by the defence. Moreover, reliance on such evidence impacts on a chamber's assessment of the evidence in its ultimate determination of guilt or innocence, given the opaqueness of such reports.

In its decision adjourning the hearings on the confirmation of charges pursuant to article 61(7)(c)(i) of the Rome Statute, Pre-Trial Chamber I in the case of *Prosecutor v Laurent Gbagbo* of 3 June 2013 aptly summarized the evidentiary challenges arising from a parties' reliance on NGO/IO reports for both the chamber and for the defence:

> Heavy reliance upon anonymous hearsay, as is often the basis of information contained in reports of non-governmental organizations ("NGO reports") and press articles, is problematic for the following reasons. Proving allegations solely through anonymous hearsay puts the Defence in a difficult position because it is not able to investigate and challenge the trustworthiness of the source(s) of the information, thereby unduly limiting the right of the Defence under article 61(6)(b) of the Statute to challenge the Prosecutor's evidence, a right to which the Appeals Chamber

---

1 A version of this chapter was published in Geert-Jan A. Knoops and Sara Pedroso, 'The evidentiary value of NGO and IO reports at the ICC' (2022), *The Global Community Yearbook of International Law and Jurisprudence*.

attached "considerable significance". Further, it is highly problematic when the Chamber itself does not know the source of the information and is deprived of vital information about the source of the evidence. In such cases, the Chamber is unable to assess the trustworthiness of the source, making it all but impossible to determine what probative value to attribute to the information.

[...]

In light of the above considerations, the Chamber notes with serious concern that in this case the Prosecutor relied heavily on NGO reports and press articles with regard to key elements of the case, including the contextual elements of crimes against humanity. Such pieces of evidence cannot in any way be presented as the fruits of a full and proper investigation by the Prosecutor in accordance with article 54(l)(a) of the Statute. Even though NGO reports and press articles may be a useful introduction to the historical context of a conflict situation, they do not usually constitute a valid substitute for the type of evidence that is required to meet the evidentiary threshold for the confirmation of charges.[2]

The OTP's excessive reliance on NGO reports and press articles to prove key elements of its case in the *Gbagbo* case was deemed so egregious that Pre-Trial Chamber I adjourned the hearing on the confirmation of charges against Mr Gbagbo and enjoined the Prosecution to consider conducting further investigations with respect to all charges. This decision is exemplary of the caution which should be exercised upon considering IO/NGO reports in the context of international criminal proceedings.

16.2 The Problematic Nature of NGO/IO Reports Used as Evidence

The capacity of a chamber to assess the reliability of a piece of evidence is essential for performing its overall assessment of the weight to be attached to that evidence. In the ICC regime, the admissibility of an item of evidence depends not only on its reliability, but also on its probative value and the weighing of any prejudicial effect the admission may have on the defence.

As held by ICC Trial Chamber II in *Katanga and Ndgudjolo*, NGO reports "can be considered *prima facie* reliable if they provide sufficient guarantees of

---

[2] *Prosecutor v Laurent Gbagbo* (Decision adjourning the hearing on the confirmation of charges pursuant to article 61(7)(c)(i) of the Rome Statute) ICC-02/11-01/11-432, PTC I (3 June 2013) paras 29, 35.

non-partisanship and impartiality", but they should include sufficient information on their sources and methodology used to compile and analyze the evidence used to make factual assertions.[3] However, the Chamber held that if such particulars are not available, it cannot not assess the reliability of the content of the reports and is therefore unable to qualify those documents as sufficiently reliable to be admitted into evidence. The Chamber further cautioned that where such reports are based for the most part on hearsay information, especially when that information was twice or further removed from its source, the "reliability of their content was seriously impugned".[4] In this particular case, for these reasons, the Chamber rejected the admission of a Human Rights Watch report from a prosecution bar table motion given it lacked probative value.[5]

Hearsay and anonymous evidence contained in NGO/IO reports typically cannot be fully scrutinised or tested in the courtroom, for instance through examination and cross-examination, in order to determine its reliability and probative value given the anonymity of the underlying sources. In other words, this type of evidence remains outside the ambit of judicial scrutiny. As held by the Appeals Chamber in the *Milošević* case at the ICTY, with respect to summarized statements amounting to hearsay evidence, the opportunity to examine the persons who summarized statements "does not overcome the absence of the opportunity to cross-examine the person who made them".[6] The Trial Chamber in *Milošević* considered *inter alia* the importance of verifying whether the hearsay evidence is "firsthand" hearsay.[7] Similarly, the Trial Chamber in the ICTY *Milutinović* case denied the admission of Human Rights Watch reports on the basis that it was not "in a position to assess the reliability of the factual contentions contained therein".[8] The Trial Chamber further added that "neither the report's acknowledgement of these problems, nor the

---

[3] *Prosecutor v Katanga and Ngudjolo Chui* (Decision on the Prosecutor's Bar Table Motions) ICC-01/04-01/07-2635, T Ch II (17 December 2010) para. 30.

[4] *Ibid*.

[5] *Ibid* para. 36; See also *Prosecutor v Katanga* (Version publique expurgée de « Décision relative à trois requêtes tendant à la production d'éléments de preuve supplémentaires et à un accord en matière de preuve » (ICC-01/04-01/07-3217-Conf)) ICC-01/04-01/07-3217-Red, T Ch II (4 January 2012), para. 13, where the Chamber rejected the LRV's request for the admission of a Human Rights Watch report titled « En quête de justice : Poursuivre les auteurs de violences sexuelles commises pendant la guerre au Congo ».

[6] *Prosecutor v Milošević* (Decision on Admissibility of Prosecution Investigator's Evidence) IT-02-54-AR73.2, A Ch (30 September 2002) para. 22.

[7] *Ibid*.

[8] *Prosecutor v Milutinović et al.* (Decision on evidence tendered through Sandra Mitchell and Frederick Abrahams) IT-05-87-T, T Ch (1 September 2006) para. 21.

opportunity to cross-examine one of the authors and editors of the report, can adequately replace the opportunity to test the reliability of any of the person's making the statements".[9] In the case of anonymous hearsay evidence, the verification of whether information is first, second, or third hand information cannot be effectuated.

This problem stems partly from the fact that given several NGO/IOs implement a policy of confidentiality with regard to the protection of sources of information. As indicated in a 2011 Manual on Human Rights Reporting published by the Office of the United Nations High Commissioner for Human Rights:

> As a general rule, the identities and other personally identifiable data (PID) of victims, witnesses, alleged individual perpetrators and other sources of information (e.g., date of birth, address, phone number) must be kept confidential at all times. This means that HROs [human rights officers] must conceal (e.g., using code names) or omit any information from reports that could lead to such a person being identified. Such information should be included only in the corresponding case file, which should be securely stored in the field presence's information management system.[10]

The Manual on Human Rights Reporting further indicates that a person's identity may be disclosed in a report only under 'exceptional circumstances', where informed consent is obtained and following a careful security assessment by the organization.[11] Such is the policy of several NGOs such as Human

---

9   *Prosecutor v Milutinović et al.* (Decision on evidence tendered through Sandra Mitchell and Frederick Abrahams) IT-05-87-T, T Ch (1 September 2006) para. 22; In the *Krajišnik* Trial Judgment at the ICTY, the Trial Chamber indicated that although hearsay evidence is not inadmissible *per se*, "in those cases where a witness did not specify the source of the hearsay, the Chamber has generally not relied on the hearsay", *Prosecutor v Krajišnik* (Judgement) IT-00-39-T, T Ch I (27 September 2006) para. 1190.

10 United Nations Human Rights Office of the High Commissioner, 'Chapter 13: human rights reporting' (2011) Manual on human rights monitoring <www.ohchr.org/sites/default/files/Documents/Publications/Chapter13-MHRM.pdf> accessed 10 October 2023, page 8.

11 United Nations Human Rights Office of the High Commissioner, 'Chapter 13: human rights reporting' (2011) Manual on human rights monitoring <www.ohchr.org/sites/default/files/Documents/Publications/Chapter13-MHRM.pdf> accessed 10 October 2023, page 9.

Rights Watch, who ensures the anonymity and confidentiality of persons interviewed.[12]

The fact that Human Rights Watch workers could not divulge the organisation's sources of information was also confirmed during the testimony of a Human Rights Watch staff who testified before the ICC.[13] In the case of *Gbagbo and Blé Goudé*, the defence for Mr Blé Goudé had requested the Chamber to exclude the anticipated testimony of a Human Rights Watch investigator or alternatively, to restrict the scope of his testimony.[14] While ultimately finding that the request was premature, Trial Chamber I held that Witness P-369 should not be asked to pronounce himself on the conclusions he drew from his research in Ivory Coast and he should not be asked to give his personal views as to the trustworthiness of any individuals he spoke to as part of his inquiry. The Chamber observed that it could not "simply rely on the impressions of NGO representatives or other third persons" in relation to the trustworthiness of any relevant evidence.[15] Significantly, the Chamber noted that "this restriction applies with even greater force when the identity of the sources of the Witness is not disclosed to the parties and the Chamber", in other words, where a witness is anonymous.[16] As result of this reasoning, Trial Chamber I concluded:

> Finally, since the Chamber has decided that Witness P-369 is not permitted to keep his sources anonymous; it will not allow the Prosecutor to question Witness P-369 on facts which he learned from anonymous sources, regardless of whether the Witness had a single or multiple sources for a particular fact. The reason for this is clear: when the sources remain anonymous, the Chamber has no independent means to ascertain the trustworthiness of those sources or to determine whether different sources genuinely corroborate each other.[17]

---

12   Human Rights Watch, 'About Our Research' <www.hrw.org/about/about-us/about-our-research#5> accessed 10 October 2023.
13   *Prosecutor v Gbagbo and Blé Goudé* (Public Transcript) ICC-02/11-01/15-T-42-ENG ET WT, T Ch I (19 May 2016) page 35.
14   *Prosecutor v Gbagbo and Blé Goudé* (Defence's Motion to Preclude and Exclude the prospected Evidence of Witnesses P-369, or, in the alternative, to restrict the Scope of Witness P-0369's intended Evidence) ICC-02/11-01/15-509, T Ch I (10 May 2016).
15   *Prosecutor v Gbagbo and Blé Goudé* (Decision on 'Defence's Motion to Preclude and Exclude the prospected Evidence of Witness P-369, or, in the alternative, to restrict the Scope of Witness P-0369's intended Evidence') ICC-02/11-01/15-539, T Ch I (13 May 2016) para. 7.
16   *Ibid*.
17   *Ibid* para. 8.

Trial Chamber 1's finding that whether a witness relied on a single or multiple sources is irrelevant is based on the acknowledgment that the reliability of those sources remained beyond the reach of judicial checks and balances. Another principle which is at the core of this reasoning is the fundamental principle that an accused is entitled to be apprised of the evidence used against him or her, as further developed below. In his reasons to the judgment acquitting Laurent Gbagbo and Charles Blé Goudé at the no case to answer stage, Judge Henderson presented further guidance as to the use of NGO/IO reports containing anonymous hearsay:

> It is important to emphasize that simply knowing the identity of the source is not sufficient. Just as in the case of in-court testimony, in order to determine what weight should be given, it is necessary to have reliable information about how the source of the information came to know it, if there are any concerns about his or her memory and whether or not there may be reasons to think that the source may have deliberately given information which he or she did not believe to be correct.
>
> Accordingly, when the only evidence in relation to a particular proposition is based primarily on anonymous hearsay without adequate information about the reliability and credibility of the source, the Chamber must conclude that such a proposition is unsupported.[18]

At the European Court of Human Rights, a distinction was made between absent witnesses and anonymous witnesses, in the 2012 *Ellis and Simms and Martin v the United Kingdom* case. In that case, the ECtHR held that unlike absent witnesses, anonymous witnesses were confronted in person by defence counsel, who was able to cross-examine them and question inconsistencies in their account. The witness' presence, albeit anonymously, allowed the judge, jury and counsel to observe the witness' demeanor and to view as to the reliability of the witness testimony. The ECtHR drew from the ECHR *Al-Khawaja and Tahery v United Kingdom* case to recall that article 6(3)(d) ECHR[19] imposed three requirements concerning reliance on anonymous witnesses: (i) there had to be a good reason to keep secret the identity of the witness; (ii) the Court had

---

18 *Prosecutor v Gbagbo and Blé Goudé* (Public Redacted Version of Reasons of Judge Geoffrey Henderson) ICC-02/11-01/15-1263-AnxB-Red, T Ch I (16 July 2019) paras 44–45.

19 Providing that a person charged with a criminal offence has the right to "examine or have examined witnesses against him and to obtain the attendance and examination of witnesses on his behalf under the same conditions as witnesses against him". In the US, the opportunity for a defendant to challenge her or his accusers is protected under the sixth amendment. See also Article 14(3) of the ICCPR.

to consider whether the evidence of the anonymous witness was the sole or decisive basis of the conviction; and (iii) where a conviction was based solely or decisively on the evidence of anonymous witnesses, the Court had to satisfy itself that there were sufficient counterbalancing factors, including strong procedural safeguards, to permit a fair and proper assessment of the reliability of that evidence to take place.[20] In other words, the ECtHR jurisprudence has established that an applicant should not be prevented from testing an anonymous witness' reliability, and safeguards must be implemented to ensure that an accused' fair trial rights are guaranteed in such exceptional circumstances.

In the case of NGO/IO reports, the sources of information which are kept confidential are akin to "absent" witnesses, whose accounts cannot be questioned or verified by either defence counsel or by a chamber. In such cases, the defence and the Chamber are simply not in a position to make their own assessment of the reliability of anonymous hearsay evidence contained in such reports. In contrast to the *Ellis* case, in most cases where the Prosecution relies on NGO reports, there is no "substantial disclosure about the anonymous witness which had provided extensive material for cross-examination".[21] Moreover, most often there is no other evidence which could attest to the reliability and credibility of the sources contained in the NGO/IO statements. It cannot be said that such evidence may be therefore corroborative.

In addition, NGO/IO reports covering conflict and post-conflict situations are often drafted on the basis of fact-finding missions. As explained by Stephen Wilkinson, a specialist in international humanitarian law and human rights in armed conflict, fact finding missions have, by nature, "a limited and restricted mandate, work under strict time constraints, have no powers of enforcement, [and therefore] are not in a position to apply the same levels of scrutiny to their findings that would be expected of formal judicial processes".[22] These factors should be taken into consideration in the context of international criminal proceedings, when assessing the evidentiary value of IO/NGO reports, and in particular, the reliability of such evidence.

---

20 *Ellis and Simms and Martin v United Kingdom* App nos 46099/06 and 46699/06 (ECtHR 10 April 2012) paras. 73–74, relying on the *Al-Khawaja and Tahery v the United Kingdom* App nos 26766/05 and 22228/06 (ECtHR, 15 December 2011) paras 119, 147.

21 *Ellis and Simms and Martin v United Kingdom* App nos 46099/06 and 46699/06 (ECtHR 10 April 2012) para. 87.

22 Stephen Wilkinson, 'Standards of Proof in International Humanitarian and Human Rights Fact-Finding and Inquiry Missions' (2015) Geneva Academy of International Humanitarian Law, <www.geneva-academy.ch/joomlatools-files/docman-files/Standards%20of%20 Proof%20in%20Fact-Finding.pdf.> accessed 10 October 2023, p. 49.

16.3 The Use of NGO/IO Reports at Different Stages of ICC Proceedings

Hearsay evidence is not inadmissible *ab initio*, although it is typically given a lower probative value and approached with caution.[23] Judges at the ICC have typically approached hearsay evidence as a matter of probative value rather than admissibility, reflecting a rather inclusionary (albeit *sui generis*) approach to evidence.[24] ICC Chambers have taken a "cautious approach" to anonymous hearsay and have found that due consideration must be given to the "impossibility of cross-examining the information source" with this type of evidence.[25]

Article 69(4) of the Rome Statute provides that the criteria for assessing the relevance and admissibility of a piece of evidence at the ICC are (i) probative value and (ii) any prejudice that such evidence may cause to a fair trial or to a fair evaluation of the testimony of a witness. Rule 63(2) of the ICC Rules of Procedure and Evidence provides for the judges' discretionary power "to assess freely all evidence submitted in order to determine its relevance or admissibility in accordance with article 69."

Article 61(6) of the Rome Statute provides the right of a suspect before the Court to "challenge the evidence presented by the Prosecutor". Article 67(1)(e) of the Rome Statute expressly provides for the right of an accused to "examine, or have examined, the witnesses against him or her and to obtain the attendance and examination of witnesses on his or her behalf under the same conditions as witnesses against him or her". These are fundamental fair trial guarantees matching several legal systems worldwide, including the framework provided by the ECHR, as indicated above.

At the pre-trial level, where the evidentiary threshold is that of "reasonable grounds to believe", ICC chambers have indicated that "there is nothing in the Statute or the Rules which expressly provides that the evidence which can be considered hearsay from anonymous sources is inadmissible *per se*".[26] However, they have warned that this type of evidence "may cause difficulties

---

[23] *Prosecutor v Ngudjolo Chui* (Judgment pursuant to article 74 of the Statute) ICC-01/04-02/12-3-tENG, T Ch II (18 December 2012) para. 55; *Prosecutor v Katanga and Ngudjolo Chui* (Decision on the confirmation of charges) ICC-01/04-01/07-717, PT Ch I (30 September 2008) para. 137;

[24] *Prosecutor v Lubanga Dyilo* (Decision on the confirmation of charges) ICC-01/04-01/06-803-tEN, PT Ch I (29 January 2007) paras 101–103.

[25] *Prosecutor v Ngudjolo Chui* (Judgment pursuant to article 74 of the Statute) ICC-01/04-02/12-3-tENG, T Ch II (18 December 2012) para. 56.

[26] *Prosecutor v Lubanga Dyilo* (Decision on the confirmation of charges) ICC-01/04-01/06-803-tEN, PT Ch I (29 January 2007) paras 101–103; *Prosecutor v Bemba Gombo* (Decision pursuant to article 61(7)(a) and (b) of the Rome Statute on the charges of the prosecutor against Jean-Pierre Bemba Gombo) ICC-01/05-01/08-424, PT Ch II (15 June 2009) para. 50.

for the defence because it is deprived of the opportunity to challenge its probative value".[27] In *Bemba*, the Pre-Trial Chamber found that the use of anonymous witness statements was permitted at the pre-trial stage because of the lower evidentiary threshold (compared with the trial stage), but that this evidence must be given low probative value because of the disadvantage caused to the defence:

> With regard to direct evidence emanating from an anonymous source, the Chamber shares the view, adopted in other pre-trial decisions, that it may cause difficulties to the Defence because it is deprived of the opportunity to challenge its probative value. This also holds true for summaries of witness statements. The Chamber is fully aware that the use of anonymous witness statements and summaries is permitted at the pre-trial stage, particularly because the evidentiary threshold is lower than the threshold applicable at the trial stage. However, to counterbalance the disadvantage that it might cause to the Defence, such evidence is considered as having a rather low probative value. More specifically, the probative value of anonymous witness statements and summaries is lower than the probative value attached to the statements of witnesses whose identity is known to the Defence.[28]

Similarly, in *Lubanga*, the Pre-Trial Chamber held that as a general rule, it will only rely on anonymous hearsay evidence – such as NGO reports and press articles – to corroborate other evidence, "mindful of the difficulties that such evidence may present to the Defence in relation to the possibility of ascertaining its truthfulness and authenticity".[29] The Pre-Trial Chamber also held,

---

27   *Prosecutor v Bemba Gombo* (Decision pursuant to article 61(7)(a) and (b) of the Rome Statute on the charges of the prosecutor against Jean-Pierre Bemba Gombo) ICC-01/05-01/08-424, PT Ch II (15 June 2009) para. 50, citing *Prosecutor v Lubanga Dyilo* (Decision on the confirmation of charges) ICC-01/04-01/06-803-tEN, PT Ch I (29 January 2007) para. 106; *Prosecutor v Katanga* (Decision on the confirmation of charges) ICC-01/04-01/07-717, PT Ch I (30 September 2008), para. 11.

28   *Prosecutor v Bemba Gombo* (Decision pursuant to article 61(7)(a) and (b) of the Rome Statute on the charges of the prosecutor against Jean-Pierre Bemba Gombo) ICC-01/05-01/08-424, PT Ch II (15 June 2009) para. 50.

29   *Prosecutor v Lubanga Dyilo* (Decision on the confirmation of charges) ICC-01/04-01/06-803-tEN, PT Ch I (29 January 2007) para. 106; *Prosecutor v Katanga* (Decision on the confirmation of charges) ICC-01/04-01/07-717, PT Ch I (30 September 2008) paras 159–160, also cited *inter alia* by the Pre-Trial Chamber in *Prosecutor v Banda and Jerbo* (Corrigendum of the "Decision on the Confirmation of Charges") ICC-02/05-03/09-121-Corr-Red, PT Ch I (7 March 2011) para. 41; *Prosecutor v Callixte Mbarushimana* (Decision on the confirmation

relying on ECtHR jurisprudence, that the use of anonymous statements as sufficient evidence to found a conviction may be irreconcilable with article 6 of the ECHR:

> Furthermore, ECHR jurisprudence evinces that the European Convention does not preclude reliance at the investigation stage of criminal proceedings on sources such as anonymous informants. Nevertheless, the ECHR specifies that the subsequent use of anonymous statements as sufficient evidence to found a conviction is a different matter in that it can be irreconcilable with article 6 of the European Convention, particularly if the conviction is based to a decisive extent on anonymous statements.
>
> Accordingly, the Chamber considers that objections pertaining to the use of anonymous hearsay evidence do not go to the admissibility of the evidence, but only to its probative value.[30]

In the same vein, Pre-Trial Chamber I in the *Gbagbo* case stated that heavy reliance upon anonymous hearsay evidence, specifically in NGO reports and press articles, is problematic for multiple reasons, namely because the Defence can difficultly "investigate and challenge the trustworthiness of the source(s) of the information, thereby unduly limiting the right of the Defence under article 61(6)(b) of the Statute to challenge the Prosecutor's evidence, a right to which the Appeals Chamber attached "considerable significance"."[31] Also, it is difficult for the Chamber to determine the probative value to attribute to the

---

of charges) ICC-01/04-01/10-465-Red, PTC I (16 December 2011) para. 49; *Prosecutor v Ruto and Sang* (Decision on the Confirmation of Charges Pursuant to Article 61(7)(a) and (b) of the Rome Statute) ICC-01/09-01/11-373, PT Ch I (23 January 2012) para. 78; *Prosecutor v Kenyatta and Ali* (Decision on the confirmation of charges) ICC-01/09-02/11-382-Red, PT Ch II (23 January 2012) para. 90; The Trial Chamber in *Mladić* at the ICTY similarly held that "the Chamber considers that it is most appropriate to allow the parties to clarify any unclear, vague, or hearsay portions of a statement during the testimony of the witnesses. In the absence of any clarification, the Chamber may attach less weight, if any, to such portions", see *Prosecutor v Mladić* (Public Transcript) IT-09-92-T, T Ch II (30 August 2012) page 2001.

30 *Prosecutor v Lubanga Dyilo* (Decision on the confirmation of charges) ICC-01/04-01/06-803-tEN, PT Ch I (29 January 2007) paras 102–103, citing ECtHR jurisprudence *Kostovski v The Netherlands* App no. 11454/85 (ECtHR, 20 November 1989) para. 44; see also *Prosecutor v Callixte Mbarushimana* (Decision on the confirmation of charges) ICC-01/04-01/10-465-Red, PT Ch I (16 December 2011) para. 49.

31 *Prosecutor v Laurent Gbagbo* (Decision adjourning the hearing on the confirmation of charges pursuant to article 61(7)(c)(i) of the Rome Statute) ICC-02/11-01/11-432, PT Ch I (3 June 2013) para. 29.

information because it does not have all the relevant tools to assess the trustworthiness of the source.[32]

In the ICC Decision on the confirmation of charges in the case against Mr Abu Garda, the Pre-Trial Chamber recognized that the Rome Statute and ICC Rules of Procedure and Evidence expressly permitted the Office of the Prosecutor to rely on anonymous witness summaries at the confirmation stage. The Pre-Trial Chamber noted, however, that the Office of the Prosecutor's right to rely on such summary evidence must be balanced with the right of the Defence, in accordance with article 61(6) of the Statute, to challenge the evidence presented by the Prosecution. It concluded that therefore, statements of anonymous witnesses will be given a lower probative value and will be evaluated on a case-by-case basis, according to whether the information contained therein is corroborated or supported by other evidence tendered into the case file.[33]

At the trial stage, the assessment of NGO/IO reports at trial does not differ significantly from that at the pre-trial stage. In assessing the admissibility of an NGO report,[34] the Trial Chamber in *Lubanga* rejected the admission of the document both on the basis of its low probative value and of it causing material prejudice to the parties:

> the authors of the report are not to be called, and counsel will be unable, through questioning, to investigate the significant criticisms that have been made of its contents [...] it follows that, if admitted, this document is likely to cause material prejudice to the parties.[35]

---

32 *Ibid.*

33 *Prosecutor v Abu Garda* (Decision on the Confirmation of Charges) ICC-02/05-02/09-243-Red, PT Ch I (8 February 2010) para. 42; For this finding, it relied on the Pre-Trial Chamber's finding in the *Katanga* case, which stated that while "there is no requirement per se that summaries of the statements of anonymous witnesses are corroborated in order for them to be admissible, the Chamber is of the view that lack of support or corroboration from other evidence in the record of the proceedings could affect the probative value of those summaries or statements", *Prosecutor v Katanga* (Decision on the confirmation of charges) ICC-01/04-01/07-717, PT Ch I (30 September 2008) para. 160.

34 "Report of the Panel of Experts on the illegal exploitation of natural resources and other forms of wealth of the Democratic Republic of the Congo".

35 *Prosecutor v Lubanga* (Decision on the request by the legal representative of victims a/0001/06, a/0002/06, a/0003/06, a/0049/06, a/0007/08, a/0149/08, a/0155/07, a/0156/07, a/0404/08, a/0405/08, a/0406/08, a/0407/08, a/0409/08, a0149/07 and a/0162/07 for admission of the final report of the Panel of Experts on the illegal exploitation of natural resources and other forms of wealth of the Democratic Republic of the Congo as evidence) ICC-01/04-01/06-2135, T Ch I (22 September 2009) paras. 33-34.

Relatedly, the Trial Chamber noted that the issues from the report were already addressed in oral evidence and admitted in documentary form, that some conclusions in the report were controversial and open to criticism and that none of its content is directly relevant to the charges against the accused.

In the *Katanga and Ngudjolo Chui* case, the Trial Chamber held that:

> Once the authenticity of a document has been established, the Chamber must ascertain whether the evidence displays such qualities that, when considered alone, it could reasonably be believed. The Chamber notes in this respect, that Trial Chamber I has held that "if [...] it is impossible for the Chamber to conduct any independent evaluation of the evidence – if there are *no adequate' and available means of testing its reliability* [emphasis added] – then the court will need consider carefully whether the party seeking to introduce it has met the test of demonstrating, *prima facie*, its probative value.[36]

The Trial Chamber further confirmed that in determining reliability, one of the key factors would be "whether the source of the information has an allegiance towards one of the parties in the case or has a personal interest in the outcome of the case, or whether there are other indicators of bias."[37] Following this reasoning, the anonymity of the source negatively impacts the reliability of the document's content.

In her partially dissenting opinion from the majority decision admitting NGO reports into the *Ntaganda* case, Judge Ozaki explained:

> The Majority holds that these reports "contain sufficient details of their sources of information and methodology" and therefore bear sufficient indicia of authenticity and reliability. The reports contain information relevant to the crimes with which the accused is charged. However, the identities of the authors and the sources of the information relied on in the reports are not revealed with sufficient detail, and as a result it is not possible to fully investigate their reliability. The three FIDH reports and the AI report admitted into evidence by the Majority are based almost entirely on information obtained from other NGOs, journalists, or

---

36   *Prosecutor v Katanga and Ngudjolo Chui* (Decision on the Prosecutor's Bar Table Motions) ICC-01/04-01/07-2635, T Ch II (17 December 2010) para. 26.
37   *Ibid* para. 27.

unidentified eyewitnesses, thus rendering it very difficult to adequately assess the reliability of the accounts contained therein.[38]

Judge Ozaki concluded that the lack of guarantees concerning the reliability of the NGO reports' sources, in the absence of witness testimony of the authors of the reports render their probative value very low, while at the same time posing a high potential prejudice for the defence.[39] Significantly, Judge Ozaki held that the Majority's reasoning that the NGO reports could be admitted "for the limited purpose that the information contained therein may serve to corroborate other pieces of evidence" did not justify their admission into evidence.

In *Bemba*, in the context of an abuse of process motion, Trial Chamber V held that NGO reports had little, if any, evidential weight, given that their provenance and reliability were entirely uninvestigated and untested.[40] Interestingly here, the motion was determined on the standard of balance of probabilities; as a logical extension, if NGO reports are found to be unreliable on this lower standard, they would surely not meet the more rigorous standard of beyond reasonable doubt, as applied in the course of trial.[41]

The Majority to the Appeals Judgment in *Bemba* further held that the trial chamber had "failed to properly analyse [anonymous hearsay] evidence and address its potentially extremely low probative value".[42] As held by Judges Van den Wyngaert and Morrison in their separate opinion to the Appeals Judgment, "[w]hereas hearsay is not per se inadmissible before the Court, this does not mean that it is permissible to make findings beyond a reasonable doubt on this basis, especially when the Trial Chamber does not seem to have tried to establish the reliability of the source of the information". The Judges reasoned that although the Trial Chamber accepted the need to be cautious when relying on hearsay evidence, "it appears that in practice it often threw its own caution to the wind". Thus, it is insufficient for a trial chamber to simply express caution;

---

38 *Prosecutor v Bemba* (Partly Dissenting Opinion of Judge Ozaki on the Prosecution's Application for Admission of Materials into Evidence Pursuant to Article 69(4) of the Rome Statute) ICC-01/05-01/08-2300, T Ch III (6 September 2012) para. 11.
39 *Ibid* para. 12.
40 *Prosecutor v Bemba Gombo* (Decision on the Admissibility and Abuse of Process Challenges) ICC-01/05-01/08-802, T Ch III (24 June 2010) paras. 235, 254–25.
41 This was argued by the Sang Defence in *Prosecutor v Ruto and Sang* (Sang Defence Response to the Prosecution's Application for Admission of Documents from the Bar Table Pursuant to Article 64(9)) ICC-01/09-01/11-1130, T Ch V(A) (24 December 2013) para. 34.
42 *Prosecutor v Bemba Gombo* (Judgment on the appeal of Mr Jean-Pierre Bemba Gombo against Trial Chamber III's "Judgment pursuant to Article 74 of the Statute") ICC-01/05-01/08-3636-Red, A Ch (8 June 2018) para. 183.

such caution must be applied in practice in order to pass muster. Further, Judges Van den Wyngaert and Morrison also referred to the inherent unreliability of hearsay evidence, emphasizing the distinction between hearsay and anonymous hearsay evidence, concluding that in the latter case, reliability could simply not be established:

> One of the central findings of the Conviction Decision is contained in paragraph 563, where the Trial Chamber found that there was "consistent and corroborated evidence that MLC soldiers committed many acts of rape and murder against civilians throughout the 2002–2003 CAR operation". However, closer inspection of the relevant footnote reveals that the evidence in question consists mainly of documentary and testimonial hearsay evidence. As set out above, we have grave concerns about excessive reliance on hearsay evidence, especially if the reliability of the source of the information cannot be established. We also reject the Trial Chamber's apparent conclusion that weak testimonial evidence can somehow be corroborated by weak documentary evidence, especially if one or both are based on (anonymous) hearsay.[43]

Significantly, the Judges found that "holistic fact-finding should not be an excuse or a reason for making findings beyond a reasonable doubt on the basis of a collection of weak evidence". In their view, this "creates the risk that the Chamber may consider evidence that is not relevant or has no evidentiary weight to speak of and make findings under the illusion of corroboration".[44]

> There is indeed a difference between claiming that one has 'twenty' coins and that one has 'many' such coins. However, in the end one can only legally prove that one has 'many' coins by defining how much 'many' is and then presenting evidence to prove the existence of each individual coin. It is thus certainly not true that a 'piecemeal' approach would lead the Chamber to exclude potentially relevant evidence. On the contrary, the Prosecutor's proposed 'cumulative' approach creates the risk that the Chamber may consider evidence that is not relevant or has no evidentiary weight to speak of and make findings under the illusion of corroboration. As indicated above, the dangers of the Prosecution's suggested approach

---

43 *Prosecutor v Bemba* (Separate opinion Judge Christine Van den Wyngaert and Judge Howard Morrison) ICC-01/05-01/08-3636-Anx2, A Ch (8 June 2018) footnote 5.

44 *Prosecutor v Bemba* (Separate opinion Judge Christine Van den Wyngaert and Judge Howard Morrison) ICC-01/05-01/08-3636-Anx2, A Ch (8 June 2018) para. 67.

are illustrated by the impugned Conviction Decision. We refer to our concerns expressed above about the opacity of the reasoning, the reliance on (anonymous) hearsay evidence and the findings beyond a reasonable doubt based on dubious circumstantial evidence.[45]

The debate around the use of NGO/IO reports also arose in the context of a defence request for interim release. Judges Ušacka and Van den Wyngaert held, in their dissenting opinions, that the Pre-Trial Chamber II "erred in its sole reliance on anonymous hearsay evidence contained in press releases, blog articles and two UN group of expert reports". In her dissenting opinion, Judge Van den Wyngaert held that such evidence "must be treated with utmost caution in the context of a criminal trial and without considerably more, independently verified, information cannot, [be] safely relied upon to justify the continued detention of Mr Bosco Ntaganda".[46]

It appears from there is a jurisprudential foundation at the ICC to reject the admission of NGO/IO reports in the context of pre-trial and especially trial proceedings, particular when containing anonymous hearsay. Anonymous hearsay evidence, which often forms the basis of such reports, is inherently unreliable and should not be used by a chamber to found a conviction.

16.4 The Admissibility of NGO Reports Based on Anonymous Sources

Thus far, this chapter has touched upon the use of NGO/IO reports based on anonymous sources in trial proceedings, however this section seeks to further elucidate this topic by looking precisely into the admissibility of NGO reports based on anonymous sources, as well as how the admissibility of this evidence was dealt with in *ad hoc* tribunals.

At the ICC, as made clear form the above sections, there is no general rule regarding the admissibility of this type of evidence; therefore, one needs to examine the jurisprudence to determine the position held by different Chambers in respect to the case they had at hand. What emanates from the jurisprudence is an obligation to disclose the source from which the information comes from. In the *Lubanga* case, the prosecution tried to admit into evidence a document relating to the Union des Patriotes Congolais (UPC)'s objectives,

---

45   *Prosecutor v Bemba* (Separate opinion Judge Christine Van den Wyngaert and Judge Howard Morrison) ICC-01/05-01/08-3636-Anx2, A Ch (8 June 2018) para. 67.
46   *Prosecutor v Ntaganda* (Dissenting Opinion of Judge Christine Van den Wyngaert) ICC-01/04-02/06-271-Anx2, A Ch (5 March 2014) para. 2.

structure and organization, which provided contextual and background evidence to the charges.[47] The author of the document was unknown, though the said material would have been received from a high high-ranking member of the UPC. The Trial Chamber held that the admissibility of documents from unknown source and origin was not a strong application for admissibility.[48] As for the admissibility of hearsay evidence, the same Chamber ruled that the timing of *when* a witness became aware of certain information was a material consideration in the assessment of the admissibility and weight attributes to the evidence, holding that information that a witness becomes aware of 'at the time that events were unfolding' is likely to be of 'greater value in those circumstances than if this was something that he happened to hear many years later when talking to somebody who was unconnected with the events.'[49]

The identity of the individual author of a document is a key component of its reliability: the organization can attest to the authenticity of the report i.e. that it is an official report emanating from that organization – but it cannot attest to the reliability. Hence, when assessing the hearsay evidence, the Trial Chamber in *Hadzihasanovic* held that to asses probative value it was necessary to know the source of information, the identity of the initial source, how the source learned about the facts and the number of intermediaries through which the information has passed.[50]

In *Boskoski*, the Trial Chamber refused to admit a document from the embassy of a foreign state (originating from defence department of that state). Although it came from a country which was actively involved in the region, the creator and the source of document were unknown and thus there was no sufficient reliability to justify admission. The Chamber held that comments of the witness to the document recorded in the transcript were sufficient and there was no need to admit the whole document in evidence (see portion of the transcript below).[51] Again, in *Milutinovic* OSCE documents for which there was no indication as to who generated documents as well as no explanation is given why the documents were not used with witnesses who could have commented on it were not admitted.[52]

---

47   *Prosecutor v Lubanga Dyilo* (Public Transcript) ICC-01/04-01/06-T-170-ENG, T Ch I (7 May 2009) pages 17–19.
48   *Ibid*.
49   *Prosecutor v Lubanga Dyilo* (Public Transcript) ICC-01/04-01/06-T-125-Red3-ENG, T Ch I (12 February 2009) pages 66–67.
50   *Prosecutor v Hadžihasanović & Kubura* (Judgment) IT-01-47-T, T Ch II (15 March 2006) para. 272.
51   *Prosecutor v Boskoski*, (Public Transcripts) IT-04-82-T, T Ch III (14 November 2007) p. 7793–7795.
52   *Prosecutor v Milutinovic et al.* (Decision on Lukic Defence Motions for Admission of Documents from Bar Table) IT-05-87-T, T Ch III (11 June 2008) paras 35, 37–38.

16.5 Conclusion

In conclusion, there seems to be a consensus among international criminal tribunals, such as the ICC, that caution must be exercised in assessing NGO/IO reports. Such reports, used as evidence, most often stand at odds with an accused's right to confront the evidence presented against him or her, which is an essential requirement of a fair trial.[53] The evidentiary value of such reports should be assessed with extreme caution due to the absence of any opportunity for the participants in these proceedings to know the source of the information, the identity of which may be vital for the truth. Moreover, as the ICC jurisprudence has shown, caution must also be exercised and demonstrated by the judges with respect to reliance on NGO/IO reports for corroborative purposes. Furthermore, hearsay where the source is known should be distinguished from anonymous hearsay, given the latter, as opposed to the former, cannot be verified, by either the parties to a trial or by the judges.

In addition, the potential use of anonymous hearsay at the pre-trial and trial stages at the ICC may be distinguished. If anonymous hearsay evidence may at times, be used, as an "introduction to the historical context of a conflict situation", or to corroborate other evidence at the pre-trial stage, this cannot be true at the trial stage, where the evidentiary threshold is much higher. At the trial phase, anonymous hearsay evidence should be excluded altogether, or given extremely little to no weight by the chamber in its determination of guilt or innocence. Reliance on IO/NGO reports in international criminal proceedings may contaminate the truth-finding mandate of international courts and tribunals.

---

53   *Prosecutor v Gbagbo and Blé Goudé* (Separate Opinion of Judge Henderson annexed to 'Decision on the Prosecutor's Application to protect the confidentiality of the sources of P-0369') ICC-02/11-01/15-466-Conf-Anx, T Ch I (21 March 2016) para. 8.

CHAPTER 17

The Evidentiary Value of Social Media at the ICC

17.1 Introduction[1]

Bearing in mind that smartphones are currently used by an estimated 4.6 billion users,[2] social media is profoundly changing the landscape of international criminal investigations. Especially in international crimes theatres which investigators can sometimes hardly access, social media content can assist the prosecution in its mission to collect evidence and investigate crime scenes. In fact, any individual with a smartphone and Internet access can create and disseminate digital content globally. As such, for over a decade, people have used social media platforms to document international crimes and human rights abuses in conflicts. For instance, the Syrian conflict is "characterised by the extensive use of online social media platforms by all sides involved".[3] Regarding Libya, the ICC OTP issued, in 2017, an arrest warrant against Libyan military commander Mahmoud Mustafa Busayf Al-Werfalli, based considerably on videos of executions in Libya found on social media platforms.[4] More recently, civil society organisations in Ukraine have been collecting user-generated content from Telegram, YouTube, Twitter and Facebook posts to build a digital picture of events on the ground in real time.

Although social media content opens up the landscape of international crime investigations to new actors in ways that may ultimately be beneficial,

---

1   This chapter is based on a version that previously appeared in Geert-Jan A. Knoops, Elsa Bohne and Aline Petersen, 'The Evidentiary Value of Social Media in International Criminal Proceedings' (2021), 18 3(71) International Studies Journal 53.
2   Number of smartphones Users Worldwide from 2013 to 2028 (in billions), STATISTA <https://www.statista.com/forecasts/1143723/smartphone-users-in-the-world> accessed 1 October 2023.
3   Derek O'Callaghan, Nico Prucha, Derek Greene, Maura Conway, Joe Carthy and Pàdraig Cunningham, 'Online social media in the Syria conflict: Encompassing the extremes and the in-betweens' (2014), IEEE/ACM International Conference on Advances in Social Networks Analysis and Mining <https://doras.dcu.ie/20485/1/IEEE_Version.pdf> accessed 17 August 2023. *See also* Melik Kaylan, 'Syria's War Viewed Almost in Real Time' (2013), The Wall Street Journal <http://www.wsj.com/articles/SB10001424127887324492604579083112566791956> accessed 30 September 2023 (noting that between January 2012 and September 2013 "*over a million videos have been uploaded [on YouTube] with hundreds of views*").
4   *Prosecutor v Mahmoud Mustafa Busayf Al-Werfalli* (Warrant of Arrest) ICC-01/11-01/17-2, PT Ch I (17 August 2017).

it nonetheless involves "a significant degree of risk".[5] As such, the growing reliance on social media content in current or future international criminal proceedings raises the question of the extent and conditions of its admissibility as evidence to prove international crimes.

17.2 Definitions and Relevant Concepts

The term "social media" is often used to refer to new forms of media that involve interactive participation.[6] Facebook, YouTube, WhatsApp, Instagram, TikTok, Telegram or Twitter are amongst the most popular social media platforms.[7] Though social media may take different forms, they can be characterised by two main features: (i) social media are interactive Internet-based applications and (ii) they are fuelled by user-generated content (e.g. written or image posts, comments to posts, live videos or so-called "stories").

Mobile Instant Messaging apps ("MIM apps") allow mobile users to "send real-time text messages, voice messages, picture messages, video messages, or files to individuals or groups of friends."[8] Facebook Messenger and WhatsApp remain the most popular MIM apps, with up to 2 billion active users per month.[9]

The concept of "deep fake" circulates within the area of user-generated evidence to refer to digital manipulation of sound, images, or video to impersonate someone or make it appear that a person did something – and to do so in a manner that is increasingly realistic, to the point that the unaided observer cannot detect the fake.[10] Metadata are data about data. Metadata

---

5   Rebecca Hamilton, 'New Technologies in International Criminal Investigations' (2018), Proceedings of the ASIL Annual Meeting <https://sci-hub.3800808.com/10.1017/amp.2019.18> accessed 28 September 2023.
6   Jimmie Manning, 'Definition and classes of Social media', *Encyclopedia of social media and politics* (Thousand Oaks, CA: Sage 2014).
7   Most popular social networks worldwide as of January 2023, ranked by number of monthly active users (in millions), STATISTA <https://www.statista.com/statistics/272014/global-social-networks-ranked-by-number-of-users/> accessed 1 October 2023.
8   Yongjin Choi, 'Mobile Instant Messaging Evidence in Criminal Trials' (2017), Cath. U. J. L. & Tech 1 <http://scholarship.law.edu/jlt/vol26/iss1/3> accessed 30 September 2023.
9   Most popular global mobile messenger apps as of January 2023, based on number of monthly active users (in millions), STATISTA <https://www.statista.com/statistics/258749/most-popular-global-mobile-messenger-apps/> accessed 1 October 2023.
10 Robert Chesney, Daniel Citron, 'Deep Fakes: A Looming Crisis for National Security, Democracy and Privacy?' (2018), LAWFARE <https://www.lawfaremedia.org/article/deep-fakes-looming-crisis-national-security-democracy-and-privacy> accessed 1 October 2023.

often include a file's characteristics and history (name, size, dates of creation or modification, chain of custody).

17.3 General Evidentiary Pitfalls of Social Media Content

The significant degree of risk involved in social media evidence mostly pertains to its probative value and more specifically to its reliability.[11]

17.3.1 *Authenticity and Risk of Manipulation*

The issue of deep fake is a key challenge for social media evidence since "technology [now] enables even those with minimal technical skills to create forgeries that are undetectable to the lay eye."[12] The growing number of deep fakes reveals that social media evidence can easily be manipulated and tempered with. Recent domestic law practice involving social media evidence reveals these risks of manipulation and the importance of the element of social media authenticity.

In several United States cases the issue of authenticity became of main concern and did impact the overall assessment by the judiciary. For instance, in *United States v Vayner*, the defendant was convicted of a single count of unlawful transfer of false identification documents. Upon appeal, a Ukrainian, resident in Brooklyn, testified that the defendant gave him a forged birth certificate showing that this Ukrainian citizen was the father of a made-up infant daughter. The prosecution provided a printout of a webpage through a special agent of the State department's diplomatic security service, while the prosecution asserted that this was the defendant's profile page on VK.com, a Russian social media website comparable to Facebook. On the basis of Federal Rule of Evidence 901, the defence objected against the admissibility of this VK.com page, arguing that it had not been properly authenticated. The Court rejected the defence's objection and admitted the VK.com page as evidence.

However, the US Court of Appeals for the Second Circuit came to a different conclusion. It held that the government had failed to provide a sufficient basis to justify the conclusion that the printout belonged to the defendant. The Appeals Court accepted that the VK.com page reflected information about the defendant but was not convinced that the defendant had created the page himself. More specifically, the Court ruled that "the mere fact that a page with [the defendant's] name and photograph happened to exist on the Internet at

---

11 For general considerations on probative value and reliability, see Chapter 11 *supra*.
12 *Ibid* (n 5).

the time of [the investigator's] testimony does not permit a reasonable conclusion that this page was created by the defendant or on his behalf."[13] However, the judgement of the Court of Appeals, did not define the required threshold for a proper authentication of a social media page. It observed though, that the mentioned Federal Rule 901 "required that there be some basis beyond [the defendant's] own testimony on which a reasonable juror could conclude that the page in question was not just any Internet page, but in fact Defendant's profile."[14]

17.3.2 *Insufficient Contextualisation*

A potential lack of contextualisation might create further evidentiary vulnerability of social media evidence in international criminal cases. Where the tendered evidence consists in photos or videos, the item itself usually cannot stand alone to support a particular proposition.

For instance, if an image depicts the dead body of a man in a desert setting, the prosecution may infer that the man was killed by armed group X, in location Y and at Z period in time. Nevertheless, without substantiation, the identity of the victim and perpetrator, or the location and date of the crime, cannot reasonably be inferred from the image alone. In this respect, several European national cases studied further below reveal how substantiation and corroboration are key to the contextualisation of social media content.[15]

17.3.3 *Biased Sources and Misinformation*

Because social media evidence is characterised by its mostly user-generated content, its reliability may be heavily impugned when the source of the content has an allegiance towards one of the parties in the proceedings or has a personal interest in the outcome of the case. As conflicts are driven by political and ideological interests, the accessibility and widespread audience of social media platforms makes them a channel of choice for the dissemination of misinformation and propaganda by those seeking media attention or social and political credibility.[16]

---

13   *United States v Vayner*, WL 4942227 (2d Cir. 2014).
14   *Ibid.*
15   See section 5.2 *infra*.
16   A study carried out on a dataset that includes 317 million Telegram messages sent between 2015 and 2019 reveals that links to known sources of misleading information were shared more often than links to professional news sources. *See* Aliaksandr Herasimenka, Jonathan Bright, Aleksi Knuutila, Philip N. Howard, 'Misinformation and professional news on largely unmoderated platforms: the case of Telegram' (2022), Journal of Information

Although Trial Chamber V of the ICC has yet to rule, the matter of fake news being propagated on Facebook in the context of the 2013–2014 Central African conflict has already been touched upon by witnesses in the case of *The Prosecutor v Alfred Yekatom and Patrice-Edouard Ngaïssona*. For instance, when confronted to several of his Facebook conversations, one of the witnesses admitted to having said "silly" or incorrect things on Facebook, and also that many people would share incorrect information in order to gain attention, visibility, or establish networks.[17]

17.3.4 *Confirmation Bias*

Aside from that of the content creator's, bias may also well originate in the individual or body interpreting the content, such as the investigators, the prosecution, the defence or the court. Human nature tends to interpret the information contained in user-generated evidence in conformity with their own pre-established theory, or, in the context of criminal proceedings, the theory of the case the prosecution or defence has in mind.[18] Visual material distributed on social media may well lead to visual biases that may distort the reality.[19]

Accordingly, cognitive errors can easily occur when one interprets user-generated evidence. Consequently, any naturally biased party to a criminal trial, namely the prosecution and the defence, should always strive to be aware of and correct for their own biases, and avoid to the extent possible to reconstruct the content of tendered items in a way that would fit their narrative, while ignoring or excluding contradictory evidence.

17.3.5 *Lack of Contemporaneousness*

Contemporaneousness is another difficulty in assessing the admissibility of social media evidence. Evidentiary reliability requires that the information or content was obtained and recorded simultaneously or shortly after the events

---

Technology and Politics <https://www.tandfonline.com/doi/full/10.1080/19331681.2022.2076272> accessed 1 October 2023.

17   *Prosecutor v Alfred Yekatom and Patrice-Édouard Ngaïssona* (Transcript of hearing) ICC-01/14-01/18-T-108-Red-ENG, T Ch V (9 March 2023) page 78, lines 9–16, and page 80, lines 5–14.

18   Wayne A. Wallace, 'The Effect of Confirmation Bias on Criminal Investigative Decision Making' (2015) Walden University Scholar Works <https://scholarworks.waldenu.edu/cgi/viewcontent.cgi?article=1406&context=dissertations> accessed 1 October 2023 (explaining confirmation bias as a process by which investigators search for or believe information that supports their favoured theory of a case "while ignoring or excusing disconfirmatory evidence").

19   *Ibid* (n 5).

to which it pertains or whether the record was created at a later stage.[20] Yet, the permanence and availability of online information is often precarious: users may choose to delete or edit their own content, making once public information henceforth unavailable. Accordingly, the collection and analysis of the content metadata is necessary – in addition to any other relevant verifications – to determine the circumstances of the content's generation, dissemination or potential alteration.

17.3.6 *User Identification*

User identification on social media is a real challenge since parties identify themselves by their user names. If usernames may consist of a unique name, they may also consist of a "set of characters", in other words, a pseudonym. The risk of anonymity associated with the use of pseudonyms on social media makes user identification more complicated than for traditional communication methods. For instance, in a phone conversation, "identifying the voices of a conversation typically authenticates the evidence."[21] Likewise, in an email communication, "the parties who exchange emails know each other personally or the server administrators know their identities";[22] therefore, the parties to the conversation may identify each other, or the server administrator may produce the logs and IP addresses of the parties.

In order to easily identify its users, most social media platforms require, at least, a valid email address and valid phone number to sign up for their service.[23] Nevertheless, social media users can circumvent those restrictions and anonymise themselves by resorting to disposable email addresses or phone numbers. In order to provide further guarantees of authenticity, some platforms have developed "Verified badges".

For instance, the Meta group – including platforms such as Facebook or Instagram – proposes a verification service named "Meta Verified", which is a paid subscription designed to confirm that the account is validated and authentic.[24] Accordingly, for an individual, business or organisation to

---

20 *Prosecutor v Germain Katanga and Mathieu Ngudjolo Chui* (Decision on the Prosecutor's Bar Table Motions) ICC-01/04-01/07-2635, T Ch II (17 December 2010), para. 27 (c).
21 Yongjin Choi, 'Mobile Instant Messaging Evidence in Criminal Trials' (2017), Cath. U. J. L. & Tech 1 <http://scholarship.law.edu/jlt/vol26/iss1/3> accessed 30 September 2023.
22 *Ibid.*
23 See for instance the Facebook Help page, in the section named 'Create a Facebook Account' <https://www.facebook.com/help/570785306433644/?helpref=hc_fnav> accessed 8 October 2023.
24 See Instagram's Eligibility requirements for Meta Verified profiles <https://help.instagram.com/2419286908233223?cms_id=2419286908233223> accessed 8 October 2023.

subscribe their profile to Meta Verified, they must fulfil a series of eligibility criteria such as, *inter alia*, age, minimum activity requirements, valid photo ID that matches their profile name and profile picture and the "two-factor authentication" enabled on their profile.[25]

However, these verification policies and subscription are designed and implemented by the platforms themselves. Yet, the authentication criteria of the platforms do not necessarily match the higher standard of authentication required in the context of the assessment of the admissibility of evidence in international criminal proceedings. Accordingly, the collection and analysis of the metadata is, again, necessary – in addition to any other relevant verifications – to determine the user's identity and the content's authorship.

17.3.7 *Role of Social Media Platforms and Content Moderation*

Another risk associated with social media evidence in international criminal cases is that it implies the involvement of the social media platforms themselves. Due to domestic regulations, social media platforms' hosts are more and more under an obligation to remove crime-related or other violent or graphic content. For instance, the Facebook Community Standards on "Violent and graphic content" indicate that the platform will remove any imagery of

> people or dead bodies in non-medical settings if they depict dismemberment, visible internal organs, partially decomposed bodies, charred or burning people unless in the context of cremation or self-immolation when that action is a form of political speech or newsworthy, victims of cannibalism, throat-slitting [or] live streams of capital punishment of a person.[26]

The issue is that this type of regulations may lead to "over-removal of content,"[27] and thus might create an obstacle to international criminal investigations.

---

[25] The "two-factor authentication" protects a Facebook or Instagram account by requiring a code if there is a log in attempt from a device that is not recognised by the platform <https://help.instagram.com/566810106808145?helpref=faq_content> accessed 8 October 2023.

[26] See Facebook Community Standards on Violent and Graphic Content <https://transparency.fb.com/en-gb/policies/community-standards/violent-graphic-content/> accessed 8 October 2023.

[27] Ibid (n 5).

17.4 Specificities of MIM Evidence

Because MIM evidence consists in conversation threads, it may well be used by the prosecution to attribute some speech or ideological position directly to the author of a message or sender of a photo or video content, in order to establish their criminal responsibility. As such, MIM evidence bears inherent risks in terms of authentication and authorship. Some of these risks have been identified by the Court of Criminal Appeals of Texas in *Tienda v State*, where the Court held that "computers can be hacked [...] and cell phones can be purloined."[28] Especially because "the applications are usually always turned on at all times while the mobile device is turned on", an illegitimate possessor of the mobile device – hacker or thief – may make use of a MIM app without having to log in with identifying credentials.

However, beyond hacking and theft, the MIM app can merely be used by someone whom the owner of the MIM account allowed access using their credentials. In this respect, the Court in the case of *State v Smith* rejected the Government's MIM evidence holding that "there [was] no evidence of whether, [...], [the defendant] allowed others access using his password or any unique qualities regarding the messages themselves from which one may assert [that it was the defendant who] sent the messages."[29]

Thus, regarding the inherent risks associated to it, MIM evidence must be "independently authenticated" by corroborating elements, such as the testimony of a knowledgeable witness or other accepted means. For that reason, the Court of Criminal Appeals of Texas in the *Tienda* case has held that the circumstance that "the respondent in an internet chat room dialogue purports to identify himself" cannot be "without more" regarded as sufficient to support a finding of authenticity.

Likewise, the US Court of Appeals for the Third Circuit[30] has rejected the Government's theory of self-authentication because the Government could only show that "the communications took place as alleged between the named Facebook accounts", but could not demonstrate that these accounts were actually used by their legitimate owner. On the same note, the Court in *State v Smith* held that "[N]o evidence or testimony was offered as to whether [the defendant] created the account and/or profile on the social media platform or

---

28 *Tienda v State*, 479 S.W.3d 863 (Tex. App. 2015).
29 *The State v Smith*, 192 So.3d 836, at 842 (4h Cir. 2016).
30 *Tienda v State*, 479 S.W.3d 863 (Tex. App. 2015).

whether he had ever accessed the platform."[31] Therefore, it appears that "user identification is the key to authenticating MIM evidence."

17.5 Legal Framework in Construction

So far, social media evidence has been apprehended in a largely *ad hoc* manner, whether by international criminal courts, investigative mechanisms or national war crimes units. Although the ICC and other international criminal tribunals have yet barely touched upon the admissibility of social media evidence, domestic courts have been developing an enlightening case-load due to increasing international criminal cases being prosecuted nationally. Besides, the need for comprehensive and harmonised guidelines has led regional and international organisations to elaborate general principals on approaching digital evidence.

17.5.1 *The Limited International Case Law on Admissibility of Social Media Evidence*

There has not yet been a case where the ICC has fundamentally ruled upon the issue of the admissibility of social media evidence in international criminal cases. Yet, this type of evidence has been used and/or relied upon in several cases, such as in the case of *The Prosecutor v Ahmad Al Faqi Al Mahdi* (*"Al Mahdi"*).[32] This was the first ICC case in which a defendant was charged with the destruction of cultural heritage as a war crime and the first to plead guilty before the ICC. The defendant was identified through videos which were posted on social media as promotion of Ansar Dine's attack on cultural heritage sites in Timbuktu.[33] The prosecution's evidence included YouTube video's and satellite images from before and after the destruction as well as archive photographs, audio and video recordings which showed the destruction at the time of the attack.[34] Trial Chamber VIII in its judgement, relied on a video to find that the charged attacks on mosques and mausoleums was an affront to

---

31 *The State v Smith*, 192 So.3d 836, at 842 (4h Cir. 2016).
32 *Prosecutor v Al Mahdi*, case no. ICC-01/12-01/15.
33 Lindsay Freeman, 'Digital Evidence and War Crimes Prosecutions: The Impact of Digital Technologies on International Criminal Investigations and Trials' (2018), Fordham International Law Journal <https://ir.lawnet.fordham.edu/ilj/vol41/iss2/1/> accessed 30 September 2023.
34 *Prosecutor v Al Mahdi* (Transcript of hearing) ICC-01/12-01/15-T-4-Red-ENG (22 August 2016), p. 28–29.

the values of the Constitution of the UNESCO.[35] While this case would have been an opportunity for the Trial Chamber VIII to address the issue of admissibility of social media evidence in international criminal cases, the Chamber was not called upon to do so specifically, because the evidence was agreed upon by the parties and therefore the defence did not challenge the authenticity of the YouTube videos. Nonetheless, the Chamber did rely on social media evidence so as to conclude that the defendant was guilty in that case.

Also, in the *Bemba et al. case*,[36] the Prosecution introduced into evidence photographs taken from a Facebook account in order to link individuals and corroborate other evidence. The defence challenged the Facebook evidence introduced by the Prosecution, namely by arguing that the photographs were not "prima facie authentic or reliable".[37] Despite the defence challenging the admissibility of Facebook evidence, Trial Chamber VII did not fundamentally address that issue. This might be explained by the fact that the Facebook photographs which were submitted to prove the defendant's guilt were already evidenced through witness testimony.

If the ICC has not yet fundamentally ruled upon the issue of the admissibility of social media evidence, Trial Panel II of the ICTY however has had to determine whether a Facebook post, dated 15 September 2020, originating from the account of Mr Gucati, could be submitted into the *Gucati and Haradinaj* case evidentiary record. The Panel found that the item was apparently authentic and relevant, and had some probative value "insofar as it pertains to circumstances referred to by Mr Gucati in both his testimony and his statement".[38] The Panel noted, however, that the Facebook post had not been shown to Mr Gucati during his testimony; accordingly, the Panel specified that "[t]his fact will be considered by the Panel when deciding what weight, if any, to give to that information."[39] In short, if the item was eventually admitted into evidence, the Panel expressed reservations as to its evidentiary weight.

---

35 *Prosecutor v Capitol A* (Judgement and Sentence) ICC-01/12-01/15-171, T Ch VIII (27 September 2016) (27 September 2016), p. 27, footnote 101.
36 *Prosecutor v Bemba et al*, case no. ICC-01/05-01/13.
37 *Prosecutor v Bemba et al* (Transcript of hearing) ICC-01/05-01/13-1245-Red (9 October 2015), p. 83.
38 *Prosecutor v Hysni Gucati and Nasim Haradinaj* (Decision on the Defence Request for Admission of Items through the Bar Table and Related Matters) KSC-BC-2020-07/F00502, TP II (17 December 2021), paras 42–43.
39 *Ibid.*

17.5.2 Increasing Domestic Case Law on Admissibility of Social Media Evidence

European national case law related to foreign terrorist fighters (FTFs) posing in front of dead bodies can be enlightening. In these cases, the charges were based on Facebook posts where purported FTFs could be seen posing triumphantly next to alleged enemies' dead bodies. In the end, the charged FTFs were convicted for war crimes of outrages upon personal dignity (art. 8(2)(c)(ii) Rome Statute).[40] The conclusion to draw from such case law is that these photos were deemed to be a sufficient ground for conviction for war crime of outrages upon personal dignity. However, these same photos in themselves were not to be seen as sufficient for conviction for war crime of murder, since they do not clarify anything about the element of perpetration. As a matter of fact, the key factor is contextualisation. Indeed, the photos could tell that the charged FTF was inflicting degrading treatments to dead bodies by proudly posing next to them; however, the photos could not tell that the charged FTF had himself killed those persons whose dead bodies were exposed.[41]

In order to contextualise the social media content tendered into evidence, these cases show that courts usually rely on substantiating and corroborating information. For instance, in a case before the Higher Regional Court of Berlin, an Iraqi national was convicted under Section 8(1), subparagraph 9 of the Code of Crimes against International Law[42] for being depicted, in a picture shared on Facebook, holding up by the hair two human heads which have been severed from their bodies. It is apparent from the reasons of the judgment the

---

[40] District Court of Pirkanmaa (18 March 2016) Judgment no. 16/112431; District court of Kanta-Häme (22 March 2016) Judgment no. 16/112863; Scania and Blekinge Court of Appeal (11 April 2017) Case no. B 3187-16; German Federal Court of Justice (27 July 2017) Judgment no. StR 57/17.

[41] Note that there is one case however where the charged FTF was convicted under Swedish law for crime against international law of extra-judicial execution. See *Prosecutor v Haisam Omar Sakhanh*, Svea Court of Appeal (31 May 2017) Case no. B 3787-16 (in addition to the Facebook photo where the defendant was posing triumphantly next to enemies' dead bodies, there was a YouTube video depicting the defendant as he was taking an active part in the extra-judicial execution of the persons whose dead bodies were exposed; in such a case, there was sufficient ground for conviction for crime against international law of extra-judicial execution, since the YouTube video allowed contextualization of the Facebook photo.).

[42] Code of Crimes against International Law, Section 8(1), subparagraph 9 ("(1) Whoever in connection with an international armed conflict or with an armed conflict not of an international character (…) 9. treats a person who is to be protected under international humanitarian law in a gravely humiliating or degrading manner shall be punished").

Facebook-derived content was authenticated by the defendant's own testimony and admission of his guilt.[43]

In addition, expert witnesses may be called to testify to provide their insights and assist the court in its assessment of social media evidence. For instance, expert witnesses may testify as to the context within which some social media content should be understood. Finnish courts have had to decide on a case involving the publication of a picture on Facebook showing the accused posing with the head of a decapitated enemy soldier.[44] Although the accused – a member of the Iraqi Special Operations Forces involved in combat operations against ISI – admitted that it was indeed him in the photo and that he had posted it on Facebook, he denied having decapitated the deceased. The District Court of Kanta Häme noted that the conditions in which the accused was raised differed significantly from those found in Finnish culture and that such cultural background had to be considered when legally evaluating the accused's conduct.[45] An expert witness was called to help the District Court of Kanta Häme interpret the meaning of the Facebook post.[46] Based on the expert witness' testimony, the accused was eventually convicted for war crime under Chapter 11(5)(2) of the Criminal Code of Finland.

Lessons learned from these domestic cases should inform future efforts in establishing a comprehensive case-load to enable international criminal tribunal apprehend social media content when tendered in the case evidentiary record.

17.5.3 *The Berkeley Protocol on Digital Open Source Investigation*

The absence of any settled international case law, and the increasing number of investigations and case openings, before both national and international courts, has further heightened the need for common standards for capturing, preserving and analysing open source information that can be introduced as evidence in international criminal trials.

On 30 January 2019, the Committee of Ministers of the Council of Europe adopted guidelines on Electronic evidence in civil and administrative

---

[43] Higher Regional Court of Berlin 2a Criminal Division (1 March 2017) Case no. (2A) 172 OJs 26/16 (3/16).

[44] District court of Kanta-Häme (22 March 2016) Judgment no. 16/112863.

[45] *Ibid.*

[46] Namely, the expert witness explained that the aim of these sort of photos was to strengthen an individual's position within an armed group by demonstrating that its members form a brutal team and send the enemy a clear message that where necessary, the party depicted in the photos is able to carry out such acts.

proceedings.[47] These guidelines however only contain very general principle pertaining to the collection, relevance, reliability or preservation of digital evidence and is limited to civil and administrative proceedings.

However, more recently, in 2022, the Office of the United Nations High Commissioner for Human Rights (OHCHR), and the Human Rights Centre at the University of California have released the Berkeley Protocol on Digital Open Source Investigations, a "Practical Guide on the Effective Use of Digital Open Source Information in Investigating Violations of International Criminal, Human Rights and Humanitarian Law".[48] Although the purpose of the present publication is not to provide an exhaustive commentary of the Berkeley Protocol, the following principles are worth highlighting.

17.5.3.1 Data Minimisation

The collection and seizure of social media content shall be limited to what is strictly necessary. Pursuant to the Berkeley Protocol:

> The principle of data minimisation prescribes that digital information should only be collected and processed if it is: (a) justified for an articulable purpose; (b) necessary for achieving that purpose; and (c) proportional to the ability to fulfil that purpose.[49]

It follows that data minimisation invites investigators and parties to favour targeted collection rather than bulk and automated collection. Avoiding over-collection of social media content is even more important that it also helps preserve the privacy and data protection of the social media users, whether they are the defendant, witnesses or third parties.

17.5.3.2 Preservation

While data minimisation is designed to prevent over-collection, the principle of preservation rather seeks to avoid under-collection. Given that social media platforms may remove content pursuant to their policy on violent and graphic content,[50] and that users may choose to delete or edit their own content,[51] an

---

47 Council of Europe, Electronic Evidence in Civil and Administrative Proceedings: Guidelines and Explanatory Memorandum (2019).
48 OCHCR, Practical Guide on the Effective Use of Digital Open Source Information in Investigating Violations of International Criminal, Human Rights and Humanitarian Law (2022).
49 Berkeley Protocol, para. 31.
50 See section 3.7 *supra*.
51 See section 3.5 *supra*.

active and diligent preservation of the relevant content shall be ensured, so that the digital material is to remain accessible and usable for future accountability mechanisms.

17.5.3.3 Verification

Another principle worth highlighting is that of verification. Pursuant to the Berkeley Protocol "[o]pen source investigators should determine whether the information or claims in digital content are *prima facie* reliable by reviewing and evaluating the content as well as the contextual information contained in the file."[52] This could include checking the original source, any linked information related for instance to the author, uploader or host of the source, or the content's embedded metadata such as IP addresses or dates and times of alterations.

17.6 Social Media Evidence and the Right to a Fair Trial: the ECtHR Perspective

On 26 September 2023, the Grand Chamber of the European Court of Human Rights delivered its judgment in the Case of *Yüksel Yalcinkaya v Turkiye*. The case concerns a Turkish teacher who was convicted in 2017 of the offence of membership of an armed terrorist organization. The conviction was based decisively on his use of an app called 'ByLock'. Messages sent on this app were encrypted, and Turkish Courts were convinced that the app was created for and only used by members of the terrorist group considered to be behind the attempted coup d'état of 15 July 2016. The electronic evidence was by far the most important evidence in this case.

Overall, the ECtHR found that the procedural shortcomings in the criminal proceedings amounted to a breach of Article 6(1) of the Convention. Indeed, the Strasbourg Court found that the Turkish courts had failed to put in place enough safeguards to ensure that the applicant had had a genuine opportunity to effectively challenge the evidence against him. The Court noted that national courts may not use evidence in a way that undermines the fundamental principles of a fair trial, regardless of whether the evidence is electronic or not. Indeed, although in the fight against terrorism it may be important to use electronic evidence, the proceedings as a whole, including the manner in which the evidence was obtained and presented, must be fair. In particular,

---

52 Berkeley Protocol, para. 149.

this implies that the accused should be given the opportunity to challenge the evidence and oppose its use.

At the outset, the Court acknowledged that electronic evidence has become ubiquitous in criminal trials and that it can be very important in the fight against organized crime.[53] It further noted the many differences between electronic evidence and traditional forms of evidence.[54] However, the Court emphasized that in abstract the safeguards under Article 6(1) should not be applied any differently to electronic evidence, neither more strictly nor more leniently.[55] In this regard, the Court stressed that the main concern is – as is also the case with traditional evidence – whether the overall fairness of the proceedings was ensured through the lens of the procedural and institutional safeguards and the fundamental principles of a fair trial inherent in Article 6 of the Convention.[56]

With regard to the quality of electronic evidence, the Grand Chamber acknowledged that, although it is not for the Court to pronounce on whether and in what circumstances and format this may be used in criminal proceedings as evidence, the reliability may be more likely called into question in certain instances.[57] The Court explicitly mentions cases where the collection or processing of electronic evidence is not subject to prior independent authorisation or supervision, or a post factum judicial review, or where it is not accompanied by other procedural safeguards or corroborated by other evidence.[58]

Moreover, with regard to the defendant's ability to challenge electronic evidence during the proceedings, the Court held that Article 6(1) of the ECHR requires the disclosure of all material evidence for or against the accused as an aspect of the right to adversarial proceedings.[59] Indeed, even if the defendant has had access to the electronic evidence reports, it does not necessarily mean that he or she does not have the right or interest to request access to the original data from which those reports were generated.[60] However, when the evidence in the possession of the Prosecution consists of a large amount of electronic information, it may not be possible/necessary to disclose this

---

53   *Ibid* para. 312.
54   *Ibid*.
55   *Ibid* para. 313.
56   *Ibid*.
57   *Ibid* para. 316.
58   *Ibid*.
59   *Ibid* para. 327.
60   *Ibid*.

information to the defence in its entirety.[61] Indeed, there may be legitimate reasons not to disclose all the information.[62]

The Court must examine whether any prejudice sustained by the defendants on account of the non-disclosure of the electronic evidence was counterbalanced by adequate procedural safeguards and thus whether there was a proper opportunity to prepare the defence within the meaning of Article 6(1) of the Convention.[63] In this regard, the Court found that "(...) while the Court acknowledges that it is in no position to determine whether, in what form and to what extent the relevant data should have been shared with the applicant, it cannot but note that the applicant was given no explanation by the domestic courts as to why, and upon whose decision, the raw data – particularly to the extent that they concerned him specifically – were kept from him. He was therefore deprived of the opportunity to present any counter-arguments, such as to contest the validity of those reasons or to dispute that all efforts had been made to strike a fair balance between the competing interests at play and to ensure the rights of the defence. The Court reiterates that maintaining the need for disclosure under the assessment of the competent court, keeping the defence duly informed and permitting the accused to make submissions and participate in the decision-making process as far as possible are important safeguards in this regard".[64]

In addition, the Grand Chamber stated that the domestic court's failure to respond to the accused's request to have the raw data submitted to an independent examination – even if only to explain why such independent examination was not deemed necessary – was problematic.[65] This was especially the case since the accused had a legitimate interest in seeking this examination, for the data had never been subjected to examination for verification of their integrity.[66] The Court considered that the inability of the defence to have direct access to the evidence and to test its integrity and reliability first-hand places a greater responsibility on the domestic courts to subject questions from the defence regarding the reliability of the evidence to the most searching scrutiny.[67]

It is emphasized by the Court that even if it is not possible to share raw data with a defendant, the requirement of a "fair balance" between parties at

---

61   *Ibid* para. 329.
62   *Ibid*.
63   *Ibid* para. 330.
64   *Ibid* para. 331.
65   *Ibid* para. 333.
66   *Ibid*.
67   *Ibid* para. 334.

least requires the proceedings to be conducted in a manner that enables the defendant to comment on the full extent of the decrypted material concerning him, including, in particular, the nature and content of his activity over that application.[68] As a matter of fact, the opportunity for a defendant to acquaint himself with the decrypted electronic evidence is an important step in persevering his defence rights.[69]

> The Court notes the findings in the MIT technical analysis report that the ByLock application had been downloaded more than 100,000 times from Google Play store and 500,000 to 1 million times from APK download sites (see paragraph 115 above). As noted above, the technical analysis indicated that while it was not possible to verify the accuracy of these figures, they did not appear to be inconsistent with there being 215,092 users on ByLock servers, considering, inter alia, the number of people who may have downloaded it on multiple devices or deleted and re-downloaded it (ibid.). It observes moreover from the expert report submitted by the applicant (see paragraph 134 above), which was not refuted by the Government, that the configurations required to establish communication with other users following download, as well as many other technical features relied on to support the exclusivity argument, were not of a nature to limit the use only to a defined group, but were in fact found in many widely available applications, a point that the applicant also raised before the domestic courts (see paragraph 90 above). It further refers to statements from some FETÖ/PDY suspects, cited in the Constitutional Court's Ferhat Kara judgment, explaining how they had downloaded ByLock from an application store after hearing about it from "friends in the cemaat" and how its use had spread across the cemaat at some point (see paragraph 176 above), suggesting that the application may have also been downloaded and used outside a strict organisational hierarchy. It is important to highlight in this regard that while the original test set out in the landmark Court of Cassation judgments indicated that the use of ByLock would constitute proof of connection with the FETÖ/PDY if it was established that a person had "joined the network on the instructions of the organisation" (see paragraph 160 above), neither the Court of Cassation itself, nor the courts in the applicant's specific case, subsequently engaged in a separate assessment to that effect. Nor did they

---

68   *Ibid* para. 335.
69   *Ibid* para. 336.

provide any explanation as to why that assessment was not deemed necessary in the circumstances.[70]

Therefore in the case at hand, the Court concluded that there had not been enough safeguards in place to ensure the applicant would have a genuine opportunity to challenge the evidence against him and conduct his defence in an effective manner and on an equal footing with the Prosecution.[71] The domestic court's failure to respond to the applicant's specific and pertinent requests and objections raised a legitimate doubt that they were impervious to the defence arguments and that the applicant had not been truly "heard".[72]

In the Court's view, the domestic courts' failure to put in place appropriate safeguards vis à vis the key piece of evidence at issue to enable the applicant to challenge it effectively, to address the salient issues lying at the core of the case and to provide reasons justifying their decisions was incompatible with the very essence of the procedural rights under Article 6 § 1 of the Convention.[73] The Court thus concluded that Article 6 § 1 of the Convention had been breached.[74]

17.7 Conclusion

Although user-generated evidence might seem attractive as an alternative to prosecute suspects of international crimes in situations where other evidence is difficult to collect, the invocation of this type of evidence – considering the abovementioned vulnerabilities and risks – questions the legitimacy of serious charges such as genocide, crimes against humanity and war crimes. The prosecution, resorting to social media evidence to prove these types of charges, might therefore undermine the acceptance and legitimacy of judgements which rely on social media evidence. It is therefore important to observe that in most cases where social media evidence was found admissible, this type of evidence in itself was not deemed sufficient to prove a criminal charge, requiring additional evidence to establish authenticity and prove that someone was the perpetrator.[75] Absent any settled set of rules on the matter, practitioners, whether investigators, prosecutors, defence counsels or even judges, still enjoy

---

70   *Ibid* para. 339.
71   *Ibid* para. 341.
72   *Ibid* para. 341.
73   *Ibid* para. 345.
74   *Ibid* para. 346.
75   *Renee v State of Texas* 49 So. 3d. 248 (2010).

a certain flexibility and leeway when confronted to the evidentiary value of social media content, and may therefore demonstrate some sort of legal creativity in this regard. However, they should always be aware of the vulnerabilities described in this Chapter whenever tendering, disputing or assessing the evidentiary value of social media content.

PART 6

The Extent of Disclosing Exculpatory Criminal Evidence

CHAPTER 18

The Extent of Disclosing Exculpatory Criminal Evidence

18.1 Introduction

As written by the authors May and Wierda in their book 'International Criminal Evidence': the issue of disclosure goes to the heart of the modern international criminal process and its adversarial form.[1] Not only at the national level, but also at the international level, failure to disclose exculpatory evidence might well be a cause for a miscarriage of justice.[2] Since the defence is not privy to the (preliminary) investigation results of the Prosecutor, the primary responsibility to disclose exculpatory information rests upon the Prosecutor.

It is for this reason that most legal systems place the burden to disclose such evidence on the prosecution.[3] Within the ICC legal framework this principle is laid down in article 67(2) of the Rome Statute and Rule 77 of the Rules of Procedure and Evidence which Rule attributes to the Prosecution the duty to disclose objects that are material to the preparation of the defence. Indeed, the Prosecution must, as soon as practical, disclosure the evidence in its possession that is exculpatory, mitigates the guilt of the accused, or that affects the credibility of the prosecution evidence. The pivotal question though is how to understand the terms 'exculpatory' and 'material'. This chapter intends to discern the legal contours of these terms.

18.2 The Evidentiary Meaning of 'Exculpatory Evidence'

At the outset, it follows from jurisprudence of international criminal tribunals that the obligation which primarily rests upon the Prosecution to disclose exculpatory evidence is not a 'secondary one' since it is as important as the

---

[1] Richard May and Marieke Wierda, *International Criminal Evidence* (*International and comparative Criminal Law Series*) (vol 9, Transnational Publishers Inc. 2002) 73.
[2] Geert-Jan A. Knoops, *Redressing miscarriages of justice practice and procedure in (international) criminal cases* (2nd rev. ed., Martinus Nijhoff Publishers 2013).
[3] *Ibid* (n 1).

obligation to prosecute the case with due diligence.[4] When determining the legal scope of the term 'exculpatory evidence', doctrine and jurisprudence of international criminal tribunals reveal three elements which constitute this type of evidence:

(i) Any material which suggests the innocence of the accused, which might entail testimony, documents and other objects.[5]
(ii) Any material which tends to mitigate the guilt of the accused
(iii) Any material which may affect the credibility of the prosecution evidence[6]

The problem though lies in the entity that is to determine if one of these three situations occur, and how this is to be determined. As to the first question, it is the Prosecution Service that at the beginning of a criminal case is endowed with the task to ascertain if such material exists, and if so, disclose it to the Court and the defence. The ICC Appeals Chamber ruled in this regard that "(...) rule 77 of the Rules leaves to the Prosecutor the assessment of whether objects are 'material to the preparation of the defence'".[7]

Within the ICC system, it lays this in the hands of the prosecutor to decide which material in its possession is relevant to the defence case.[8] This system places on the defence the burden to indicate with a certain degree of specificity which information might be in possession of the prosecution and why this information is 'material' to its case.[9] This triggers the next question as to what the term 'material' entails. One can find an attempt to define this term in the ICC case of *Prosecutor v Jean-Paul Bemba*, where ICC Trial Chamber III held that:

> An item will be considered material to the preparation of the defence if it 'would undermine the prosecution case or support a line of argument of the defence' or 'significantly assist the accused in understanding the incriminating and exculpatory evidence and the issues in the case'.[10]

---

4 *Prosecutor v Barayagwiza* (Decision on Prosecution Request for Review of Reconsideration) ICTR-97-19-AR72, A Ch (3 March 2000) para. 64.
5 *Ibid* (n 1) page 77.
6 *Ibid*, 76.
7 *Prosecutor v Ntaganda* (Judgment on the appeal of Mr Bosco Ntaganda against the "Decision on Defence requests seeking disclosure orders and a declaration of Prosecution obligation to record contacts with witnesses") ICC-01/04-02/06-1330, A Ch (20 May 2016) para. 23.
8 *Ibid*.
9 *Ibid*.
10 *Prosecutor v Bemba Gombo* (Decision on the "Defence Motion on Prosecution contact with its witnesses") ICC-01/05-01/08-3070, T Ch III (22 May 2014) para. 23; cited in

In order to meet the threshold of 'material to the defence case', the ICC Trial Chambers expect from the defence more than just to indicate that the particular item 'may potentially' entail relevant information. At the least, the defence is bound to illustrate a direct connection to the charges or a live issue in the case.[11]

This notion was further set out in jurisprudence of various Trial Chambers in the *Ongwen, Al Hassan* and *Lubanga* cases. Indeed, in which cases it was held that when information is disputed by the prosecution as 'material', the defence bears the burden of showing the material importance of the information at stake; this requires, according to these rulings, a form of 'substantiation' on part of the defence.[12]

Yet, a limitation to this burden is to be noted. The Appeals Chamber of the ICC has held that any assessment of whether information is material to the preparation of the Defence pursuant Rule 77 should be made on a *prima facie* basis, which 'place a low burden on the defence'.[13] Importantly, the ICC Appeals Chamber also stressed that it "may be that information that is material to the preparation of the Defence is ultimately not used as evidence at the trial or may not turn out to be relevant to it. Yet, the defence is still entitled to this information on the basis of a *prima facie* assessment."[14]

To conclude, the ICC legal framework on disclosure of potentially exculpatory evidence, thus creates a certain legal monopoly for the prosecution on the scope of disclosing exculpatory evidence. Moreover, it requires that the prosecution places itself in the mind of the defence, which is a questionable task.

Prosecutor v Yekatom and Ngaïssona (Prosecution's Response to the Yekatom Defence Urgent request for access to evidentiary materials in possession of the Office of the Prosecutor (ICC-01/14-01/18-1604-Conf) ICC-01/14-01/18-1609, T Ch V (13 October 2022) para. 15.

11 See *Prosecutor v Ongwen* (Decision on Defence Request for Remedies in Light of Disclosure Violations) ICC-02/04-01/15-1734, T Ch IX (22 April 2020) para. 22.

12 *Ibid*; See also *Prosecutor v Lubanga Dyilo* (Decision on the prosecution's request for an order on the disclosure of tu quoque material pursuant to Rule 77) ICC-01/04-01/06-2147, T Ch I (2 October 2009) and *Prosecutor v Al Hassan* (Rapport du Greffe en application de la Décision du 20 mars 2019) ICC-01/12-01/18-359, Registrar (29 May 2019).

13 *Prosecutor v Banda and Jerbo* (Judgement on the appeal of Mr Abdollah Banda Abakaer Nourain and Mr Salah Mohammed Jerbo Jamus against the decision of Trial Chamber IV of 23 January 2013 entitled "Decision on the Defence's Request for Disclosure of Documents in the Possession of The Office of the Prosecutor") ICC-02/05 03/09-501, A Ch (28 August 2013) para. 42.

14 *Ibid*.

18.3 Practical Implications Pertaining to the Defense Disclosure Burden

The aforementioned monopoly position of the prosecution and the subsequent burden on the defence to demonstrate *prima facie* the 'materiality' of the evidence for which it asks the disclosure, has several practical consequences.

First, although the initial assessment of whether evidence is exculpatory within the meaning of Article 67(2) Rome Statute and Rule 77 is primarily endowed to the discretion of the prosecution,[15] the prosecution cannot be said to have fulfilled its disclosure obligations (...) by simply acknowledging her obligations under the Rules of Procedure and Evidence stating that she has complied with them.[16]

Second, even if it is the case that the prosecution cannot dispose of its obligations by simply stating that it has complied with the disclosure rules, the question is what mechanisms are available for the defence to challenge this. The only remedy accessible to the defence is to litigate the matter before the Trial Chamber. In that situation, the defence still incurs the obligation to present to the judges of the Trial Chamber *prima facie* or if the fact that the prosecution is in possession of the particular exculpatory evidence.[17]

Third, when prosecuting a disclosure request to the Trial Chamber, apart from the mentioned *prima facie* burden, such request should at the least indicate the nature and type of the documents sought by the defence; in other words, such a request should go beyond a mere 'fishing expedition'.[18]

Fourth, one of the disclosure obligations of the prosecution, as mentioned in Article 67(2) of the Rome Statute, relates to information that is in the prosecution's possession or control which 'may' affect the credibility of the prosecution's evidence. The word 'may' implies that the defence's burden to show that the information sought might affect the credibility of the prosecution evidence is low in that no absolute proof is required. For instance, one of the prosecution witnesses' criminal record might, from the prosecution's perspective, not undermine the witness' credibility as such, while for the defence this record can be an important piece of information for the examination of the

---

15   *Ibid* (n 1) page 76, referring to *Prosecutor v Delalic et al.* (Decision on the Defence Motion to Compel the Discovery of Identity and Location of Witnesses) ICTY TC (18 March 1997) para. 19.
16   *Ibid* (n 1) page 76, referring to *Prosecutor v Blaskic* (Decision on the Production of Discovery Materials) IT-95-14, TC (27 January 1997) para. 47.
17   *Ibid* (n 1) page 77, referring to the *Prosecutor v Blaskic* (Decision on the Production of Discovery Materials) IT-95-14, TC (27 January 1997) para. 50.
18   *Ibid.*

witness and lead to a cross-examination which can convince the judges to discredit the witness.

Also here, the question arises as to what the exact scope of the words 'might affect the credibility of Prosecution evidence' is. This depends to a large extent on whether the case file already reveals some indicia for the apparent non-credibility of the particular witness.

In addition, the views of the prosecution and defence will in most instances diverge. For example, in the case of *Prosecutor v Patrice Ngaïssona*, one of the prosecution witnesses withdrew during the trial in 2021–2022 his cooperation with the Prosecution, while in the same timeframe his house was searched by the local authorities at the request of the ICC Prosecutor. The defence deemed the information underlying the witnesses' decision to no longer cooperate important for the preparation of its case and sought disclosure of the said information leading to the witness' decision. After opposition by the prosecution, the defence asked for the intervention of the Trial Chamber, claiming that the information concerning the withdrawal of cooperation by a prosecution witness was, in that case material to the preparation of the defence and, as such, disclosable under Rule 77 of the RPE.

18.4 Towards a Different Disclosure System

Still, in light of the burden which the defence bears – albeit a 'low' one – and the fact that litigation to obtain disclosure of exculpatory evidence is time-consuming, it could also be considered to change the disclosure system such that in the event of disputes between the prosecution and defence about what constitutes 'materiality', the information which the prosecution has in its possession and is not willing to disclose as purportedly not 'material' to the preparation of the defence, is handed over to the Trial Chamber without having to formally litigate the matter. It is then an independent organ, the Trial Chamber, which can determine the exculpatory nature of the said information.

18.5 Disclosure Mechanisms to Prevent Miscarriages of Justice

One has to bear mind that any deficiencies in the disclosure system might potentially result in a miscarriage of justice.[19] In the United Kingdom, disclo-

---

19   *Ibid* (n. 2) page 21.

sure of evidence has been the subject of scrutiny for over a decade.[20] Within the jurisdiction of the United Kingdom several high-profile cases have illustrated the vulnerability of the disclosure system which led to a review of the system.[21]

One of the cases that led to a review of the disclosure system in the United Kingdom was the trial of *R. v Allan* in 2017. This case pertained to a defendant charged with rape and sexual assault, Mr Liam Allan. In this case the police supressed the disclosure of several text messages which were considered to be exculpatory to the defence and also the prosecution, until the day of the trial. Allan was charged with six counts of rape and six counts of sexual assault, which charges were brought against him after a woman with whom Allan had a relationship reported him to the police. The woman in question claimed that the relationship was unhappy and abusive, and she did not want sex. The messages held back by the police contained statements that amounted to the woman 'being extremely happy for the defendant to come back to her after they broke up and extremely happy with the sex,'[22] and thus were considered exculpatory.

Upon disclosure on the day of the trial, the Prosecution Service came to the conclusion that there no longer existed a case for them and the charges were dismissed.[23] The *R. v Allan* case prompted the United Kingdom Joint National Police Chiefs Council, the College of Policing and the Crown Prosecution Service to produce a 'National Disclosure Improvement Plan' (NDIP) aiming at improving the way disclosure obligations were to be performed.[24]

Importantly, also for International Criminal Trials, were the recommendations and actions that resulted from the NDIP (second) report of 2019 in order to improve disclosure practices.[25] In short, the main measures proposed were the following:

---

20 Claire Brader, 'Disclosure of Evidence in Criminal Proceedings' (2020) House of Lords Library Briefing 1, 2.
21 *Ibid*, referring to the cases *R. v Mouncher and others* (2011) and *R. v Allan* (2017).
22 Lizzie Dearden, 'Rape Trial Collapse over Undisclosed Sex Messages Blamed on Police Funding Cuts' (2017) Independent <www.independent.co.uk/news/uk/crime/rape-trial -collapse-sex-text-messages-police-funding-cuts-liam-allan-disclosure-phone-innocent -miscarriages-of-justice-a8113011.html>, accessed 17 October 2023.
23 *Ibid* (n 20) pages 3–4.
24 *Ibid* (n 20) pages 1 and 4.
25 Report National Police Chiefs' Council, College of Policing and Crown Prosecution Service, 'National Disclosure Improvement Plan: Phase Two – Embedding Culture Change and Continuous Improvement' (2018) <https://www.cps.gov.uk/sites/default /files/documents/publications/National-Disclosure-Improvement-Plan-Phase-Two -Nov-18.pdf>, pdf, 2.

i. To improve police and prosecution capability when dealing with extensive amounts of digital material[26]
ii. To transform the (police) culture in order to accept disclosure as being an integral part of the criminal investigation and prosecution.[27]
iii. To improve communication between prosecution and defence with regard to materials which have to be disclosed.[28]

Especially the action sub ii above seems vital to prevent miscarriages of justice such as the one prevented in R. v. Allan. Apart from the NDIP reports, also the UK House of Commons Justice Committee, based on an inquiry into Disclosure Practices in Criminal Cases initiated in January 2018, produced a report.[29] In this report, a direct relation was made between disclosure obligations and the prevention of miscarriages of justice.[30]

In the context of preventing miscarriages of justice which can be caused by improper disclosure, in so far as this arises from police culture (factor sub i above) two other problems emerge:

i. The disclosure test is not always correctly applied by police investigators and prosecutors. This problem was identified in a report of the UK Attorney General's office in November 2018, called 'Review of the Efficiency and Effectiveness of Disclosures in the Criminal Justice System'.[31]
ii. Prosecutors must always make the proper inquiries themselves to prevent failure of disclosure obligations.[32]

The disclosure test as mentioned sub i hereabove is codified in the UK Criminal Procedure and Investigations Act 1996. The essence of this test is to ensure that the police and prosecution services provide to the defence all the necessary material if this material "[...] might reasonably be considered capable of undermining the case for the Prosecution against the accused, and/or of assisting the case for the accused and which has not previously been disclosed."[33]

---

26   *Ibid.*
27   *Ibid*, 7; *Ibid* (n 20) page 5.
28   *Ibid* (n 25) page 9.
29   House of Commons Justice Committee, 'Disclosure of Evidence in Criminal Cases' (2018) <https://publications.parliament.uk/pa/cm201719/cmselect/cmjust/859/859.pdf>, pdf; discussed in Claire Brader, 'Disclosure of Evidence in Criminal Proceedings' (2020) House of Lords Library Briefing 1, 6–7.
30   House of Commons Justice Committee, 'Disclosure of Evidence in Criminal Cases' (2018) <https://publications.parliament.uk/pa/cm201719/cmselect/cmjust/859/859.pdf>, pdf, 18.
31   *Ibid*, 7; See also Claire Brader, 'Disclosure of Evidence in Criminal Proceedings' (2020) House of Lords Library Briefing 1, 8.
32   *Ibid.*
33   Claire Brader, 'Disclosure of Evidence in Criminal Proceedings' (2020) House of Lords Library Briefing 1, 2.

It is the combination of the abovementioned measure sub ii (i.e. to transform the police culture) with proper training on and prosecutorial supervision of the described disclosure test, which is pivotal to prevent wrongful prosecutions. In addition, the implementation of this disclosure test is to be performed "[...] from the onset rather than as an afterthought".[34]

18.6 Conclusion

Disclosure of exculpatory materials in criminal trials, both nationally and internationally, pertains to the right of an accused person to have access to investigation material that is capable of refuting the prosecution's case and/or assisting the defence case in establishing the innocence or in mitigating the accused's guilt.[35]

As the UK Ministry of Justice conceded in a report of 18 December 2018: "Ensuring the process of disclosure is done correctly and considerably is essential to maintaining a fair justice system [...]."[36] The same report, referring to "systemic problems with disclosure" calls for "sustainable culture change and improvement."[37]

These observations and subsequent recommendations equally should be transposed onto the 'materiality' principle which is applied by the ICC Trial Chambers. Fair disclosure of criminal evidence is ultimately a matter of professional integrity, notwithstanding the level at which the accused person is tried.

---

34   *Ibid*, 8.
35   *Ibid*, 1.
36   Ministry of Justice, 'Government Response to the Justice Select Committee's Eleventh Report of Session 2017–2019: Disclosure of Evidence in Criminal Cases' (2018) <https://assets.publishing.service.gov.uk/government/uploads/system/uploads/attachment_data/file/763763/gov-res-jsc-report-disclosure-evidence-criminal-cases.pdf>, pdf, 3; quoted by Claire Brader, 'Disclosure of Evidence in Criminal Proceedings' (2020) House of Lords Library Briefing 1, 8.
37   *Ibid*.

PART 7

Weighing Evidence at ICC Trials

∴

CHAPTER 19

Evidence Presentation in ICC Trials

19.1 Practices at the ICC

In the case of *Yekatom and Ngaïssona*, the Trial Chamber of the ICC repeatedly recalled that it is not the written statement of a witness that is ultimately decisive, but the oral testimony under oath during the trial.[1] This view is an exponent of an adversarial model of presenting evidence at trial.[2] Within this model, also partially endorsed by the Rome Statute, each party, Prosecution and Defence, may present their own evidence to support their case.[3]

Accordingly, similar to the ICTY and ICTR, the ICC framework sets forth the following model of presentation of evidence:

(i) Introduction of witnesses and experts (and documentary evidence) by the Prosecution;[4]

(ii) Introduction of witnesses by the Legal Representatives of Victims (LRV);[5]

---

1 See for example *Prosecutor v Yekatom and Ngaïssona* (Decision on the Prosecution Requests for Formal Submission of Prior Recorded Testimonies under Rule 68(3) of the Rules concerning Witnesses P-1962, P-0925, P-2193, P-2926, P-2927, P-1577 and P-0287, and the Ngaïssona Defence Motion to Limit the Scope of P-2926's Evidence) ICC-01/14-01/18-907-Red, T Ch V (1 April 2021) para. 14.

2 Robert Cryer, Darryl Robinson and Sergey Vasiliev, An Introduction to International Criminal Law and Procedure (4th edn, Cambridge University Press 2019) 406; Kai Ambos, Treatise on International Criminal Law: International Criminal Procedure, vol 3 (Oxford University Press 2016) 5–6.

3 Richard May and Marieke Wierda, *International Criminal Evidence*, vol 9 (Brill 2021) 144 <https://brill.com/display/title/13900#navigation> accessed 14 June 2023.

4 *Prosecutor v Gbagbo and Blé Goudé* (Directions on the conduct of the proceedings) ICC-02/11-01/15-205, T Ch I (3 September 2015) para. 12; *Prosecutor v Yekatom and Ngaïssona* (Initial Directions on the Conduct of the Proceedings) ICC-01/14-01/18-631, T Ch V (26 August 2020) para. 16; *Prosecutor v Ongwen* (Initial Directions on the Conduct of the Proceedings) ICC-02/04-01/15-497, T Ch IX (13 July 2016) para. 9.

5 *Prosecutor v Gbagbo and Blé Goudé* (Directions on the conduct of the proceedings) ICC-02/11-01/15-205, T Ch I (3 September 2015) para. 12; *Prosecutor v Yekatom and Ngaïssona* (Initial Directions on the Conduct of the Proceedings) ICC-01/14-01/18-631, T Ch V (26 August 2020) para. 16; *Prosecutor v Ongwen* (Initial Directions on the Conduct of the Proceedings) ICC-02/04-01/15-497, T Ch IX (13 July 2016) para. 9.
   However, this introduction is limited, as it is for the Prosecution to establish the alleged crimes. Therefore, the questioning shall be limited "to matters relevant to the personal interests of the victims. This may, for instance, include questions about harms which the witness personally suffered or harms of other victims which the witness observed". Cf. *Prosecutor v Yekatom and Ngaïssona* (Initial Directions on the Conduct of the Proceedings) ICC-01/14-01/18-631, T Ch V (26 August 2020) para. 19.

(iii) Introduction of witnesses and experts by the Defence;[6]
(iv) Potential rebuttal evidence by the Prosecution;[7]
(v) At any time during the presentation of evidence, calling of witnesses by the Trial Chamber and order to produce documents and other evidence if necessary for the determination of the truth.[8]

With regard to the order of examination of witnesses at trial, ICC practice – similar to common law procedure – has in principle adopted the following sequence:

(i) Examinations in chief by the calling party;[9]
(ii) Examination by the non-calling party (also known as cross-examination);[10]
(iii) Potential re-examination by the calling party. This type of examination is essentially limited to areas that were only raised during cross-examination and could not be foreseen by the calling party.[11]
(iv) When the Prosecution is the calling party, the LRV may question the witness thereafter (if leave is granted).[12] When the Defence is the calling party, the LRV may question the witness after the examination by the non-calling party (with leave).[13]

---

6   *Prosecutor v Gbagbo and Blé Goudé* (Directions on the conduct of the proceedings) ICC-02/11-01/15-205, T Ch I (3 September 2015) para. 12; *Prosecutor v Yekatom and Ngaïssona* (Initial Directions on the Conduct of the Proceedings) ICC-01/14-01/18-631, T Ch V (26 August 2020) para. 16; *Prosecutor v Ongwen* (Initial Directions on the Conduct of the Proceedings) ICC-02/04-01/15-497, T Ch IX (13 July 2016) para. 9.

7   *Prosecutor v Gbagbo and Blé Goudé* (Directions on the conduct of the proceedings) ICC-02/11-01/15-205, T Ch I (3 September 2015) para. 12; *Prosecutor v Ongwen* (Initial Directions on the Conduct of the Proceedings) ICC-02/04-01/15-497, T Ch IX (13 July 2016) para. 9.

8   Article 64(6)(b) and Article 69(3) RS; Rule 140(2)(c) ICC RPE; *Prosecutor v Gbagbo and Blé Goudé* (Directions on the conduct of the proceedings) ICC-02/11-01/15-205, T Ch I (3 September 2015) paras 12 and 27.

9   *Prosecutor v Gbagbo and Blé Goudé* (Directions on the conduct of the proceedings) ICC-02/11-01/15-205, T Ch I (3 September 2015) paras 27–29; *Prosecutor v Ongwen* (Initial Directions on the Conduct of the Proceedings) ICC-02/04-01/15-497, T Ch IX (13 July 2016) para. 10; *Prosecutor v Bemba et al.* (Directions on the conduct of the proceedings) ICC-01/05-01/13-1209, T Ch VII (2 September 2015) para. 10.

10 *Prosecutor v Gbagbo and Blé Goudé* (Directions on the conduct of the proceedings) ICC-02/11-01/15-205, T Ch I (3 September 2015) paras 27–29.

11 Ibid (n 10) para. 38., where the Chamber held: "in exceptional circumstances, the calling party may be permitted to reexamine its witness, but shall be limited to issues raised for the first time during questioning by the non-calling parties or the LRV. If the Chamber permits the Prosecution to re-examine its witness, the Defence teams will be permitted to ask any final questions of the witnesses in accordance with Rule 140(2)(d) of the Rules".

12 Ibid (n 10) para. 28.

13 Ibid (n 10) para. 29.

ICC Chambers have quite some discretion in issuing guidelines on how to conduct trial proceedings. For instance, in the case of *Yekatom* and *Ngaïssona*, the Trial Chamber came to a specific direction for the two Defence teams:

> With a view to ensuring the most efficient and streamlined presentation of evidence by the Defence, the Chamber considers that if the Defence elects to present evidence, their presentation is to take place by topic, rather than one Defence team after the other. The Chamber considers that this will be the best manner specifically to avoid overlap and to maintain a meaningful structure of the presentation, with a view to best assisting the Chamber in making its determinations. The Chamber therefore directs the Defence to organise their presentation of evidence in the following thematic order, to the extent possible:
> - Contextual/background evidence;
> - Individual criminal responsibility;
> - Attack in Bangui on 5 December 2013 and events thereafter;
> - Events at Yamwara School Base;
> - Events concerning PK9-Mbaïki axis;
> - Children under the age of 15 years alleged to be associated with the Anti-Balaka; and
> - Attack in Bossangoa on 5 December 2013 and events thereafter.[14]
>
> Having regard to the proceedings and conduct of the Defence teams to date, the Chamber trusts that within this thematic order, the Defence teams will be able to agree between themselves in which order they will call witnesses. Equally, the Defence teams are to agree inter partes on any witnesses common to their presentation of evidence.[15]
>
> Witnesses will first be questioned by the Defence team calling them, followed by the other Defence team, the Prosecution, and the CLRV, if leave is granted. The non-calling Defence team may ask leave to question the witness further after the questioning by the Prosecution and the CLRV, if any. The presenting Defence team shall have the right to be the last to question a witness, in accordance with Rule 140(2)(d) of the Rules. If a witness is common to the presentation of evidence of both Defence

---

14 *Prosecutor v Yekatom and Ngaïssona* (Further Directions on the Conduct of the Proceedings (Presentation of Evidence by the CLRV and the Defence)) ICC-01/14-01/18-1892, T Ch V (29 May 2023) para. 25.
15 *Ibid* para. 26.

teams, they shall agree inter partes on the order of questioning between themselves.[16]

Thus, in deviation from the normal order, whereby defence teams present evidence one after the other, in this case the presentation of evidence essentially meant a 'joint presentation' by topic. Important for the presentation of the defence's case is the Court's reference to the right of the defence, presenting the witness, to be the last to question a witness. This may allow the defence to re-emphasise the most important part of the testimony.

19.2 Presentation of Evidence by Way of Leading Questions

In common law systems, the use of leading questions is accepted as a main principle of adversarial proceedings.[17] Leading questions are questions that directly suggest to the witness the answer the interviewer desires, and are usually considered appropriate – among other cases – during cross-examination or when questioning hostile or adverse witnesses.[18] Yet, the person conducting the cross-examination may not mislead the witness by adducing facts that the witness must admit and which have no basis in fact.[19]

At the International Criminal Court, the Trial Chambers allow non-calling parties to (cross)examine the calling party's witnesses beyond the scope of direct examination, particularly when the credibility of the witness is at stake. This departs from the closed system of the U.S. Federal Rules of Procedure and Evidence.[20]

In fact, one of the main purposes of cross-examination is also to subject the calling party's witness to the non-calling party's narrative when the latter contradicts the calling party's evidence.[21] Apart from the argument of fairness to the witness, so that he or she can respond to the opposing party, it is an opportunity for the non-calling party to question the calling party's evidence.[22]

---

16   *Ibid* para. 27.
17   Thomas Mauet, *Trials: Strategy, Skills, And the New Powers of Persuasion* (1st edn, Aspen Publishers 2005) 212; *Ibid* (n 3).
18   *Ibid*; 'Leading Question', *Legal Information Institut* (Cornell University insignia) <https://www.law.cornell.edu/wex/leading_question#content> accessed 3 November 2023.
19   *Ibid*.
20   Thomas Mauet, *Trials: Strategy, Skills, And the New Powers of Persuasion* (1st edn, Aspen Publishers 2005) 213.
21   *Ibid* (n 3).
22   *Ibid*.

After all, cross-examination serves not only to question the credibility of the witness, but also to reveal facts that support the non-calling party's case. Importantly, Thomas Mauet introduces the so-called '90-percent rule' by saying: "during cross-examination you should be doing almost all of the talking (90 percent), and the witness should be giving one-word or short answers (10 percent)".[23]

Overall, the questioning of a witness based on leading questions remains a controversial topic at the ICC.

19.3 Presenting Evidence at Opening and Closing Statements

As Thomas Mauet claims: 'the essence of effective closing arguments is argumentation, which goes beyond the mere summarizing the evidence.'[24] The aim of closing arguments is to put the evidence in perspective and to show how and why it deconstructs the narrative of the adverse party. To this end, closing arguments should include two important elements:

(i) They should start with the strongest argument or piece of evidence which disproves the charges;
(ii) They should re-construct the own narrative based on facts or inference of facts which are in evidence.[25]

At the International Criminal Court, the Defence may present an opening statement directly after the Prosecution's opening statement, or postpone the opening statement until the beginning of the Defence's case. The advantage of presenting an opening statement directly after the Prosecution's opening statement could be that the Defence's opening statement may counterbalance the allegations and narrative of the Prosecution already at the beginning of the trial. This may already have an impact on the perception of the prosecution's case by the court and the public.

Thomas Mauet, in his important work on trial strategies, provides the following suggestions:

1. 'Work backward. Plan your closing argument first, because everything else then follows.
2. When you have outlined your planned closing argument, you will also know what should be in your opening statement.

---

23 Thomas Mauet, *Trials: Strategy, Skills, And the New Powers of Persuasion* (1st edn, Aspen Publishers 2005) 218.
24 *Ibid*, page 463.
25 *Ibid* 463–468.

3. It is important to make sure that your opening statement and closing argument are consistent.
4. Your opening statement has to bring out your theory of the case [...] it must anticipate what your opponent is likely to say in his opening statement.'[26]

As for the opening statement, also at the ICC, it is for the defence lawyer to present not only the narrative and theory of the defence case, without arguing the alleged evidence, but also, if possible, to personalise the defendant to the Court. Consequently, both opening and closing statements can be an important tool of the defence to convince the judges that the defence's case is more probable than the prosecution's case.

19.4 Conclusion

The order of presentation of evidence at the International Criminal Court, as illustrated in this chapter, remains a matter in which the ICC Court Chambers have considerable room for manoeuvre. The same applies to the modalities of cross-examination. This implies that a defendant, depending on the Trial Chamber, may be subject to a different regime than another defendant tried by another Chamber. A more uniform system could therefore benefit legal certainty.

---

26   *Ibid* 19.

CHAPTER 20

No Case to Answer Proceedings at the ICC

20.1 Introduction

This chapter deals with the standards of review regarding 'no case to answer' motions. In order for such motions to be successful, two elements are required. The first element entails showing that the Prosecution's case is on the 'brink of collapse' (also commonly referred to as 'completely breaking down). The second element refers to the evidence presented being 'incapable of belief'.

This chapter aims to analyse these two elements, which includes identifying the factors that are considered in their assessment.

20.2 Historical Background on 'No Case to Answer' Motions

A 'no case to answer' motion is filed to argue that the Prosecution has not presented sufficient evidence to reasonably support a conviction. It can also be filed simply to argue that a reasonable case was not presented which a reasonable Trial Chamber could support. Essentially, the aim and effect of a successful 'no case to answer' motion is to issue a full or partial judgment of acquittal.[1] Put differently, it allows trial chambers to assess and evaluate witness credibility which in turn would avoid the continuation of a trial for several years with no real prospect of a conviction.[2]

The history of the 'no case to answer' motion goes back centuries. It is a procedural rule originating in common law systems, which naturally follows from the presumption of innocence: an accused should not have to defend themselves if the Prosecution has not produced sufficient evidence that could support an actual case against them.[3] Indeed, if the evidence presented does not constitute a case, it does not merit a response.

---

1 *Prosecutor v Ruto and Sang* (Decision No. 5 on the Conduct of Trial Proceedings (Principles and Procedure on 'No Case to Answer' Motions)) ICC-01/09-01/11-1334, T Ch V(a) (3 June 2014) para. 22.
2 *Prosecutor v Ruto and Sang* (Public redacted version of: Decision on Defence Applications for Judgments of Acquittal) ICC-01/09-01/11-2027-Red-Corr, T Ch V(a) (5 April 2016) Separate reasons of Judge Fremr, para. 144.
3 Ady Niv, 'The Schizophrenia of the "no Case to Answer" Test in International Criminal Tribunals' (2016) 14 Journal of international criminal justice 1121, 1121–1122; *Prosecutor v*

'No case to answer' motions also promote efficiency and judicial economy. As a matter of fact, it would be superfluous for the trial to proceed if no charge has been brought against a defendant.[4] The case of *R. v Galbraith*[5] – considered to be the *locus classicus* of the 'no case to answer' motions in the UK and as the basis of the standard for this type of procedure in international courts and tribunals – summarises the criteria for a successful 'no case to answer' motion by elaborating a two-limb test:

(1) If there is no evidence that the crime alleged has been committed by the defendant, there is no difficulty – the judge will stop the case.
(2) The difficulty arises where there is some evidence but it is of a tenuous character, for example because of inherent weakness or vagueness or because it is inconsistent with other evidence.
   (a) Where the judge comes to the conclusion that the prosecution evidence, taken at its highest, is such that a jury properly directed could not properly convict upon it, it is his duty, upon a submission being made, to stop the case.
   (b) Where however the prosecution evidence is such that its strength or weakness depends on the view to be taken of a witness's reliability or other matters which are generally speaking within the province of the jury and where on one possible view of the facts there is evidence upon which a jury could properly come to the conclusion that the defendant is guilty, then the judge should allow the matter to be tried by the jury.[6]

The second limb shows that the standard was originally intended for jury trials. Nevertheless, international criminal tribunals – where judges are both judges of fact and judges of law – have considered this motion possible before such courts as well. Thus, this second part of the test is generally 'translated' into the answer to the question 'whether the Prosecution has produced evidence on the basis of which a reasonable trier of fact could be convinced beyond reasonable doubt of the guilt of the accused'.[7]

Gbagbo and Blé Goudé (Judgment in the appeal of the Prosecutor against Trial Chamber 1's decision on the no case to answer motions) ICC-02/11-01/15-1400, A Ch (31 March 2021).

4 Ady Niv, 'The Schizophrenia of the "no Case to Answer" Test in International Criminal Tribunals' (2016) 14 Journal of international criminal justice 1121, 1122.

5 *R v Galbraith* [1981] 1 WLR 1039.

6 'No Case to Answer' (*Defence-Barrister.co.uk*) <https://www.defence-barrister.co.uk/submission-of-no-case-to-answer> accessed 17 December 2023; Ady Niv, 'The Schizophrenia of the "no Case to Answer" Test in International Criminal Tribunals' (2016) 14 Journal of international criminal justice 1121, 1122.

7 *Ibid* 1123.

After the establishment of the ICC Rules of Procedure and Evidence in 2002, a group of experts recommended the adoption of a 'no case to answer' mechanism at the ICC. They stated that:

> [If] the defence chooses not to coordinate 'its case' with the prosecution case and a more adversarial form of presentation of evidence is adopted, there may be a possibility, after presentation of the prosecution evidence, to 'purge' the case, dropping those charges and incidents that have not been sufficiently substantiated by the evidence (the so-called, 'no case to answer' test in common law jurisdictions, leading to an advanced judgment of acquittal). Application of this procedural device will shorten the presentation of evidence by the defence, since the defence need only respond to charges that have passed a 'no case to answer' test. This is not explicitly provided for in the Statute or the Rules but would probably still be a possible tool for the Court to employ. It may be, however, that there will not be much room for using this device due to the test conducted when the charges are confirmed.[8]

However, despite a general recognition of the 'no case to answer' institution in the Rules of international ad hoc courts and tribunals,[9] this procedure is not yet covered by the ICC Rules of Procedure and Evidence. So far, there have been only two precedents in which the motion was filed, and a third in which its admissibility was questioned, although eventually seen as not inherently incompatible – and therefore permissible – under the Court's legal framework.[10]

---

[8] ICC-OTP, 'Informal Expert Paper: Measures Available to the International Criminal Court to Reduce the Length of Proceedings' (International Criminal Court 2003) para. 91 <https://asp.icc-cpi.int/sites/asp/files/asp_docs/library/organs/otp/length_of_proceedings.pdf> accessed 17 December 2023.

[9] Cf. Rule 98bis of the ICTY Rules, Rule 98bis of the ICTR Rules, Rule 98 of the SCSL Rules, Rule 167 of the STL Rules, Rule 130 of the KSC Rules, and Rule 121 of the IRMCT Rules; *Prosecutor v Gbagbo and Blé Goudé* (Judgment in the appeal of the Prosecutor against Trial Chamber I's decision on the no case to answer motions) ICC-02/11-01/15-1400, A Ch (31 March 2021) footnote 208.

[10] *Prosecutor v Ntaganda* (Judgment on the appeal of Mr Bosco Ntaganda against the "Decision on Defence request for leave to file a 'no case to answer' motion") ICC-01/04-02/06-2026, A Ch (5 September 2017) paras 43–45.

20.3 Jurisprudence of International *ad hoc* Tribunals

At the International Criminal Court, the Trial Chamber in the case of *Ruto & Sang* adopted the same general standard as consistently applied by ICTY and ICTR trial chambers when assessing motions pursuant to Rule 98*bis* of their respective Rules of Procedure and Evidence. Indeed, these Rules 98*bis* contain provisions similar to the 'no case to answer' procedure as in practice before the ICC, as will be seen in this chapter.

This section will evaluate the jurisprudence relating to the similar provisions of a 'no case to answer' motion across international courts and tribunals (ICTY, ICTR, and SCSL), while the next sections will focus on the International Criminal Court. Before proceeding to an assessment of such jurisprudence, it should be recalled that the basic question is whether a reasonable trier of fact could convict the accused on the basis of the prosecution evidence.[11] The function of a motion under Rule 98*bis* (Rule 98 motion) is foreshadowed in the case of *Strugar*, where the Trial Chamber observed that:

> Rule 98*bis* is a safeguard where the object and proper orientation of the Rule should not be lost sight of. Its essential function is to bring an end to only those proceedings in respect of a charge for which there is no evidence on which a chamber could convict, rather than to terminate prematurely cases where the evidence is weak.[12]

Notably, Rule 98*bis* does not apply on appeal.[13] Instead, it places an obligation on Trial Chambers after the close of the Prosecution's case and after hearing oral submissions of the parties, to enter a judgment of acquittal on any count if there is no evidence capable of supporting a conviction.[14]

20.3.1 ICTY Jurisprudence

Rule 98bis concerning the judgment of acquittal at the ICTY read as followed:

> At the close of the Prosecutor's case, the Trial Chamber shall, by oral decision and after hearing the oral submissions of the parties, enter a

---

11 *Prosecutor v Kubura* (Appeals judgment) IT-01-47-A, A Ch (22 April 2008) para. 51.
12 *Prosecutor v Kubura* (Decision on Motions for Acquittal pursuant to Rule 98 bis of the Rules of Procedure and Evidence) IT-01-47-T, T Ch (27 September 2004) para. 20.
13 *Ibid* (n 11).
14 *Prosecutor v Krajisnik* (Decision on Appeal of Rule 98 bis Decision) IT-00-39-AR98bis.1, A Ch (4 October 2005) para. 3.

judgement of acquittal on any count if there is no evidence capable of supporting a conviction.[15]

20.3.1.1   ICTY Standard for a 98bis Judgement of Acquittal

The general test to be applied in order to determine whether there is a no case to answer at the end of the Prosecution's case is 'whether there is evidence upon which, if accepted, a reasonable tribunal of fact could be satisfied beyond reasonable doubt of the guilt of the accused on the particular charge in question'.[16] Therefore, the key concept is not whether the Chamber could arrive at a conviction beyond reasonable doubt based on the prosecution's evidence, but rather *the test is whether or not a reasonable trier of fact could do so*. Hence, the Prosecution's evidence must be capable of belief by a reasonable trier of fact.

In this regard, 'belief' is established in the context of the prosecution's evidence which, if believed, is sufficient to allow a reasonable trier of fact to potentially conclude a conviction. A Trial Chamber must conclude that a reasonable trier of fact could be satisfied beyond reasonable doubt that the evidence adduced, if believed, could sustain a finding of guilt.

20.3.1.2   Origins

After an examination of a range of national legislation, the Trial Chamber in the case of *Kordić and Čerkez* was the first to establish the two primary elements needed for a successful 'no case to answer' (or Rule 98*bis* motion). In particular, the Chamber stated:

> The test that the Chamber has enunciated – evidence on which a reasonable Chamber could convict – proceeds on the basis that generally the Chamber would not consider questions of credibility and reliability in dealing with a motion under Rule 98 bis, leaving those matters to the end of the case. However, there is one situation in which the Chamber is obliged to consider such matters; it is where the Prosecution's case has completely broken down, either on its own presentation, or as a result of such fundamental questions being raised through cross examination as to the reliability and credibility of witnesses that the Prosecution is left without a case.[17]

---

15 Adopted 10 July 1998, amended 17 Nov 1999, amended 8 Dec 2004.
16 *Prosecutor v Karadzic* (Appeals judgment) IT-95-5/18-AR98bis.1, A Ch (11 July 2013) para. 21.
17 *Prosecutor v Kordić and Čerkez* (Decision on Defence Motions for Judgment of Acquittal) IT-95-14-2, T Ch (6 April 2000) para. 28.

The Rule 98*bis* standard was further refined in the case of *Brdjanin*, where the Trial Chamber agreed with the *Amicus Curiae* Prosecutor, making the following submissions – in line with the jurisprudence of the Tribunal:[18]

a) In applying the test, the Trial Chamber should not assess the credibility and reliability of the Prosecution evidence unless the "evidence is so manifestly unreliable or incredible that no reasonable tribunal of fact could credit it", i.e., unless the Prosecution case can be said to have 'completely broken down' in that no trier of fact could accept the evidence relied upon by the Prosecution to maintain its case on a particular issue.[19]

b) In that regard, inconsistencies in the Prosecution evidence are matters for consideration in assessing credibility and reliability of the evidence, and, thus, are matters for consideration at the conclusion of the case, not at this stage.[20]

c) The Trial Chamber should not consider evidence favourable to the Respondent. It is at the conclusion of the proceedings, not at this midway point, that the Trial Chamber should consider the extent to which any evidence is favourable to the Respondent, and the overall effect of such evidence in light of the other evidence of the case.[21]

However, the case of *Kordić and Čerkez*, as well as section A of the submissions of the *Amicus Curiae* Prosecutor, do not elaborate further on what is meant by the 'Prosecution's case completely breaking down', but reiterate that the Chamber in this case is not required to consider questions of credibility and reliability at this stage of the proceedings, except in the two aforementioned limited circumstances.

The Defence for Kordić submitted that the Prosecution evidence only touched upon persecutions in 9 municipalities, and therefore, the remaining 22 municipalities should be dismissed. The Trial Chamber disregarded this claim and submitted that "the Prosecution case relates to the participation of the accused in the highest levels of government, and the Defence should prepare its case accordingly. In particular, the Defence will not be expected to

---

18 *Prosecutor v Brdjanin* (Decision on Motion for Acquittal pursuant to Rule 98 bis) IT-99-36-R77, T Ch (19 March 2004) para. 9.

19 *Prosecutor v Kordić and Čerkez* (Decision on Defence Motions for Judgment of Acquittal) IT-95-14-2, T Ch (6 April 2000) para. 28; *Prosecutor v Galić* (Decision on the Motion for the entry of Acquittal of the Accused Stanislav Galic) IT-98-29-T, T Ch (3 October 2002) para. 11.

20 *Prosecutor v Kupriskic et al.* (Appeal judgment) IT-95-16-A, A Ch (23 October 2001) paras 332–334.

21 *Prosecutor v Brdjanin* (Decision on Motion for Acquittal pursuant to Rule 98 bis) IT-99-36-T, T Ch (28 November 2003) para. 62; *Ibid* (n 18).

call evidence concerning municipalities about which no evidence has been given".[22] Thus, making evident here that definitive linkage to each of the municipalities is not a requirement and further does not fall under the very limited exceptions of Rule 98*bis*.

20.3.1.3 Cannot 'Pick and Choose'

On a separate but related note, Trial Chambers cannot 'pick and choose' parts of the evidence. Indeed, a Trial Chamber is required to assume that the evidence presented by the Prosecution is entitled to credence, unless it is incapable of belief, and that the evidence must be taken at its highest.

At the International Criminal Court, this point was further highlighted by Judge Eboe-Osuji in the case of *Ruto & Sang*. Judge Eboe-Osuji considered the ICTY jurisprudence, citing the *Karadžic* Appeal Chamber which had famously held: "in deciding a no-case submission at that Tribunal, a Trial Chamber 'cannot "pick and choose among parts of [the prosecution] evidence" in reaching its conclusion'".[23]

This can be emulated to highlight the difficulty of a Trial Chamber in, first, assuming the Prosecution's evidence is taken at its highest unless it is incapable of belief, but second, and most importantly, that it cannot pick and choose which evidence to use in reaching its conclusion. Indeed, it would be an error of law not to consider evidence favourable to the accused elicited during the prosecution's case when deciding a motion for judgement of acquittal[24] and crucially, the Prosecution's evidence shall be presumed credible and reliable at the Rule 98*bis* stage unless a witness is so lacking in credibility or reliability that no reasonable trial Chamber could find them credible or reliable.[25]

A final example where this standard was used, applies to situations where the Trial Chamber did not consider evidence which might be favourable to the Accused, essentially implying that the evidence presented by the Defence in its favour during the Prosecution case had been completely ignored. As

---

22 *Prosecutor v Kordić and Čerkez* (Decision on Defence Motions for Judgment of Acquittal) IT-95-14-2, T Ch (6 April 2000) paras 30–32.

23 *Prosecutor v Ruto and Sang* (Public redacted version of: Decision on Defence Applications for Judgments of Acquittal) ICC-01/09-01/11-2027-Red-Corr, T Ch V(a) (5 April 2016) reasons of Judge Eboei Osuji, para. 51; *Prosecutor v Karadzic* (Appeal judgment) IT-95-5/18-AR98bis.1, A Ch (11 July 2013) para. 21.

24 *Prosecutor v Kubura* (Appeal judgment) IT-01-47-A, A Ch (22 April 2008) para. 55.

25 *Prosecutor v Mladić* (Public Redacted Version of Decision on Defence Interlocutory Appeal from the Trial Chamber Rule 98 bis Decision) IT-09-92-AR73.4, A Ch (24 July 2014) para. 20.

previously illustrated, such approach would amount to an error of law.[26] The *Kubura* Appeal judgement provided examples to this effect:

> where the Defence has cross-examined a witness to good effect or has obtained evidence in an accused's favour during cross-examination, *this evidence must be used to assess whether the Prosecution evidence is incapable of belief* [emphasis added].[27]

The Trial Chamber in this case had previously recognized this principle, but had referred in its Rule 98*bis* decision to the entirety of the testimonies, without excluding the cross-examination of the witnesses.

20.3.1.4   Evidence

On the issue of evidence, the *Jelsic* Appeals Judgement held that "The Trial Chamber was required to assume that the prosecution's evidence was entitled to credence unless incapable of belief".[28] Moreover, in *Kordić and Čerkez* it was stated that it is not necessary to define what is meant by evidence on which a reasonable trier of fact could convict, but rather that there must be some evidence which could properly lead to a conviction.[29] Furthermore, in *Strugar* it was held that 'if there is no evidence of an offence charged, or if it is unusual and the only relevant evidence when viewed as a whole is incapable of belief, then it could not properly support a conviction, even when taken at its highest for the Prosecution, a rule 98*bis* motion for acquittal will succeed.[30] "The evidence is insufficient to sustain a conviction" means a case in which in the opinion of the Trial Chamber, the prosecution evidence, if believed, is insufficient for any reasonable trier of fact to find that guilt has been proved beyond reasonable doubt.[31]

The evidence favourable to the accused may only be used to assess whether a piece of evidence is clearly unreliable and incapable of belief. Accordingly, a motion for acquittal will be granted only when there is no evidence capable of sustaining a conviction or when there is one or several pieces of evidence, but even when taken at their highest, this evidence the Trial Chamber could not

---

26 *Ibid* (n 24) para. 55.
27 *Ibid*.
28 *Prosecutor v Jelisic* (Appeal judgment) IT-95-10-A, A Ch (5 July 2001) para. 55.
29 *Ibid* (n 22) para. 26.
30 *Prosecutor v Strugar* (Decision on Defence Motion requesting Judgment of Acquittal pursuant to Rule 98 bis) IT-01-42-T, T Ch II (21 June 2004) para. 18.
31 *Prosecutor v Jelisic* (Appeal judgment) IT-95-10-A, A Ch (5 July 2001) para. 37.

sustain or decide for a conviction because the only evidence is clearly unreliable and incapable of belief.[32]

20.3.2 ICTR Jurisprudence

Turning to the jurisprudence of the ICTR, the Trial Chamber would not consider questions of credibility and reliability until the end of the case; however, there is one exception where Trial Chambers are obliged to consider issues of credibility and reliability under Rule 98*bis*:

> At the close of the Prosecutor's case, the Trial Chamber shall, by oral decision and after hearing the oral submissions of the parties, enter a judgement of acquittal on any count if there is no evidence capable of supporting a conviction.[33]

This exception is where the Prosecution's case has completely broken down, either on its own presentation, or as a result of such fundamental questions being raised through cross-examination as to the reliability and credibility of witnesses that the Prosecution is left without a case.[34]

20.3.2.1 ICTR Standard for a 98bis Judgement of Acquittal

Similar to the ICTY, in order to assess a situation regarding the credibility of Prosecutions witnesses, Trial Chambers must "assume that the prosecution's evidence [is] entitled to credence unless incapable of belief". The inquiry is simply to determine whether the evidence – assuming that it is true – could

---

32 *Prosecutor v Šešelj* (Public transcript) IT-03-67 (4 May 2011) pp. 16829 (lines 16–19), 16830 (lines 5–8), and 16831 (lines 1–8). Available at: http://www.icty.org/x/cases/seselj/trans/en/110504ED.htm.

33 Adopted 10 July 1998, amended 17 Nov 1999, amended 8 Dec 2004.

34 *Prosecutor v Kamuhanda* (Decision on Kamuhanda's Motion for Partial Acquittal Pursuant to Rule 98 bis of the Rules of Procedure and Evidence) ICTR-99-54A-T, T Ch II (20 August 2002) para. 19; *Prosecutor v Mpambara* (Decision on the Defence's Motion for Judgement of Acquittal) ICTR-2001-65-T, T Ch I (21 October 2005) para. 4; *Prosecutor v Muvunyi* (Decision on Tharcisse Muvunyi's Motion for Judgement of Acquittal Pursuant to Rule 98 bis) ICTR-2000-55A-T, T Ch II (13 October 2005) para. 37; *Prosecutor v Rwamakuba* (Decision on Defence Motion for Judgement of Acquittal) ICTR-98-44C-T, T Ch III (28 October 2005) para. 7; *Prosecutor v Zigiranyirazo* (Decision on the Defence Motion Pursuant to Rule 98 bis) ICTR-2001-73-T, T Ch III (21 February 2007) para. 11; *Prosecutor v Nchamihigo* (Decision on Defence Motion for Judgement of Acquittal) ICTR-2001-63-T, T Ch III (8 March 2007) para. 13; *Prosecutor v Ndindiliyimana et al.* (Decision on Defence Motions for Judgement of Acquittal) ICTR-2000-56-T, T Ch II (20 March 2007) para. 7.

not possibly sustain a finding of guilt beyond a reasonable doubt.[35] Thus, the standard that must be met is that a reasonable trier of fact, based on the Prosecution's evidence, could find the accused guilty of the crime charged.[36]

Importantly, contradictory evidence can still be reliable. The Trial Chamber in *Muvunyi* stipulated that there is no justification for discounting evidence given by a Prosecution witness who contradicted another witness as a reasonable motion for acquittal.[37] In this regard, the Trial Chamber in *Karemera et al.* declined to find a 'no case to answer' regarding contradictory witness testimonies as it preferred to wait until it heard all of the evidence before it would make a credibility determination.[38] The Chamber further extended this reasoning towards witnesses who recanted their testimonies during the Prosecution's case as it also preferred to wait until the end of the case whereby an investigation could take place regarding the false testimony of the witness.[39]

The test to be applied is whether the evidence, assuming it is true, could not possibly sustain a finding of guilt beyond reasonable doubt. That will only be the case where there is no evidence whatsoever which is probative of one or more of the required elements of a crime charged, or where the only such evidence is incapable of belief.[40]

A Rule 98*bis* motion will succeed if an essential ingredient for a crime was not made out in the Prosecution's case; or, if on the basis of evidence adduced

---

35 *Prosecutor v Bagosora et al.* (Decision on Motions for Judgement of Acquittal) ICTR-98-41-T, T Ch I (2 February 2005) para. 6; *Prosecutor v Nyiramasuhuko et al.* (Decision on Defence Motions for Acquittal Under Rule 98 bis) ICTR-98-42-T, T Ch II (16 December 2004) para. 71.

36 *Prosecutor v Bagosora et al.* (Decision on Motions for Judgement of Acquittal) ICTR-98-41-T, T Ch I (2 February 2005) para. 3; *Prosecutor v Nyiramasuhuko et al.* (Decision on Defence Motions for Acquittal Under Rule 98 bis) ICTR-98-42-T, T Ch II (16 December 2004) para. 71; *Prosecutor v Mpambara* (Decision on the Defence's Motion for Judgement of Acquittal) ICTR-2001-65-T, T Ch I (21 October 2005) para. 4; *Prosecutor v Muvunyi* (Decision on Tharcisse Muvunyi's Motion for Judgement of Acquittal Pursuant to Rule 98 bis) ICTR-2000-55A-T, T Ch II (13 October 2005) para. 35; *Prosecutor v Rwamakuba* (Decision on Defence Motion for Judgement of Acquittal) ICTR-98-44C-T, T Ch III (28 October 2005) para. 5; *Prosecutor v Ndindiliyimana et al.* (Decision on Defence Motions for Judgement of Acquittal) ICTR-2000-56-T, T Ch II (20 March 2007) para. 6.

37 *Prosecutor v Muvunyi* (Decision on Tharcisse Muvunyi's Motion for Judgement of Acquittal Pursuant to Rule 98 bis) ICTR-2000-5A-T, T Ch II (13 October 2005) para. 42.

38 *Prosecutor v Karemera et al.* (Decision on Joseph Nzirorera's Omnibus Motion on the Testimony of Ahmed Mbonyunkiza, Notice of 15th Violation of Rul e72(E), and Motion to Strike the Prosecution's Response) ICTR-98-44-T, (19 November 2008) para. 9.

39 *Prosecutor v Karemera et al.* (Decision on Joseph Nzirorera's Second Motion for Finding of No Case to Answer and Motion for Reconsideration) ICTR-98-44-T, (3 July 2008) para. 4.

40 *Prosecutor v Bizimungu et al.* (Decision on Defence Motions Pursuant to Rule 98 bis) ICTR-99-50-T, (22 November 2005) para. 4.

NO CASE TO ANSWER PROCEEDINGS AT THE ICC 307

by the Prosecution, an ingredient required as a matter of law to constitute the crime is missing, that evidence would also be insufficient to sustain a conviction.[41]

20.3.3 SCSL Jurisprudence

Similar to the ICTY and ICTR, the SCSL Trial Chamber stipulated that the plainer language of the amended Rule leaves no doubt that what must be considered by the Trial Chamber is not the reliability or credibility of the evidence, but merely its capability of supporting a conviction. Simply put, if one possible view of the facts may support a conviction,[42] then the Trial Chamber cannot enter a judgement of acquittal under Rule 98 that read:

> If after the close of the case for the Prosecution, there is no evidence capable of supporting a conviction on one or more counts of the indictment, the Trial Chamber shall enter a judgment of acquittal on those counts.[43]

Importantly, this jurisprudence held:

> To be incapable of belief, the evidence must be obviously incredible or unreliable; the Chamber should not be drawn into fine assessments of credibility or reliability. Needless to say, a finding that the evidence is not obviously incredible does not foreclose the Chamber, at the end of the trial, from finding that the evidence is, in fact, neither credible nor reliable.[44]

20.3.3.1   Necessary to acquit on an entire count

As a final caveat on the jurisprudence of the ad hoc tribunals, this paragraph will address the necessity to submit motions regarding an entire count and the charges within, rather than on partial portions of a count.

At the ICTY, *Mladić's* request for acquittal under Rule 98bis was rejected. The Trial Chamber confirmed that it was only appropriate to consider motions of acquittal regarding entire counts, rather than charges within a count. The Trial Chamber stated there is no good reason to depart from the well-established practice of the ICTY and look within each individual count and examine

---

41 *Nahimana et al.*, Reasons for Oral Decision of 17 September 2002 on the Motions for Acquittal (TC); *Ntagerura et al.*, T. 6 March 2002 (oral argument and decision) para. 19.
42 *Prosecutor v Brima, Kamara and Kanu* (Decision on Defence Motions for Judgement of Acquittal Pursuant to Rule 98) SCSL-04-16-T, T Ch II (31 March 2006) para. 8.
43 Amended on 14 May 2005.
44 *Ibid* para. 11.

whether or not the accused may be acquitted of partial portions of each count. Thus, the defence must present a 'no case to answer' motion on an entire count. In this case, *Mladić* sought acquittal on two counts of genocide and charges relating to individual crimes. However, the Trial Chamber found evidence that there was perpetrators" genocidal intent and that the accused significantly contributed to the Joint Criminal Enterprises implementation.[45]

20.4   Overview of 'No Case to Answer' Proceedings at the ICC

At the International Criminal Court, 'no case to answer' proceedings are relatively new features. To date, there have only been two instances in which the Defence was able to file such a motion.

Firstly, in the *Ruto & Sang* case, where both accused submitted an application for a ruling of a 'no case to answer' on all counts,[46] thus seeking an acquittal.[47] The application was successful: the Trial Chamber decided to vacate the charges against the accused. As a result, the Chamber 'discharged the accused without prejudice to their prosecution afresh in the future'.[48]

Secondly, in the *Gbagbo & Blé Goudé* case, where the Appeal Chamber found that "judgments of trial chambers for full acquittal of a defendant – following a no case to answer motion – fall entirely within the purview of article 74 of the Statute".[49] In this regard, the Chamber explained that "(t)his is primarily

---

45   Judgement Summary, Rule 98bis judgement summary in the case of Ratko Mladic. The Hague, 15 April 2014, CS/MS/16ooe available at: http://www.icty.org/en/press/tribunal-rejects-ratko-mladi%C4%87%E2%80%99s-request-acquittal

46   Following Rule 98bis under the ICTY, A trial chamber is only expected to determine whether the Prosecution has adduced enough evidence for each count taken as a whole as opposed to all the various charges making up that particular count. This also allows the defence the possibility not to answer all of the allegations contained in a count for which it feels that the prosecution failed to lead any evidence. *Prosecutor v Šešelj*, IT-03-67, 4 May 2011 Transcript, P. 16829, Lns. 16–19 and P. 16830 Lns. 5–8.

47   *Prosecutor v Ruto and Sang* (Public redacted version of "Corrigendum of Ruto Defence Request for Judgment of Acquittal", ICC-01/09-01/11-1990-Conf-Corr, 26 October 2015) ICC-01/09-01/11-1990-Corr-Red, T Ch V(A) (26 October 2015); *Prosecutor v Ruto and Sang* (Public Redacted Version of Sang Defence 'No Case to Answer' Motion, filed on 23 October 2015) ICC-01/09-01/11-1991-Red, T Ch V(A) (6 November 2015).

48   *Prosecutor v Ruto and Sang* (Public redacted version of: Decision on Defence Applications for Judgments of Acquittal) ICC-01/09-01/11-2027-Red-Corr, T Ch V(A) (5 April 2016) reasons of Judge Eboe-Osuji.

49   *Prosecutor v Gbagbo and Blé Goudé* (Judgment in the appeal of the Prosecutor against Trial Chamber I's decision on the no case to answer motions) ICC-02/11-01/15-1400, A Ch (31 March 2021) para. 109.

because that provision is intended to regulate Trial Chamber's final judgment that puts an end to the trial – either by way of a conviction or by way of an acquittal. It is true that an unsuccessful no case to answer motion does not, as such, contemplate a conviction of the defendant, and thus does not bring a case to a final conclusion. However, the incident of the motion is different in the event of a full acquittal of the defendant, following a successful no case to answer motion. The case is brought to conclusion, and the plea of double jeopardy – or ne bis in idem – fully attaches. For that reason, such judgments of acquittal fall entirely within the ambit of article 74. And they are to be fully regulated accordingly, in the same manner as a judgment resulting from a plenary trial. The Appeals Chamber is persuaded by the pronouncement of the ICTY Appeals Chamber to the same effect".[50]

Notably, in *Ntaganda* the Appeal Chamber found that defendants before the ICC are not entitled to file 'a no case to answer' motion as a right, but rather that Trial Chambers would have broad discretion over the matter. In particular, the Chamber held:

> While the Court's legal texts do not explicitly provide for a 'no case to answer' procedure in the trial proceedings before the Court, it nevertheless is permissible. A Trial Chamber may, in principle, decide to conduct or decline to conduct such a procedure in the exercise of its discretion.[51]

20.4.1 *What Is a 'No Case to Answer' Motion?*

As anticipated, before the ICC the 'no case to answer' motion was successfully used in the *Ruto and Sang* case. The Trial Chamber released Decision No. 5 to provide guidelines and specifically address the issue of witness credibility, stating that such issues would not be considered unless it could be shown that the Prosecution's case was on the 'brink of collapse' or when the evidence was 'incapable of belief'.[52]

---

50   *Prosecutor v Gbagbo and Blé Goudé* (Judgment in the appeal of the Prosecutor against Trial Chamber I's decision on the no case to answer motions) ICC-02/11-01/15-1400, A Ch (31 March 2021) para. 109; *Prosecutor v Karadzic* (Appeals judgment) IT-95-5/18-AR98bis.1, A Ch (11 July 2013) para. 9.

51   *Prosecutor v Ntaganda* (Judgment on the appeal of Mr Bosco Ntaganda against the "Decision on Defence request for leave to file a 'no case to answer' motion") ICC-01/04-02/06-2026, A Ch (5 September 2017) para. 1; *Prosecutor v Gbagbo and Blé Goudé* (Judgment in the appeal of the Prosecutor against Trial Chamber I's decision on the no case to answer motions) ICC-02/11-01/15-1400, A Ch (31 March 2021) para. 108.

52   *Prosecutor v Ruto and Sang* (Decision No. 5 on the Conduct of Trial Proceedings (Principles and Procedure on 'No Case to Answer' Motions)) ICC-01/09-01/11-1334, T Ch V(a) (3 June 2014) para. 24.

Thus, Decision No. 5 stipulated that questions of witness credibility would not be considered unless two elements could be established. The first element requires proving that the Prosecution's case is on the 'brink of collapse', which is also commonly referred to as 'completely breaking down'. The second element refers to the evidence presented being 'incapable of belief'.

This section aims to define these two elements, also identifying the factors that are taken into account in their evaluation.

20.4.2 Standard of Review

To begin, the Prosecution's evidence is intended to be taken 'at its highest' with the burden of proof set to be 'beyond a reasonable doubt'. Notably, Judge Eboe-Osuji stated that Decision No. 5 does not alter the standard under which the Prosecution bears the burden of proof. In this regard, he held:

> the assessment of witness credibility and the application of the standard of proof beyond reasonable doubt – are constant requirements of criminal litigation; even if it is accepted, for the sake of argument, that they are not questions appropriately engaged at the stage of no case to answer litigation. From the beginning to the end, the Prosecution was always required to prove its case beyond reasonable doubt and with credible evidence. Decision No. 5 did not alter those requirements – even if it is considered appropriate to hold off, until a later stage, the review of the evidence according to those standards. That being the case, it is only a matter of submission for the Prosecution to address, at any stage that they are called upon to do so, the constant question whether the prosecution evidence has met the requirements of credibility and the standard of proof beyond reasonable doubt. There is no prejudice involved.[53]

Moreover, Judge Fremr made it clear that the beyond any reasonable standard must be understood as a standard under which "a reasonable Trial Chamber could convict" and that such Chamber "could be satisfied beyond reasonable doubt of the guilt of the accused";[54] or, in the words of Judge Eboe-Osuji, "[i]n more concrete terms, then, the point is about the presence of acceptable

---

53 *Prosecutor v Ruto and Sang* (Public redacted version of: Decision on Defence Applications for Judgments of Acquittal) ICC-01/09-01/11-2027-Red-Corr, T Ch V(a) (5 April 2016) Separate reasons of Judge Eboe-Osuji, para. 88 [emphasis added].

54 *Prosecutor v Ruto and Sang* (Public redacted version of: Decision on Defence Applications for Judgments of Acquittal) ICC-01/09-01/11-2027-Red-Corr, T Ch V(a) (5 April 2016) para. 18.

evidence upon which the reasonable trier of fact 'could properly' convict".[55] However, there are instances where the evidence presented could, and should, be challenged. This may be done in the form of a 'no case to answer' motion.

As mentioned above, there is no explicit provision, either in the Rome Statute or in the Rules of Procedure and Evidence, which regulates the 'no case to answer' procedure. It is because of this absence in the law of the International Criminal Court that the Trial Chamber in *Ruto & Sang* took up the challenge of setting out the guidelines for a no case to answer motion under Article 64 of the Rome Statute.[56] Decision No. 5 set out the test for a no case to answer motion by stating that:

> [T]he test to be applied in determining a 'no case to answer' motion, if any, in this case is whether there is evidence on which a reasonable Trial Chamber could convict. In conducting this analysis, each count in the Document Containing the Charges will be considered separately and, for each count, it is only necessary to satisfy the test in respect of one mode of liability, as pleaded or for which a Regulation 55 of the Regulations notice has been issued by the Chamber. The Chamber will not consider questions of reliability or credibility relating to the evidence, save where the evidence in question is incapable of belief by any reasonable Trial Chamber.[57]

Taking the test into consideration, in his reasoning Judge Eboe-Osuji confirmed that "there is a 'no case to answer' only if the evidence is not capable in law of supporting a conviction".[58] this way, he implied that there must be room for doubt about the credibility of the evidence presented by the prosecution, to make it unreasonable to support a conviction.

In her Dissenting opinion, Judge Herrera Carbuccia considered that the only exception to the principle where the Chamber should consider matters of credibility and reliability is when the Prosecution's case has completely broken

---

55   *Prosecutor v Ruto and Sang* (Public redacted version of: Decision on Defence Applications for Judgments of Acquittal) ICC-01/09-01/11-2027-Red-Corr, T Ch v(a) (5 April 2016) Separate reasons of Judge Eboe-Osuji, para. 47.
56   *Ibid* (n 52) para. 32.
57   *Ibid*.
58   *Questions of Law Reserved on Acquittal (No 2 of 1993)* 61 SASR 1 [Supreme Court of South Australia, Full Court], para. 18, per King CJ. As seen in: *Prosecutor v Ruto and Sang* (Public redacted version of: Decision on Defence Applications for Judgments of Acquittal) ICC-01/09-01/11-2027-Red-Corr, T Ch v(a) (5 April 2016) Separate reasons of Judge Eboe-Osuji, para. 70.

down, either on its own presentation, or as a result of such fundamental questions being raised through examination as to the reliability and credibility of witnesses that the Prosecution is left without a case.[59] This opinion introduces the factors to be considered for the exception of a 'no case to answer' to be allowed, i.e. when the Prosecution's case has completely broken down, or secondly when the reliability of the evidence is questioned.

20.4.3   The Concept of 'Brink of Collapse'

This section will turn to what it means for the Prosecution's case to be on the 'brink of collapse' or alternatively, 'completely broken down'. To begin, the question of what it means to be on the brink of collapse is under-discussed and under-used in practice. Judge Fremr shares a similar sentiment, when stating: "I appreciate that one can differ in the understanding of when a case has 'completely broken down'".[60] However, in his reasoning, he focuses on the evidence provided by the witnesses.

The first factor to be considered is whether the prosecution's entire case hangs on the testimony of a sole witness: where initially it was intended to rely on multiple witnesses, it can certainly be argued that the case teeters on the brink of breaking down.[61] In other words, if the Prosecution's entire case rests on the evidence of only one witness, or if some crucial elements of the charges rest on the evidence of only one witness, the accused cannot be substantially held accountable and the case is therefore bound to be on the brink of collapse. All in all, to make a crucial element of the charges rely on the evidence of only one witness is first and foremost implausible, since it can be argued that such substantial evidence for the prosecution's case would require several witnesses to corroborate it, and thus shows that the prosecution has gambled on a case that is about to collapse.

The second factor to be considered is a central element and depends on the weight attached to the specific testimony of the witness in question. If it is central, as evident in *Ruto & Sang*, it can be concerned to fulfil the element and thus be found to be on the brink of collapse.

After assessing these factors, the third factor to take into account is the question, according to Judge Fremr, of whether there is a point in continuing the

---

[59]   *Prosecutor v Ruto and Sang* (Annex I Dissenting Opinion of Judge Herrera Carbuccia) ICC-01/09-01/11-2027-AnxI, T Ch V(a) (5 April 2016) para. 20.

[60]   *Prosecutor v Ruto and Sang* (Public redacted version of: Decision on Defence Applications for Judgments of Acquittal) ICC-01/09-01/11-2027-Red-Corr, T Ch V(a) (5 April 2016) reasons of Judge Fremr, para. 57.

[61]   *Ibid.*

trial proceedings.[62] If both factors are met, it can be held that the Prosecution's case is on the 'brink of collapse', or more eloquently put, when the 'prosecution case has collapsed under the sheer weight of its own weakness,'[63] then the Trial Chamber can assess the credibility of the witnesses.

As a final note, it should also be considered that Judge Fremr accepts the inevitable discrepancies that occur when a witness has difficulty remembering details several years after the events, or when the story is told several times.[64] This does not prove that a non-credible witness is worthy of collapsing a prosecution's case. However, when a witness omits or no longer remembers the essential part of the information relevant to the case, this is considered 'wholly unconvincing'.[65]

20.4.4 When the 'Brink of Collapse' Can Be Applied

It is submitted that in applying the test, issues of reliability and credibility should be noted by the Chamber in circumstances where the prosecution's case has 'completely broken down', either during presentation or through fundamental issues raised by the defences cross-examination, such that the Prosecution is 'left without a case'- a practice akin to that of the ICTY and ICTR.[66] Furthermore, the majority of the *Ruto and Sang* Trial Chamber – Judge Fremr and Judge Eboe-Osuji – agreed that Trial Chambers are able to enter an assessment either at the 'no case to answer' stage, or beyond as well, where 'the prosecution's case can be viewed on the brink of breaking down [...]. In trials of this nature, with a significant duration, it cannot be the case that a Trial Chamber should only consider, as suggested by the Prosecution, the quantity of the evidence, and not the quality".[67] Therefore evidencing the importance of assessing the quality of the evidence provided by the prosecution instead of taking the quantity of evidence at its highest value.

---

62   *Ibid*.
63   *Ibid* (n 55) para. 55.
64   *Prosecutor v Ruto and Sang* (Public redacted version of: Decision on Defence Applications for Judgments of Acquittal) ICC-01/09-01/11-2027-Red-Corr, T Ch v(a) (5 April 2016) reasons of Judge Fremr, para. 58. which will be considered in the following section discussing 'incapable of belief'.
65   *Ibid*.
66   *Ibid* (n 52) para. 18.
67   *Prosecutor v Ruto and Sang* (Public redacted version of: Decision on Defence Applications for Judgments of Acquittal) ICC-01/09-01/11-2027-Red-Corr, T Ch v(a) (5 April 2016) reasons of Judge Fremr, para. 144; reasons of Judge Eboe-Osuji para. 87 [emphasis added].

20.4.5 'Incapable of Belief'

This section will consider what it means for the Prosecution's case to be 'incapable of belief'. In brief, a Trial Judge may assess the credibility of a witness when the evidence provided is 'incapable of belief' from any reasonable point of view.[68]

While the standard of review is to take the prosecution's evidence 'at its highest', Decision No. 5 indicates that the aforementioned standard of review stands unless the evidence is 'incapable of belief'. In essence, in Decision No. 5 it was stated that the Chamber will not consider questions of reliability or credibility relating to the evidence unless the evidence in question is incapable of belief by any reasonable Trial Chamber.[69]

Judge Fremr further explained that 'incapable of belief' can be understood to mean, "circumstances where a witness has demonstrated such a far-reaching willingness to manipulate the truth, the resulting evidence is incapable of being relied upon by a reasonable Trial Chamber."[70] Several examples from *Ruto & Sang* may help support this point.

Firstly, Witness 658's testimony taken at its highest was incapable of proving the Prosecution's allegations that the Network mobilised the youth to carry out the attacks, and was thus found 'incapable of believing' the prosecution's theory.[71] In other words, the evidence presented was too far-reaching to be credible.

Secondly, Witness 800 gave evidence regarding an alleged cleansing ceremony. In this regard, Judge Fremr noted that even if the evidence was not fully incapable of believe, it was highly implausible that such a large event would

---

68 *Prosecutor v Ruto and Sang* (Public redacted version of: Decision on Defence Applications for Judgments of Acquittal) ICC-01/09-01/11-2027-Red-Corr, T Ch v(a) (5 April 2016) para. 66.

69 Something to note, is that Judge Ebo-Osuji states in her reasoning that the above passage raises the understandable concern that a no case to answer assessment may only arise where the "destitution is evident beyond all dispute". Problematically, the Chamber may only focus on the apparent strengths of the prosecution evidence while ignoring its apparent weaknesses, thus signalling the importance, pursuant to Article 64, for the Trial Chamber to assess the credibility of a witness when the evidence provided is 'incapable of belief' and not allow the quantity of evidence to blind the narrative of the case. *Prosecutor v Ruto and Sang* (Decision No. 5 on the Conduct of Trial Proceedings (Principles and Procedure on 'No Case to Answer' Motions)) ICC-01/09-01/11-1334, T Ch v(a) (3 June 2014) para. 32.

70 *Prosecutor v Ruto and Sang* (Public redacted version of: Decision on Defence Applications for Judgments of Acquittal) ICC-01/09-01/11-2027-Red-Corr, T Ch v(a) (5 April 2016) para. 43.

71 *Ibid* para. 98.

have gone unnoticed at the alleged time.[72] The word to highlight here by Judge Fremr is 'highly implausible', as an element of incapable of belief. This would evidence that an entire testimony does not need to be incapable of belief, but rather the larger contextual elements surrounding the evidence that are incapable of belief. Examples of this nature could concern a sole witness testifying on specific events, or details of a larger event, and being the sole person who witnessed it. It would seem incapable of belief, that they were the only witness to have seen the relevant evidence being testified. In this particular incident, it is also important to note that there were no other reports of the event, even though the witness testified 'all the youth' attended.[73]

Domestic legislation could also shed light on the matter. For example, Judge Eboe-Osuji in his reasoning referred to Chief Justice King of the Supreme Court of South Australia, who stated that he did not understand the law to be 'that there can be a case to answer on circumstantial evidence which is incapable of producing in a reasonable mind a conviction of guilt beyond reasonable doubt. If the evidence is incapable of producing that state of mind, it is not capable in law of proving the charge'.[74]

Finally, it should be noted that it was found that the evidence provided by several prosecution witnesses could not be considered reliable by a reasonable Criminal Chamber. Therefore, they were found to be 'incapable of belief'.

20.5 Conclusion

In conclusion, the Trial Chamber is only able to assess the credibility of a witness when one of two elements is satisfied. The first element is to show that the Prosecution's case is on the 'brink of collapse', while the second element refers to the evidence presented being 'incapable of belief'. It is clear that for the Prosecution's case to be on the 'brink of collapse' three factors must be met:

1. The first factor relates to whether the entire Prosecution's case rests on the testimony of one witness;
2. The second factor concerns the amount of weight accorded to that specific witness in proving the prosecution's theory. If it can be proven that a

---

72 *Ibid* para. 116.
73 *Ibid*.
74 *Questions of Law Reserved on Acquittal (No 2 of 1993)* 61 SASR 1 [Supreme Court of South Australia, Full Court], para. 18, per King CJ (emphasis added). As seen in *Prosecutor v Ruto and Sang* (Public redacted version of: Decision on Defence Applications for Judgments of Acquittal) ICC-01/09-01/11-2027-Red-Corr, T Ch V(a) (5 April 2016) reasons of Judge Eboe-Osuji, para. 70.

large amount of weight is accorded to a single witness to prove the prosecution's case, then it can be held that the prosecution's case is on the 'brink of collapse'.
3. Finally, taking both of these factors into consideration, it should be weighed whether or not there is a point in continuing the trial proceedings.

The second element concerns whether or not the evidence presented by the prosecution is 'incapable of belief'. In order to better understand this notion, several examples and factors have been expressed.

One must consider whether the witness manipulated the truth, or whether their testimony is so far-reaching that it is 'incapable of belief'. Also, one must consider whether the evidence presented is highly implausible, either because the witness was the only one who saw the event or because no other accounts of the event were provided. Moreover, it has been found that contradictory evidence provided by multiple witnesses on the same issue does not automatically imply that a reasonable Trial Chamber would find the evidence reliable or credible. In particular, this notion can be seen as an umbrella term to accommodate different expressions of 'unbelievable', but it leaves no room for contradictory testimony nor for witnesses fatigued by the memory of events who provide inaccurate recollections after several years have passed.

CHAPTER 21

The Legal Position of the Acquitted Person at the ICC

21.1 Introduction

The sophistication of a law system might be measured by the way the legal position of an acquitted person is respected and preserved. The law systems which ensure a right to financial compensation for an acquitted person are in the minority compared to those where such a legal right is absent.

In Europe, the Kingdom of the Netherlands is one of the few countries which has codified such a right for the acquitted person, in article 533 of the Dutch Code of Criminal Procedure, which stipulates that:

1. If the case ends without imposition of a punishment or measure or with such imposition, but on account of an offence for which pre-trial detention is not permitted, the court may, at the request of the former suspect, award him compensation from the national treasury for the damage he has suffered as a result of being placed under detention, clinical observation or pre-trial detention. Damage shall be understood to include harm other than pecuniary loss.
2. (...)
3. The request may only be submitted within three months of the termination of the case. The hearing of the request by the chambers shall take place in public.
4. The chambers shall as far as possible be composed of the members who sat on the case at the hearing.
5. The award shall be made by the court of factual instance before which the case was or was to be prosecuted during its termination or was otherwise last prosecuted.
6. (...)

Yet, this provision is not a commonplace in national or international criminal jurisdiction.

This article discerns the question as to how the International Criminal Court envisions the possibility for an acquitted person to obtain reparations for potential wrongful incarceration and whether the stance taken by the ICC meets the standards of international criminal justice.

21.2 The (Non-)Right to Compensation for Any Acquitted Person at the ICC

21.2.1 *Statutory Obstacles*

The drafters of the Rome Statute opted in 1998 to include a provision in this Statute which at its face introduces a non-automatic right to compensation for an acquitted person. On the basis of this provision, "(…) in exceptional circumstances, where the Court finds conclusive facts showing that there has been a grave and manifest miscarriage of justice, it may, at its discretion, award compensation, according to the criteria provided in the Rules of Procedure and Evidence to a person who has been released from detention following a final decision of acquittal or a termination of the proceedings for that reason".

Several procedural hurdles are incorporated in this provision. First, the Court has to find 'conclusive facts' as to the existence of a 'grave and manifest miscarriage of justice'. Second, the Court has to be convinced that compensation is justified, as it is at the Court's discretion to award it.

Yet, there is a third procedural barrier that the acquitted person has to overcome within the ICC framework in order to receive compensation. This threshold is to be found in Rule 173(2) of the ICC Rules of Procedure and Evidence. This Rule requires that any request for compensation shall be submitted no later than six months from the date the person making the request '(…) was notified of the decision of the Court concerning (…) (a) The unlawfulness of the arrest or detention under article 85, paragraph 1; (b) The reversal of the conviction under article 85, paragraph 2; (c) The existence of a grave and manifest miscarriage of justice under article 85, paragraph 3.'

As set forth by the ICC Trial Chambers, a request for compensation pursuant to article 85(3) of the Rome Statute must therefore be preceded by a 'decision of the Court', finding that such a grave and manifest miscarriage of justice took place.[1]

---

[1] *Prosecutor v Ngudjolo Chui* (Decision on the "Requête en indemnisation en application des dispositions de l'article 85(1) et (3) du Statut) ICC-01/04-02/12-30/ENG, T Ch II (16 December 2015) para. 3; see also *Prosecutor v Charles Blé Goudé* (Decision on Mr. Blé Goudé's request for compensation) ICC-02/11-01/15-1427, Article 85 Ch (10 February 2022) para. 20.

In practice this procedural threshold has been partially remedied by the ICC Trial Chambers in that the Trial Chamber which is seized of a compensation request, despite the absence of a specific decision of the Court as envisioned by Rule 173(2) of the Rules of Procedure and Evidence, identifying a miscarriage of justice, can simply entertain the request by first assessing whether a grave and manifest miscarriage of justice did occur. This approach was taken in *Prosecutor v Matthieu Ngudjolo* in its decision of 16 December 2015 on the art. 85(1) and (3) application of Mr. Ngudjolo who was acquitted on 18 December 2012 of several charges relating to crimes against humanity and war crimes.[2]

As the Trial Chamber observed in *Ngudjolo*: "(...) there is no provision in the applicable legal texts which states that a prior decision concerning any of the situations listed in Rule 173(2) of the Rules, should be issued by a chamber other than that seized of the request for compensation."[3]

In *Prosecutor v Charles Blé Goudé*, in its decision dated 10 February 2022 regarding compensation, the ICC judges conceded with the approach in the *Ngudjolo* case and pursued a "two-fold approach". The Chamber resumed this approach by the following: "First, it will determine whether a grave and manifest miscarriage of justice occurred. If this is found to have been the case, the Chamber will, as a second step, consider whether it will exercise its discretion to award compensation."[4] In light of these three procedural obstacles to obtain compensation after acquittal at the ICC, one can conclude that no automatic right to such compensation exists.

This view was explicitly set forth in the compensation decision of *Prosecutor v Charles Blé Goudé*, saying – based on the drafting history of Article 85 – that the drafters of the Rome Statute did not intend, "(...) to go so far as to vest an acquitted person with a right to benefit from compensation by mere virtue of the fact that the acquittal was preceded by time spent in custody, (...) however lengthy (this) might have been."[5]

---

2 *Prosecutor v Mathieu Ngudjolo* (Decision on the "Requête en indemnisation en application des dispositions de l'article 85(1) et (3) du Statut) ICC-01/04-02/12-30/ENG, T Ch II (16 December 2015) para. 16.
3 *Ibid*, para. 16.
4 *Prosecutor v Blé Goudé* (Decision on Mr. Blé Goudé's request for compensation) ICC-02/11-01/15-1427, Article 85 Ch (10 February 2022) para. 23; this approach was also adopted by the ICC Pre-Trial Chamber II in *Prosecutor v Bemba Gombo* (Decision on Mr. Bemba's claim for compensation and damages) ICC-01/05-01/08-3694, PT Ch II (18 May 2020) paras 21–22.
5 *Prosecutor v Blé Goudé* (Decision on Mr. Blé Goudé's request for compensation) ICC-02/11-01/15-1427, Article 85 Ch (10 February 2022) para. 24, referring to *Prosecutor v Jean-Pierre Bemba Gombo* (Decision on Mr. Bemba's claim for compensation and damages) ICC-01/05-01/08-3694, PT Ch II (18 May 2020) para. 44.

In the case of *Prosecutor v Blé Goudé*, the acquitted person, Mr Blé Goudé spent 2731 days in ICC detention prior to the acquittal by the Trial Chamber on 15th January on the basis of a no case to answer-procedure, which decision was confirmed by the Appeals Chamber on 31 March 2021. The Trial Chamber held, according to the press release of the ICC and the summary of the judgement:

> In its judgment, the Appeals Chamber rejected, by majority, the Prosecutor's two grounds of appeal, namely that the Trial Chamber's decision to acquit Mr Gbagbo and Mr Blé Goudé (i) had violated statutory requirements and (ii) was taken without properly articulating and consistently applying a clearly defined standard of proof and its approach to assessing the sufficiency of the evidence. The Appeals Chamber found inter alia that, whilst trial chambers should ideally deliver both the verdict and reasons concurrently, a delay between the issuance of a verdict and its reasons cannot necessarily invalidate an entire trial process. There may, on the contrary, be clear justification for such separation in the particular circumstances of a case; most obviously in this regard is when the liberty of an acquitted defendant is at stake. The Appeals Chamber also rejected the argument that the two judges of the Trial Chamber who had formed the majority had failed to articulate and consistently apply the standard of proof. The Appeals Chamber noted in this regard that both judges had found that the evidence against the two accused had been 'exceptionally weak'.[6]

Moreover, the majority of the Trial Chamber was very critical of the quality of the investigation by the Prosecution, as evidenced by, inter alia, the following observations by the majority:

> Your Honours, the Chamber in appeal unequivocally found that both Judge Henderson and Judge Tarfusser, I quote, "shared the view that the evidence […] was 'exceptionally weak', and that the fundamental flaw of the Prosecutor's case lay in the numerous divergencies between the Prosecutor's 'one-sided' narrative and the facts emerging from her own evidence." Unquote. And you will find this in paragraph 328 also in the appeals judgment.[7]

---

[6] *Prosecutor v Blé Goudé* (Public Transcript) ICC-02/11-01/15-T-242-Red-ENG CT WT, Article 85 Ch (13 December 2021).

[7] *Ibid*, lines 10–14, page 13.

THE LEGAL POSITION OF THE ACQUITTED PERSON   321

>As pointed out by Judge Henderson in his reasons, and you can find it in paragraph 90, 9-0, of Judge Henderson's reasons, I quote: "[...] the Prosecutor should not be allowed to hide behind large volumes of submitted evidence and an indeterminate 'system of evidence' to avoid scrutiny of her case.[8]
>
>In his preliminary statement, he emphasised that, upon scrutiny, the Prosecution systematically omitted or downplayed significant factual elements which resulted in a highly misleading and somewhat skewed version of the events, which did not reflect the reality of the case. Paragraph 66 of Judge Henderson's reasons.[9]
>
>And in the same paragraph [referring to paragraph 36 of Judge Henderson's reasons] Judge Henderson does say that: "This is especially true in a case like ..." here, "where much of the evidence was essentially provided by the current government, which [was] headed by political opponents of the accused. Indeed, under these circumstances" – as Judge Henderson mentions – "the Chamber would have expected the Prosecution to take further steps to ensure that important documentary evidence was properly and demonstrably authenticated before being submitted" to the Court.[10]

In the absence of an automatic right to compensation, the question of perennial concern is how trial chambers define the boundaries of the axiom 'grave and manifest miscarriage of justice.'

21.2.2   Defining a 'Grave and Manifest Miscarriage of Justice'
21.2.2.1   General Remarks

In order to ascertain the ramifications of these procedural criteria for the legal position of the acquitted person within the ICC-system, this section will delve into the substantive meaning of the most prominent criterion, i.e. the existence of a grave and manifest miscarriage of justice.

First it has to be observed that within the ICC-system, an acquitted as such is not perceived as constituting a 'grave and manifest miscarriage of justice.' In *Prosecutor v Charles Blé Goudé*, the Article 85 Trial Chamber in paragraph 21 did not find that "(...) the decision of Trial Chamber I to acquit the applicant or the Appeals Chamber's decision confirming the acquittal, in and of themselves, constitute a grave and manifest miscarriage of justice, or that either of

---

8   *Ibid*, lines 23–25, page 18.
9   *Ibid*, lines 18–22, page 19.
10   *Ibid*, lines 3–9, page 22.

the Chambers explicitly found that a grave and manifest miscarriage of justice had taken place".[11]

What should one understand to be a 'grave and manifest miscarriage of justice'? This criterion is nowhere defined or circumscribed in international instruments, let alone the ICC's legal framework.[12] The ICC judges have attempted to delineate this criterion, by saying that 'a grave and manifest miscarriage of justice "(...) is a certain and undeniable miscarriage of justice following, for example, an erroneous decision by a Trial Chamber or wrongful prosecution."[13] Even this description does not assure legal certainty for an acquitted person as to what he or she should understand this criterion to be. The question is whether an overall definition of this criterion is possible at all.

Importantly though is that this description by the ICC Trial Chambers does include the phenomenon of a "wrongful prosecution" as a potential exponent of a grave and manifest miscarriage of justice. In fact, no acquittal could be otherwise subject to Article 85 since it is obvious that from the perspective of the acquitted person, an acquittal can never be a miscarriage of justice. However, the underlying prosecution could be wrong. Therefore, subjecting the way the prosecution was performed in a certain case, to the scope of Article 85 is justified. Otherwise, Article 85 would be totally superfluous. Consequently, the question arises as to what a 'wrongful persecution' entails.

21.2.2.2 The Meaning of a 'Wrongful Prosecution' within the ICC Framework

If one touches upon the discussion as to what a 'wrongful prosecution' actually means, the most controversial question seems to be whether Article 85, i.e. wrongful prosecutions, also applies to 'failed' prosecutions. It seems without dispute that a 'malicious' prosecution does meet the standard of Article 85, as such prosecutions are instituted from wrongful or improper motives and without probable cause.[14]

However, what about 'failed' prosecution? What is a 'failed' prosecution? In *Prosecutor v Charles Blé Goudé*, the Chamber addressed these questions

---

11 *Prosecutor v Charles Blé Goudé* (Decision on Mr. Blé Goudé's request for compensation) ICC-02/11-01/15-1427, Article 85 Ch (10 February 2022) para. 21.
12 *Ibid* para. 26.
13 *Ibid*; see also *Prosecutor v Mathieu Ngudjolo* (Decision on the "Requête en indemnisation en application des dispositions de l'article 85(1) et (3) du Statut) ICC-01/04-02/12-30/ENG, T Ch II (16 December 2015) para. 45.
14 This differentiation between 'malicious prosecution' and 'wrongful prosecution' was made by the Prosecution in the Ble Goude compensation case; see para. 28 of the Ble Goude compensation decision.

in order to clarify the boundaries of a 'wrongful prosecution' to its reading of Article 85. In paragraph 29 of the compensation decision, the Chamber writes that "(...) a 'failed' prosecution' (ergo, resulting in an acquittal from the bench) does "not necessarily mean, that the prosecution was 'wrongful', irrespective of whether the accused spent time in detention."[15] In an attempt to further shed light on the legal contours of the term 'wrongful prosecution', the Chamber in paragraphs 30–31, relying on previous ICC case law, provided the following parameters:

- A 'miscarriage of justice' under Article 85, including a wrongful prosecution, must have given rise to 'a clear violation of the applicant's fundamental rights' and (cumulatively) must have 'caused serious harm to the applicant'.
- Therefore, not every error committed in the course of the proceedings is automatically considered a 'grave and manifest miscarriage of justice'.
- As the threshold set by Article 85(3) is particularly high, for it to be met "(...) the violation must be so serious and exceptionable as to indicate that (...) the proper administration of justice was compromised."[16]

The foregoing implies that, as also confirmed by the ICC trial chambers, in cases whereby the evidence, tested at trial, falls short of the "beyond reasonable doubt"-test, these outcomes do not pass the threshold of "so serious and exceptional".[17]

As the ICC trial chambers therefore require, for the application of article 85, that the applicant show that the purported wrongful prosecution amounted to a violation of the applicant's fundamental rights so serious and exceptional such that the proper administration of justice was compromised, this raises the question as to the extent the burden of proof thereto rests upon the acquitted person.

---

15 *Ibid* (n 11) para. 29.
16 *Ibid* paras. 30–31; referring also to *Prosecutor v Mathieu Ngudjolo* (Decision on the "Requête en indemnisation en application des dispositions de l'article 85(1) et (3) du Statut) ICC-01/04-02/12-30/ENG, T Ch II (16 December 2015) para. 45; and *Prosecutor v Jean-Pierre Bemba Gombo* (Decision on Mr. Bemba's claim for compensation and damages) ICC-01/05-01/08-3694, PTC II (18 May 2020) para. 42.
17 *Ibid* (n 11) para. 31.

21.2.2.3   (Non-)Reversal of the Burden of Proof?
This section discerns the issue of the burden of proof in relation to article 85, more specifically what this burden of proof embraces for the acquitted person.

At the outset, it should be noted that the European Court of Human Rights, in its landmark judgement of 25 August 1993, in Sekanina v. Austria, unanimously held that article 6(2) of the ECHR was violated, the decisive paragraphs 29–31 read as follows:

> 29. Notwithstanding this decision, on 10 December 1986 the Linz Regional Court rejected the applicant's claim for compensation, pursuant to section 2(1)(b) of the 1969 Law (see paragraphs 12 and 16 above). In its view, there remained strong indications of Mr Sekanina's guilt capable of substantiating the suspicions concerning him; it listed them relying on the Assize Court file. The evidence in question could, in its opinion, still constitute an argument for the applicant's guilt. The court inferred from the record of the jury's deliberations that in acquitting the applicant they had given him the benefit of the doubt (see paragraph 12 above).
>
> The Linz Court of Appeal went further in the grounds of its decision of 25 February 1987. It considered that section 2(1)(b) of the 1969 Law, according to which compensation is confined to persons that have been not only acquitted but also cleared of all suspicion, was in conformity with the Austrian Constitution and Article 6 para. 2 (art. 6-2) of the Convention. In this respect it did not regard itself as bound by the Assize Court's acquittal. On the other hand, it referred to its own decision of 30 April 1986 authorising detention on remand for a year (see paragraph 7 above); it saw this as confirmation of the gravity of the suspicions concerning the applicant. After having drawn up a comprehensive list of items of evidence against Mr Sekanina, in its view not refuted during the trial, and after having carefully examined the statements of various witnesses, it concluded: "The jury took the view that the suspicion was not sufficient to reach a guilty verdict; there was, however, no question of that suspicion's being dispelled" (see paragraph 13 above).
>
> 30. Such affirmations – not corroborated by the judgment acquitting the applicant or by the record of the jury's deliberations – left open a doubt both as to the applicant's innocence and as to the correctness of the Assize Court's verdict. Despite the fact that there had been a final decision acquitting Mr Sekanina, the courts which had to rule on the claim for compensation undertook an assessment of the applicant's guilt on the basis of the contents of the Assize Court file. The voicing of suspicions regarding an accused's innocence is conceivable as long as the

conclusion of criminal proceedings has not resulted in a decision on the merits of the accusation. However, it is no longer admissible to rely on such suspicions once an acquittal has become final. Consequently, the reasoning of the Linz Regional Court and the Linz Court of Appeal is incompatible with the presumption of innocence.

31. Accordingly, there has been a violation of Article 6 para. 2 (art. 6–2).

For the relevance to the interpretation of article 85 of the Rome Statute and especially the application of the burden of proof, the observation of the European Court in paragraph 30 is of importance, where it is said that after an acquittal has become final, it is no longer admissible to rely on suspicions regarding an accused's innocence. Does the fact, as observed by the ICC Trial Chambers, that compensation proceedings are not "criminal in nature" but more alike "civil or administrative proceedings" alter this observation or the division of the burden of proof?[18] The answer is that this different character of the proceedings, in view of the ICC case law partially changes the application of the burden of proof.

In the Ble Goude Compensation Decision, the Chamber, relying on previous case law and the text of the ICCPR, explain this view as follows:

- Article 85(3) of the Rome Statute requires, as mentioned earlier, that 'conclusive facts' support the existence of a miscarriage of justice, meaning the presentation of a 'fact' that 'conclusively' shows such a miscarriage.[19]
- In the absence of a clear definition in the ICC legal framework of what 'conclusive facts' entail, the ICC judges impose (implicitly) on the acquitted person the burden to provide "(...) concrete evidence on the basis of which the Chamber is satisfied that a grave and manifest miscarriage of justice took place, that is, evidence of a violation so serious and exceptional resulting in the proper administration being compromised."[20]
- Yet, the Chamber in the Ble Goude compensation decision limited this burden on the acquitted person by saying that the applicant "(...)

---

18   *Ibid* (n 11) para. 32.
19   *Ibid* (n 11) para. 33, whereby the ICC Trial Chamber refers to the text of articles 14(6) ICCPR and article 3 of Protocol no. 7 to the ECHR.
20   *Ibid* para. 34.

need not his or her claim to rise to the standard of beyond reasonable doubt."[21]

After having assessed that the ICC Trial Chambers do attribute to the acquitted person the burden to establish 'conclusive facts' that he or she was subjected to a wrongful prosecution, the next section will go into the question how this theoretical model operates in practice.

21.3   Establishing a 'Grave and Manifest Miscarriage of Justice' in Practice

The proliferation of the criterion 'grave and manifest miscarriage of justice' in the law practice of the ICC tends to proof of 'male fides' actions by the prosecution, and thus seems to put the acquitted person on quite a burdensome "showing of conclusive facts" which implicitly requires him or her to establish 'male fides' prosecutorial behaviour.[22]

In the Ble Goude Compensation procedure and hearing of 16 December 2021, the Defence was asked by the Bench to provide a definition of a 'wrongful prosecution'. In response to this question by the bench, it was submitted by counsel for the applicant that the wrongful prosecution in that case was based on "(...) firstly, the systematic failure in investigation in accordance with the burden of proof. Secondly, the tunnel vision, one-sided narrative acknowledged by the majority of the judges at appeal and first instance; and thirdly, the Prosecution against all odds (...) continued with this one-sided narrative."[23] These three categories could also apply to what 'wrongful prosecutions' in general entail.

In its ruling of 10 February 2022, in paragraph 42, the Chamber addresses this view of the Defence. The Trial Chamber arrives at the following findings:
– First, it holds that it has not been presented with any evidence of 'male fides' by the Prosecution;
– Secondly, the Chamber opines that a deficient internal review process by the Prosecutor – which should have led the Prosecutor to change its initial theory – which is indicative for the fact that the Prosecution suffered from 'tunnel vision', do not constitute a wrongful prosecution tantamount to a 'grave and manifest miscarriage of justice'.

---

21   *Ibid.*
22   *Ibid* para. 42.
23   *Ibid* para. 27.

The sentence which attracts attention within the Chamber's findings reads:

> However 'shortcomings' on the side of the Prosecutor and poorly prosecuting a case, while undesirable – especially at the international level, with the type of interests which tend to be at stake – do not constitute a wrongful prosecution that amounted to a 'grave and manifest miscarriage of justice'.[24]

The Court also was confronted with the defence argument that the Prosecution failed to re-evaluate its case theory, notwithstanding clear instructions from the Trial Chamber after closure of the Prosecution case, and therefore violated article 67(1)(c) of the ICC Statute. In this regards, the Chamber in the Ble Goude compensation decision accepted this stance, holding that the Prosecution ought to have (properly) re-evaluated its case at any stage during trial when the evidence, as presented, warranted a review of the case theory, while stressing that the Prosecution is "(…) under a duty to do such".[25]

However, the overall assessment of the Trial Chamber was such that it did not find that the "(…) Prosecution's errors were so serious and exceptional that the proper administration of justice was compromised."[26] The chamber at the end of its ruling concluded that the applicant "(…) has not presented evidence to that effect (…)".

21.4 The Future of Acquitted Persons at the ICC: towards a Right to Compensation?

The question arises whether the ICC compensation system meets the demands of respect for human rights of acquitted persons. In order to answer this question, one should bear in mind the following two circumstances:

(i) First, the observation that international criminal trials and especially at the ICC, since these are predominantly based on an adversarial process model, prolong for many years. The case of the Prosecutor v. Charles Ble Goude lasted, including pre-trial stage and appeal, almost eight years.

(ii) Secondly, the ICC provisional release system hardly creates a realistic option for accused persons to benefit from provisional release. This is due

---

24   *Ibid* para. 42.
25   *Ibid* para. 44.
26   *Ibid* para. 45.

to the apparent unwillingness of States to host persons accused of international crimes pending a trial. As of to date, only two states, Belgium and Argentina have signed an agreement with the ICC to host accused persons who are provisionally released. In the absence of States willing to cooperate with the Defence or the ICC to accommodate an accused who might be eligible for provisional release, no accused persons at the ICC has until so far been released pending trial.

These two factors result in practice in a situation whereby the accused at the ICC remains for years in provisional custody up to at least the judgement in his or her case. By then, in case of an acquittal, the personal implications of such a lengthy detention are for the acquitted person almost irreversible.

In light of these implications, while bearing in mind the practical obstacles for an accused person to be subject to provisional release, it would be justified to re-consider the compensation system at the ICC. Two alternatives arise:

(i) First, one could opt for the Dutch system of compensation after acquittal or termination of proceedings in that there is a right to compensation if the Court finds this 'reasonable'.[27]

(ii) Second, one could maintain the text of Article 85 of the Rome Statute, albeit that the Trial Chamber reverse the current burden of proof which rests on the applicant and instead take as a starting point that in case of acquittal or termination of proceedings, there is an assumption of a wrongful prosecution pursuant to Article 85. Consequently, it is up to the Prosecution to show 'facts' that the administration of justice was not compromised.

In his article "Towards the international right to claim innocence", Professor Brandon L. Garrett, one of the leading authors on wrongful convictions, concludes his analysis by saying:

> The time is ripe to begin to think of the right to claim innocence as a general and consistent practice that deserves (…) international recognition and perhaps eventually as a matter of legal obligation and a principle of customary international law.[28]

Transposed on the position of the acquitted person at the ICC, one can say that the time is perhaps ripe to re-consider the judicial ambit of Article 85.

---

27   Article 530 Dutch Criminal Code of Procedure.
28   Brandon L. Garrett, "Towards the international right to claim innocence". California Law Review, vol. 105"1173–1221, 1220.

21.5 Conclusion

The compensation case of Prosecutor v. Charles Ble Goude illustrates that the materialization in practice of the main criterion of article 85, namely the existence of a "grave and manifest miscarriage of justice" as defined by the ICC Trial Chamber, remains problematic from the perspective of the acquitted person. The combination of both the non-existence of a legal right to compensation and the de facto imposition of the burden of proof to show "conclusive facts" thereto on part of the acquitted person, seems to make a successful recourse to article 85 impossible. This might be exemplified by the fact that until so far, none of the compensation requests under art. 85 filed to the Court have resulted in award of damages.

Overall Concluding Remarks and Recommendations

The purpose of this book was to illuminate the main evidentiary principles applicable within the system of the ICC, in particular to enable defence counsel to perform their duties as professionally as possible. Analyzing these principles, one has to conclude that the various Trial Chambers of the ICC display a lack of one coherent evidentiary system of law. This lacuna is especially visible with regard to the processing of documentary, forensic and social media evidence, as determined in the chapters.

This observation has also implications from the perspective of the accused person. Depending on which Trial Chamber and its composition an accused is facing, the evidentiary rules might vary. This differentiation is also fueled by the legal background of a particular judge, that is to say whether they are educated and legally raised within a civil or common law system.

A particularly telling example is the introduction of NGO reports into evidence. One of the major risks associated with such reports is that they often rely on anonymous witness interviews. As described in Chapter XVI, due to the lack of reliability in these unknown sources, some Trial Chambers have not allowed the authors of such reports to testify about these sources, but have rather limited their testimonies to the extent of their own findings. Other Trial Chambers have shown a different approach and permitted that NGO workers, testifying in court, could refer to these anonymous findings.

The lack of clarity within the evidentiary system of the ICC could also be attributed to the aspiration of the ICC as being a truth-seeking body. From this perspective it might explain why the Trial Chambers do not endeavor strict and uniform evidentiary principles but rather pursue a case-by-case approach in order to serve the overall truth-seeking mandate of the ICC.

One of the main issues regarding ICC evidentiary rules, is the distinction made by Trial Chambers between the admission and submission regimes. As further developed in Chapter XV, the submission regime, which is held applicable by most Trial Chambers, constitute the problem that defence counsel. Indeed, defence counsel sometimes faces thousands of documents submitted by the prosecution and they all have to be addressed at the end of the trial, in the closing arguments, because the court has deferred the admissibility decision to that stage.

This means that the potential probative value and overall evidentiary weight of a certain piece of evidence remains unclear until the end of the trial instead of being decided upon when tendered. This raises important questions regarding the rights of the accused, especially in terms of legal predictability and transparency of the Chamber's reasoning.

The evidentiary system of the ICC being driven by the 'truth finding' nature of the Court, creates thus a potential disbalance with the defence position, which also visible with regard to the provision of Rule 74(2) of the Rules of Procedure and Evidence which enables the Court to provide to a witness an assurance with respect to self-incrimination.

This provision clearly reflects the notion that witnesses are encouraged to give evidence against accused persons, even so-called insiders who in most instances were themselves involved in potential crimes, but are given by the ICC-judges de facto immunities from prosecution before the ICC and national courts. In chapter 17.6 of this book, it was already illustrated, based on a judgement of the ECtHR of 1 June 2023, that such a practice contravenes the principle of fair trial.

At the end of this survey into the evidentiary system of the ICC, one can conclude that this raises the question whether its application comports with the true nature of criminal rules of evidence, namely the protection of individuals, who are confronted with the power of an institution that has the ability to deprive that person from his or her freedom against an abuse of such power (see chapter 1).

The international community does not always perceive an acquittal at the level of international criminal tribunals as on exponent of "justice".[1] Yet, the apparent assumption by the international community, individuals charged with international crimes by the ICC are *eo ipso* guilty and should be convicted, should never transpire into a law system such as the ICC that proclaims to the uphold fair trial rights of accused persons.

Rules of evidence should thus not only serve to channel the case of the prosecution service, but rather to safeguard the accused person from a prosecution based on evidentiary rules that might create miscarriages of justice. Having determined the evidentiary system of the ICC, the overall conclusion is justified that it would benefit from more uniformity, while its application should be more balanced towards the principal position of the accused person within a criminal trial.

---

[1] See for instance the address of the Japanese ambassador during the ASP of December 2020 on the acquittal of the former ICC suspects Laurent Gbagbo and Charles Ble Goude.

Bibliography

Books

Amann P and Dillon MP, 'Electronic Evidence Management at the ICC: Legal, Technical, Investigative and Organizational Considerations', in A. Babington-Ashaye A, Comrie A and Adeniran A, *International Criminal Investigations* (Eleven international publishing 2018).

Ambos K, Treatise on International Criminal Law: International Criminal Procedure, vol 3 (Oxford University Press 2016).

Appazov A, *Expert Evidence and International Criminal Justice* (Springer 2016).

Boot M, *Genocide, Crimes Against Humanity, War Crimes: Nullum Crimen Sine Lege and the Subject Matter Jurisdiction of the International Criminal Court* (Intersentia 2002).

Brooks J, *You Might Go to Prison, Even Though You're Innocent* (University of California Press 2023).

Cryer R, Robinson D and Vasiliev S, *An Introduction to International Criminal Law and Procedure* (4th edn, Cambridge University Press 2019).

De Smet S, 'A Structural Analysis Of The Role Of The Pre-Trial Chamber In The Fact-Finding Process Of The ICC' in Carsten Stahn and Göran Sluiter (eds), *The Emerging Practice of the International Criminal Court* (Brill 2009).

Farthofer H, 'The Development of Witness Evidence Law at the International Criminal Court' in Alexander Heinze and Viviane E. Dittrich (eds), *The Past, Present and Future of the International Criminal Court* (Torkel Opsahl Academic EPublisher 2021) <https://www.toaep.org/nas-pdf/5-dittrich-heinze> accessed 28 December 2023.

Finlay B, Cromwell TA and Latrou N, Witness Preparation – A Practical Guide Aurora, (Law Book, 2010).

Gaynor F, "Law of Evidence: Admissibility of Documentary Evidence" in Göran Sluiter and others (eds), *International Criminal Procedure: Principles and Rules* (Oxford University Press 2013).

Gill P, *Misleading DNA Evidence: Reasons for Miscarriages of Justice* (Elsevier Inc 2014).

Kassin S, *DUPED: Why Innocent People Confess – and Why We Believe Their Confessions* (Prometheus 2022).

Khan KA, Buisman C, and Gosnell C (eds), *Principles of Evidence in International Criminal Justice* (Oxford University Press 2010).

Klamberg M (ed), *Commentary on the Law of the International Criminal Court* (Torkel Opsahl Academic EPublisher 2017) <https://www.toaep.org/ps-pdf/29-klamberg> accessed 30 December 2023.

Klamberg M, *Evidence in International Criminal Trials: Confronting Legal Gaps and the Reconstruction of Disputed Events* (Brill 2013).

Knoops G-JA, *Redressing Miscarriages of Justice: Practice and Procedure in (International) Criminal Cases* (2nd edn, Martinus Nijhoff Publishers 2013).

Laroche X and Baccard E, 'International Courts and Forensic Sciences', in Siegel JA et al. (eds) *Encyclopaedia of Forensic Sciences* (Academic Press 2013).

Levy E, *Examination of Witnesses in Criminal Cases*, (Carswell, 2004).

Locke J, *The Second Treatise of Civil Government and A Letter Concerning Toleration* (Blackwell 1948).

Manning J, 'Definition and classes of Social media', in K. Harvey (ed.), *Encyclopedia of social media and politics* (Sage 2014).

Mauet TE, *Trials: Strategy, Skills, And the New Powers of Persuasion* (Aspen Publishers 2005).

May R and Wierda M, *International Criminal Evidence* (Brill 2021) <https://brill.com/display/title/13900#mainContent> accessed 28 December 2023.

O'Callaghan D, Prucha N, Greene D, Conway M, Carthy J and Cunningham P, *Online social media in the Syria conflict: Encompassing the extremes and the in-betweens* (IEEE/ACM International Conference on Advances in Social Networks Analysis and Mining, 2014).

Office of the United Nations High Commissioner for Human Rights (OHCHR), 'Human Rights Reporting', *Manual on Human Rights Monitoring (Revised edition)* (2nd edn, United Nations 2011) <https://www.ohchr.org/en/publications/policy-and-methodological-publications/manual-human-rights-monitoring-revised-edition#main-content> accessed 29 December 2023.

Roberts P and Zuckerman A, *Criminal Evidence* (3rd edn, Oxford University Press 2022).

Rohan C, 'Protecting the Rights of the Accused in International Criminal Proceedings: Lip Service or Affirmative Action?' in Schabas WA and McDermott Y (eds), *Critical perspectives* (Routledge 2013).

Schabas WA, *The UN International Criminal Tribunals: The Former Yugoslavia, Rwanda and Sierra Leone* (Cambridge University Press 2006).

Schuttpelz, KO, *Witness Preparation in International and Domestic Legal Proceedings*, (Nomos, 2014).

Singh A, 'Expert Evidence' in Karim A.A. Khan, Caroline Buisman and Chris Gosnell (eds), *Principles of Evidence in International Criminal Justice* (Oxford University Press 2010).

Sluiter G and others (eds), *International Criminal Procedure: Principles and Rules* (Oxford University Press 2013).

Spencer J, *Hearsay Evidence in Criminal Proceedings* (Hart Publishing 2008).

Wallace WA, *The Effect of Confirmation Bias on Criminal Investigative Decision Making* (Walden University Scholar Works 2015).

Zahar A and Sluiter G, *International Criminal Law: A Critical Introduction* (Oxford University Press 2008).

Academic Articles

Applegate, JS, 'Witness Preparation' (1989) 68 Texas Law Review 277.

Ambos K, 'International Criminal Procedure: "Adversarial", "Inquisitorial" or Mixed?' (2003) 3 International Criminal Law Review 1.

Chesney R, Citron DK, 'Deep Fakes: A Looming Challenge for Privacy, Democracy, and National Security' (2018) 107 California Law Review 1753.

Chlevickaite G and Hola B, 'Empirical Study of Insider Witnesses' Assessments at the International Criminal Court' (2016) 16 International Criminal Law Review 673.

Choi Y, 'Mobile Instant Messaging Evidence in Criminal Trials' (2017), Cath. U. J. L. & Tech 1.

Combs NA, 'Grave Crimes and Weak Evidence: Fact-Finding Evolution in International Criminal Law' (2017) 58 Harvard International Law Journal 47.

Van den Eeden CAJ, De Poot CJ and Koppen PJ, 'The Forensic Confirmation Bias: A Comparison Between Experts and Novices' (2019) 1 Journal of forensic sciences 64.

Freeman L and Llorente R, 'Finding the Signal in the Noise: International Criminal Evidence and Procedure in the Digital Age' (2021) 19 Journal of International Criminal Justice 163.

Freeman L, 'Digital Evidence and War Crimes Prosecutions: The Impact of Digital Technologies on International Criminal Investigations and Trials' (2018) 41 Fordham International Law Journal 283.

Garrett BL, 'Towards the International Right to Claim Innocence' (2017) 105 California Law Review 1173.

Gillett M and Schuster M, 'The Special Tribunal for Lebanon Swiftly Adopts Its Rules of Procedure and Evidence' (2009) 7 Journal of International Criminal Justice 885.

Groenhuijsen M and Selçuk H, 'The Principle of Immediacy in Dutch Criminal Procedure in the Perspective of European Human Rights Law' (2014) 126 Zeitschrift für die Gesamte Strafrechtswissenschaft 248.

Herasimenka A, Bright J, Knuutila A, Howard PN 'Misinformation and professional news on largely unmoderated platforms: the case of Telegram' (2022), 2 Journal of Information Technology and Politics 20.

Klinker M, 'Forensic Science Expertise for International Criminal Proceedings: An Old Problem, a New Context and a Pragmatic Resolution' (2009) 13 The International Journal of Evidence and Proof 102.

Knoops G-JA, 'The Proliferation of Forensic Sciences and Evidence before International Criminal Tribunals from a Defence Perspective' (2019) 30 Criminal Law Forum 33.

Knoops G-JA, Bohne E, and Petersen A, 'The Evidentiary Value of Social Media in International Criminal Proceedings' (2022) 18 International Studies Journal 53.

Mansour Fallah S, 'The Admissibility of Unlawfully Obtained Evidence before International Courts and Tribunals' (2020) 19 The Law and Practice of International Courts and Tribunals 147.

Mcdermotty Y, 'The Admissibility and Weight of Written Witness Testimony in International Criminal Law: A Socio-Legal Analysis' (2013) 26 Leiden Journal of International Law 971.

O'Sullivan I and Montgomery D, 'The Erosion of the Right to Confrontation Under the Cloak of Fairness at the ICTY' (2010) 8 Journal of International Criminal Justice 511.

Safer M, 'Educating Jurors about Eyewitness Testimony in Criminal Cases with Circumstantial and Forensic Evidence' (2016) 47 International journal of law and psychiatry 86.

Wald P, 'To "Establish Incredible Events by Credible Evidence": The Use of Affidavit Testimony in Yugoslavia War Crimes Tribunal Proceedings' (2001) 42 Harvard International Law Journal 535.

Wise R, 'An Examination of the Causes and Solutions to Eyewitness Error' 5 Frontiers in Psychiatry 102.

Blogs and Online Journals

'Delivering Justice, Faster' (*Coalition for the International Criminal Court*) <https://www.coalitionfortheicc.org/fight/strong-icc/delivering-justice-faster#main-content> accessed 29 August 2023.

'Human Rights Watch Memorandum for the Twelfth Session of the International Criminal Court Assembly of States Parties' (*Human Rights Watch*, 12 November 2013) <https://www.hrw.org/news/2013/11/12/human-rights-watch-memorandum-twelfth-session-international-criminal-court-assembly#main-content> accessed 14 July 2023.

'The Application of Call Data Records in Corporate Forensic Investigations' (*CYFOR*) <https://cyfor.co.uk/the-application-of-call-data-records-in-corporate-investigations/> accessed 18 August 2023.

Dearden L, 'Rape Trial Collapse over Undisclosed Sex Messages Blamed on Police Funding Cuts Innocent Student Liam Allan Cleared as Judge Warns over Potential Miscarriages of Justice' *The Independent* (15 December 2017) <https://www.independent.co.uk/news/uk/crime/rape-trial-collapse-sex-text-messages-police-funding-cuts-liam-allan-disclosure-phone-innocent-miscarriages-of-justice-a8113011.html#main-content> accessed 29 December 2023.

Hamilton R, 'New Technologies in International Criminal Investigations' (Proceedings of the ASIL Annual Meeting, January 2018) <https://www.researchgate.net/publi

cation/331956933_New_Technologies_in_International_Criminal_Investigations> accessed 5 January 2024.

Heller K, 'Not All Hearsay Rules Are Created Equal' (*OpinioJuris*, 29 July 2008) <http://opiniojuris.org/2008/07/29/not-all-hearsay-rules-are-created-equal/> accessed 14 June 2023.

Knoops G-JA, 'De Rechtsstaat in Het Geding; Essay Gerechtelijke Dwalingen' (*De Groene Amsterdammer*, 24 April 2013) <https://www.groene.nl/artikel/de-rechtsstaat-in-het-geding> accessed 20 July 2023.

Van Schaack B, 'ICC Assembly of States Parties Rundown' (*A Forum on Law, Rights, and U.S. National Security*, 27 November 2013) <https://www.justsecurity.org/3862/icc-assembly-states-parties-rundown/#primary> accessed 14 June 2023.

Reports

'Amendments to the Rules of Procedure and Evidence' (International Criminal Court 2013) ICC-ASP/12/Res.7.

Brader C, 'Disclosure of Evidence in Criminal Proceedings' (House of Lords Library Briefing 2020) https://lordslibrary.parliament.uk/research-briefings/lln-2020-0010/ accessed 5 January 2024.

'Establishment of a Study Group on Governance' (International Criminal Court 2010) ICC-ASP/9/Res.2.

'Report of the International Tribunal for the Prosecution of Persons Responsible for Serious Violations of International Humanitarian Law Committed in the Territory of the Former Yugoslavia since 1991', A/62/172-S/2007/469 (1 August 2007).

'Working Group on Lessons Learnt: Second Report of the Court to the Assembly of States Parties' (International Criminal Court 2013) ICC-ASP/12/37/Add.1.

'Report of the Panel of Experts on the Illegal Exploitation of Natural Resources and Other Forms of Wealth of DR Congo' (United Nations 2001) S/2001/357.

Wilkinson S, 'Standards of Proof in International Humanitarian and Human Rights Fact-Finding and Inquiry Missions' (Geneva Academy of International Humanitarian Law and Human Rights 2015) <https://www.geneva-academy.ch/joomlatools-files/docman-files/Standards%20of%20Proof%20in%20Fact-Finding.pdf> accessed 29 December 2023.

Dictionary and Encyclopedia Entries

'Business Records Exception', *Legal Information Institut* (Cornell University insignia) <https://www.law.cornell.edu/wex/business_records_exception#content> accessed 15 August 2023.

'Evidence', *Legal Information Institut* (Cornell University insignia) <https://www.law.cornell.edu/wex/evidence#content> accessed 20 July 2023.

'Hearsay Rule', *Legal Information Institut* (Cornell University insignia) <https://www.law.cornell.edu/wex/hearsay_rule#content> accessed 4 August 2023.

'Witnesses' (United Nations, International Criminal Tribunal for the former Yugoslavia) <https://www.icty.org/sid/158#main-content> accessed 2 August 2023.

Web Pages

House of Commons Justice Committee, 'Disclosure of Evidence in Criminal Cases' (2018) <https://publications.parliament.uk/pa/cm201719/cmselect/cmjust/859/859.pdf>, pdf.

Human Rights Watch, 'About Our Research' <www.hrw.org/about/about-us/about-our-research#5> accessed 10 October 2023.

Ministry of Justice, 'Government Response to the Justice Select Committee's Eleventh Report of Session 2017–2019: Disclosure of Evidence in Criminal Cases' (2018) <https://assets.publishing.service.gov.uk/government/uploads/system/uploads/attachment_data/file/763763/gov-res-jsc-report-disclosure-evidence-criminal-cases.pdf>, pdf.

Report National Police Chiefs' Council, College of Policing and Crown Prosecution Service, 'National Disclosure Improvement Plan: Phase Two – Embedding Culture Change and Continuous Improvement' (2018) <https://www.cps.gov.uk/sites/default/files/documents/publications/National-Disclosure-Improvement-Plan-Phase-Two-Nov-18.pdf>, pdf.

Report National Police Chiefs' Council, College of Policing and Crown Prosecution Service, 'National Disclosure Improvement Plan: Progress Update' (2019) <https://www.cps.gov.uk/sites/default/files/documents/publications/National-Disclosure-Improvement-Plan-progress-update-March-19.pdf>, pdf.

Scottish Government, 'The not proven verdict and related reforms: consultation' (13 December 2021) <www.gov.scot/publications/not-proven-verdict-related-reforms-consultation> accessed 21 September 2023.

Wex Definitions Team, 'Corroborate' (*Legal Information Institute*, June 2021) <www.law.cornell.edu/wex/corroborate> accessed 21 September 2023.

The Crown Prosecutor Service, 'Bad character evidence' (*Legal Guidance*, updated 10 September 2021) https://www.cps.gov.uk/legal-guidance/bad-character-evidence accessed 25 September 2023.

The Crown Prosecutor Service, 'Expert evidence' (*Legal Guidance*, updated 5 August 2022) <www.cps.gov.uk/legal-guidance/expert-evidence> accessed 26 September 2023.

UK Law Reform Commission, Expert Evidence in Criminal Proceedings in England and Wales, Law Com No 325 (21 March 2011), presented to Parliament pursuant to section 3(2) of the Law Commissions Act 1965, <www.lawcom.gov.uk/app/uploads/2015/03/lc325_Expert_Evidence_Report.pdf>, pdf.

Index

Acquitted persons
    Acquitted   72, 169, 308
    Acquitted person   317–329
Ad hoc Tribunals
    Evolution and context   52
    Jurisprudence on cross-examination of witnesses   157
Admission
    Admission   9–18, 42, 55, 58, 69–72
    Admission of documents   64–65
    Admission of evidence   36, 39
Anonymous evidence   245
Antithetically obtained evidence   15

Biased sources   263–266
Brink of collapse   298, 309, 312–315
Burden of proof   323, 325–329
Business documents   36–37
'Bad Character Evidence'   193–200

Circumstantial evidence   44, 167–174
    Ad hoc Tribunals application   170
    Evideniary value   172
Civil Law   133, 175, 187, 216
    Hearsay evidence   38
Closing Statements   295
Command Responsibility   58–59
Common Law   72, 133
    Witness preparation   142–147
    Shepered Direction   173
    Corroboration   175–178
    Character evidence   193–194
    Admissibility of Propensity Evidence   197
Confirmation Bias   226, 264
Contemporaneousness   264
Content Moderation   266
Contextualisation   263, 270
Corroboration   205
    Evidentiary Principles   175–185
Cross-examination
    Cross-examining witness   156–158

Data minimisation   272
Digital Open Source Investigation   271–272

Direct evidence   29
Disclosure
    Expert Evidence   226
    Exculpatory criminal evidence   281–288
Documentary evidence   89
    Hearsay evidence   36
    ICTY   45, 53–54
Due Process notion   20

Electronic evidence   271
    ECtHR   273–276
Expert evidence
    Admissibility   203–230
Eyewitnesses   30–33

Failed prosecution   322–323
Forensic sciences
    Admissibility   203
    Testing   214–218

Guidelines
    Expert evidence   218
    Cross-examine experts   221
    Witness preparation   153

Hearsay
    Anonymous hearsay evidence   36–46
    NGO and IO Reports   243–252
Holistic and atomistic approach   12
Human rights   9, 15–16, 22–23
    Rule 68   129–131

Incapable of belief   297, 303–316
Insider witnesses   47–50
IO reports   243–259

Leading questions   156–161, 294

Manipulation   261–262
MIM evidence   267
Miscarriage of justice   281, 318–329
Misinformation   263

NGO reports   243–259
'No case to answer' motion   297–316

INDEX

Opening statements 13–14
    Presenting Evidence 295–296

Pattern evidence 189–192
Preservation 221, 239–41
    Social Media 272–273
Probative value 7, 9–14, 20, 28, 38–43
Propensity evidence 187

Reliability 203
    Evidence 210–213
    Forensic Sciences 214–216
Right to compensation 318
Rule 68, 52–136
Rule 92bis 52
    ICTY 55–62

'Shepherd direction' doctrine 173

Social media
    Evidentiary 260–277
    Documentary evidence 239
Submission 10, 13
    Documentary evidence 235–240

Tailoring of evidence 151
Transcripts 60, 88, 116

User identification 265, 268

Verification 273
    User identification 265

Witness preparation 141–154
Witness reliability 185
Wrongful prosecution 322–328